CHANGING JOBS:
A HANDBOOK FOR LAWYERS FOR THE 1990s

Heidi L. McNeil
Editor

Contributing Editors:
Lynne Albert
Sheila Anderson
Nancy Bronson
Hillary J. Mantis
Lawrence G. Sirhall, Jr.

Published jointly by the
American Bar Association
Young Lawyers Division
and
Section of Law Practice Management

The Section of Law Practice Management, American Bar Association, offers an educational program for lawyers in practice. Books and other materials are published in furtherance of that program. Authors and editors of publications may express their own legal interpretations and opinions, which are not necessarily those of either the American Bar Association, the Young Lawyers Division, or the Section of Law Practice Management unless adopted pursuant to the By-laws of the Association. The opinions expressed do not reflect in any way a position of the Section or the American Bar Association.

Library of Congress Catalog Card Number 94-070030
ISBN 0-89707-964-7

95 96 97 98 5 4 3 2

Discounts are available for books ordered in bulk. Special consideration is given to state bars, CLE programs, and other bar-related organizations. Inquire at Publications Planning and Marketing, American Bar Association, 750 N. Lake Shore Drive, Chicago, Illinois 60611.

TABLE OF CONTENTS

Chapter 2.A
Personality Factors and Career Choice 34
Larry Richard

Chapter 2.B
Interpreting the Results of Self-Assessment Techniques:
Will Career Testing Really Help You? 44
Anthony Monahan

Chapter 3
How to Counterattack If You Are Losing Your Job 52
David S. Machlowitz

Chapter 4
How to Improve Your Satisfaction with Your Current Career 57
Mindy Friedler

PART III
Getting the Offer   **115**

ACKNOWLEDGMENTS

The Career Issues Committee of the American Bar Association Young Lawyers Division (ABA-YLD) published the first edition of *Changing Jobs: A Handbook for Lawyers* in 1988. As a result of the dramatic change in the economic condition of the legal market during the late 1980s and early 1990s, an update to the prior book was felt necessary. *Changing Jobs: A Handbook for Lawyers for the 1990s* is prepared with the hope that it will remain viable for job changers throughout the 1990s.

As with any undertaking, numerous individuals have contributed to the success of this book. First and foremost, without the support and cooperation of the experts and professionals who generously donated their time to researching and writing their chapters, this handbook would not be possible.

Playing equally important roles in the process were Career Issues Committee Vice-Chair Larry Sirhall and Planning Board Members Lynne Albert, Sheila Anderson, Nancy Bronson, and Hillary Mantis, who served as editors for a number of the chapters. In addition, Hillary Mantis (who is serving as Committee Chair during the 1993–1994 bar year) was extremely helpful in locating authors for many of the chapters. David Delpierre and Jill Gelineau (Chairs of the ABA-YLD Publications Committee for 1992–1993 and 1993–1994, respectively) provided invaluable editorial guidance, as did Susan Fahey, member of the Publications Committee. ABA-YLD Chairpersons Mark Sessions (1992–1993) and Dan Gourash (1993–1994), Assistant Staff Director Dirk Behrends, and former Staff Director Ronald Hirsch were supportive and helpful in assuring that the book was timely and successfully routed through the proper ABA channels.

Special thanks to my secretary, Gina Bresee, and all the members of the Word Processing Department of my law firm, who were responsible for typing, revising, and proofing the various chapter drafts. In this regard, my law firm of Snell & Wilmer (Phoenix, Arizona) deserves special credit for permitting me to take on this project and utilize firm resources and personnel.

Finally, I remain grateful to my husband, Bill Staudenmaier, for patiently enduring the time that I spent in the office late at night and on the weekends working on this book. I also thank him for continuing to enthusiastically support my numerous bar activities at local, state, and national levels. None of my bar work would be possible without this support.

Heidi L. McNeil
Director
American Bar Association Young Lawyers Division

Introduction

Introduction

Heidi L. McNeil

Given the change of economic conditions in the legal profession and the practice of law in general over the past ten years, I am probably a rarity among lawyers graduating from law schools since the early 1980s. I have practiced law with the same law firm since graduating in 1985—the same firm where I spent my second year of clerking in 1984. And barring any unforeseen circumstances or unlikely appointments to the U.S. Supreme Court, this will probably be the place where I will remain until retirement.

My husband, on the other hand, has had three different legal jobs since graduating from law school in 1987. (This does not include a one-year federal clerkship immediately after law school.) His changes have come about for various reasons, ranging from more manageable hours to changing the focus of his practice to something more interesting and challenging (i.e., from collections to environmental work).

These days, changing law jobs—even getting out of the practice of law entirely—is more the norm than the exception. Indeed, statistics show that most lawyers change jobs at least once during their first ten years of practice. The reasons are varied: Some claim the hours required in private practice outweigh the compensation, thus making government work or in-house positions more desirable. Others seek greater intellectual stimulation or challenge through changing practice areas. Even more so, lawyers complain that the practice of law has become less civil and more stressful and leaves no time for one's self, family, or outside pursuits.

Changing Jobs: A Handbook for Lawyers for the 1990s is designed to assist those of you who are thinking about changing your current legal positions or even leaving the law business entirely. The Career Issues Committee of the American Bar Association Young Lawyers Division (ABA-YLD) enlisted the gracious assistance of nearly 50 experts in the fields of career planning and placement for lawyers to write this second edition. Furthermore, our focus is not to assist only *young* lawyers, but also lawyers out of law school for ten years or more. Moreover, this handbook is intended to provide career assistance throughout the 1990s and, hopefully, beyond, depending on any further changes that may occur in the legal market.

Part II of the book deals with the strategies and techniques for successful career planning. First, do you *really, really* want to be a lawyer, or do you want to do something else? This question is answered from a variety of angles, ranging from techniques on self-assessment and assessment of the market to bouncing back from an involuntary job termination. Other chapters deal with the career transition process, career opportunities for minorities, and how to improve your satisfaction with your current career.

Once you have put some thought into planning your career and the path that you wish to take, the next task is successfully identifying how to go about the job search. Part III focuses on various job-finding techniques and resources, such as networking, law school career-services offices, third-party intermediaries, bar associations, and other informational sources.

The job search process is further explored in Part IV, where the fundamental skills required of a successful job hunter are addressed in depth. For example, the experts explain how to write an effective résumé and cover letter, interview for success, negotiate salary and benefits, and make the "right" decision once you get the offer.

Part V provides detailed analyses of employment opportunities for experienced lawyers within various public-sector and private-sector practice settings. Separate chapters are devoted to specific geographic areas, substantive practice areas (i.e., "what's hot, what's not"), law firms, solo practitioners, corporations, government, judgeships, teaching, legal aid, legal services, public-interest organizations, and part-time/contract work. And for those lawyers who find that perhaps law is not quite what they wanted after all, there is a chapter on how to switch gears completely and look at nonlegal opportunities.

The final part of the book is a comprehensive bibliography of career-planning and job-finding resources.

Hopefully, the tips and guidelines offered by the experts in *Changing Jobs: A Handbook for Lawyers for the 1990s* will streamline the career-change process, making it more focused and productive. More importantly, you will have the confidence that whatever the future holds with respect to your legal career, you have carefully planned a road map to long-lasting satisfaction.

PART I

Career-Planning Strategies

Is the Grass Greener? How Does Your Current Career Compare with Others Across the Country?

Ronald L. Hirsch

You obviously are thinking seriously about changing your job, otherwise you would not be reading this book. Most of you are considering a job change because you are dissatisfied with some aspect of your current jobs, some of you have been laid off, and yet others want to change jobs for reasons unrelated to the specifics of your current employment. If you have a choice in the matter, the first question you must ask yourself is, "Should I really change jobs?" For all of you, the major conundrum is what your next job should be.

This chapter will provide you with a rough tool with which to measure your current job against jobs nationwide. The data that will be presented are from the National Survey of [Lawyers'] Career Satisfaction/Dissatisfaction conducted by the ABA-YLD in 1984 and 1990 ("National Career Surveys").[1] These data show a trend of deterioration in the lawyer workplace that will likely continue until law firms and other employers begin to address the management practices that are causing the problem.

You Are Not Alone

The first thing that you have to realize as you think about changing jobs is that you are in good company. In 1990, 18 percent of all lawyers (16 percent in private practice, 21 percent in corporate legal departments, and 30 percent in government jobs) said that they planned to change jobs in the next two years. Another 48 percent of all lawyers indicated that while they were not planning on changing jobs, they *would* if they felt they had a reasonable alternative!

Why do all of these lawyers want to change their jobs? Table 1.1 shows the reasons considered very important by those lawyers planning on changing their jobs.

Clearly, these lawyers are dissatisfied with a number of different aspects of their current jobs. What should that tell you? It tells you that many lawyers in many law firms and other job settings have problems with their workplace

TABLE 1.1

Reasons Considered Very Important in the Decision to Change Jobs

	Private	Corporation	Government
General job dissatisfaction	59%	53%	24%
Limited/no advancement potential	32	73	45
Experienced gender bias	5	12	15
Want more time for self or family	40	26	20
Desire more financial reward	42	56	61
Pressure to bill hours	23	NA	NA
Job tension/personalities	38	18	11
Other	34	52	59

environment. It tells you that you better think twice about whether your current job really is that bad. It tells you that you have to very carefully investigate the alternatives before you accept another job offer.

Testing Your Current Job

To start the process of assessing your current job in relation to the alternatives, you must ask yourself the same questions that were asked of the respondents to the National Career Surveys. The following few questions, culled from the complete 25-page questionnaire, will provide you with a point of comparison with the data that will be presented in this chapter.

1. The following will be descriptive of your current employment to a greater or lesser extent. For each phrase, indicate the extent to which it describes your job using a four-point scale ranging from "very descriptive" to "just the opposite."

	Very Descriptive	Somewhat	Not Very	Just the Opposite
The financial rewards are great......	1	2	3	4
I have enough time for myself.......	1	2	3	4
The opportunity for me to advance is very good....................	1	2	3	4
Atmosphere is warm and personal ..	1	2	3	4

Advancement is determined more by quality than by the quantity of one's work...................	1	2	3	4
Political intrigue and backbiting are almost nonexistent..............	1	2	3	4
Level of pressure or tension on the job is minimal..................	1	2	3	4
The intellectual challenge of my work is great...................	1	2	3	4
Superiors provide frequent instruction or training...........	1	2	3	4

2. In thinking about your current job, *overall* how satisfied or dissatisfied are you, or do you feel neutral?

Very satisfied 1
Somewhat satisfied 2
Neutral............................ 3
Somewhat dissatisfied 4
Very dissatisfied 5

The Experience of Other Lawyers

As will be seen, both the 1984 and 1990 National Career Surveys found that the majority of both male and female lawyers were satisfied overall with their jobs. The data, however, do reflect that the legal workplace environment has deteriorated, that increases in the hours worked and the resulting decrease in personal time have become a major problem, that the status and acceptance of women has not improved in the intervening six years, and that, as a result of all of these changes, dissatisfaction has increased throughout the profession.

Table 1.2 shows that there has been a marked increase in the percentage of lawyers who are dissatisfied. It also shows that, as in 1984, significantly more women are dissatisfied with their jobs than men in private practice. Furthermore, this greater level of dissatisfaction exists regardless of position—that is, women partners, junior associates, and solo practitioners all feel much more dissatisfied than their male colleagues.[2]

This same table shows that dissatisfaction increased only minimally for male and female junior associates, while dissatisfaction for partners, senior associates, and solo practitioners increased significantly. Clearly, dissatisfaction no longer is primarily a junior associate issue.

Table 1.3 shows how all lawyers in corporate legal departments and government agencies compare with those in private practice. While the decrease in those lawyers who are very satisfied is similar across all job settings, the increase in those dissatisfied is most striking for those working in corporate legal departments; for government lawyers, there was actually a slight decrease in dissatisfaction.

TABLE 1.2

Job Satisfaction in Private Practice

	(Sat = Very Satisfied + Somewhat Satisfied + Neutral)							
	1990				1984			
	Male		Female		Male		Female	
	Sat	Dis	Sat	Dis	Sat	Dis	Sat	Dis
Partner	78%	22%	58%	42%	88%	9%	84%	15%
Senior associate	68	32	67	33	84	13	74	25
Junior associate	77	23	60	40	77	19	57	40
Solo practitioner	57	43	45	55	77	18	75	21
All	72	28	59	41	83	13	69	29

Comparison of Tables 1.2 and 1.3 also shows a generational change. While 19 percent of all lawyers in private practice are dissatisfied, when comparing only lawyers who graduated from law school after 1967, the percentage of dissatisfied lawyers rises to 31 percent.

Many of you may think that lawyer dissatisfaction is especially prevalent in larger and medium-sized firms. Table 1.4, however, shows that there is no substantial variation of satisfaction by size of firm. To the extent there is, more solo practitioners are very dissatisfied and more lawyers in small firms and solo practitioners are very satisfied.

TABLE 1.3

Dissatisfaction by Job Setting

| | Private Practice | | Corporate Legal Department | | Government | |
	1990	1984	1990	1984	1990	1984
Very satisfied	32%	40%	31%	42%	26%	42%
Somewhat satisfied	44	40	42	38	53	4
Neutral	5	4	5	7	6	4
Somewhat dissatisfied	14	3	16	11	12	16
Very dissatisfied	5	3	7	2	4	3

TABLE 1.4

Dissatisfaction by Size of Firm

	Solo	2–3	4–9	10+
Very satisfied	35%	31%	34%	29%
Somewhat satisfied	38	45	43	47
Neutral	5	5	6	5
Somewhat Dissatisfied	18	11	11	15
Very dissatisfied	5	8	5	5

What Causes Dissatisfaction?

The results of the analyses show that although there is some variation in dissatisfaction levels by job setting, size of firm, and type of position, as well as by gender, these factors are not in themselves statistically significant in determining whether an individual is dissatisfied as opposed to satisfied. These factors are not causative.

Rather, it is the work environment, the particular mix of positive and negative work environment factors, that accounts for most of the variation in satisfaction/dissatisfaction levels. The different figures in the tables just show the extent to which these countervailing factors are present in the various positions for each gender. Another way of looking at this is to say, put someone in a negative work environment and that person will be dissatisfied. Put that same person in a positive environment and that person will be satisfied.

The analysis shows that the reason for the decrease in lawyer satisfaction lies in the increased number of lawyers who reported negative experiences in the workplace in 1990 compared with 1984, as shown in Table 1.5. Your answers to the first question in the current job test that you completed earlier provide a point of comparison for you.

Table 1.6 shows reports of negative workplace experiences by size of firm. This table shows a mixed picture: For several items, size of firm does not have a significant impact; on others it does. And while the direction generally is in favor of smaller firms, on the issue of financial reward, clearly those in smaller firms not only describe their financial rewards as being less, but the data also show that more are dissatisfied with their earnings (34 percent in firms of nine or less; 15 percent in firms of ten or more). This would seem to belie the often-stated theory that people who go into small-firm or solo practice make a conscious trade-off of less money for more freedom, etc. For most, that does not seem to be the case.

Why, then, are women lawyers more dissatisfied? The answer is apparent: Across the board, regardless of position, women continue to experience

TABLE 1.5

Percentage of Lawyers in Private Practice Reporting Negative Experiences on Selected Workplace Environment Variables

	1990	1984
Advancement is not determined by the quality of work ..	30%	14%
No good opportunity to advance	24	18
Political intrigue and backbiting......................	28	18
Not much time for self.............................	54	46
Not much time for family...........................	44	36
No good opportunity for professional development	18	11
Not very warm and personal atmosphere	12	9

TABLE 1.6

Percentage of Lawyers in Private Practice Reporting Negative Experiences on Selected Workplace Environment Variables (by Size of Firm)

	Solo	2–3	4–9	10+
Advancement is not determined by the quality of work..	16%	16%	25%	30%
No good opportunity to advance	27	29	25	21
Political intrigue and backbiting	NA	17	17	36
Not much time for self	50	56	47	59
Not much time for family	36	32	40	51
No good opportunity for professional development	18	26	17	15
Not very warm and personal atmosphere..............	9	7	9	17
Level of pressure/tension on job is high..............	75	73	70	77
Financial rewards are not good......................	35	34	32	15

a more negative work environment than men do. Some of the reasons for this are as follows:

- Only 18 percent of women are partners compared with 45 percent of men. And because this figure considers only those who have graduated from law school after 1967, the figure is not skewed.
- More women report that they do not have a good chance to advance (30 percent versus 21 percent) and that advancement is not determined by the quality of one's work (32 percent versus 24 percent).
- More women report that political intrigue and backbiting is present (33 percent versus 28 percent).
- More women report that their work atmosphere is not warm and personal (21 percent versus 15 percent).
- More women report that they do not have enough time for themselves (61 percent versus 55 percent).
- Women continue to be worse off financially than their male colleagues in most positions as can be seen in Table 1.7.

Thus, women experience less of the positive and more of the negative work environmental factors. The result is greater dissatisfaction among women.

Are these different experiences the result of gender bias? The survey asked whether the respondents have observed differences in opportunities

TABLE 1.7
Job Income for Private Practice

"What was your income from your primary job in 1989, after deducting business expenses, but before taxes and other deductions?"						
	Solo Practitioner		Junior Associate		Partner	
	Male	Female	Male	Female	Male	Female
Less than $15,000	9%	21%	2%	4%	2%	4%
$15,000–$24,999	10	27	6	10	2	6
$25,000–$39,999	19	27	32	35	3	9
$40,000–$54,999	21	18	30	27	13	25
$55,000–$74,999	13	3	20	21	15	17
$75,000–$99,999	16	3	10	1	18	8
$100,000–$199,999	11	0	1	2	29	25
$200,000 or more	1	0	0	0	18	8

provided male lawyers as opposed to female lawyers or whether female law-yers are provided equal opportunities. Table 1.8 shows that a large percentage of women and a significant percentage of men reported that opportunities are better for men. After reviewing all the data, there is strong support for the proposition that gender bias is a significant factor in the greater extent of negative work experiences reported by women lawyers; one cannot discount gender bias as merely the perception of women.

Again, however, the majority of women do not report problems in their work environments and differential opportunities. Thus, while a serious problem exists in many law firms, in many gender bias does not appear to be a factor. So, if gender bias is an important issue for you and you are not happy with your current firm, many alternatives are available for you.

TABLE 1.8

Percentage Reporting Better Opportunities for Men in Law Firms (No Solo) and Nonprivate Practice (Corporate, Government, and Other) Settings

	Law Firms (No Solo)		Nonprivate Practice Settings	
	Male	Female	Male	Female
Firm management involvement	29%	54%	16%	41%
Promotions	13	44	10	34
Job assignments	9	38	7	26
Litigation work	17	42	5	22
Transactional work	9	30	2	16
Compensation	9	38	9	24

The Time Famine

In looking at the deterioration in the lawyer workplace, one of the most sig-nificant shifts is the increase in the number of lawyers who report that they do not have enough time for themselves and their families—what has been called by some "the time famine."

Table 1.9 shows that lawyers are working more now than they did in 1984; 50 percent of all lawyers in private practice now work 2,400 hours a year or more and 45 percent bill 1,920 hours a year or more. How do your hours compare?

TABLE 1.9

Hours Worked and Billable Hours in Private Practice

	Hours Worked Per Month			Billable Hours Per Month	
	1990	1984		1990	1984
240 and more	13%	4%	200 plus	16%	N.A.
200–239	37	31	160–199	29	
160–199	34	40	120–159	35	
Less than 160	16	25	Less than 120	20	

Several other important points should be noted regarding the issue of time. First, working long hours has a cumulative effect. People can handle time deprivation for a year or two, but as the years go on and there is no relief, the impact on an individual's psyche increases.

Added to all of these factors is the pressure stemming from the small amount of vacation time actually taken by lawyers. Fifty percent report taking two weeks or less vacation during the past year, while only 30 percent were restricted to that amount of time off.

Not surprisingly, given all of this data, the problem is not just one of not having enough time for one's family or oneself; lawyers are also increasingly just worn out. While 61 percent of all lawyers reported in 1984 that they "frequently feel fatigued or worn out by the end of the workday," that percentage had risen to 71 percent in 1990. Furthermore, in comparing male and female lawyers (which again are those graduating after 1967), the percentage is 71 percent for males and 84 percent for females.

Communication

While not measured by the survey, the managing partners at an American Bar Association (ABA) national conference held in April of 1991 to discuss the survey results and possible solutions[3] felt almost universally that an important problem was the breakdown of communication within the office. This was true in several critical areas:

- Associates have little information about what is happening in the firm. Despite the fact that they sacrifice their lives for the chance of financial and professional security with the firm, they are kept in the dark regarding important administrative matters and their input is not sought. Participants also indicated that even partners outside the inner power circle frequently do not have good information and are not asked for input; they, too, then effectively are excluded from management decisions. As one participant put, "Management by mystery is the downfall of a firm. It is important that all lawyers are consulted." The result of this lack of communication is that associates and partners feel insecure and less in control of their professional lives.

- Associates' evaluations, probably one of the most important forms of communication, often are cursory, vague, and generally not helpful. Associates are not given a clear understanding of what the firm expects of them, how their work is viewed, or their chances of attaining partnership.
- Another point made was that much of the communication that did take place regarding the law firm's philosophy and expectations, both to law students and within the firm, was false. This was expressed in the following way: "When the chips are down, when money is paid out, what are the criteria for compensation. There is a great dissidence between what is talked about and what is done in a firm."

The result of this breakdown in communications is political intrigue and a lack of trust within the firm. This conclusion is supported by data from the National Career Surveys, which show that 28 percent of lawyers in private practice report that political intrigue and backbiting are common, and that 30% feel that advancement is not determined by the quality of work. Another result of the poor communication within law firms is the isolation of lawyers, which a number of participants felt was an important factor in lawyer depression.

What Role Does Your Personality Play?

While the National Career Surveys did not contain a personality inventory (which will be discussed in other chapters in this book), it did contain measures of several psychological factors, including hardiness (a measure of one's strength in adversity) and coping (a measure of the impact of stress). The analyses conducted show that hardiness and coping skills have less of an impact on job satisfaction than the work environment does. The issues are primarily systemic rather than personal.

Perhaps the clearest reflection of the predominant role of the work environment vis-à-vis personality can be seen in the data on the longitudinal respondents—those who responded to both the 1984 and 1990 surveys. These individuals, who one would assume were the same personality types in 1990 that they were in 1984, reported significantly reduced satisfaction despite the fact that they were further along in their careers, more successful, and thus, by rights, should be more satisfied. This reduced satisfaction was caused by the more negative work environment that many of them experienced in 1990 compared with 1984.

Psychological factors, however, even as measured by the National Career Surveys, definitely play a role in lawyers' satisfaction, albeit a less significant one than the impact of the work environment. Thus, you are encouraged to carefully assess your psychological needs and how a job opportunity meets those needs, together with the other factors that have been discussed, before making employment decisions to ensure the best fit between you and your future work environment.

Where Do You Go from Here?

Now you have a rough idea of how your current job and work environment compare with those across the nation. This initial assessment must be followed by a very detailed assessment of both your current job and the alternatives available in your community before you make any decisions. The remaining chapters in this book will help you through that process.

Notes

1. The 1984 survey was a random sample of all lawyers in the country, ABA members and nonmembers, both young and old. The 1990 survey followed all those who responded to the 1984 survey plus questioned a new sample of those who graduated from law school since 1984. The surveys achieved a 76 percent and 67 percent response rate, respectively, and the data are representative of the profession. The survey report, *State of the Legal Profession 1990*, is available from the ABA.

2. Please note that all the data comparing men and women lawyers are based on data for those graduating from law school after 1967, to remove any bias that might be present if all lawyers were compared because women only started entering the profession in large numbers during the late 1960s. All other data are based on all respondents to the survey.

3. The conference report, *At the Breaking Point: The Emerging Crisis in the Quality of Lawyers' Health and Lives—Its Impact on Law Firms and Client Services*, is available through the ABA.

CHAPTER 2

Career Self-Assessment: An Overview

Maureen A. Provost

Whatever your dream job, identifying it may help you move toward it.
—Robert O. Snelling, Sr.

The late 1980s and early 1990s have not been pleasant years for lawyers. The heyday of the 1980s, followed by the recession and the resultant layoffs, created an apparently stagnant, shrinking marketplace. In response, lawyers have been forced to take a creative approach to the job market to pursue new opportunities. Those who have been laid off and those who merely became disenchanted with the profession have become exposed to the value of career planning and goal setting. Many have used the insights that they gained to move up or laterally within the profession; others changed to nonlegal positions in a variety of settings.

Self-assessment can be enjoyable and reveal new possibilities for a lawyer's career. Why, then, is it so often an overlooked step in the job search campaign? It is human nature, when faced with the legitimate crisis of a job search, to at once engage in tasks that might have an immediate payoff. Thus, candidates hastily revise their résumés and call headhunters and personal contacts very early, perhaps *too* early, in the campaign.

When confronted with the necessity of a job hunt, clients are advised by counselors to stop, take a deep breath, and assess their past to plan their future. The process of career self-assessment provides the equivalent of a road map defining the destination at which to arrive; without the road map, one can be lost or sidetracked. Job searches are more informed and more efficient when the candidate has a clear sense of direction and a sense of purpose. For many reasons, the resulting job will more likely create greater job satisfaction. Morale is improved when one's work is in sync with one's values, skills, goals, and higher purpose.

18

The paradox of the job search is that one must simultaneously be focused and open to possibilities. Too often, candidates feel at the mercy of a bad job market, that job satisfaction is a luxury, and that they need to take just any job rather than the "right" job. Youthful idealism has been replaced by a weary realism that they must accept their lots in life.

Historical Perspective

During the 1960s, the concepts of the human potential movement, and in particular, Maslow's pyramid model of a hierarchy of needs, raised the possibility of "self-actualization" and helped shift the perception and expectation of work as a necessity to work as a pleasurable, self-enhancing, and rewarding activity.

The early popularization of these concepts was achieved through the work of such career-planning authors as Richard Bolles (*What Color Is Your Parachute?*, *The Three Boxes of Life*, *The Quick Job Hunt Map*, and *How to Find Your Mission in Life*), Bernard Haldane (*Career Satisfaction and Success*), and John Crystal (*Where Do I Go from Here with the Rest of My Life?*). They asserted that one can do work that is deeply meaningful and that taps talents, skills, knowledge that one enjoys using—that one could describe the components of an "ideal job" and achieve it, first by identifying it.

The Goals and Benefits of Self-Assessment

Introspection leads to insight and insight leads to action and commitment. Self-assessment formalizes the introspective process to extract information and make it usable for planning purposes.

The following results can be achieved through the self-assessment process:

- Clarity of objectives and focus; goals articulated;
- Increased self-confidence;
- Ability to describe and market oneself in an interview;
- Ability to evaluate employment options informed by your needs and desires;
- Ability to ask questions designed to evaluate the suitability of an employment option;
- Ability to create employment opportunities;
- Sense of being in control by designing one's future;
- A more efficient job search, fewer "wild goose chases"; and
- Renewed enthusiasm; a positive expectation of the future.

The self-assessment process allows one to shift from the passive posture of a victim to that of a powerful, in-charge person.

In *How to Find Your Mission in Life*, Richard Bolles discusses the purpose of self-assessment as follows:

We are to begin deciphering our unique Mission by studying our talents and skills, and more particularly which ones (or One) we most rejoice to use . . . which talent gives us the greatest pleasure from its exercise (it is usually the one which, when we use it, causes us to lose all sense of time) . . . the kind of work God usually calls you to do is the kind of work (a) that you need most to do and (b) the world needs most to have done. The place God calls you to is the place where your deep gladness and the world's deep hunger meet.

Career self-assessment guides the job seeker to articulate and define the following:

- Accomplishments and achievements;
- Motivated, functional, transferable skills and success pattern (including both legal and other skills);
- Personality traits and style;
- Work values, preferred working conditions, and the extent to which the current job "fits" these criteria;
- Lifestyle needs (including geographic preference);
- Interest areas and areas of expertise, including compelling topics, causes to address, problems to be solved; and
- Potential professional/personal weaknesses to overcome.

In *The Quick Job Hunt Map*, Bolles advises the job seeker to identify the following factors as part of the process of identifying the ideal job:

1. Physical setting, including geographic location;
2. Salary level;
3. Tasks that are appealing, organized by the necessity to work with data, people, or things;
4. Kinds of information that will be handled;
5. Types of things/issues to be worked on;
6. Short-range and long-range outcomes of the job;
7. Spiritual and emotional setting that is compatible with the job seeker's philosophy of life and values; and
8. Kinds of people the job seeker likes to work on behalf of (as clients or customers) and likes to have as colleagues.

Ultimately the candidate is able to synopsize as follows (here adapted for lawyers):

I want to work as a _____ in a setting such as _____ using my special knowledge and expertise in the area(s) of _____ on behalf of the following kinds of clients: _____.

For midcareer lawyers, this type of early or midcareer analysis and introspection provides an opportunity for realignment and redirection into more suitable employment. Lawyers are naturally proficient in analysis and synthesis of data. For most people, the most fascinating subject they can study is themselves. Thus, the process often is found to be practical as well as enjoyable.

Career Self-Assessment: How to Do It

Many excellent books have been published during the past decade on the topic of job searching; several contain excellent chapters on self-assessment. A small but growing number of authors have tailored their discussions to the specific career-assessment issues for lawyers.

Notably, Deborah Arron's *What Can You Do With a Law Degree?*, Mark Byers's *Lawyers in Transition*, and Don Samuelson's workshop materials, *Legal Career Planning: Planning A Life in the Law*, have made major contributions to the area of career-planning exercises for lawyers. Although written for a general audience, Bolles's *What Color Is Your Parachute?*, Barbara Sher's *Wishcraft*, Marsha Sinetar's *Do What You Love and the Money Will Follow*, and Gerald Sturman's *If You Knew Who You Were, You Could Be Who You Are* are valuable resources.

To assist law students and lawyers in quickly addressing their self-assessment process, various exercises can be used in the process. Several such exercises (Figures 2.1 through 2.12) appear throughout this chapter. They include several techniques of self-assessment that will require you to write your answers to exercises on paper. You may want to use a notebook or a personal computer for this purpose. After completing the exercises, the job seeker will have a notebook filled with narrative and ideas for a suitable career path.

Career consultants assist clients in the process of discovering their talents and interests. A variety of methods are used to profile the client, ranging from formal personality and career testing, card-sort processes to paper-and-pencil exercises. If you do not have access to a career counselor, this process can be performed individually or with a friend who is willing to meet with you to discuss the various issues.

Skills Identification

One of the most important aspects of the career-planning process is the identification of your most enjoyable skills, or "success pattern" (see Figures 2.1–2.3). This provides valuable information for interviews and for designing a job for which you will be well-suited. Career counselors Richard Bolles, the late John Crystal, and Bernard Haldane first developed a workable procedure.

Several career counselors insist that clients write lengthy autobiographies to collect data and analyze the patterns, but the shorter process described here works nearly as well.

Checklists also can provide an easy and effective means of self-analysis. In Bolles's *What Color Is Your Parachute?* and *The Quick Job Hunt Map*, he lists hundreds of skills and suggests that the job seeker indicate the number of times that these skills were utilized for each of the seven accomplishment stories being analyzed. The success pattern emerges very clearly.

It is not enough, however, only to identify skills. To do a thorough job, skills must be evaluated in terms of ability *and* amount of satisfaction the use of the skill provides. Dr. Dory Hollander, in her excellent book *The Doom Loop*

FIGURE 2.1

Skills Identification
EXERCISE 1: An Overview of the Key Events of Your Life

Draw four columns on a piece of paper. In the first column, indicate all five-year incre-
ments for your life span. In each of the other columns across the top, write LEISURE,
EDUCATION, and WORK/CAREER. For the duration of your life span, starting with zero to
five years of age, jot down key words to signify events in each of these areas,
including jobs and degrees attained at various schools. Examples: winning a spelling
bee or science competition, being on a debate team or the Model U.N., volunteering
at a hospital, serving as an intern to a judge, learning a language, traveling abroad,
arguing in court or Moot Court, writing a thesis, working on a transaction, and so on.

System, takes skills analysis to a new level. She asserts that some skills are
enjoyable to use and others have ceased to be or never were enjoyable to use.
Therefore, a person may be good at something, even proficient, but no longer
delights in using this skill. Thus, once a list of skills has been developed,
analyze each as enjoyable, no longer enjoyable, or the extent to which one is
motivated to develop them. Dr. Hollander believes that growth in one's career
comes from developing skills in areas that are enjoyable but in which proficiency has not as yet been achieved. The "Doom Loop" occurs when a professional feels caught in a job that requires the use of skills that no longer are
enjoyable or skills that one does not have and does not enjoy.

Other checklists include:

- The "Inventory of Legal Skills" in Mark Byers's *Lawyers in Transition*;
- The list of skills necessary for success as a lawyer that resulted from
  the Harvard Career Paths Study (see Figure 2.4 on page 24);
- The performance evaluation used by the job seeker's organization (A
  job seeker might ask for a copy and evaluate himself or herself.);

FIGURE 2.2

Skills Identification
EXERCISE 2: List of Accomplishments and Success Stories

List twenty accomplishments or achievements from your work/career, leisure, or
education columns. (Accomplishments can be as simple as the first time you cooked
a complicated dish or taught a child to ride a bicycle, or as intricate as winning a
trial.) The only rule is that the achievement had to be satisfying to you.

Select seven accomplishments to examine in greater detail. For each, write a
paragraph describing what steps you took, from beginning to end, to achieve the
result.

FIGURE 2.3

Skills Identification
EXERCISE 3: What are your transferable skills?

List all the skills that were utilized for each of the seven stories. Richard Bolles suggests that skills be described not only with a verb but also an object of a verb. Hence, "writing" is not nearly as descriptive as "writing performance manuals."

A pattern should emerge from the seven stories. Which skills appear several times or consistently in every story? Each of us has hundreds of skills, but which skills do you consistently, characteristically, and happily use when faced with problems or challenges? Because of the practice you have had in the exercise of these competencies, you have become proficient in them, possibly noticeably better than your peers.

Often, other people observe you and rely on your ability to handle situations in a certain way. It is especially helpful to have another person listen to the stories and tell you the skills he or she notices. You also might solicit people who have worked with you to get feedback on your competencies. Out of humility or lack of observation, you may take your own skills for granted, especially the ones that come easily to you.

- Deborah Arron's *What Can You Do With a Law Degree?*;
- Gerald Sturman's *If You Knew Who You Were, You Could Be Who You Are* is excellent if one must assess not only strengths but weaknesses, and includes many additional self-analysis worksheets.

Knowledge Areas

The job seeker's experience gained before, during, and after law school has developed expertise in a specific area of the law or in dealing with the problems of certain types of people or organizations. It is important to conduct an inventory of this experience. (See Figures 2.4–2.6.)

Consultant Don Samuelson's approach to assessment utilizes a cube format in which the candidate's legal experience is analyzed in terms of the types of clients represented, the practice area, and the skills used. He advocates "filling in the cube" to create a complete portfolio of lawyer skills, helping one eventually to become a well-rounded generalist. Other career counselors advocate repeating the experiences from the past that were satisfying; this advice may more quickly lead to becoming a specialist.

Candidates must consider whether they intend to stay in their current area(s) of practice or to shift to others. This type of shift might be achieved as easily as requesting new assignments or a change of practice area. The candidate may need to accumulate additional training, such as studying for an LL.M. or taking Continuing Legal Education (CLE) courses.

FIGURE 2.4

Skills of Successful Lawyers
EXERCISE 4: In which "lawyer skills" are you most proficient?

In the first column, indicate your level of proficiency on a scale of 1–5, 1 as not proficient, 3 as average, and 5 as excellent. In the second column, check those skills that you like and want to develop in your next position, regardless of how proficient you presently are. (These skills were largely drawn from the results of the Harvard Career Paths Study, in which 1,300 lawyers were asked to identify the traits that were necessary for success in the practice of law.)

Skill Level	Want to Develop?	SKILL CLUSTERS
_____	_____	Analytical abilities
_____	_____	Writing, legal drafting
_____	_____	Research, fact gathering, legal research
_____	_____	Oral advocacy, public speaking
_____	_____	Mediation
_____	_____	Negotiation
_____	_____	Adversarial skills
_____	_____	Business planning
_____	_____	Strategy formulation
_____	_____	Financial management, financial analysis
_____	_____	Assembling deals, structuring deals
_____	_____	Interviewing, client counseling
_____	_____	Management, manage complex tasks
_____	_____	Staff management, manage people
_____	_____	Business development, marketing
_____	_____	Client relations, client communications
_____	_____	Ability to build networks, networking
_____	_____	Productivity, work well under pressure
_____	_____	Quality control, attention to detail
_____	_____	Solve problems creatively
_____	_____	Commitment, drive, willing to put in long hours
_____	_____	Good judgment, common sense
_____	_____	Get along with colleagues, team player, political judgment
_____	_____	Leadership
_____	_____	Ability to inspire confidence

FIGURE 2.5

Areas of Practice and Interests
EXERCISE 5: What do you want your work to be about?

In which areas of practice do you have experience at present? Which do you find interesting? In which do you hope to continue to develop expertise?

What interests do you have, both law-related and non-law-related? What are the causes about which you feel most strongly? Which articles do you always stop to read in newspapers and magazines? What is the subject matter of the books you read and purchase? What seminars do you attend or wish you had the time to attend?

If you had five lives to lead, what five different careers would you pursue during those lifetimes?

An index of a continuing education catalog can be used to pinpoint and cluster your interests. First, highlight all of the topics you find interesting, then organize those by headings which capture sense of the group. How can these be combined with the law or with each other to create a satisfying career path?

FIGURE 2.6

Skills and Experience
EXERCISE 6: What do your billing records reveal about your experience?

Review the last few years of your billing or other work records to determine the types of work you have done in each practice area. Make a chart or outline organized by practice area with the details of the experience you have in each area. On what types of transactions did you work? On behalf of what types of clients? How substantial were the amounts of money involved? If a litigator, what types of litigation were involved; what were the issues and the tasks required? What was the result for the client? What types of documents did you write or utilize? On which transactions or procedures did you work?

This research will be invaluable when you are marketing yourself to prospective employers as a candidate for a position. In effect, a document such as this (called a "Summary of Experience") will be translating for interviewers the work you can do (because you have done it already), the problems you can solve, and the projects that can be given to you immediately because of the nature of your experience.

Values

Another area for exploration would be values (also referred to as motivators, satisfiers, or "anchors"). (See Figures 2.7–2.9.) In addition to the checklists of values in Byers's *Lawyers in Transition* and Arron's *What Can You Do With a Law Degree?*, one also can examine how past jobs and the present or last position have been satisfying or unsatisfying, in an effort to compile a profile of factors to seek in the next position and factors to avoid.

FIGURE 2.7

Work Values

EXERCISE 7: What factors are crucial for your job satisfaction?

Consider each item separately and rate each

        A = very important,
        B = moderately important, and
        C = not very important.

_____ Achievement	_____ Pleasant surroundings
_____ Advancement	_____ Pleasure and fun
_____ Affiliation	_____ Prestige, status
_____ Authority/Power	_____ Public or client contact
_____ Autonomy/Independence	_____ Reasonable hours
_____ Being needed	_____ Recognition
_____ Boss you respect	_____ Respect
_____ Challenge	_____ Responsibility
_____ Competition	_____ Results of work seen
_____ Control	_____ Reward
_____ Creativity	_____ Salary
_____ Direct impact	_____ Stability
_____ Discovering new things	_____ Self development
_____ Ethics/Morality	_____ Self expression
_____ Excellence	_____ Service
_____ Excitement	_____ Structured environment
_____ Improving the world	_____ Training, mentoring
_____ Influencing people, leadership	_____ Traveling
_____ Intellectual stimulation	_____ Variety of work
_____ Interesting work	_____ Working alone
_____ Interpersonal relationships	_____ Working on teams
_____ Job security	_____ Other:
_____ Mentoring	_____ Other:

    Review those values marked "A" and rank-order those from 1 through 10 in order of their importance to you as follows: 1—most important, 2—next most important, and so on.

FIGURE 2.8

> **Values Clarification**
> EXERCISE 8: How happy are you in your present job?
>
> List your top ten values down the left-hand column of a chart. Across the top, list all the jobs you have held. For each of the jobs and each of the values, assign a 1 to 5 point score, 1 for "not satisfied" and 5 for "very satisfied."
>
> To what extent does your present or most recent job satisfy your most important values?
>
> Consider which past jobs were more satisfying. Why?
>
> Which factors are so important to you that you will ensure that they be present in your next job?

For instance, a job seeker might realize that interesting work, a boss you respect, autonomy, and challenge (see the exercise in Figure 2.8) are the factors without which he or she is unhappy, even miserable. These priorities will enlighten his or her evaluation of future opportunities, and the absence of these important values may explain the mismatch experienced in past jobs.

Edgar Schein's Career Anchors model also lends insight into an evaluation of values and priorities. Schein believes that eight "anchors" or patterns of work values, motivators, and satisfactions exist, which include:

1. Security/stability/organizational identity,
2. Autonomy/independence,
3. Technical/functional competence,
4. Managerial competence,
5. Entrepreneurial creativity,
6. Sense of service/dedication to a cause,
7. Pure challenge, and
8. Lifestyle integration.

FIGURE 2.9

> **Past Experiences**
> EXERCISE 9: What did you like and dislike about your past jobs?
>
> List all jobs you have held since high school, including volunteer jobs and internships. For each position, list the aspects you liked and did not like.
>
> What factors do you want to include in your next and future positions? Which factors do you want to avoid? Which factors are the most important contributors to your job satisfaction?

The job seeker's top three anchors describe the nature of a satisfying job and create a sense of focus for the job search by identifying the components that should be present in the next position. They also may explain the lack of fit experienced in past jobs.

Settings

The exercise in Figure 2.10 asks the candidate to select appealing types of organizations in which to work. Preferences for work setting are related to values and suggest possible target employers, especially when cross-referenced with areas of practice in which the job seeker has interest or expertise. For example, if a lawyer was interested in pursuing elder law in the government, a hospital, a corporation, or a nonprofit organization, he or she would think, "What kinds of jobs exist in each of these settings in the area of elder law?" The next step would be to generate a list of possible job titles in these settings and research them.

Lawyers work in a variety of both traditional and nontraditional settings, ranging from law firms, corporate legal departments, accounting firms, prosecutorial offices, government and public-interest agencies, and the judicial system. Nontraditional options are many, and for this one should read Arron's books *What Can You Do with a Law Degree?* and *Running from the Law.*

Personal and Professional Style

One of the most enlightening and encouraging components of the self-assessment process is discovering your characteristic and preferred personality style. Several theories of personality typology exist, but some have become quite popular and have yielded interesting and useful insights related to the strengths, skills, job/person "fit," and interaction strategies for lawyers (see Figures 2.11–2.12).

During the past ten years, the Myers-Briggs Type Indicator (MBTI) has become increasingly popular as an assessment tool. In a nutshell, this inventory gives a sense of an individual's preferences for an attitude of Extraversion or Introversion, and Perceiving or Judging as a lifestyle orientation. In addition, the candidate's preferred style of absorbing information, either Intuitive or Sensing, is measured, as is the likely method of evaluating and deciding—Thinking (objective) or Feeling (subjective). The MBTI is discussed in greater detail in Chapter 2.A.

The results suggest that the job seeker might fit the description of one of 16 personality types and one of four temperaments. The results also suggest the type of lawyer one might be happiest as—the area of practice, the setting and supervisor's style to which one would be best matched, and the strategies to overcome clashes of style. Paul Tieger's new book, *Be What You Are,* is an excellent resource on the relationship of type to career choice and ultimate satisfaction. A counselor qualified to administer the inventory can assist the candidate in taking the inventory and making full use of the results, but it is possible to discern one's type by reading the profiles in Tieger's book and other discussions of typology.

FIGURE 2.10

Preferred Settings

EXERCISE 10: Where might your talents be used?

Which of the following would be appealing settings in which to work? (Check all that apply, then rank-order.)

_____ Accounting Firm

_____ Advertising Agency

_____ Bar Association (National, State, or Local)

_____ Community Organization

_____ Consulting Firm

_____ Continuing Legal Education Provider

_____ Corporation

_____ Educational Institution (Law or Graduate School, College or University, Secondary School)

_____ Entertainment Industry

_____ Entrepreneurial Start-up

_____ Financial Institution (Bank, Credit Union, Savings & Loan)

_____ Government (Federal, State, or Local)

_____ Hospital

_____ Investment Bank

_____ Insurance Company

_____ Labor Union

_____ Law Firm

_____ Library or Bookstore

_____ Lobbying Organization

_____ Military

_____ Nonprofit Organization

_____ Political Organization

_____ Prepaid Legal Plan

_____ Private Foundation

_____ Publishing House

_____ Trade Association

_____ Transit Company

_____ Trust Company

_____ Other: _____

Place an asterisk next to all types of organizations for which you have already worked. A lawyer considering building a practice might also use this exercise to decide which types of clients he or she would like to have.

FIGURE 2.11

Conditions for Peak Performance
EXERCISE 11: What brings out the best in you?

Select two or three times when you felt you did your *best* work, when you experienced the psychological state called "flow," when you were proud of your work product and everything seemed to go well and obstacles were handled without difficulty.

   Analyze these instances for the common themes that run throughout them, the skills and personality traits you have that contributed to the achievement of the goal, the reasons that you were inspired to do your best work, the factors in the environment that enabled you to perform to this standard of excellence.

   What are the implications for the type of work or projects you should seek out in the future? How can this information be used to describe you to a prospective employer in an interview?

A lawyer's preferred style of interaction is not only the source of greatest strength but potentially the source of greatest weakness as well. There are many examples of a strength taken to an extreme and becoming a weakness: for instance, the perfectionist who exhibits great attention to detail who is unwilling to relinquish a project until it is absolutely perfect or the intuitive strategist who continues to generate possibilities long after a decision was needed.

   Lawyers are uniquely stressed because they must exhibit proficiency in all eight MBTI dimensions, yet they possess natural strengths and preferences for one set of behaviors over another. For instance, an Intuitor will be valued for an ability to see the possibilities but may be tripped up by his or her lack of attention to detail or unwillingness to complete time records for client billing purposes. The ability to compensate for a potential weakness will help one succeed as much as emphasizing one's strengths. An awareness of one's supervisor's style can help meet his or her expectations and facilitate good working relationships.

   Nontraditional style assessments such as the Heroic Myth Index (HMI), found in Carol S. Pearson's *Awakening the Heroes Within: Twelve Archetypes to Help Us Find Ourselves and Transform Our World*, also can yield valuable insights from another perspective. Pearson's HMI indicates the most active "archetypes" presently being experienced by the individual, including: Innocent, Orphan, Care Giver, Warrior, Seeker, Destroyer, Creator, Lover, Ruler, Magician, Fool, and Sage. Many lawyers in transition have discovered through such assessments that their natural style was compatible with or in conflict with their supervisors' or the overall "corporate culture" of their organizations and were then able to seek more suitable settings as a result.

   For instance, a lawyer scoring high on "Care Giver" will be unhappy in a law firm with a "Warrior" style, unless he or she works in the trusts and estates practice area. A Warrior-style lawyer may be naturally drawn to liti-

FIGURE 2.12

Visualization
EXERCISE 12: What would your ideal job be like?

Imagine it's five years from now and you are reporting for work in a job for which you are very well-suited and in which you experience a great deal of satisfaction.

How long is your commute? If you go to an office, how do you get there? What type of physical setting are you in? Is it formal or informal? How are you and your coworkers dressed? Do you work in a team or alone, or both? How much time do you spend in and out of the office?

What type of hours do you keep? What relationship do you have with your boss or supervisor (if you have one)?

What types of clients do you have and what types of problems do you solve for them? How much pressure do you experience? What are the particular satisfactions of this work?

---

gation or mergers and acquisitions or marketing activities. A "Ruler" or "Sage" lawyer will experience a sense of "fit" in a same-style law firm and will be perceived positively by coworkers and supervisors because of the good fit.

Holland Code

Finally, a fundamental aspect of style assessment is the mesh between your personality and the types of jobs to which you are drawn. Career theorist John Holland developed a theory of careers that has been used for 50 years to analyze jobs and the fit between people and certain career possibilities.

The theory is based on an assumption that there are six types of people and six types of jobs and that people are naturally drawn to jobs in which they could be themselves, use their strengths, and be surrounded by like-minded individuals. Various methods are used by career counselors to determine an individual's Holland Code, including card sorts and the Strong Interest Inventory.

The six types are Social, Enterprising, Artistic, Investigative, Realistic, and Conventional. Lawyers, formerly classified as Enterprising, Artistic, and Social, recently have been reassigned to the "Artistic" category. Holland noticed that Artistic types possess innovating, intuitional abilities and like to work in unstructured situations using imagination and creativity. They describe themselves as independent, unconventional, original, and tense. It is common to find a lawyer who in his or her life had strong interests in other types of artistic pursuits (e.g., the fine or performing arts) or who originally trained in an enterprising field (e.g., accounting or business).

Those lawyers who have strong interests in areas other than artistic may experience restlessness or dissatisfaction in a traditional associate's role. The

Holland Code for a lawyer may indicate the area of practice for which he or she will be best suited:

- If Artistic is the lawyer's type, communication through words, visual images, or music is the theme. Does the lawyer want to be a creative person or will it be satisfying to have creative people as clients? If the lawyer wants more artistic activity in his or her life, can the present job be expanded to include such activity or can the individual's leisure pursuits more actively include artistic activities?
- If a lawyer has a Realistic preference, he or she may enjoy work that allowed time outside the office "in the field," such as environmental or construction law.
- If Social is the style of the lawyer, the importance of helping, counseling, and protecting the interests of individuals and families will be satisfying. These lawyers will actively seek out pro bono assignments to augment their work experience.
- If Investigative is the style, scientifically based practice areas will be suitable, for instance, patent, environmental, medical malpractice, and health-law careers will fit.
- Conventional lawyers will enjoy using their computers and will be drawn to financial, tax, and accounting. They will not mind the detail required in discovery and may be excellent at litigation-support projects.
- Enterprising lawyers will enjoy building a practice and counseling clients on the full range of problems encountered by businesses and corporations. Because of their strong leadership skills, they may enjoy the role of in-house corporate counsel, especially if they have the opportunity to participate in business decision making.

Pulling It All Together

To pull together the results of one's self-analysis into a coherent statement of immediate and long-range goals and objectives, the job seeker should consider enlisting the support of a career counselor, friend, or fellow job seeker. Job-search support groups are being organized by bar associations, law schools, and nonlegal groups; these might be suitable settings in which to explore your options and generate possibilities.

If the job seeker is working on this alone, arrange the key facts on a large piece of poster board using Post-it notes. Note all findings, one key factor per Post-it note. Arrange them and rearrange them in clusters on the poster board to see how the whole picture fits together.

Show the poster board to a friend and brainstorm the possible jobs that would fit all or most of the criteria.

Before giving up a current job, a lawyer might want to consider whether the job can be redesigned or changed in some way to better fit strengths, preferences, and goals. Can projects be taken on that allow for development in the direction desired?

The experience of looking for a new position can be a valuable opportunity not only to reassess one's career path, but to explore positive qualities, strengths, and potential. A thorough analysis of the past can lead to a portrait of a more satisfying future. A synthesis of the findings will allow one to honor preferences and strengths in order to step confidently into the future, designing it, rather than merely surviving it.

CHAPTER 2.A

Personality Factors and Career Choice

Larry Richard

Finding job satisfaction in the practice of law has become a greater challenge during the past few years. With increasing time pressures, declining civility, and an increase in assembly-line legal work, many of your colleagues are facing difficulty in finding a work environment in which they can enjoy the practice of law.

To find true work satisfaction, though, you must do more than simply avoid an unpleasant work environment. What is needed is a thorough understanding of how your own personality fits key aspects of the job that you select. The better the fit between your personality and your job, the greater your likelihood of job satisfaction will be.

A simple example suffices: A lawyer with a personality characterized by warmth, nurturance, and a high need for intimacy is more likely to report job satisfaction in a firm with an open, informal, and friendly "culture," and less likely to report job satisfaction in a firm with a more impersonal, austere, "eat-what-you-kill" atmosphere.

The first step in matching your personality to a job is to understand the most common personality factors that can be used to describe both the individual and the job itself. This chapter will describe a system of personality that will enable you to do just that—Jung's Theory of Psychological Types.

This system of personality has withstood the test of time for more than 40 years, has been used extensively by career counselors assisting individual job seekers, and has spawned a psychological test that has become widely used to help people in general, and lawyers in particular, to better match their personalities to their jobs.

Jung's theories inspired the well-known and widely used Myers-Briggs Type Indicator (MBTI). The MBTI is a formal professional tool that can be administered only by a licensed psychologist or someone specifically trained and certified to do so. Many career counselors, placement officials, guidance counselors, therapists, and others have been so certified. To find a qualified professional, check with your local law school placement office or university counseling center. You also may contact the Center for Applications of Psychological Type in Gainesville, Florida at (800) 777-CAPT. The center may be able to identify someone in your local area trained to administer the MBTI.

Jung's Theory of Psychological Types

Carl Jung, the Swiss psychoanalyst, developed an insightful system of personality classification based on the idea that much of the patterned, habitual behavior of people can be explained by their preferences on four[1] scales:

1. Extraversion[2] versus Introversion
2. Sensing versus Intuition
3. Thinking versus Feeling
4. Judgment versus Perception

Jung conceived each scale as a dichotomy. He reasoned that although everyone utilizes both sides of a given scale on a regular basis, over time each individual develops a psychological comfort for one side in favor of the other. The preferred side thus tends to exert greater influence over a person's thoughts and behavior and eventually forms recognizable personality patterns. Preferences tend to be stable, long term, and pervasive.

The MBTI reports one's preferences in the form of a letter score (E or I, for example) for each of the four scales, along with a numerical score that indicates how strong each score is.[3]

Each person maintains an independent preference on each of the four scales. The author, for example, prefers Extraversion over Introversion, Intuition over Sensing, Feeling over Thinking, and Perception over Judgment. Collectively, these four preferences constitute one's MBTI "type." The author thus would be said to prefer the Extraverted Intuitive Feeling Perception type, or ENFP. (The "N" is used to designate Intuition so as not to confuse it with Introversion, which also begins with an "I".) There are 16 such combinations possible in the MBTI system as shown in Figure 2.A.1.

Let us look at the four MBTI scales to understand the differences that they represent.[4]

Extraversion Versus Introversion

This scale measures one's preferred source of psychological energy. People who prefer Extraversion are energized by the world outside their psyche, by stimuli coming from outside the self. People who prefer Introversion are energized by their inner world, by stimuli from inner thoughts, feelings, and sensations.

Extraverts are more likely to be gregarious, to enjoy client contact, to prefer discussing a legal matter more than writing about it. They may tend to think out loud, more to clarify their own thoughts than to engage in meaningful conversation. They may positively enjoy the rainmaking process, are more

FIGURE 2.A.1
Possible MBTI Combinations

ISTJ	ISFJ	INFJ	INTJ
ISTP	ISFP	INFP	INTP
ESTP	ESFP	ENFP	ENTP
ESTJ	ESFJ	ENFJ	ENTJ

likely to join clubs and bar associations, and will prefer breadth and variety in their work.

Introverts, on the other hand, tend to be more reserved, prefer working alone or in one-on-one relationships, and enjoy analyzing and writing about a legal issue. Their thinking usually is done silently. They tend to prefer concentrating on a topic in depth, thinking it through and reflecting on it. The same events that an Extravert finds exciting and energizing—parties, crowds, fast-breaking events—may be experienced by an Introvert as overstimulating, "too much," or simply not enjoyable.

In the United States, Extraverts constitute a clear majority among the general population. Approximately 75 percent of all men and women prefer Extraversion. The author's study, however, showed that among lawyers, 56 percent prefer Introversion (see Figure 2.A.2). Also, unlike the general population, a gender difference exists. Fully 58 percent of male lawyers prefer Introversion, while 51 percent of women lawyers do.

Despite the fact that more Introverts are attracted to law, both male and female Extravert lawyers report slightly higher job satisfaction than their Introverted counterparts. One possible explanation might be that Introverted lawyers may be weary from too much client contact. Another possibility is that Extraverts tend to report greater job satisfaction in surveys in general.

This particular personality trait can influence your comfort level in the office environment. Strong Introverts can feel really out of place in a boisterous, high-energy Extraverted office. While less common, the opposite can be true for Extraverts. If you are thinking about accepting a particular job offer,

FIGURE 2.A.2
Extraversion Versus Introversion Scale

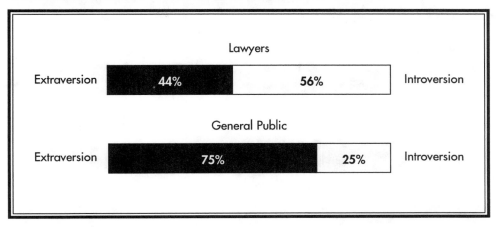

spend some time in the office of your potential employer and pay attention to energy.

As indicated previously, 56 percent of all lawyers prefer Introversion, while the remaining 44 percent prefer Extraversion. In the author's research, three legal specialty areas were found to attract significantly more Extraverts: torts and insurance, litigation, and labor law (53 percent of all labor lawyers preferred Extraversion). If you have a strong preference for Extraversion yourself, you may consider exploring any of these fields. Work setting also can be important. The author's study also found that more than 64 percent of all government lawyers in the study preferred Introversion.

Sensing Versus Intuition

This scale determines how you gather information. Sensors are more comfortable with concrete, specific, factual data—the kinds of information that you get from your five senses. Intuitives are more comfortable with abstract, impressionistic, or theoretical information—the kinds of information you get from your sixth sense.

Sensors usually prefer low ambiguity, well-defined tasks, and a no-nonsense approach to work. Intuitives thrive on creativity, imagining what could be, and finding meaning behind the data.

This scale is highly correlated with many kinds of occupational choices. For example, more Sensors than Intuitives are attracted to the fields of engineering, bookkeeping, chemistry, and budget analysis. More Intuitives than Sensors are attracted to the fields of philosophy, psychotherapy, the fine arts—and law. While 70 percent of all men and women in the United States prefer Sensing, 56 percent of all lawyers (see Figure 2.A.3) prefer Intuiting.

FIGURE 2.A.3
Sensing Versus Intuition Scale

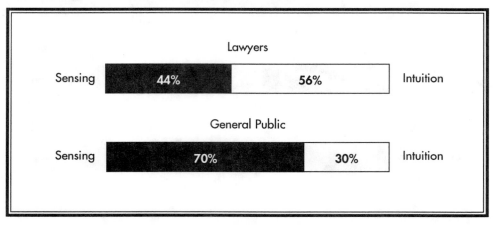

Thus, there are more Intuitives in the population of lawyers than in the general population.

Typical tasks in the early years of law practice are more Sensing than Intuiting. Much of the work assigned to a young associate in the early years of practice is tilted toward the Sensing side of the scale—research on individual points of law, drafting and reviewing documents, combing through transcripts of depositions and answers to interrogatories, etc. As one advances in one's career, more responsibility probably will be conferred on the lawyer, leading ultimately to more "big-picture" case responsibilities and dealing with the larger issues.

If you are a Sensor, you most likely have some affinity for Intuiting as well. Lawyers who prefer Sensing to the exclusion of Intuiting are a small minority. If you fall into this minority, your best path is to develop an expertise in a particular substantive area, preferably one with low ambiguity. Regulatory and code-based practice areas such as tax, securities, and many administrative law specialties will feel much more natural to the strong Sensor. If you are comfortable with both Sensing and Intuiting, most areas of law will fit. And if you are a strong Intuitor, be patient and choose a practice area that will expose you to conceptual issues or one in which gray areas abound.

More than 56 percent of all lawyers prefer Intuiting. The remaining 44 percent prefer Sensing. The author's research identified three legal specialty areas that attract more than their fair share of Sensors: general practice (54 percent), real estate (57 percent), and tax/trusts/estates (57 percent). Likewise, three practice areas attracted a disproportionate number of Intuitives: criminal law (64 percent), labor law (67 percent), and litigation (65 percent). While none of these figures is overwhelmingly tilted in one direction, the trend is clear. If you have a strong Sensing or Intuition preference, you may wish to explore one of the six practice areas previously mentioned.

Your choice of a work setting also may be influenced by your preference on the Sensing versus Intuition scale. In the author's study, two settings attracted a disproportionate number of Intuitives: judicial clerkships (78 percent), and legal-aid and public-defender offices (74 percent). This makes sense for most clerkships offer the promise of dealing with legal jurisprudence, the kinds of conceptual and philosophical issues that Intuitives find appealing. Sensors prefer more practical objectives and thus are more likely to look for a first job that allows them to roll their sleeves up and get to work as a lawyer, such as a position in a traditional law firm. Lawyers who choose poverty-law positions possibly do so out of a motivation to achieve some philosophical end. It makes sense that Intuitives would be attracted to such a practice.

By the same token, it makes sense that 75 percent of the military lawyers in the author's study preferred Sensing. Other studies of military officers have found a preponderance of Sensing types among them.

Thinking Versus Feeling

This scale describes two very different modes of decision making. Thinkers rely on logic and objective analysis to reach their conclusions. They may have strong feelings about the thing to be decided, but they usually make a conscious attempt to put those feelings aside and not allow them to influence their thinking.

Feelers, on the other hand, use a more personal, subjective strategy. Typical questions that a Feeler might ask of himself or herself include "Do I like X?" or "Do I want X?"

Thinkers tend to be critical and to receive criticism from others as mere data, while Feelers allow the emotions in along with the data. Thus, Feelers tend to have their feelings bruised more easily. Because of this, Feelers also pay more attention to maintenance behaviors—harmonizing, avoiding conflict, paying compliments, etc.

Thinkers are attracted to the realm of the mind. Ask a thinker "Why did you go into law?" and you'll most likely hear the words "intellectual challenge" as the answer. Ask a Feeler the same question and you may hear answers such as "to help people" or "to promote social justice."

The Thinker-Feeler scale (see Figure 2.A.4) is the only one that is distributed differently for men and women in the general population. Roughly 60 percent of all men prefer Thinking, as opposed to 35 percent of all women. The Thinking preference is one of the hallmarks of the legal profession. In the author's study, 66 percent of all women lawyers and 81 percent of all men lawyers preferred Thinking.

In the author's study, Thinker lawyers had a slightly higher level of job satisfaction than Feeler lawyers. Despite the minority status of Feelers in the profession, however, many of them have found satisfaction.

It is not known why Feelers have been able to find nearly equal levels of satisfaction in what is clearly a Thinker profession. Possibly, it is by choosing work environments or substantive areas wisely. For example, nearly 44 per-

FIGURE 2.A.4
Thinking Versus Feeling Scale

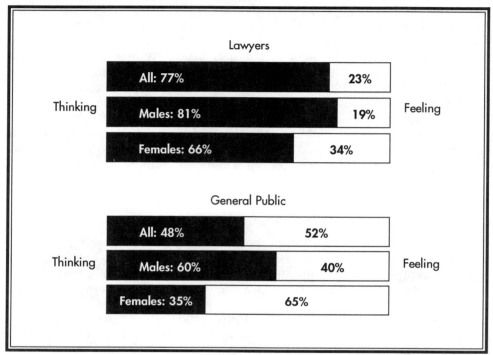

cent of the lawyers working for legal-aid or public-defender offices were Feelers compared to all lawyers as a whole, of whom only 24 percent prefer Feeling.

Thirty-four percent of all female lawyers prefer Feeling. The author's study found two legal specialties that attract greater proportions of Feeler women: labor law (44 percent female Feelers/56 percent female Thinkers) and litigation (41 percent female Feelers/59 percent female Thinkers). For all Feelers, litigation can be a two-edged sword—many Feelers are attracted to the field because it holds the promise of effecting social change (a value for many Feelers); on the other hand, it represents the area of the law with perhaps the greatest percentage of ongoing interpersonal conflict (a situation that most Feelers disdain).

Only 19 percent of all male lawyers prefer Feeling. The author's study found three legal specialties that attract greater proportions of Feeler men: general practice, criminal law, and matrimonial law, all of which attracted 28 percent male Feelers and 72 percent male Thinkers.

Lawyers with a Thinker preference—male and female alike—have found job satisfaction in nearly every legal specialty imaginable.

Judging Versus Perceiving

This scale measures one's style in dealing with tasks and people. This scale is the most readily recognizable in others. Judgers prefer a life that is planned, decisive, and orderly. Perceivers prefer a life that is open-ended and spontaneous. Judgers like to have control; Perceivers like to keep their options open.

To maintain control, Judgers tend to employ one or more of the following strategies: doing only one thing at a time; completing assignments in an orderly and timely manner to avoid the last-minute rush; keeping small manageable lists of things to do, and methodically checking off completed items; making decisions at the earliest possible point, without waiting for all information; scheduling their time carefully, and giving a great deal of respect to their schedule; keeping a neat desk; and planning for all possible contingencies in advance.

Perceivers like to keep their options open and they do so by employing one or more of the following strategies: juggling many tasks, often doing more than one at a time; "playing it by ear"; making many lengthy lists (and sometimes losing them); putting off decisions to gather more complete information; maintaining piles in their office, any one of which can be worked on; acting spontaneously; avoiding committing themselves to plans until the last minute; and enjoying surprises.

The author's study (see Figure 2.A.5) found that more lawyers prefer Judging (63 percent) compared to the general public (55 percent). Moreover, Judger lawyers tend to have stronger numerical scores on the Judging scale than they do on the other three MBTI scales. In other words, many lawyers identify quite strongly with the Judger traits described previously. It makes sense that a profession that has many deadlines and requires a great deal of organizational skills from its practitioners would attract more people with personality traits that favor these kinds of skills.

FIGURE 2.A.5
Judging Versus Perceiving Scale

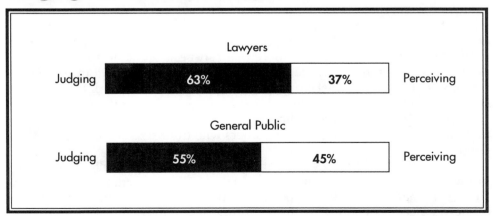

Not only are Judgers more prevalent in the legal profession, but they enjoy greater job satisfaction as well, according to the author's study. Less than 20 percent of all Judger lawyers reported job dissatisfaction, compared to more than 25 percent of all lawyers.

What strategies can you adopt if you have a strong Perceiving preference? The author falls into this category and made the difficult choice to leave the law after ten years of practice. It was a good decision for the author but certainly is not the only option for you.

The only work setting to which significantly more Perceivers are attracted is legal-aid and public-defender offices (57 percent prefer Perceiving compared to 37 percent of all lawyers.) If this type of work appeals to you for other reasons, you may find that your Perceiving preference fits right in.

In terms of practice areas, Labor lawyers reported more Perceivers than any other area (47 percent compared to 37 percent of all lawyers). Other areas with somewhat more Perceivers than Judgers include criminal law (43 percent), general practice (42 percent), and litigation (42 percent). As with the Feeling realm, Perceivers in litigation are using a two-edged sword. While the "play-it-by-ear" style of the Perceiver can cope well with a fast-breaking change in circumstances quite common to litigation, and thus provide the Perceiver with satisfaction, many Perceivers also tend to be a bit on the disorganized side, and in litigation, the consequences of this style can be more harsh and immediate than perhaps any other legal specialty.

The best advice for lawyers with strong Perceiver preferences is to surround themselves with support staff—secretaries, paralegals, etc.—who have Judging preferences and to count on them to help out in the weakest areas. This strategy can enable even the strongest Perceiver to find increased satisfaction in the law.

Overview

Perhaps the most important finding of the author's research is that it is possible for lawyers of every kind of MBTI preference to find job satisfaction. There was no single MBTI preference, and none of the 16 MBTI types, that contained more dissatisfied lawyers than satisfied lawyers.

Although this chapter has focused on job satisfaction, one added benefit of learning about your Myers-Briggs type preferences is worth noting. A true understanding of typological differences can be a valuable tool in understanding others in the workplace and becoming more effective in communicating with them. An underlying premise of the MBTI is that all the different styles of behavior are legitimate and that no single style is better or worse than any other. By truly understanding type preferences, you can gain a deeper understanding and appreciation for others who think and act differently than you do.

You also should be aware that several other key personality variables influence your job satisfaction besides your MBTI preferences. Examples include personal values (helping people, status, security, fun, etc.), psychological needs (need for control, inclusion, intimacy, achievement, etc.), motivated skills (writing, analyzing, persuading, etc.), and career interests (technology, health care, real estate, international trade, etc.). The more of these variables that you pay attention to in formulating your job search, the more likely you are to achieve job satisfaction. Your local library or bookstore is full of excellent self-help books that cover most of these areas. Also, any good career counselor can help you identify your key personality traits and fit them to the job.

Finally, keep in mind that a job is just the first step in a career. Career satisfaction requires job satisfaction plus a clear game plan for the long term. Those who formulate long-term career goals and put them in writing are more likely to achieve what they want.

Notes

1. For Jungian purists, Jung explicitly identified three dichotomies. The fourth, Judgment versus Perception, was added by the developers of the MBTI, Katherine Briggs and Isabel Myers, because it was implicit in Jung's theory.

2. In Jungian and Myers-Briggs literature, it is customary to spell "Extraversion" with an "a" in contrast to the term "extroversion," which is commonly used in colloquial English.

3. Purist alert: Orthodox MBTI theory holds that the numerical score indicates how clear or certain one is of one's preference for the particular side of the dichotomy, and that it does not indicate the strength of the score. How could it, for we are theoretically dealing with a dichotomy and not a continuum. This point is the subject of much scholarly debate within the academic world, and in fact, the assertion that Type is dichotomous is one of the vulnerable points of Jungian theory. In actual practice, most laypersons and many counselors treat the numerical score as a strength score, as in "He has a strong preference for Extraversion. . . ." or "She has a mild preference for Intuition. . . ."

4. Most of the generalizations offered in the balance of this chapter are drawn from the personal experience of the author in working with the MBTI over the past 12 years of providing career counseling to lawyers. The remaining generalizations are drawn from empirical research conducted by the author in 1992. The research investigated the relationship of the MBTI to job satisfaction among U.S. lawyers. Research-based conclusions will be identified as such; all other observations can be assumed to be based on the author's personal counseling experience.

Interpreting the Results of Self-Assessment Techniques: Will Career Testing Really Help You?

Anthony Monahan

"Remember why you became a lawyer?" was the recruitment pitch of a general-membership ABA section a few years ago, playing on aspirations of law as a lifetime journey, not an eight-to-six timesheet. We are pretty clear about when we became lawyers, memories framed by certificates and graduation snapshots; it is the *why* that grows fuzzy and distorted.

Still, we think we can become more competent lawyers—through hard work, later hours, by being smarter, tougher. But what if we want more? What if we want that elusive thing called "happiness"? The professional world offers many ways to assess our careers and job choices, as this book and this chapter describe. What we learn about ourselves, however, may not be the most valuable lesson.

"In any Myers-Briggs Type Indicator session I've been in," says one lawyer about a popular self-assessment process, "I've never heard anyone say, 'I want to change, I want to be a litigator,' or, 'I don't know what I'm doing; how can this help me?' You learn that you can't change people, but that you can recognize and appreciate how they deal with others, how you can adjust. You begin to understand how other people tick, and then begin learning about yourself."

Dissatisfaction Among the Ranks

First, however, what is the problem? Is it simply young lawyer "dissatisfaction"? Recent news implies something worse, that despondency is just around the corner. ABA-YLD surveys profile a profession edgy and uneasy, with self-doubts echoing off hotel ballroom walls in career seminars across the country. In just one practice area, "the dissatisfaction rate for corporate counsel has jumped an astonishing 77 percent . . . across the board, there has been a dramatic reduction in lawyers who are very satisfied. . . ." Nearly 75 percent of all lawyers and 84 percent of women in practice responding to one survey feel "worn out" at the end of each workday; 17 percent said their marriages were undermined; 20 percent of women lawyers and 13 percent of male lawyers reported looking for focus in a bottle, downing more than six drinks a day. The survey results are discussed in greater detail in Chapter 1.

Is it post-1980s disillusionment, predictable way-after-hours griping, or a deeper love-loathing relationship with the law and life? One legal career counselor, Larry Richard, President of Richard Consulting Group, Inc., reports that of all young lawyers who complete his firm's most intensive career evaluation, more than half actually leave the profession. These are the worst cases—"for them, the law is a bad fit"—but he senses a wider malaise: "I'm seeing a nonstop increase in lawyers very unhappy, very distressed."

We could get depressed about all this. In fact, we *are* getting depressed: Lawyers are 3.6 times more likely to suffer depression than people in any other occupation, according to the November, 1990, *Journal of Occupational Medicine*. Researchers at Johns Hopkins University evaluated health surveys of 12,000 people in 105 occupations. Among the criteria for depression were two or more consecutive weeks of "sadness," and abrupt changes in sleep, appetite, and energy. "Juggling their jobs and their values" could be one cause of lawyer depression, according to a survey report. "Some lawyers engage in activities they know to be questionable or are very conflicting. This can be depressing."

There is, we know, no mass exodus from the law, although 37 percent of young lawyers in private practice who are actively considering changing jobs say they would look at nonlegal careers. The most damaging, and lasting, effect is on the majority of lawyers who stay. "There are serious problems," reported Ronald L. Hirsch, a former YLD staff director and a principal investigator for YLD career dissatisfaction surveys. "These lie in the increasing social dysfunction or destructive behavior by lawyers and the impact of this behavior on themselves, their families, their quality of work and productivity, their firms, and their clients."

A major nemesis is the demand for more billable hours, professional burnout with its numbing effect in family and personal life. Other suspects cited in YLD surveys are a lack of intellectual challenge, capricious job-advancement policies, few "warm and personal" work settings, and "political intrigue and backbiting." Are the culprits, then, external—senior lawyers and managers, unreasonable clients, law firm profit pressures? Is it "their" fault?

Of course not; it is *your* fault. Ironically, you are both the problem and the solution, according to psychological theorists who specialize in soothing career nightmares. Who *am* I? How can I understand, then change, myself? Are there tests that I can take to determine the rest of me, the best of me? You might learn that it is still your fault, but at least you will know who to blame.

You could, for example, be succumbing to the Imposter Phenomenon (IP). "This goes hand in hand with the idea of success," says clinical psychologist Dr. Joan C. Harvey. "It is based on intense, secret feelings of fraudulence in the face of success and achievement . . . victims are caught in a cycle of emotions, thoughts, and actions that can virtually control their lives." Up to "70 percent of all successful people" are victims of "temporary or chronic IP." In her book, *If I'm So Successful, Why Do I Feel Like a Fake?*, she cites one IP sufferer, Jessie, a law firm associate who had written a brief highly praised by her senior partners:

"I *knew* that brief wasn't good. It wasn't bad, but it was so easy for me to do . . . I felt if it's not difficult, it's not really worth anything, it's not good. I thought, 'Those poor guys, they've never seen a good brief in their lives.' "

"How many people have achieved less than they should have, or given up their careers completely, due to the Imposter Phenomenon?" asks Dr. Harvey. How are our IP tendencies revealed? One quick way is through her test, the Harvey IP Scale, which includes a 14-question multiple-choice questionnaire (question number 8: "I tend to feel like a phony," with answers ranging from "not true" to "very true").

There is the *Sustainer versus Achiever* battle for control of ourselves: "The world of work divides people into two distinct and telling categories, Sustainers and Achievers," writes Los Angeles–based career coach Adele M. Scheele, Ph.D.

Sustainers are most of us who do our jobs well, "learning to wait for others to tell us how good our work is, instead of noting our mistakes . . . waiting for our bosses to appreciate out loud our last negotiation, instead of asking if that was all we could get. When waiting doesn't work—and it doesn't—we become resentful . . . we pay with our lives." Achievers grab control of their work and careers, while trusting "Sustainers believe in a 'fair' system. Achievers negotiate their way along, making new rules, wanting to both give and get more. They are often labeled aggressive by those too timid to try."

Can *we* become Achievers, too? In *Skills for Success: A Guide to the Top*, Dr. Scheele lists Achiever career strategies (from "Experience Doing" to "Use Catapulting"), allowing us to test ourselves, if we are tough enough.

There is still time to survive the climb to the top, and even enjoy it. Or "find yourself lying awake after another day at your fascinating job, feeling bored, disappointed and uneasy," warns behavioral scientist Robert M. Bramson, Ph.D., in his 1990 book, *Coping With the Fast Track Blues*. "Worse, you wake up to an empty bed, an empty bottle, a drawer full of unpaid bills, a headache from trying to figure out how anyone who's making such good money and seems so accomplished could have such a messed-up life."

Ouch—shoot me your personality quiz, doc, quick!

Self-Assessments

To determine your candidacy for the career-bending blues, Dr. Bramson offers several self-assessments, including a "Mini-Quiz on Power Motivation and Hubris." First, a 14-question self-evaluation test assesses your risk of career crack-up: "1. Are you extraordinarily competent? Do you feel exhilarated by your control over your work, other people, important events . . . 11. Have you been told that you're more angry, indecisive, overly social, withdrawing, or intimidating lately?" Answer yes, maybe, even "sometimes" to more than half of the questions, and you fit "the fast-track template."

Most of us, however, still want it all: stimulating, rewarding careers; strong, fulfilling personal relationships, and some measure of self-awareness. Is there a career-planning personality measurement that seems especially responsive to the wavering dreams of lawyers?

1. Are you usually
   (a) a "good mixer," or
   (b) rather quiet and reserved?
2. If you were a teacher, would you rather teach
   (a) fact courses, or
   (b) courses involving theory?
3. Do you more often let
   (a) your heart rule your head, or
   (b) your head rule your heart?

—from Myers-Briggs Type Indicator,
© 1985 Consulting Psychologists Press

In young-lawyer gatherings across the country, and at state and local bar meetings, cryptic codes are overheard: Are you an ESTP, "the ultimate realist," an ISTP, "ready to try anything once," or an ENTJ, "a natural leader"?

According to Von S. Heinz, a former director for the YLD, one of the most popular programs at past Young Lawyer meetings has been career-evaluation, audience-participation sessions. "The programs use the Myers-Briggs Type Indicator to analyze lawyers' personal likes and dislikes, strengths and weaknesses, to indicate their suitability for certain areas of practice. The large number of lawyers attending Myers-Briggs programs demonstrates a very strong interest among young lawyers in analyzing their own personalities and their particular interests in the law."

Personality Type Theories

Will we ever be in the right place at the right time in our careers? The Myers-Briggs Type Indicator, developed in the 1940s and 1950s by Isabel Briggs Myers and Katherine C. Briggs, based on psychologist Carl Jung's theories of personality preference, gives clear answers, using shorthand terminology.

Myers-Briggs begins with a questionnaire—92 multiple-choice and word-preference questions, for example, on a self-scoreable measurement. The result is a four-letter indicator of your type: Extraversion (E) or Introversion (I); Sensing (S) or Intuition (N); Thinking (T) or Feeling (F); Judging (J) or Perceiving (P). Sixteen basic letter-code personality types, then, are indicated by the Myers-Briggs system.

The type most frequently found in law, according to Larry Richards and lawyer-author Susan Bell in a 1989 paper, is ESTJ. "Extraverts are more energized by the outer world, focusing more on social interaction than inner reflection. Sensers use all their senses to take in information, thus are likely to be no-nonsense, realistic, pragmatic people who look for facts rather than theory. Thinkers are logical in decision making, more comfortable being detached, objective, sensible. Judgers are organized and decisive, keep projects on schedule, want to get to the point. The ESTJ style can be described as the natural manager."

Other personality types drawn to law are ENTJs ("the 'take charge' people in many law firms"); ISTJs ("the most meticulous, overprepared, the classic perfectionists"), and ENTPs ("the legal profession's entrepreneurs, risk-takers, frequently scattered").

"Personality type theory is not intended to pigeonhole people, or explain everything," says Richards. "It does offer a way to understand and appreciate differences. Type theory helps explain different ways that people take in information and make decisions with that information, which helps explain some of our behavior."

Since the Myers-Briggs Indicator was first published in 1956, it has become the most widely used personality measurement of its kind, with an estimated two million people taking the "test" each year. Law firms have used it to improve office communication, manage partnership conflicts, and aid in recruiting and hiring. ("Firms, however, should not use any psychological instrument to exclude candidates on the basis of personality," warns Richards. "This exclusion may well be illegal, and at the least goes against the spirit of the instrument. The Myers-Briggs Indicator motto is 'understanding and appreciating differences,' not 'using differences to discriminate.' ")

"Of course, the 16 personality types and the four temperaments explored . . . can never capture all the nuances of our individual uniqueness," says Dr. Charles Seashore of Johns Hopkins University in *Type Talk*, a 1988 book on type theory and the Myers-Briggs Indicator by Otto Kroeger and Janet M. Thuesen. "But what is amazing is just how much ground can be covered. The combinations of eight letters help us to move easily from alphabet soup to a direct, plain-folks understanding of behavior."

Reactions to Personality Measurement

At young lawyer meetings, the use of Myers-Briggs in career workshops remains a long-running hit. As the workshops wind down, and people huddle to analyze and compare their personality codes, rooms fill with chatter, a sense of involvement and fun—and some doubts about Myers-Briggs's ultimate relevance in making hard career choices.

"The first time I took the indicator, in Denver at the 1989 midyear YLD meeting," says James Whitehill, a young Tucson lawyer, "four guys together, all in pin-striped suits, had the exact same characteristics; the YLD activists in our group also were the same, ESTJs." (ESTJs, according to *Type Talk*, are "life's administrators.")

"In every Myers-Briggs session I've been in, though, you learn as much about others, how they think and react, as you learn about yourself."

"Some people who take Myers-Briggs are disappointed," says Michael A. Bedke, a Tampa lawyer. "They think a bright light will come on, a voice saying something like, 'be a real estate practitioner in a midsized firm.' The expectation is for great, sage advice—'if you work in a 9.3-person firm, practicing medical malpractice defense, *then* you'll be happy.'

"We walk away from the workshop," says Bedke, a real estate practitioner, "it's been sort of fun, some chuckles, and we go over it again at dinner. But would we go out and really change? Most of us say, 'I wish I'd had the information earlier, but to change now, I've got to take this big financial hit.' The fact is, nobody is willing to pay me enough to do what I really love to do. And we think we have problems, but with the money we're making anyway, these are not terrible, life-or-death choices."

It is hazardous to use a single test in making career choices, says Larry Richard, a former trial lawyer, psychologist—and an ENFP. "First, why are you in law?" says Richard. "Did you go to law school by default, you wanted to be a professional but didn't want to be a doctor or accountant, you liked what you saw on *L.A. Law* or *Perry Mason*? Law schools have become the great repositories for liberal arts students who don't know what they want to do. What are your personal values, psychological needs, your real interests? Myers-Briggs can explain much about your personal fit in the profession." Richard details Myers-Briggs in greater detail in Chapter 2.A.

Personality Types in the Legal Field

Who tend to be the most unhappy lawyers? Certain personality types indicated by Myers-Briggs could be roughed up by the legal culture. Feelers are hard to satisfy in law, where Thinkers predominate. (In Myers-Briggs interpretations, Feelers make decisions through a process of personal valuing, based on how important something is to them, not on whether it is "right" or not. Thinkers, those analytical logic lovers, rarely become personally invested in their decisions.)

"Imagine being a Feeler in a firm of 100 Thinkers," Richards says. "The values with which a Feeler is most comfortable—an interpersonal, harmonious environment, strong personal relationships—are just not there." Lawyers with both Sensing and Feeling scores are particularly vulnerable: "Virtually every Sensing-Feeling lawyer I've counseled finally says, 'I want out.' "

For anyone considering a career change, Richard advises to step out carefully and with self-knowledge. "Even if the change is within the profession, clarity is important before you make any move. What do you really want? It's a big mistake to examine the job market, your 'options,' before achieving that clarity. Before looking 'out there,' you should look 'in here,' look at what you can learn about yourself."

What is your Myers-Briggs sign? A growing number of young lawyers today can describe their four-letter type more accurately than their checkbook balances. Much of the profession, however, still does not know ESFP from ERISA and would resist any typecasting movement.

"Let's face it, most lawyers, and certainly law firms as organizations, have great reluctance about anything that sounds 'touchy-feely,' " says Carol Jordan, a San Francisco–based management consultant with Altman & Weil, a legal consulting firm. Much of the work using Myers-Briggs is in improving law firm communications: "It's a good tool in helping people see how they relate to others, in team-building, getting everyone with their own sense of beliefs pulled into a firm's decision-making process. Tax people, for example, are very Sensing and Judging ('orderly, organized, seeking closure'). If you have someone who is an Extravert and a Perceiver (the procrastinating, messy, list-loser), and you put these folks together, then it's time for some attitude adjustment, some understanding."

Among the benefits of test-yourself approaches, says Washington, D.C., lawyer and author Susan Bell, is looking realistically at professional unease and dissatisfaction. "When you get a sense of basic personality differences, a sense of why you or others clash with other people, then you discover there's no reason to take it personally," says Bell, author of *Full Disclosure*, a career-choice guide for those considering law.

"I think dissatisfaction is worse today than we see in surveys," she says. "A problem with this generation of lawyers is that it's more of a business than they thought they were getting into. Many people got into law for the wrong reasons, they feel trapped, and there are tremendous financial pressures—we know that average salaries are much different than those few big-firm salaries we read so much about. Most law firms certainly aren't taking the problems seriously, so we should commend those people who do try to understand themselves, who try and understand what might really be behind unhappy situations."

The Effects of Self-Analysis

Can lawyer dissatisfaction, edginess, even that "sadness" found by the Johns Hopkins researchers, be confronted, perhaps cured by self-analysis? Professional maturity might be realizing that instead of becoming great, famous lawyers, we have become good, honest advocates. Personal growth might mean looking into that mirror and saying, pretty fair, I can live with that.

"I went through a two-year period when I was very unhappy, simply didn't know what I was suited for," says Larry Caniglia, a civil litigator in Trenton, New Jersey. "I was depressed all the time, hated the thought of going to work each day." He thought strongly about nonlegal work, then signed up for an intensive career-evaluation program including personality type testing.

"Myers-Briggs did help me focus on what I was unhappy about," he says. "It gave me hints on other careers—I might make a travel agent, or a very good florist—but what shocked me were the final indications: I was meant to be a lawyer! I was not unhappy about being a lawyer, but about the way I was working. It helps you see what it is about yourself that drives you crazy about yourself. I learned I would never, ever, be happy being a law office manager, which is what I thought I wanted to do.

"It might sound simple to say, 'understand your strong points, if you want to try cases, try cases.' Or it sounds simple to say, 'free yourself up,' do what you're best at, what is most fulfilling for you. But most of us need some help to see things that clearly, especially about ourselves."

CHAPTER 3

How to Counterattack If You Are Losing Your Job

David S. Machlowitz

"Two weeks ago, I had a great job, a great salary, and a performance review that said I was headed for even greater things. Now, like dozens of other lawyers in my firm, all I've got is two months' severance, a student loan, a mortgage and a draft of a résumé." The speaker is one of the hundreds of lawyers laid off in recent years. Unfortunately, the economic climate is unlikely to improve enough to cause a repeat of the "go-go" 1980s. Accordingly, lawyer layoffs remain a reality in the 1990s.

The psychological impact on the fired lawyers is often horrendous, especially because for many of them it is the first setback after an unbroken string of successes in school. As one of them recalls, "It was devastating to my self-worth. Everyone else is going to work and you're not going to work. After a while, you wonder whether you're ever going to work again." The economic impact, of course, can be devastating as well, especially for those with student loans to repay and families to support. The days when associates from top firms could always land good jobs are long gone.

Is a layoff easier to take—or at least survive—if you are part of a two-income family? Not necessarily, says Debbie, a Los Angeles lawyer married to another lawyer: "Yes, we had two incomes, but we also had two sets of student loans. We had to have two cars, which our firms insisted be expensive enough to impress clients. We have to pay $17,000 a year of after-tax income to our child's care giver. So that we could see the baby more, we bought a home in the expensive area near our offices. When I was laid off, none of these expenses went away. We're eating into what savings we have now. If my husband is fired before I find a job, we're bankrupt."

What is behind the wave of layoffs? Some of the most lucrative aspects of business law—mergers and acquisitions, real estate, and stock and bond offerings—are slumping. Less work means either the same lawyers earn fewer dollars or fewer lawyers earn the same dollars. Years ago, most firms would have accepted fewer dollars (perhaps even enjoying the fewer hours worked) to save their colleagues' jobs. Now, forget it!

As law firms grew, it became easier to fire partners and associates you barely knew. *The American Lawyer* magazine, and that 1980s' invention, the law firm business consultant, harped incessantly on profits per partner as if it were the only reason to practice law. Avaricious headhunters encouraged partners to jump ship for slightly more money. No one should doubt that firms are businesses and that nonperforming partners and associates should not have perpetual employment, but the late Judge Irving Kaufman of the U.S. Second Circuit Court of Appeals said that the then current wave of firings in the late 1980s was "a disgrace" and "immoral."

And what about in-house lawyers? Because few corporations have hundreds, or even dozens, of lawyers, there have been only one or two reports of mass firings of corporate counsel. Corporate hiring and salary freezes, however, remain common. In addition, to some extent in-house lawyering is countercyclical. When employees are laid off, in-house lawyers are busy with termination plans and discharge suits. When business is off, work formerly sent outside may be brought in-house to save money.

In addition, in-house counsel face some disasters all their own. At best, lawyers of companies that have been taken over or relocated find themselves reporting to people they do not know who are hundreds of miles away. Then there was the 1980s' wave of leveraged buy-outs (LBOs), which is being followed by a 1990s' wave of those companies being broken up and sold off, or even worse, going bankrupt. The post-LBO general counsel of a New Jersey company conceded to a prospective recruit: "Don't think of this job as a career."

Michael Luskin had been a partner at New York's Gelberg & Abrams for two years when the senior partners dissolved the firm. Now a partner at Luskin & Stern, he looks back on the situation: "I worked hard for years to achieve my goal. It was very, very upsetting for me to watch a phenomenally successful firm—and my career—torn apart by small-minded people for no good reason. Gelbert & Abrams fell apart, not for financial reasons, but because of personal animosities among the partners.

"Dealing with the betrayal and the dishonesty is impossibly difficult," Luskin says. "You put out for these people, and then you get shafted. The bitterness never goes away, but there is nothing you can do about having bad people as partners. It is not productive to blame them.

"I called everyone I knew. I spent at least four hours a day on the phone. Yes, you have to answer ads and see headhunters, but most of all, call everyone on your Rolodex. You have to be disciplined about it. It was very gratifying that my friends—even people I had not seen in years—really helped me out. They set up interviews and made phone calls on my behalf. Now, I always help anyone who asks me."

How can you tell when trouble is on the horizon? What can you do about it? First of all, do not panic, but do not just sit around, either. Headhunter turned outplacer Carol Kanarek advises: "Find out what your true situation is before you do anything rash."

The following provides some practical pointers on identifying the warning signs of a layoff, preparing oneself for the layoff, and "picking up the pieces."

Warning Signs of a Layoff

There are many indications of an impending layoff. Some are readily apparent, while others are more difficult to discern. Have the firm's or company's revenues dropped? These days, many partners will not accept small drops in income to save associates' careers. Have competitors laid off lawyers recently? Once one firm takes the public-relations heat, others follow.

Have partners left the firm? If a major rainmaker has left, disaster is brewing. If service partners have been forced out, what hope is there for associates? Is the new CEO from a different city? Many New York Fortune 500 corporations spent millions of dollars relocating to Connecticut to save their CEOs a 50-mile commute. If the CEO is from 500 miles away, watch out.

Are merger discussions under way? "Redundant associates" will be fired before the handshake is concluded. Have salary increases been delayed or reduced? Next, entire salaries will be reduced—perhaps including yours. Have performance reviews been delayed? If profits are dropping, firms will not give good reviews to associates who soon will be terminated.

Are partners spending unusual amounts of time in closed-door meetings? They are not wasting that much billable time to pick out new stationery. Are the firm's clients or the company's customers hurting? You will be hurting next. Are memos demanding a decrease in minor expenses circulating? The firm will save more money firing people than saving cab fare.

Are bills being padded? Suicidal as it often is, firms often churn cases to raise cash, hoping that clients will not notice. Has hiring of new lawyers been reduced? The next step is firing of old lawyers.

How to Prepare for a Layoff

You can take several steps to prepare for a layoff. For example, you should:

- Increase your personal client base, which is the only real security in today's market.
- Develop a "hot" specialty, for being a "good litigator" or "solid generalist" is not enough any more.
- Step up your networking efforts.
- Make a purely social call to everyone you think might help if you later have to make a "know of any jobs?" call. It will make the later call seem less self-serving.
- Build up your savings. Why have financial pressure added to professional pressure?
- Rely on liquid investments. Long-term bonds will not pay short-term rent.
- Try to get assignments from the most powerful potential mentors. They will be the ones swinging the ax.
- Think about what you would like your next job to be and what would make you more likely to get it. Pick your future targets when you are not panicking.

- Talk to lawyers who have found new positions recently about what techniques worked for them. They have the most relevant advice.
- Update your résumé. You want it ready to go before any positions are filled. Prepare different résumés emphasizing your different specialties.
- Get the names of any reputable headhunters in your area. The disreputable ones—and there are many—will find you.
- Draft a cover letter describing your strengths to possible new employers. This should be sitting in the drawer with your résumés.

If You Are Laid Off: Picking Up the Pieces

If you are laid off, you must prepare to face the consequences. Negotiate as good a severance deal as you can. This means not only money, but access to a telephone, a secretary, and someone who will take messages. Find out what type of reference you will receive. While you are still at the firm, be psychologically prepared to be treated as a leper. The partners may be justifying their decision to fire you and the associates may be afraid or embarrassed to associate with you. Being angry is natural and perhaps justified, but it will not help you. Redirect your rage into determination to find a new job fast.

Eliminate unnecessary expenses. It may be a long struggle after the severance pay runs out. Buy an answering machine and good stationery. Treat your job search as a full-time job.

Let everyone know that you are looking (but not that you were fired). You never know from whom a lead will come. Ask people not only if they know of openings, but if they know of anyone who might know of openings. You may have only 50 contacts, but if each of them gives you only three or more names, you have 200. Ask for help. None of us likes begging, but your contacts' contacts will respond better to a call from them than from you. If you can ask a jury for $10 million in damages or a seller to reduce his or her asking price, you can ask a friend for help.

Contact associations. Your city and state bar associations and the local and national chapters of the American Corporate Counsel Association may maintain lists of openings and also may provide support groups and workshops on résumé writing, interviewing, networking, and starting your own practice. Contact your law school or college alumni association for help. Alumni of your law firm might also lend a hand.

Search for the right search firm. Be very selective about which recruiters you use, but if you find several who seem ethical and energetic, use them all—do you think you are their only candidate? Just keep careful lists of who suggested which opening. Press them for more than listings of jobs: comments on your résumé, inside information about firms, and suggestions about how to discuss your firing with an interviewer. Follow up with the recruiters monthly.

Do not rely exclusively on headhunters. Some can be notoriously sleazy, generally unresponsive to people more than four years out of law school and often they are willing to send you to the worst sweatshop in town for a fee.

Be wary of "career counselors" or "outplacement consultants." Many are just failed headhunters. If possible, contact desirable employers directly. If you do not need a headhunter to suggest openings, contact them yourself. Not having a headhunter's fee attached to your hiring may help.

Consider government positions. The work is often interesting and far more socially meaningful than private practice, the security is great, and you may learn a marketable specialty. Or consider relocating. Boston may be slumping but Orlando is not. Or consider setting up your own firm. If you have clients, or think you can get them, maybe it is time to be your own boss.

Perhaps you should switch from outside counsel to in-house, or vice versa. A former client may have an opening, or you can consult the *Directory of Corporate Counsel*. If your in-house work is a specialty now in demand at law firms, such as Employee Retirement Income Security Act (ERISA), environmental law, or patents, consider private practice.

Whatever you do, keep working. To stay solvent and keep from getting rusty, consider part-time work, pro bono projects, court-appointed cases, or work as a temporary lawyer. Lesley Friedman of Special Counsel, Inc., in New York, which places lawyers in temporary positions, has been flooded with résumés: "They're people from the best firms and the best law schools. It's really heartbreaking and scary." Part-time work also can generate new contacts.

Do you really want to be a lawyer? Being laid off may be the opportunity you need to start afresh. New York headhunter Laura Colangelo says that "overwhelming numbers of lawyers are fed up with law firm life and are desperate to find something else."

Help your family cope. They are anxious, too. The impact on children can be especially severe.

Stay visible. Use some of your time to line up speaking assignments or write articles. It may pay off with a job or with clients later. As well as breaking up the monotony of repetitive job search, it may boost your self-esteem.

Finally, do not jump at the first opportunity that knocks. Your hardest time actually may be when you first get offered a job. If it is not what you want, think seriously about turning it down. Be realistic, but do not be desperate.

Conclusion

Despite the immediate emotional trauma of being laid off, it is certainly not the end of the world. It does not require passive acceptance. Quite the opposite, by recognizing the layoff warning signs and preparing oneself psychologically, a displaced lawyer can actively counterattack and secure another position.

CHAPTER 4

How to Improve Your Satisfaction with Your Current Career

Mindy Friedler

The first question many practicing lawyers ask nonpracticing lawyers is, "How did you get out?" The level of dissatisfaction with the practice of law is on the rise and has led to lost productivity, low morale, burnout, and expensive turnover. Changing careers, however, is no longer a viable option for many lawyers. The years of headhunters calling associates a few times a week to ask if they "knew anyone who might be interested . . ." are largely over. In addition, there are fewer opportunities for alternative careers. For years law school recruiters (and frustrated parents) sold law school to reluctant students on the theory that a law degree would open doors for them even if they did not want to practice. Unfortunately, as supply has exceeded demand, and changes in the economy have forced cutbacks in all industries, many lawyers have discovered a lack of mobility.

At times, it seems as though the term *happy lawyer* is an oxymoron. But despite what you hear, or even feel yourself, there are lawyers who find their careers satisfying, challenging, and rewarding. Although there are no magic pills to improve your life, you and your firm can take steps to improve career satisfaction.

What Are the Sources of Dissatisfaction?

Lawyers often characterize their discontent as dissatisfaction with the "quality of life" offered by the firm. But what does quality of life mean in the law firm context—it clearly is more than money and hours. Changes in the economy and other factors have dramatically altered the practice of law and the management of law firms and legal departments. Many of these changes have negatively impacted the quality of life. The following elements contribute to the quality of life.

Quantity and Quality of Work

Lawyers' level of satisfaction is affected as much by the *quality* of work as the quantity. Often, the most unhappy, stressed-out, and insecure lawyers are those who do not have *enough* to do, not those who are meeting or exceeding billable-hours requirements. The ability and willingness to cope with high billable hours tend to increase when the work is challenging and varied. Those lawyers who are working hard and feel that they are part of the client team, not just a "fungible billing unit," tend to be more satisfied.

Money

Money contributes to the quality of life, but money does not control it. Many of the most unhappy lawyers are those who earn the most money, but who feel unrewarded in their work. High starting salaries probably have caused more dissatisfaction than satisfaction because they have led to the following:

- Partner expectations of associate capabilities that may exceed actual performance and associate expectations that other aspects of their jobs will match their income. When both sets of expectations are unmet, resentment, hostility, declining morale, and "we-theyism" set in.
- Associates being more quickly stereotyped as superstars or losers. Firms cannot afford to let young lawyers develop at their own pace.
- Law school graduates who might have been happier in nontraditional positions accepting high-paying jobs in private practice because the money was too good to turn down. Many thought that they would try private practice for a few years and then reevaluate their situations. Now, however, they find that their lifestyles depend on earning a certain amount of money and joining the Peace Corps is not a realistic option.
- Increased billable-hours pressure on partners that makes them reluctant to delegate meaningful work and to spend time training and supervising associates.

Firm Environment, Collegiality, and Culture

A feeling of community and a sense of belonging contribute to the quality of life. Lawyers often feel alienated and cast adrift in firms where there is minimal communication and a high level of internal competitiveness. As firms grow, it becomes more difficult to maintain a common culture, shared values, and communication.

Lawyer Training and Development

The firm's level of commitment to associate training and development, as evidenced by mentor programs, formal training, and partners who are committed to on-the-job training and supervision, impacts the quality of life. Unfortunately, some firms have cut back on their training programs. In addition, billable-hours pressure has caused partners to spend less time supervising and training associates. Also, clients are more resistant to "paying" for training. Associates often feel that they are left to sink or swim on their own.

Opportunities for Advancement and Job Security

The track to partnership is becoming longer, more difficult, and less realistic for all but a few associates. Putting in the requisite amount of time and being a good lawyer no longer is enough to become a partner at most firms. Equity partnership is being restricted to those who meet more rigorous criteria of "value-added" beyond technical lawyering skills. Associates' perceptions that the rules are changing without notice makes them insecure, less loyal, and more paranoid about their importance to the firm. This also leads to competition for hours, work, and relationships. In addition, becoming a partner no longer means lifetime job security. Firms are asking partners to leave in record numbers.

Stability of the Firm as an Institution

Not only are lawyers insecure about their own positions, they also are insecure about the future of their firms. Mergers, dissolutions, terminations of partners, management shifts, client losses through takeovers, bankruptcies, and lawyer shopping increase the sense of insecurity of all lawyers—associates and partners alike.

How Quality of Life Relates to the Bottom Line

Partners often resist efforts to improve the quality of life because they perceive those efforts as a way to coddle whiny associates. Lawyer dissatisfaction and lower morale, however, directly affect the bottom line in the following ways.

Lawyer Turnover

Turnover is expensive. Generally, associates are not profitable until their second to fourth year of practice. Some attrition is healthy and necessary. However, if a firm loses a disproportionate number of associates (particularly those whom the firm would like to keep), the firm loses its investment.

Productivity and Client Satisfaction

Studies show that improved morale leads to improved productivity. When lawyers are professionally satisfied, they can focus their attention on serving clients instead of on how miserable they are. In addition, firms can provide continuity of service. Clients do not like being shuffled around from associate to associate, and they do not like being forced to reeducate lawyers about their business or legal needs.

Lessons from Satisfied Lawyers

There is no model for happiness. A few valuable lessons, however, can be learned from satisfied lawyers.

Take Responsibility for Your Own Development

The most important lesson to be learned from satisfied lawyers is that they do not see themselves as victims. For example:

- If you are not satisfied with the type of work you receive or the partners with whom you work, pursue other opportunities within the firm. Do not wait for someone to offer you a golden opportunity—it is not going to happen. Talk to your department chair or mentor, if you have one. Look at your firm's new matter sheets, and if you see something interesting, ask the partner in charge if you could work on it or to keep you in mind the next time that a similar matter comes into the firm. Be persistent.
- Draft a set of professional goals and objectives for yourself and ask a partner, your department chair, or the managing partner to help you meet those goals by getting you the assignments that you need or the appropriate training programs.
- If you are interested in an area of law, read about it—on your own time, if necessary. Locate appropriate training programs and submit a request to attend. Some senior practitioners have successfully retooled into new areas of law. Although not an easy process, this can help to revive a partner's interest in the practice of law.
- Ask for work when your work flow is slow. If you do not, partners will perceive you as damaged goods and will stop sending you work. Just as the rich get richer, the busy get busier. Go to a partner you have never worked with and tell him or her that you would like the opportunity. Talk to the department chair or others in management. As you become more senior, try to develop your own business. Ask for marketing-skills training.
- On the other hand, if you are too busy to handle a new assignment, say so and explain your situation. Do not wait until you are drowning before you ask for help. No one is going to tell you to go home or not to work so hard. Lack of control is extremely frustrating, but you have more control than you think.
- Ask for feedback on assignments. Do not assume that no news is good news. If you are a partner, ask your clients for feedback. This not only will help you improve your skills, it will reinforce the client relationship.

Develop Realistic Expectations about
What Life in the Law Firm Is Like

If you think the law firm and the individual partners are going to nurture you and hold your hand, you will be constantly disappointed. Even firms that sell themselves as offering a better quality of life expect you to work hard. Not all of your work will be fascinating or challenging. Often, second-career lawyers are the most satisfied and the most admired by partners, partly because they tend to have a more realistic view of what it means to have a job, to work hard, and to be accountable.

Make Sure That You Understand the Assignments

Time spent reinventing or spinning your wheels is extremely frustrating and counterproductive. When you receive an assignment, make sure you understand it. When confronted with a "dump and run" delegator, ask questions, including context, type of document, resources, time, etc. Do not spend five hours in the library staring at the digest. If the delegator is not available, ask a colleague.

Take an Active Role in Firm Life

Get involved in firm activities such as management, recruiting, training, marketing, etc. Volunteer for nonbillable projects. Offer to be a mentor for a more junior lawyer. Spend time training more junior lawyers. Partners who need a respite from practice often are rejuvenated by the challenge of learning new skills that are needed to manage the firm and train other lawyers.

Take a Client-Focused Approach to Your Practice

Lawyers often find that the most satisfying elements of their jobs are their relationships with clients. As you become more senior, you can become more involved with your clients. For example, learn more about their businesses by visiting their offices. Develop training programs for them.

Associates often complain that they do not have client contact. But for many associates, the partners are their clients. Practice client-relation skills with them. For instance, learn to return telephone calls and how to get the information you need to complete the assignment. Ask to go to meetings, even if you cannot bill the time. Get to know your peers at the client's office, even if it means a nonbillable lunch or a visit to the office.

Explore Alternative Career Tracks

Lawyers often perceive nonpartnership tracks or nonequity partnerships as booby prizes. If approached properly, however, these options can be attractive. As you advance, think about whether you really want the responsibilities that come with being an equity partner. Do you want to be an owner of a business with its attendant risks and pressure or do you simply enjoy your work and colleagues? Even as an income partner or senior associate, you will have to work hard and contribute to the firm, but without some of the additional pressures. If your firm does not have alternative tracks, develop a plan and present it to your practice leader or firm management. Make sure you sell them on the benefits to the firm.

If you are currently a partner, think about whether other alternatives might make more sense for you. Do not let ego or peer pressure keep you from exploring alternative work schedules or career tracks such as part-time or "of counsel."

Learn to Work Smarter, Not Harder

Most standard time-management courses and materials are unrealistic for people in a service industry. We all could manage our time if we did not have to answer the telephone or deal with interruptions. Most lawyers, however, can learn to manage their time and work more efficiently. To do this, you should:

- Gain a sense of control over your work and priorities. Ask for deadlines and determine priorities. Keep a list of what you need to accomplish and when. Try not to skip from one project to another.
- Get organized, even if it means coming in early a few mornings or working late. Every firm has at least a few well-organized lawyers and they often are the busiest people. Ask the ones in your firm how they manage their time. For example, the author interviewed a partner at a firm that had developed a management program on WordPerfect. He creates a directory for each case with names, telephone numbers, deadlines, trial dates, and work plans for each week, month, and longer term. He updates the files once a week. He can generate a report showing all of the tasks for that week. And no one else in the firm knew the program existed!
- Read materials on time management; there might be a few techniques that make sense for you.
- When possible, delegate work to others with the appropriate area or level of expertise. When you delegate, make sure to explain the assignment and set deadlines.
- Make more effective use of technology, especially for research and document preparation.

Get a Life

Another reason second-career people often are happier is that they have developed a life outside of work and do not look to work to meet all their social and emotional needs. Become involved in the community (which also might help with marketing), make time to read books, go to the movies, or do whatever you like to do. You need a sense of perspective about your work.

Institutional Approaches: Lessons from Law Firms

Although there are malcontents at every firm, some firms seem to produce fewer than others. The following are some characteristics of firms where the general level of discontent is within at least tolerable limits.

Strong Firm Management

Initially, lawyers tend to resist centralized management and grumble about how "no one is going to tell me how to practice law." Once they adjust, however, most find strong management to be liberating because it allows them to concentrate on practicing law without worrying about how many paper clips to order. Centralized management also helps ensure that decisions will be made by some rational, consistent process.

Strategic Planning

Management should focus substantial attention on strategic planning and client relations. Strategic planning leads to a sense of security and direction.

Lawyers want to know that their firm will be there in a few years and how they fit into the picture. Defections often begin when lawyers sense that their firm is drifting and without leadership.

Formal Policies

Many firms leave policies on personal issues (part-time, alternative career tracks, etc.) to an ad hoc, informal decision-making process. Formal written policies, however, indicate a real commitment and take the decisions out of the hands of individuals. They give the firm and lawyers guidelines and help develop a sense of fairness and consistency.

Merit-Based Compensation System

No compensation system is perfect, but those systems that emphasize personal production tend to produce the most cutthroat, competitive environments. The best systems consider each lawyer's total contribution.

Commitment to Associate Training and Development

This commitment can be seen in a number of ways, including:

- Delegating responsibility to a specific person or committee; not considering training as something to be done in a partner's or administrator's spare time;
- Work-allocation systems that go beyond allowing partners to grab associates in the hall;
- Formal training programs on a firm-wide and department basis, as well as a budget for external CLE;
- Training programs on lawyering skills, including negotiation, supervision, client relations, marketing, writing, and editing;
- Mentor programs;
- Formal evaluations;
- Career development plans for associates; and
- Associate evaluations of partners.

Clearly Defined Alternative Career Tracks

Equity partnership is neither a realistic nor an attractive option for all associates. Alternative tracks, to be attractive, must be viewed not as inferior castes but as ways to keep valuable people who have a contribution to make, yet who are not equity partnership material because of lack of business development, narrow niche, etc. Look at how the people on other tracks are treated. Do they attend meetings? See financial information? Get decent offices? Are the criteria spelled out or is it in ad hoc decisions?

Will these steps magically transform your law firm into an "up-with-people" celebration? No, but they can help.

CHAPTER 5

The Career Transition Process

Celia Paul

Lawyers interested in making career or job transitions or those forced to do so by circumstances often become discouraged before they begin their employment search process by what they have heard and read regarding the tight job market. Even though the legal market in the 1990s is tighter than it was in the 1980s, particularly in transactional work, you can locate many opportunities if you use effective job search techniques. The knowledge of these methods is critical if you are to gain the competitive edge in this tighter market.

Maintaining a steady and consistent effort throughout your search will be one of the most important factors in your success. If you work in bursts of activity, you will not be so successful even if you are a brilliant lawyer, for the job search involves constant follow-up by contacting and recontacting people. You need to continue working through the process of rejection and move on to the next call, meeting, or interview that may be the one where you land a job. If this process is not consistent, but involves many starts and stops, then the interruptions almost create new beginnings at each juncture. When you begin, therefore, make sure that you can work on your search every day even if only to make one or two telephone calls. You also must devote several hours every week to your research, letter writing, and organizing your contacts. If you are not working during the search, you should consider it your job and devote at least six hours a day to it. In this chapter, the steps involved in the career transition process are defined so that you can use your time effectively and reach your goal.

Step One: Know What You Want and What You Have to Sell

You will want to spend the first part of your transition time focused on your self assessment. (This topic is covered in Chapter 2.) The length of this period will vary depending on how much time you have to devote to it and how quickly you need to move. However, you cannot afford to omit sharpening your focus on what types of jobs are most suitable for you. Then, you can explain to others what you want to do and what you can do rather than vaguely stating that you just want another job. To obtain the assistance of others in your career transition, you must be clear on your goals and on what type of assistance you need.

The transition from self-assessment to self-promotion is accomplished by using the "skills analysis." You will use many exercises to help you analyze what types of jobs will satisfy your needs. These exercises are discussed in Chapter 2 on self-assessment. The skills analysis, which is part of self-assessment, will round out the picture to help you determine the most appropriate career paths. Then, work on clearly articulating your skills for informational as well as job interviews. Even when networking, you must interject appropriately to present your skills and ask your contacts in what organizations, firms, or their specialty areas they think these skills would be most useful.

For example, if you have three years' experience as a products-liability litigator and want to continue doing litigation but change areas of specialty, then you must emphasize the strength of your litigation skills. Among the areas you could discuss would be your ability to learn new information quickly (because each product you have dealt with is different); research, including knowing data bases, and using creativity in developing your approach; interview effectively to obtain hard-to-get information; and argue clearly and persuasively. You need to be as specific as possible and include examples so that your comments stand out from other candidates.

Employers are interested in what you can do rather than just where you went to school or where you have worked since you graduated. List your legal skills to help you define your strengths. Ask colleagues for feedback on what they see as your strengths and practice your presentation with them before you speak with important contacts in your job search.

Step Two: Identify Opportunities by a Combination of Research and Networking

After having completed your skills analysis, begin your job search process by conducting basic research. This will help you identify target firms, companies, and organizations that do the type of work you would like to do and for which you are qualified.

The use of computer data bases, particularly the on-line Martindale-Hubbell library, saves hours of research time and provides access to data by category that was previously too time consuming to locate. You can access any information that is written in the directory, including lawyers practicing in a specific area of law in a particular geographic area. You also can search through this list to find out if any of these lawyers went to your law school. You can search by lawyer age to find those who would be likely to be more senior, or conversely, to find those closer to your years of practice. If you have decided that you would prefer a certain size of firm, you can search this list to find lawyers in firms of particular sizes. If you have received a special award, you may be able to identify if any of these lawyers obtained the same distinction. You even can search for lawyers who are fluent in languages that you know.

You also may want to cross reference the target firms to see if they practice other areas of the law that you are qualified in or that you want to learn. In the example discussed previously where the litigator had products-liability experience but wanted to change fields, one could identify which firms practice both products liability and the new desired area. One then can market himself or herself by agreeing to practice some products liability in exchange for learning the new area.

Remember, however, that the information obtained from Martindale-Hubbell is only the starting point of your search and cannot be relied on as your only source. Firms and lawyers pay to be listed in this directory and they select the information that is published about them; so it is not an objective source. Also, some smaller firms as well as solo practitioners may not choose to be listed in the directory. You will be checking and augmenting your data by using other source material such as surveys published by *The National Law Journal* and *The American Lawyer*. The National Association for Law Placement (NALP) is also an excellent resource and contains substantial information about firms such as the number of lawyers practicing in specific areas, the number of men and women, the lawyer turnover rate, etc. Use *The Directory of Corporate Counsel* if you are looking for an in-house position.

Other supplementary information also can be found by using Nexis, which is part of the on-line computer data bases available. However, there will be a charge for the on-line time used, unlike the Martindale-Hubbell directory. You can manually access this information by using the directories and other written information available in the law library either at a law school or a bar association. If you have difficulty figuring out how to search for a particular piece of information or need to know which libraries to use, call Lexis/Nexis at 1-800-543-6862 (24 hours a day).

Once you have completed this phase of your research and have compiled a list of firms, companies, or organizations where your skills might fit and where you might want to work, you are ready to begin the networking process. (To assist you in your research, it may be helpful to use the format shown in Figure 5.1.) You will need to contact everyone you know, show them your list, and ask them if they know anyone in these target firms or even if they know anyone who might know someone in these organizations. They do not need to know the specific person you are trying to reach, although that is obviously most useful. Ask them to tell you anything about the person that might be helpful in approaching him or her, such as how did the person become associated with this firm; how long has the individual been working there; what aspects of his or her personality might be useful for you to know; should you approach the person formally or informally, etc. Also, be sure to ask whether you can use the contact's name and if the contact would be willing to send the individual a note or make a call preceding your approach.

You will constantly revise your target master list by adding new names as you obtain more contacts, adding new firms or organizations, and deleting some when you decide the fit is not right for you. In addition, you should

FIGURE 5.1

Target Master List

My Target Firms (or Organizations and Companies)	Name of Primary Person to Contact	Names of Others in the Firm Who Might Be Helpful	Additional Information

continue to do research on the new names and organizations that you have discovered through your networking by using the resources mentioned previously. In this way, you are prepared for your conversations and can use each dialogue to your best advantage.

Your list should be supplemented by index cards containing the following information on each: dates when contacts were made, with whom, how you obtained the name of this individual, substance of conversation, and the date for your next follow-up. Keep these cards in a file indexed by follow-up date or write the dates on your calendar. Effective time management is critical both to an efficient search and to demonstrate to prospective employers that you are conscientious and organized. If you say that you will call someone on a particular date and you are working on creating a positive impression, then you cannot afford to be late in your approach.

When you call your contacts, always ask them for suggestions and advice about your job search or career transition. *Never ask for a job.* If the individual knows of an opportunity and he or she thinks highly of you, the contact will tell you about it without your asking. Asking directly, however, will put a contact on the spot, creating discomfort and a desire to end the conversation. Because you cannot realistically expect most people to know about jobs, your goal is not to cut short your discussion but to engage in a substantial dialogue and obtain as much information as possible, including referrals to other people and places. You also want to impress each individual with your qualifications so that he or she becomes your advocate when opportunities arise in the universe of people that the contact knows.

Try to see your contacts in person; use the telephone to make the appointment and explain your purpose. If the individual will not agree to a face-to-face meeting, then you may have to ask your questions over the telephone; so be prepared when you call. As a practical matter, most people will not give you names of other colleagues unless they have met you, so the telephone will work better for your own personal contacts than for those to whom you have been referred.

If you are searching full-time, your goal should be to have four face-to-face meetings every week so that you are systematically expanding your network. If you are working while searching, then your goal should be one or two meetings each week whether it be lunch, breakfast, or after work. Additional assistance in how to conduct these meetings can be found in Chapter 10 on informational interviewing.

There may be some firms on your target list where you would like to work, and despite extensive networking, you cannot find a contact. In this case, as a last resort, you will have to write a cold letter. Use what you have learned about this firm through your research to write an individualized letter. Take the time to briefly document your qualifications that as far as you can ascertain from your information meet the firm's needs. State when you will call to follow up. A well-crafted and researched letter will give you the greatest chance of success. Mass mailings that are not individualized and sent to a large number of firms have an extremely low response rate, and they are ineffective unless you have a hard-to-find specialty or the most superior qualifications.

Step Three: Conduct an Active Search

The methods described in this chapter enable you to conduct a proactive search identifying opportunities by obtaining information through both networking and research. Such opportunities may never be advertised or referred to a recruiter because they will be filled by this informal method. In fact, according to a Harvard study, 80 percent of the positions are filled in this way. This fact does not mean that you should ignore advertisements or recruiters. Make them a part of your search, but do not rely on them to obtain a job.

Advertisements are excellent tools in your research because they show you where some hiring is taking place. You may notice advertisements from the same firm or company over a period of time. This fact may mean either that there is something wrong with the job or that this particular organization is in a hiring mode and has more than one position available. Put the firm on your target list and ask your contacts about it. You then have a reason to recontact certain individuals and remind them that you still are available. You also should send a cover letter and your résumé to the person indicated in the advertisement. When you obtain another contact in that firm through your network, you can always send a second letter. Advertisements with box numbers have the lowest rate of return and cannot be used as research tools. If you have most of the skills required, however, sending your material may produce an interview that leads to a job or, at the very least, another contact for you.

Recruiters also can be a source of information, particularly if you are trying to relocate to a new geographic area and want to learn about the local market. Obtain the names of helpful recruiters through your contacts. Register only with those whose reputations for ethical behavior are known. Never allow them to send your résumé to firms without your permission. This is extremely serious because you may already have a contact in that firm who can get you in the door. Any firm would prefer to hire you without paying the recruiter's fee and would be more likely to take a chance if you do not have all the qualifications when no fee is required. However, if you do not have any contacts in a particular organization and the recruiter can get you an interview, then this would be a time to use his or her services. Selective integration of recruiters into your search can increase your entry into targets (markets) that have been difficult for you to reach.

There are always jobs available even in the tightest market, and all you need is one position. Your task, therefore, is to identify opportunities, to promote yourself for those opportunities using the techniques and tools outlined in this chapter, and to persist until you are successful in reaching your goal.

In conclusion, your search has to be organized and actively developed in the same manner as you would your professional work product. Your strategies have to be well thought out, thorough, and creative. If a particular method does not seem to be working, then analyze the reasons and try a totally different approach. Be very clear on your product—what you have to sell and where you can sell it.

CHAPTER 6

Market Assessment: Setting Realistic Goals

Dr. Abbie W. Thorner

Although career counselors and job seekers alike appropriately focus considerable attention on self-analysis, few direct the same scrutiny on the particular external forces that will affect each individual's job search. If self-assessment requires concentration on the attitudes, experience, and goals of the individual in search of a new job, a market assessment—if it is to be relevant to an individual's career goals—must focus on the forces, patterns, and trends that set the parameters in which an individual job search occurs.

What, then, is the marketplace in which the average lawyer must broker skills and experiences to make a job change? To understand this marketplace and assess its effect on the individual job seeker, you must examine recent trends and changes in the world of law practice and turn your attention to what those trends and changes mean to you in your search for a new job.

Expansion in the Legal Market

A quick review of legal market indices of size reveals just what a "big business" law has become. With 723,000 lawyers practicing in the United States and approximately 40,000 new bar admissions each year, the profession is growing at a rate of about 25,000 new lawyers annually. As of 1988, one out of every 340 U.S. residents was a lawyer. A 1987 census of service industries reported that the 138,000-plus law offices surveyed had receipts of more than $67 billion then, or almost twice that reported by the 115,000 such offices surveyed in 1982, who produced $34 billion in revenue. Law, as a career then, attracts a significant percentage of the total U.S. population and accounts for a growing proportion of the gross national product (GNP) associated with U.S. service industries. One estimate suggests that lawyers in the United States generate about 10 percent of this GNP. Opinions differ about whether this is too much, but even critics of the profession concede that law is an important and, in some sectors, a dominant force in the economy of this nation.

During the same period (mid-1980s to late 1980s), in which the census noted such growth, important changes also occurred in the composition of the legal profession. Because of the influx of the "baby boom" generation into the economy in general, and the legal profession in particular, the profession's median age dropped from 46 in 1970 to 40 in 1980, and has remained at 39–40 since. In contrast to the previously male, nonethnic profession, many of the new lawyers emerging from law schools during recent years have been women and minorities. By 1988, 16 percent of all lawyers were women. The percentage has continued to grow because women represent 40 to 50 percent of entering law students in the 1990s (up from just over one-third in the mid-1980s). In addition, minority group members, approaching 5,000 each year, account for almost 15 percent of the 1990s entering law students, compared to just over 8 percent in 1983.

Compression in Legal Employment Opportunities

Employment statistics, however, do not reflect this growth pattern. During the late 1970s and early 1980s, statistics compiled by the NALP demonstrated a consistent trend in new lawyer employment. Within six to nine months of graduation, approximately 90 percent of the new lawyers nationwide had obtained employment. This pattern began to change, however, with the change in decades and the accompanying well-publicized decline in the economy brought by the 1990s. From a high of 92.2 percent employment in 1987, a gradual slippage began in 1988. The percentage of new lawyers employed six months after graduation plummeted almost 5 percent between 1990 and 1991, and dropped another 2.4 percent to a low of 83.5 percent in 1992. At the same time, median starting salaries that peaked nationally in 1990–1991 at $40,000 dropped 10 percent to $36,000 in 1992. This new trend has led the NALP to a rather somber summary of the marketplace in the *NALP Annual Review, 1992–1993*:

> Since the "boom" period of the late 1980s, the job market for new law graduates has undergone a dramatic change and engaged the profession in analysis of sobering new realities. During the most recent years, the protracted recession, coupled with a steady increase in the number of J.D. graduates from ABA accredited schools, has had a negative cumulative effect. Since 1989, each successive class has found it more difficult to obtain employment in general and full-time legal employment in particular than did their predecessors.

Restructuring to Support This Tension

According to the ABA Foundation's 1988 study, approximately 520,000 of 720,000 lawyers (72 percent) were in private practice. These private firms have traditionally structured their growth within a pyramidal structure. By the mid-twentieth century, most law firms' profitability—even survival—was based on a leveraged system in which associates, in numbers equal to or greater than partners, formed the base of that pyramid, with ever-decreasing numbers of lawyers existing in the firm as the approach to the pinnacle progressed:

Senior Partners
Junior Partners
Senior Associates
Junior Associates

Such a structural pattern, initiated by large firms, was ultimately adopted by medium-sized and smaller firms who openly or inadvertently acknowledged its economic promise. Associated with this structure was a series of numbers and formulas—some merely unspoken, others clearly articulated—that attempted to capture the proportions necessary for the health of this pyramidal economy. Young lawyers should be hired in roughly three to four times the number of future partners to be made. The ratio of associates to partners should be 1:1, 2:1, or 3:1, depending on the size and type of practice. Associates should be expected to bill three times their annual salary, one-third for firm overhead (space, rent, equipment, furnishings, supplies, and support services) and one-third going to profit sharing that is divided annually or biannually by the partnership. The numbers and proportions varied considerably, depending on the location, size, and style of management in the firm.

The pyramid, for its own structural soundness, required three underpinnings: (1) lawyers in appropriate numbers needed to enter the structure; (2) attrition of lawyers in appropriate percentages needed to occur; and (3) organizational growth needed to be continual.

In the 1970s and early 1980s, lawyers in growing numbers were entering the mainstream of the profession as the baby boom generation pursued legal practice in record numbers. With 50 percent to 60 percent of these 40,000 new lawyers each year entering private practice, the potential number of new associates more than exceeded the pyramid's demand for an entry-level base. Anticipating continued growth, many firms hired from this large talent pool what, in retrospect, were too many inexperienced lawyers. The optimal number of entry-level lawyers had, for many private practices, been exceeded.

The second requirement, that these lawyers leave the firms in numbers consistent with firm growth, was similarly thwarted by a change in economic forces and the mobility of lawyers themselves. As overhiring led to decreased percentages of new partners or to the need for layoffs in some firms, increased mobility within the profession ironically led to undesirable high attrition for other firms. Small, medium-sized, and large firms alike seemed to be faced with "feast or famine," along with the growing awareness that the traditional pattern of progress up or out of the pyramid no longer produced the appropriate number of lawyers.

The third requirement, that the growth of the organization must continue into perpetuity, became an unrealized pipe dream for many firms. The pyramid, if it was going to allow increasing numbers of partners with some prospect of firm profitability, had to bring into its base increasing numbers of associates. All of these personnel increases obviously heightened the need for increasing numbers of clients, client matters, and fees. The spiral could not continue indefinitely—and continue it did not. The economic downturn of the late 1970s brought with it more cost-conscious clients ready to limit legal fees; more corporations pulling legal matters in-house for cost and quality control; and fewer small businesses and private citizens willing or able to pay for professional legal services. The entire framework of the pyramid had come into question. The leveraged system of private firm profitability and the very organizational principle of many firms no longer seemed ideal. Before the existing system could be altered or adjusted, however, the severe economic downturn of the 1980s all but destroyed projected growth in the private sector and eliminated the need for growing numbers at the bottom who could sustain high earnings at the top. The economic framework no longer had a base.

A New Vocabulary: Toward Balance

The traditional jargon of the profession that had included such frequently used words as *partnership, collegiality*, and *permanency* expanded in the 1980s to include *business, competition*, and *productivity*. By the 1990s, terms such as *layoffs, downsizing*, and *outplacement* described the legal-service sector in the jargon of constricting rather than the vocabulary of professional relationships. The difference in the more traditional constructs and the new vocabulary is not merely one of semantics, but one of content. The focus among private practitioners has, out of necessity, moved to a more serious scrutiny of economic structures that will restore economic balance to private practice.

As various economic forces have led to more attrition and movement for individual lawyers coupled with less economic certainty for their primary employers, the private firms, those firms have naturally begun acting less like partnerships, and more like employers under siege. Throughout the legal profession, new personnel categories for lawyers are proliferating. The progression from associate to partner or junior lawyer to senior counsel is no longer a certain, or in some cases even probable, path of upward mobility. Terms such as *permanent associate, senior lawyer*, and *staff lawyer* have become labels for the lawyer in private practice who has become a paid employee of the firm rather than an owner or profit sharer in a partnership. Similarly, *of counsel* arrangements, which have been reserved in the past for senior lawyer consultants or those approaching or having reached retirement status, now include a wide variety of amorphous relationships between firms and lawyers who, as "of counsel," really function as private contractors. Even traditional partnerships no longer are simply partnerships, but may be split to include individuals with equity and nonequity status, or structured to include multiple distinctions of role on a hierarchical ladder of compensation and management. Temporary and contract lawyers are common in towns and cities of all sizes and locations.

This proliferation of employment categories has begun to have and will continue to have a profound effect on the attitudes of individual lawyers. As the traditional firm structure has disappeared, looser affiliations have emerged to take its place. Becoming less an elite group and more a cluster of employment categories, the profession now inspires less collegiality and loyalty because increasing numbers of its members are short-term employees rather than partner-participants in its predominant structure, the private firm.

The perceived escalating need for legal talent, which fed the recruiting frenzy of the late 1980s and fueled the salary wars in which $10,000 annual jumps "to start" were common, had ended. In its place, a "no-growth" ethic based on strict fiscal management and "right-sizing" legal personnel needs had begun to evolve. This new approach, and the vocabulary to describe it, seem to be more than a market adjustment; they are an important attempt of the profession to move toward "balance."

A New Momentum: Escalating Change

Beyond the hallways of private practice and the jargon of the legal profession is a world rapidly changing. These changes only increase the factors to be considered in any marketplace assessment:

- Globalization of economics means even more interdependence of businesses, governments, and financial institutions. Specialties in the law coupled with interdisciplinary approaches and languages skills will be in greater demand.
- Knowledge-based industries and services such as law will become even more important to this world, but will be challenged to collect, analyze, synthesize, disseminate, store, and retrieve information in more technologically advanced ways.
- Technology dependence will not demand more office equipment, but rather fully integrated office systems, satellite work sites, and "value-added" time measures. The "billable hour" will join the dinosaur as a relic of the past.
- As the nonwhite population increases to approximately 25 percent of the U.S. population by the year 2000, and minority group members become more proportionally represented in the legal profession, the cultural diversity of both clients and legal-service providers will contribute to a more truly integrated law firm environment.
- The integration of cultures and economics coupled with economic necessity will require law firms to develop ancillary businesses. Some forecasters estimate that in the year 2000, more than half of the individuals employed by law firms will be nonlawyers. Concomitantly, lawyers themselves will—out of professional necessity—become even more involved with work tasks not traditionally associated with legal practice.
- Education, continuing education, and retraining—based in technology and demanded by the accelerated accumulation of knowledge—will

reemerge in the private bar, but with added concerns about adult learning styles and assessable outcomes.

■ The aging population will affect the practice by increasing the demand for expertise in "elder law" and will affect the profession by increasing the need for creative pension-fund arrangements to accommodate the increasing number of older people who remain active in the profession longer. Retirement from the profession will come later and multiple careers—not just job changes—will be common, if not universal. Some futurists predict that career changes will occur, for most individuals, on an average of every ten years.

Setting Realistic Goals

With such dramatic changes having occurred in the marketplace and only increasing into the next century, how should the individual job seeker adjust his or her approach to the market? A five-step process is helpful:

1. *Reflect on the past.* What job, role, or function allowed you to excel, to experience job satisfaction?
2. *Visualize the future.* Identify where—with no limitations imposed— you would like to see yourself professionally, in this and future job or career changes.
3. *Build on the present.* Honestly examine the general parameters and specific jobs for which you are most marketable, given your experience, education, work attitudes, and goals. Arrange your current educational, training, and life experiences to provide bridges to future goals.
4. *Develop a package.* This includes your résumé, a cover letter, and an interview style that markets you in a way most appealing to the type of employer you seek.
5. *Make contact.* Then follow up each lead, application, letter, or interview with persistent determination. The intensity of this marketplace requires a comparable personal intensity and commitment.

This five-step process is useful regardless of the market segment you choose for your search. Initially, at least, consider all of the major market segments traditionally open to lawyers: private firms, public-interest organizations, corporations, financial services, and government entities. If none of these are appealing, look beyond them to the quasi-legal and nonlegal marketplaces, which are as numerous and broad as are categories in a dictionary of occupational titles. Occupational titles and job combinations, as well as career paths, are evolving rapidly in this marketplace.

Your task as job seeker is to know not only the general state of the market that has been discussed but also your own strengths and weaknesses that will determine just where in that market you will find the best "fit." Approach the marketplace with an awareness and utilization of the very terms that characterize it: change, globalization, value added, technology integration, and assessable outcomes. In short, base the way you market yourself on an integration of your individual self-analysis and your awareness of current market trends. In that way, a market assessment will allow you to set realistic professional goals and move toward personal satisfaction.

CHAPTER 7

Career Opportunities
for Minorities

Suzanne Baer
Londell McMillan

In general, it has been more difficult for minority lawyers to find equal opportunity in the legal profession. For this reason, affirmative-action programs were initially instituted. Although all doors may not yet be open, the playing field has begun to level, and the changes are there to be seen. Minority lawyers have worked their way into every arena of the profession, from the bench to the academy.

Today's minority lawyer, whether Hispanic, African-American, Asian, or Native American, has more opportunities to succeed in the legal profession than in the past. The magnitude of the change is demonstrated by the increased numbers of minority lawyers who have moved into positions of influence and who will help shape a profession that promotes fairness in career opportunities for all lawyers. Nonetheless, even when one is "qualified," success is not always obtainable because obstacles to opportunity remain. However, if you can see success as being ready for the struggle, if you can see limitations as temporary deficits to be overcome, if you subscribe to the concept that most everything can in fact be learned, you are well on your way to building a successful career.

But first, how do you learn what you need to know, and how do you get where you want to go? Two pathways are through networks and mentors.

Networks and Mentors: You Never Know
Who Is Going to Be Helping You

Networking is the art and science of cultivating connections. First, you begin with a recognition and support of others—"*What goes around, comes around.*" This is a critical factor in attracting attention and support for yourself. As you cultivate connections, you are always in a learning mode; interpersonal skills and leadership opportunities are continuously being developed. Here are just a few reasons articulated by minority lawyers why their networks were critical factors in building their careers:

- Networks provided them with reliable sources of practical information.
- Networks assured them of a "choir" of affirmation.
- Networks helped maintain a true sense of their self-worth and self-esteem.
- Networks bolstered their confidence in the face of the obstacles, prejudices, and inequities that were encountered.

For minority lawyers to succeed in the legal profession, they must build networks of relationships beyond their own ethnicity. Coalitions between different minority group members and effective relationships with nonminority lawyers are essential. Minorities who have already found success in the mainstream workplace developed a capacity to see beyond race while simultaneously understanding the politics of race dynamics. We all need to remember that fundamentally what really makes us alike is that we all are different.

When you start out as a practicing lawyer, make friends with everybody. You never know who is going to be able to lend a helping hand in the future. Minority lawyers are increasingly able to move into new areas—areas where they were not seen before. To accelerate this process, it is in your interest, and in that of the profession, to attend panel discussions, CLE programs, and bar association meetings whenever possible. Join committees; run for office. Find out what steps were taken that opened new specializations to minority lawyers.

Meeting the challenge of building and promoting a career in the twenty-first century will depend on your flexibility and willingness to develop new skills to meet labor market changes. Law practices will have to respond even more rapidly to the requirements of global business. The corporate world of the 1990s is leaner and less predictable, and the political world has already begun to meet the demand for improved racial and gender balance in appointed and elected officials. Lawyers must be active, committed participants in civic, social, and professional organizations. This activity will position them to benefit from new opportunities as the legal profession changes to meet the reality of a diverse workforce.

Career Advice from Minority Lawyers

When people look backward rather than forward at their career paths, frequently there is greater insight and understanding of the choices and decisions made along the way. We asked minority lawyers to look backward, and they had a lot to say:

- What were your three most successful career-development decisions?
- If applicable, what were the three most effective methods you used to make a transition from one job to the next?
- How do you feel the present conditions and trends in today's public and private marketplace affect the types of career strategies minority lawyers should pursue?

Here are some noteworthy responses from experienced minority lawyers:

- When you start out in law practice, make friends with everybody. Everyone can help you.
- Get involved in politics. Politics is the center of power. Campaign for candidates in the political party of your choice. Being political helps you get places.
- Maintain involvement in community organizations. To be truly successful you have to be able to step out of the comfort of your own community, as well as work in it.
- Network with experienced minority lawyers because you need those who have been through it to tell you how they made it.
- The best way to learn what to do is to watch people who excel at what you want to do.

Additional advice includes the following:

- *On the subject of a career in teaching law, minorities opt out and do not even apply for faculty positions.* It's a myth that you must have only perfect credentials, Law Review experience, a prestigious clerkship, et al. You have to make your interest in law teaching known to a lot of people. Many law schools are looking for minority faculty. Start by calling faculty where you went to law school to find out about the process.
- *Wisdom from a prosecutor:* I always worked to set myself apart. I went out of my way to find new responsibilities. That was my formula, keep growing, learning, and seek new responsibilities. Do more than you need to do to prepare a case and more than others do. Research every case meticulously. The time you put in, the extra lengths you go to— that is how you stand out.
- Minorities have to learn more about promoting themselves. If you do not know how to get known, start by watching a known commodity in your workplace—see what he or she does, and learn when and how to do it for yourself.
- When you meet minority lawyers who have moved from one job to another, find out how they got there. Break it down a step at a time— what did they join, whom did they know, how did they develop their expertise.
- Law is advocacy in organized, persuasive, clear language and writing. Remember, writers are made, not born. Some tips on continuing to develop your writing talent: Get on a bar association committee and write a report. Write an article or even a letter to the editor and get it published. Write a long letter to a judge about a trial issue that interests you, write a memo on a current legal issue, get on CLE panels, and keep a file of speeches. Build an impressive writing portfolio.

There was consensus around the three most effective career strategies:

1. Seek out mentors and role models. Become active in bar associations for friendship and networking.

2. Keep developing new skills.
3. Your career plan must have a focus, but you cannot plan every step. Take risks and be alert to unplanned opportunities.

Choosing an Environment Where You Can Be at Your Best

Imagine coming across this law firm in the NALP's *Annual Directory of Legal Employers*:

> 245 partners, 47 are lawyers of color and 138 partners are women. The firm's managing partner is an African-American female, the hiring partner is a white female, the Associate Committee Chair is a Hispanic male. . . .

You get the point! While you won't find a twenty-first century law firm like this yet, here are some touchstones for you to consider when choosing the environment where you can be at your best. If possible, speak with minority lawyers in the organization before accepting an employment offer and ask them to evaluate their experience and perception of the environment. Some important questions to ask are:

- Do you believe your work is consistent with and as challenging as assignments given to white peers?
- What do minority lawyers report about communication and feedback in the organization?
- Do you feel you are continually required to demonstrate your competence?
- Have minorities advanced in the organization recently to senior levels of management?
- What do minority lawyers report about being mentored; are they recommended for professional association committees and CLE presentations? Are there minorities at senior levels of the organization to assist you?

A growing number of legal organizations have undertaken an assessment and cultural analysis of their work environment. The use of a consultant to assist an organization in the retention and advancement of a diverse workforce demonstrates a serious commitment to the inclusion of minorities. Management consultants have advised Fortune 500 corporations since the early 1970s on how to create cultural environments that increase retention and promotion of minorities and women. Legal employers of the 1990s have begun to acknowledge the need for, and value of, this process.

A review of some important indices of commitment to workforce diversity include the following:

1. Frequent performance evaluations and communication of expectations at early stages in the lawyer's employment;
2. A carefully monitored work assignment system;
3. Attention to, and quality of, training;

4. An infrastructure of support for new lawyers, i.e., advisers and mentors;
5. A "safe" place in the organizational structure for troubleshooting around problematic situations without fear of reprisal;
6. Employer participation in programs to foster diversity, i.e., bar association or school-sponsored minority clerkships, minority hiring from regional law schools, participation in minority job fairs, lateral hiring of minority lawyers, support of minority-focused community activities, joint-venture projects with minority-owned law firms, and inclusion of minority vendors by the organization.

Resources: Recruitment Opportunities and Professional Networks

American Bar Association
750 North Lake Shore Drive
Chicago, IL 60611
312/988-5667

Minorities in the Profession Committee
American Bar Association
Young Lawyers Division
750 North Lake Shore Drive
Chicago, IL 60611
312/988-5611

Publications of the ABA Commission on Opportunities for Minorities in the Profession:

Minority In-House Counsel Directory
Minority Partners in Majority/Corporate Law Firms Professional Profiles
Directory of National Minority Bar Associations

American Indian Bar Association
Tricia Tingle
144-B East San Antonio Street
San Marcos, TX 78666

National Asian Pacific American Bar Association
Brian A. Sun
O'Neil & Lysaght
100 Wilshire Boulevard, Suite 700
Santa Monica, CA 90401

Hispanic National Bar Association
Wilfredo Caraballo
Seton Hall Law School
One Newark Center
Newark, NJ 07102

National Bar Association
Paulette Brown
Brown & Childress
337 South Harrison Street
East Orange, NJ 07018

Publications of the Judicial Administration Division, Task Force on Opportunities for Minorities:

Directory of the Asian/Pacific Islander Judges of the United States of America
Directory of the Hispanic Judges of the United States of America

National Association for Law Placement
1666 Connecticut Avenue, Suite 450
Washington, DC 20009-1039
202/667-1666

Directory of Minority Programs

Directory of Minority Faculty Judges in the United States
California Center for Judicial Education and Research
2000 Powell Street, Suite 850
Emeryville, CA 94608
415/464-3828

The following bar associations and city and state groups of law firms have signed Statements of Goals to increase minority representation in the profession:

Association of the Bar of the City of New York
Boston Law Firm Group
Connecticut Law Firm Group
Chicago Bar Association
Dallas Bar Association
District of Columbia Conference on Opportunities for Minorities
  in the Legal Professions
Houston Bar Association
Los Angeles County Bar
Maricopa County Bar Association (Phoenix)
New Jersey Law Firm Group
San Francisco Bar Association
State Bar of Arizona
Texas State Bar Association
Colorado Law Firms

PART II

Career Identification

CHAPTER 8

Effective Career Search Techniques and Strategies

Christine White
Jeanne Q. Svikhart

One of the frustrations of looking for a job is the amount of advice, much of it conflicting, that confronts the job seeker. This chapter focuses on specific strategies and techniques that actually work in today's legal job marketplace.

Background

During 1991 and 1992, White Svikhart & Associates consulted, on an outplacement basis, with more than 110 lawyers from private practice and several corporations. The observations in this article are based on the results of the firm's effective and successful job searches. The lawyers had a wide range of work experience, ranging from first-year associates to partners, and the distribution was approximately one-third junior associates, one-third mid-level associates, and one-third senior associates and partners. The majority of lawyers surveyed were from the Washington, D.C.–Baltimore, Maryland, metropolitan areas.

Five basic and effective job search strategies were used by the lawyers who were surveyed.

Strategy 1: Focus and Plan

Lawyers offered two types of basic advice to job changers:

1. Assess yourself: "Spend time planning, strategizing, and deciding what you really want to do."
2. Assess your market: "Don't use a shotgun approach. Know who you are, what you want, and what they want. Be specific in what you want but not exclusive."

As a first step, you need to tally your accomplishments, your strengths, your shortcomings, what you like, and what you do not enjoy so much. Once you have looked within, you are ready to look at alternatives and possibilities. Assessing the marketplace helps you draw a realistic map of your potential market and focus your efforts. If you do not know where you want to go, you are relying on luck and the vagaries of the marketplace to shape your next move. Equally important, candidates who are unable to articulate their professional goals in some detail often lose out to other applicants who are more focused and directed. If you are confused about what you are looking for or what you can offer, you can expect that the employer will be confused as well.

Strategy 2: Informational Interviews

One way to avoid the "catch-22" of a job search—you do not know what you are looking for because you do not know what is out there—is to conduct some informational interviews. Lawyers who take part in these interviews have found this strategy absolutely essential.

If, for example, you decide that you want to make a move from private law practice to a corporate legal department because you are looking for more management responsibility and want more reasonable hours, then your first step should be to use your personal, alumni, or business contacts to talk to some lawyers who hold positions in corporations. You will need to determine:

1. If your assumptions about the working environment are valid, e.g., the hours are more reasonable;
2. What the similarities/differences between private practice and an in-house position are;
3. Which aspects of your background and experience would be of particular interest to corporations; and
4. What obstacles you may encounter and what strategies you should utilize to overcome those obstacles.

Informational interviews also can be used effectively as advance work in a target market. For example, one lawyer who had been out of law school for 12 years decided to pursue an LL.M. degree before moving to a new geographic area. She assumed her seniority would be an obstacle and that an LL.M. would improve her chances of locating a new position. She used informational interviews to test her hypothesis and called a few people in the city and practice area that she had targeted. As a result, she discovered that her assumption about seniority level being a major impediment was not valid for that market and that an advanced degree would not improve her chances of getting a new position.

Another lawyer with both federal government and private practice experience decided that he wanted to return to the federal government. Through informational interviews, he discovered that he would encounter difficulties in getting the seniority level that he was seeking. With the assistance of other lawyers, he learned how best to finesse that issue, and he located an influential lawyer to "go to bat" on his behalf. Informational interviews are discussed further in Chapter 10.

Strategy 3: Allocate Your Time Properly

Every source of job leads works for somebody some of the time, but which works best? Because you have only a limited amount of time to devote to a job search, you must decide which source will be most productive for you.

The results for the sample group of lawyers surveyed were as follows:

- 68 percent found positions through personal contacts;
- 16 percent through published openings or advertisements;
- 11 percent through search firms; and
- 5 percent through mass mailings.

The message for you, the job seeker, is to allocate your time and energy properly among the various sources and "play the percentages."

Ideally, 70 percent to 80 percent of your time should be spent expanding your personal contact base. In addition, approximately 10 percent of your time should be devoted to locating and responding to published notices in local newspapers and journals, to government job listing services, and to bar association and law school placement office announcements. Mass mailings, while they do satisfy your desire for action, are one of the least effective methods for locating a position and should be viewed as a supplementary, not a primary, strategy. Search firms are worth a preliminary contact so that you can make a decision if their employer contacts are compatible with your background and interests.

Personal Contact Base

Many lawyers explained how important networking was to them:

> If possible, let as many people as you can know that you are in the market. Maintain *frequent* contact. You might miss a new job opportunity by failing to stay in touch with a contact.

> Develop a good networking interview to market yourself and then use the results and contacts to lead to the actual interview.

> Use every contact you've ever made to get an interview; if you do well in interviews, you can overcome any flaw in your credentials. The "halo" effect is still alive and well.

Published Notices

Surprisingly, many lawyers found jobs by responding to published openings. Because the lawyers in this group tended to be looking for positions in or near large metropolitan areas, it could not be determined if the same strategy would be as effective in small cities or rural areas.

One lawyer offered this advice to fellow job seekers:

Answer ads and keep your name on professional lists. Answering notices at least puts you in touch with firms with actual openings . . . in contrast with mass mailings, which are time consuming, but not very productive.

The best sources for posted jobs were the local legal newspapers, local bar associations, and specialized bar groups, such as the Federal Bar Association and the local Women's Bar Association. Local law school placement offices also can be useful sources for posted jobs.

Search Firms

Search firms seem to play a slightly less prominent position in the legal marketplace than they did in past years.

Based on the limited sample, the authors learned that senior lawyers without substantial portable business may not find search firms as useful as other resources.

Advice from successful job seekers about utilizing legal search firms included:

> Only deal with search firms who are optimistic and willing to tell you specific actions they will take and who will get your clearance before they send your résumé to any prospective employer. Avoid those who use a "shotgun" approach.

> Don't get discouraged if one search firm can't help. Try another search firm or try a different strategy instead.

> If you decide to use legal search firms, discuss at great length with prospective search firms the method, strategy, and procedures to be used.

Mass Mailings

Conducting mass mailings is the least effective of all job search strategies in today's legal, lateral job market. Networking works significantly better than mass mailings. Contacts made in person (through a personal friend, for example, who can introduce you to the key person) are far more effective than mass mailings. According to one job seeker, if a lawyer does decide to try a mass mailing, "you should be very focused—really target your letters."

Strategy 4: Devote an All-Out Effort To Locate a New Job

Job seekers who devoted 80 percent or more of their time to looking for a new job were the most successful. The amount of effort expended in locating a new position is the most important factor in any job search campaign. This held true for all levels of experience and seniority. The message, then, for all lawyers is that once you have decided to make a job change, then an "all-out campaign" is necessary to be successful. You should utilize every strategy and resource available, and keep the momentum going throughout the process by *setting weekly goals.*

Strategy 5: Develop a Good Support Network

One job seeker suggested that "support of friends, family, and mentors is the key. Job hunting is no fun but it's no disgrace either. Talk to everyone who may be helpful no matter how far removed their job is from the job sought." Obviously, this is a variant of the informational interview advice. The word *support* is the significant difference. This piece of advice from one job seeker is the key to a successful search:

> [The] most important part of the job search is keeping a positive attitude and continuing to have self-confidence in the face of inevitable rejections. Every week do at least one job search–related activity that is upbeat and reinforcing.

Twelve Steps in a Successful Legal Job Search Campaign

The following steps contribute to a successful legal job search campaign:

1. Plan and focus. Spend considerable up-front time planning, strategizing, and deciding what you really want to do.
2. Begin your search by conducting informational interviews. Be specific when asking for *advice*. Never ask for a job.
3. Allocate your time appropriately among the various sources and strategies. The majority of your time should be spent expanding your personal contact base.
4. Devote a full effort to locating a new position.
5. Target specific markets.
6. Tailor your résumé and interview to the market(s) selected.
7. Network until you drop.
8. Network some more.
9. At a minimum, allow *at least* three to six months to find a job.
10. Allow considerably more time if you are inclined to exert only half-hearted efforts to your search.
11. Keep a written record of all your efforts and make sure that you exert efforts every week to your search. Never let the momentum drop.
12. Keep your spirits up.

CHAPTER 9

Networking

Kathleen Brady

Networking rests on the basic principle that business, jobs, and careers are built on personal relationships. The true purpose of networking is to get information, advice, and referrals.

By simply meeting in person with professional and personal contacts (even if you have been out of touch for a long time), you can obtain valuable information about the ways that your talents could be used by organizations. You must utilize these relationships as a primary outreach technique to broaden your field of vision for making a good career decision. Law school classmates and professors, college friends and family members, former employers, colleagues and opponents, and bar association leaders all may be able to assist you in your quest for employment. There is no hidden agenda. At this point in your search, you simply are looking for information about where the jobs are.

According to Dr. Ronald Krannich and Caryl Rae Krannich, authors of *Network Your Way to Job & Career Success: Your Complete Guide to Creating New Opportunities*, the *advertised* job market represents only about 25 percent of actual openings. This market, they explain, tends to represent positions at the extreme ends of the job spectrum—low-paid unskilled or high-paid highly skilled jobs. Worst of all, many of these advertised jobs actually are filled prior to being advertised. The remaining 75 percent or more of all job opportunities can be uncovered through networking or "job prospecting"; therefore, this job search activity is the most important.

Developing an Effective Strategy

Because countless articles have been written extolling the virtues of networking as the best method for landing a job with techniques and gimmicks outlined to coach readers how to achieve maximum effectiveness, people often jump into the process without first developing an effective strategy. If you are not clear about what you are trying to accomplish, networking equals busy-work. You must understand what you can reasonably expect from these relationships and what is outside those bounds. When networking to uncover job opportunities, it is reasonable to expect:

- Information;
- Referrals to others who can help you;
- Feedback about résumés, cover letters, and approach;
- Testing of ideas and theories;
- Assistance in formulating plans; and
- Moral support.

It is *not* reasonable to expect that *a job* will be handed to you! While appearing to be organized and coherent, the job market really is disorganized and chaotic. Your task is to organize the chaos around your skills and interests. When approaching your contacts, keep in mind that most people do not know of many current job openings. If the first and only question posed to your contacts is "Do you know of any openings?" you will more often than not receive a "No" and an opportunity to learn valuable information may be lost. By asking "What do you do and what alternatives are out there?" you will uncover information that eventually will generate job leads and preserve your relationships.

Identifying Possible Contacts

Networking occurs naturally in all areas of life. For example, when moving into a new neighborhood, you probably would not hesitate to ask your new neighbors for recommendations about dry cleaners, grocery stores, dentists, etc. Or when planning a vacation, you would not think twice about asking friends or family to recommend hotels and restaurants. In business, it is common to ask colleagues to suggest accountants, bankers, or computer systems. But for some reason, we hesitate to ask people we know about job opportunities.

To identify possible contacts, you must:

- Review your address book/Rolodex;
- Contact the educational institutions you attended to ask for copies of alumni directories;
- Review your billing records to jog your memory about co-counsels, opposing counsels, clients, etc.; and
- Create target employer lists using basic library research skills to learn who is doing what you would like to do. (Both Lexis/Nexis and Westlaw offer extremely valuable information to aid you in your job search. Call their customer service representatives to ask for information on how to effectively use their services (Lexis—1-800-543-6862; Westlaw—1-800-937-8529). You then can ask people on your contact list if they can help you meet someone at an organization in which you have a particular interest.

Do not concentrate your efforts on only those contacts with influential positions and the power to hire you. Remember, networking should be used only as a communication process to acquire information, *not* as a manipulation used to acquire power and influence over employers. If you are playing the "advice-and-information game" when you really believe networking is nothing more than the backdoor route to a new position, you are being insincere and misleading and you will not be effective. Focus on people who are close to your level of experience—it is less uncomfortable networking with fellow professionals than with potential bosses.

Identifying Yourself

Before you approach your contacts, make sure you are able to articulate your strengths, passions, preferred workstyle, goals, enthusiasms, values, contributions, potential, ideals, interest areas, temperament, accomplishments, special knowledge, and motivations. You also should be aware of your faults so that you can minimize them. (See Chapter 2 on self-assessment.)

Once you can articulate your motives, skills, and goals, you must find out who would be interested in the "product" that you are selling. Read trade papers and annual reports to learn about current issues in various practice or geographic areas. Establish where your skills fit in today's market. Remember, do not be so narrowly focused that you cannot see options outside of what you have been doing. Think about different ways to apply your skills. If you are an intellectual-property lawyer, for example, consider computer companies, publishing companies, high-tech businesses, or entertainment enterprises. You may know enough about an industry to go into the business side. If you represent investment bankers, consider the financial-services industry. Real estate lawyers may want to present themselves as workout specialists. Once you have identified a need, you can outline and explain how you think you can fill the need.

The Proper Way to Approach a Contact for Help

To achieve maximum effect, use a well-thought-out process: approach letter, telephone call, interview, thank-you note. Write your contact a letter, then call to ask for *15* minutes of his or her time for *advice*. Do not put pressure on the individual to find you a job or to interview you. That may be a long-term result, but at this juncture, an informative conversation should be your objective.

Write a Letter of Introduction

The first step in this process is writing an approach letter such as the following:

> Bob Smith suggested that I contact you about my interest in career opportunities in environmental law (the legal community in New Jersey, etc). I am a graduate of XYZ Law School with four years' experience in . . .

> [Your next paragraph should tell something about your background. Include your prior work experience, current situation, skills, interests, academic history, connection to the geographic region, etc.]

As I venture into the job market, I hope to benefit from the experience and knowledge of others in the field (in New Jersey) who might advise me of opportunities for someone with my qualifications. I would appreciate the opportunity to meet with you for 15 minutes for your guidance. I will call your office next week to see if we can schedule a meeting.

I look forward to discussing my plans with you.

Follow Up with a Telephone Call

Prepare a script so that you can clearly and succinctly introduce yourself and articulate your needs. Your ability to present yourself and explain what you hope to gain from meeting with your contact will determine his or her response to you. Why have you chosen this particular organization and, more importantly, this particular person to contact over all of the other possibilities? What specifically do you want to find out? These types of questions will help you to clarify your objectives in networking before you call or write contacts and will increase your chances of arousing the contacts' interest in consenting to meet with you. You must be prepared to say more than "I have just lost my job and I was wondering if you know of any openings." Try instead:

Hello, Mr./Ms. _____. This is Mary Brown, I am calling at the suggestion of Bob Smith. I sent you a letter the past week explaining . . . [restate the first paragraph of your letter] and I was wondering if you might have 15 minutes sometime this week to meet with me?

Remember, do not exert pressure on this person to find you a job. The objective is to arrange for an in-person meeting to unearth information about the contact and his or her job experience.

The Appointment

Once you are in your contact's office, you must lead the conversation. You should be prepared to:

- Explain the purpose of the meeting.
- Show how your contact can be helpful.
- Present your background and skills to put the meeting in context.
- Ask questions to elicit the information you need.
- Get the names of others who could be helpful.
- Be considerate of their time.

The purpose of the meeting is to determine how your talents could be used in different settings, so you must do a good job presenting them. As you talk about your accomplishments, you are illustrating your thinking and problem-solving style. The more concrete and specific you are, the better able your contact will be to think of possibilities for you and suggest additional people you should meet.

Your goal should be to make your contacts feel good about their ability to help you. You must present yourself as positive, confident, and self-assured, not negative, needy, and desperate. Never scoff at a suggestion by saying "I've tried that and it does not work." Also, never make your contacts feel sorry for you or responsible for your situation; they will doubt their ability to help you and may begin to avoid you.

During your appointment you may want to address the following:

1. The career of the person you are visiting:
   - Background;
   - How his or her interest developed in this area;
   - What is liked best/least about the work; and
   - "Career steps" (former jobs that he or she held, what was learned from each, how he or she progressed from one job to the next).
2. Advantages and disadvantages of work with that:
   - Type of firm, agency, or corporation;
   - Type of law practice; and
   - Geographical area.
3. What the organization is like and how it operates:
   - Supervising and reporting functions; and
   - What a typical day looks like.
4. What the organization is looking for in an employee.
5. What you could do to make yourself more attractive as a potential employee including suggestions on:
   - Upgrading your résumé;
   - Interviewing techniques;
   - Additional educational and experience qualifications that you might pursue; and
   - Others in the field with whom you could speak.

Once the individual gets to know you, and you have asked questions about his or her career (showing genuine interest), it is his or her prerogative to offer further assistance. Toward the conclusion of your talk, the contact's thoughts might naturally turn to what action he or she might take on your behalf.

You should express gratitude for offers of assistance and take notes if the individual suggests that you contact colleagues. You might add, "Would it be all right if I use your name when contacting this person?" If the contact does not offer assistance or additional names of people to call, you might gently ask if he or she could suggest names of individuals to speak to who could give you more information.

You may find that the 15 minutes you asked for stretched to a conversation lasting an hour or more. This usually occurs because the individual is flattered that you came to him or her for advice and are asking about things of importance to him or her. However, it is up to *you* to stick to your preset time limit, and let your contact take the initiative to extend the meeting, if he or she desires to do so.

People love to talk about themselves. This type of conversation tends to be very warm and animated, full of goodwill. If they do not know of a job opening, they will keep you in mind when they do have one, or if a colleague is trying to fill a position, they will recommend you.

When you meet with people on your network list, take notes about the meeting. It would be helpful to start a three-by-five-inch card file for each contact. Be sure to include:

- The contact's name (be sure you have the correct spelling);
- The date of the contact;
- The results of the meeting;
- Follow up that is required and the time frame;
- The person who referred you;
- Any personal information that may be helpful; and
- Your impressions of the person and the organization.

The job search process requires that you continually make telephone calls, schedule appointments, write follow-up notes, contact new people, etc. You must record the dates and times for each activity on a pocket calendar to remind you what needs to be done; this will help you organize your days, which, in turn, will allow you to accomplish more.

Follow-Up Correspondence

Anyone who helps you should be kept apprised of your job search. If a lead results in an interview or new information about you becomes available, let him or her know. Keep people informed. A note or telephone call every month or two is appropriate. If you occasionally remind people that you are still in the job search, other opportunities may present themselves down the line.

Social and professional gatherings offer an opportunity to network comfortably. Introduce yourself to people. ("Hi, I don't believe we've met. I'm Mary Smith.") Ask people open-ended questions to learn about them. It may be helpful to imagine yourself as the host of the event with your mission being to make others feel at ease.

If you are using professional associations as sources of networking, remember that collecting business cards is not effective; being a participant is! Demonstrate your capabilities by becoming involved. Give prospective employers the opportunity to witness your abilities firsthand.

Finally, do not rush to network at every occasion. Feel out the situation and use your judgment. If all you talk about is needing a job, people will run when they see you.

Fear of Being a "User"

Many people are hesitant about "using" people or asking for help. Networking, however, should be viewed as a communication process—exchanging and receiving advice and referrals about jobs. Many people these days consider it foolish *not* to use contacts, and those in positions to help might even be insulted that they were not asked for assistance. People *like* to help others.

It makes them feel good, powerful, and important. By establishing a specific and relevant basis for a meeting—asking for ideas, opinions, a reaction to your own thoughts—there is no reason for you to be turned down. Because much of professional life operates on the "favor system," you will owe your contact a favor while perhaps helping him or her pay back a favor from someone else. Busy professionals understand the system and they know that with just a little time and some guidance from *you*, they can evaluate you for their own needs or those of their associates while still satisfying your request for information. Both you and the other person receive something. Therefore, do not feel guilty about approaching busy people for help; they will enjoy it and you will benefit by it. If you are doubtful, consider whether you would be willing to share your knowledge or give names to friends or business associates to be helpful.

You should be concerned with the process of building and using networks as a permanent aspect of your career, not just a technique you use for finding jobs and advancing your career. Keep in touch with people you meet through professional groups or at receptions. Drop them a note occasionally or send them an article you saw that made you think of them. Do not wait until you "need" something from them. You must develop, use, and nurture personal relationships throughout your career.

By adopting these basic networking techniques, you can achieve greater job and career success!

CHAPTER 10

The Informational Interview

Ellen Wayne

The informational interview can be one of the most valuable tools in your job search. It is the next natural step after determining your career goals. Once you have been able to narrow your choices, it is time to obtain as much information as possible. The purpose of the informational interview is to provide you with the resources that you need to decide whether a particular job is the right choice for you.

The informational interview is similar to a job interview in that because during both a conversation is held between two or more people after which an evaluation is made. The major difference is that *you* are the one conducting the interview and you are the one making the evaluation. The other party to the conversation is providing the information and answering questions. Typically, informational interviews are less formal than job interviews, because the purpose of the interview is to verify the goals and career choices that you have selected for yourself, *not* to seek employment with the person you are visiting.

Once you have decided to conduct some informational interviews, how should you proceed? First, create a list of possible job choices. Second, draft a list of all the organizations in which you might possibly work. Use resources in the law school career office (most law schools allow graduates to utilize their services), law library, business library, and your neighborhood research library. Directories that list trade and professional associations, as well as the *Wall Street Journal* employment listings, can be especially useful. Third, determine the particular job titles that would be appropriate. Finally, identify people holding those positions who would be willing to spend some time with you.

Available Resources

Resources that can be utilized to assist you in finding people who would be willing to speak with you include:

1. *Law school career office.* The law school career-services office often has a list or a directory of alumni and their areas of specialization. Many career services offices have established programs that will match alumni with graduates or students to discuss practice settings and career information. (Also see Chapter 11.)

2. *State, city, or local bar association.* Become a member of your bar association. The services offered can be useful. Some of the members of specialty sections can be helpful at introducing you to practitioners who are in the field of your choice. (Also see Chapter 13.)

3. *Lexis/Nexis.* An entirely new library of information now is available on-line through Lexis/Nexis. Resources on-line through Lexis include *Martindale-Hubbell Law Directory, The United States Government Manual, The Directory of Legal Aid & Defender Offices, The Public Interest Employer Directory, The Lawyers "Plum" Book,* and others. Nexis is comprised of articles from more than 700 publications nationwide and can be used to research judges, law firms, and individuals who have been mentioned in the press. Lexis provides graduates with access to the "Career Library" through special passwords distributed through the law school career-services office.

4. *Westlaw Computerized Legal Research.* The Westlaw Career Information Library includes the West Lawyer Data Base and the Law and Business Directory of Corporate Counsel. Westlaw also maintains a publications library. Access for graduates seeking to change jobs is very limited. Law schools are not authorized to provide Westlaw services to graduates, and limited assistance is available through the local Westlaw field offices.

5. *Printed materials.* Articles in law journals, books, corporate annual reports, magazines, brochures, and library references all can be resources for providing names of potential interview contacts and information about an industry or corporation.

6. *University career-placement office.* This office is a valuable resource, especially if you are searching for a nonlegal position. Universities also maintain extensive lists of graduates and their current job placements. They also may provide a network of graduates willing to meet with people, similar to that maintained by law schools.

7. *Family and friends.* They often can provide information and an introduction to people who can help to expand the network that you are trying to develop. Ask family and friends to make a list of lawyers known to them either through business contacts or social activities. Request that they contact the lawyers that you select from the list to set up an informational interview. An introduction through someone whom the lawyer knows often makes the request for a meeting more successful.

8. *Other lawyers* (those met in court, negotiation sessions, etc.). Ask for information from those people you know. Remember to ask that your inquiry be kept confidential if your present employer is unaware of your search.
9. *Faculty at your law school.* Faculty members may be able to recommend people for you to meet through their contacts with graduates of the law school and their consulting work in the business and legal community. Many faculty keep in close contact with graduates of the law school. They will be aware of lawyers who would be willing to spend some time with someone wanting information about their particular fields of practice.
10. *CLE programs or "current trends" programs in the area of specialization in which you have an interest.* Many state bar and private organization programs (ALI/ABA, PLI, etc.) attract people who have similar interests to yours.

The Contact/Network List

When you are gathering names for your contact list, begin by being inclusive rather than exclusive. It will be easier to delete names from your list as you make decisions about your areas of interest than to go back to your original sources to add names when you find that your original search was too narrow in scope.

First, establish a working copy of your network list. Then, begin to narrow down the list to the few people with whom you wish to hold an informational interview. The decision about whom to interview can be made by asking yourself questions about both the strength of your contact with the person being targeted and your interest in his or her field of law practice or work setting. If you can, choose people to begin with who have been recommended by friends or colleagues rather than initially choosing people from a resource list of specialists.

Once you have selected the people that you want to meet, your next step will be to contact them. It is best to write a letter and then telephone. (If your request to meet is to be confidential, be sure to indicate this fact, both in the letter and on the telephone.) You should enclose a résumé (for informational purposes only), inform the person about the reason for your correspondence, and indicate where you obtained his or her name (especially if you have been referred by someone). The next step is to wait a few days and then call for an appointment. Be careful to inform the person again that you are not seeking employment, just information.

Preparing for the Interview

Most informational interviews are about 20 minutes long. Prepare for the meeting by writing down several questions and by learning as much as possible about the person's work setting and area of practice before you meet with him or her. This will allow you to ask questions that will be helpful to you in your career search as well as let the interviewee know that you are taking this learning opportunity seriously. Information can be obtained from Lexis/Nexis, your law school career library, and reference books in the law library. Always keep in mind the reason for this meeting: your need for information to evaluate the career path in terms of your own goals, strengths, and weaknesses.

Remember, you are already an experienced interviewer. In most instances, you interview clients, other lawyers, and students (if you are involved with the hiring process) every day. You successfully interviewed for that first, or even second, job after law school. Nevertheless, some questions that you might consider asking include:

1. What is the educational background of the person?
2. Why did he or she choose this particular field of law (or nonlegal position)?
3. How did he or she get started in this field?
4. How did he or she develop the position that he or she now holds?
5. How would he or she describe a typical workweek?
6. What are the chances for advancement in the field?
7. What is his or her advice for someone with your experience, or who is just beginning or trying to enter his or her practice field?
8. Is his or her practice typical of others in the field?
9. Where could you find further information about this particular area of practice or work setting?
10. Are there other people whom he or she might be willing to refer you to for further information?
11. Is there any other information that he or she could supply that would be helpful to you in learning more about this field?
12. What would he or she advise that you do as your next step after you complete the informational interview process?

As with any interview, be prepared to deal with all kinds of people. Some of the people will be enthusiastic and interested in the work they are doing; some will be dull and slower to share information; others will press you to take control of the interview. Something can be learned from each of these types of people and from the manner in which they approach their career goals. Some hints for making the interview successful include:

1. Dress in business attire; make the best impression possible.
2. Take notes. This is perfectly acceptable in this setting.
3. Be aware of the time; you promised to take only 20 minutes of the person's day. You always can come back if invited.
4. Let the other person do most of the talking. You are there to learn, not to sell yourself.
5. Prepare five or six open-ended questions to begin the interview, then let the conversation guide the rest of the interview.
6. Make an attempt to really get to know the other person. Find out what he or she likes/dislikes about his or her career.

7. Obtain other names of people to contact; expand your network.
8. Do not ask for a job; *remember the purpose of the meeting.*
9. Ask if you can call again should you think of additional questions to ask or should you need more information as your search progresses.
10. Always send a thank-you note. It is the polite and professional way to indicate that you appreciated the person's time and effort. Whether to type or handwrite the note depends on the comfort level of the meeting. If the person was friendly and the interview felt informal, it would be better to send a handwritten note. If the person's style and manner were more formal, a typed note would be appropriate.

On the day of the interview, keep in mind the implicit agreement that requesting an informational interview involves. More specifically, the person you are meeting agrees to share his or her life/experiences and will give advice with the clear understanding that you will not pressure the contact for employment.

Analyzing the Interview

After each informational interview, analyze the information that you have gathered. Decide whether to continue to investigate this particular career option. Keep in mind that individual differences will exist among your contacts. (This is the reason why it is always best to interview at least two people in each area of interest.) Never disregard a field of interest unless you have received the same information from more than one source. Always remember your goals and keep revising them based on the data that you collect and the feelings that you have about the area of practice. Evaluate not only the verbal information but also the nonverbal. Ask yourself: How would I feel about working every day in this particular setting?

In some instances, employment may be offered as a result of the informational interview or the contacts suggested, but this is not the norm. Clearly, this is not the purpose of an informational interview.

Even if, after speaking with a number of lawyers in a particular practice setting, you decide not to follow the employment route being investigated, you have had the opportunity to meet with other practitioners and to extend your professional network. Even a negative choice can be positive. Instead of entering an inappropriate field that does not comport with your goals and interests, you can use the informational interview to evaluate a position before accepting a job that would not have been right for you. Take full advantage of this process as an opportunity to explore areas of practice before you commit to the next career move. You want the next position that you accept to be a fulfilling and rewarding one.

CHAPTER 11

How to Use Your Law School's Office of Career Services

Hillary J. Mantis

Most law students are familiar with their law school's office of career services. Often, they have used the office to land their first jobs through on-campus or other recruitment programs, or have met with a career counselor at some point during their years in law school. What they may not realize, however, is that the office may provide many services to them after they graduate.

Services to law school graduates have expanded tremendously in recent years because of the economic downturn. Law schools have responded to this need by beefing up their existing services and offering several new programs designed specifically for alumni in career transition. What follows is an overview of services, programs, and resources offered to graduates by many law schools.

Services

Many law graduates are unaware that they can schedule individual appointments for career counseling with a counselor at their law school's office of career services. Although most schools are not equipped to offer long-term counseling, even one appointment with a career counselor (generally this is free of charge) can provide valuable information, ideas, and a direction in which to start your career search. You generally must be a graduate of the law school to receive career counseling or other services.

For those having a hard time locating employment, career services often offers ongoing job search support groups. Again, this service is free of charge and can be a useful source of job leads and other information, as well as emotional support. In addition to job search support groups, career services will provide résumé and cover letter advisement to any graduate of their schools in the job market. In recent years, many career-services offices will provide this service by fax, thus enabling graduates who no longer live in the area to use the service.

In light of the increasing competition for every available job, many offices are providing interview-skills workshops, mock interviews, and videotaped mock interviews as new services to graduates. Videotaped mock interviews, where the career counselor interviews and then critiques the subject, are especially useful. Often the office will provide the actual videotape, so that it can be reviewed at home prior to interviews.

Another service that has been expanded in recent years is the alumni job newsletter. Nearly every law school has created a newsletter containing all of the job listings that it receives for alumni. It is mailed to alumni who request this service, for free, or for a minimal charge. Most schools publish their newsletter either monthly or bimonthly. Job newsletters can contain a wealth of information and possible job leads, for many schools receive job listings from their alumni that are not published elsewhere. Many career offices also include job listings from local newspapers or job bulletins and information such as notices of upcoming local bar association programs. A number of law schools also trade their alumni job newsletters with other schools and keep the newsletters on file for alumni, thus enabling their graduates access to job listings from other schools located in different geographic areas.

If a graduate is seeking employment in another city or geographic area, most law schools are able to arrange reciprocity for its graduates in that area for a limited duration (usually three months). Otherwise, a nongraduate of the school generally will be prohibited from using that school's career center. If granted reciprocity, the graduate usually will have access to most of the resources that the school offers to its own graduates as well as its job listings. In recent more competitive times, however, some schools have curtailed reciprocity, reserving all services for their own graduates.

Programs

Along with an increase in services to alumni, law schools also have increased programming for alumni in the job market. Among the new programs created are skills-training seminars, panels, and symposia. Topics have included networking, rainmaking, marketing skills, résumé/cover letter preparation, and how to become a solo practitioner. Some schools have instituted their own series of programs; other schools have joined efforts and offered combined programs for all law graduates of a group of schools in the same region. In addition to the informational value of such programs, many lawyers have found these programs to be excellent networking opportunities. Local area bar associations also have developed programs exclusively for lawyers in career transition. (See also Chapter 13 on bar association activities.)

Many career-services offices have similarly developed networking and other types of receptions offered jointly with their schools' Office of Alumni Affairs. Increasingly, these two departments have been working together to help their alumni. Recent graduates should take advantage of these "home court" opportunities, because alumni often are willing to help fellow graduates.

Resources

Every law school's Office of Career Services contains a mini-library where students and graduates can research job opportunities, write down job listings, and read directories, books, and periodicals relevant to the job search. By utilizing your career library in person, you can save a lot of expensive subscription costs, and you have access to a multitude of resources. In light of recent advances in technology, law schools also have been able to upgrade their resource libraries and offer many computerized on-line services. The available resources are described in further detail below.

Job Listings

Every law school has a job board or binder that contains job listings that are published for its graduates. Often, these jobs are not published elsewhere, especially those sent in by other alumni of the school. Lawyers geographically located near their law school should check the job listings in person on a weekly or biweekly basis, rather than waiting to receive the alumni job newsletter in the mail. These jobs often are filled very quickly.

Newsletters

Most law schools subscribe to weekly or monthly commercially prepared job newsletters with listings all over the country. Utilizing these newsletters can provide graduates with access to hundreds of job listings and saves the expense of an individual subscription. Often, these commercially prepared newsletters are compiled by taking job listings from local legal periodicals and condensing them. Although repetitive, looking at all of the newsletters will ensure that you are covering all bases and not missing any advertisements.

Handouts/Regional Law Firm Lists

Many graduates do not realize that law school career-services offices spend a lot of time compiling their own resources that they give to their students and graduates. Most schools put together and distribute lists of state and regional law firms and in-house corporate legal departments. Law schools often provide many handouts relating to different steps in the job search, including résumé/cover letter guides and other valuable information.

Books and Periodicals

In addition to these resources, career libraries often subscribe to many local and regional publications and to national legal periodicals such as *The National Law Journal*, *The American Lawyer*, and *The Chronicle of Higher Education*. Many popular career and self-assessment books, such as *What Color Is Your Parachute?*, also are kept in career-services libraries and may be borrowed rather than purchased.

On-Line Services

Perhaps the most important advance in recent years has been the arrival of the Martindale-Hubbell directory on Lexis and NALPLine on Westlaw. Both data bases enable the user to manipulate the directories to create a very targeted mailing list. For example, on Lexis you can request a list of personal-injury firms with two to twelve lawyers practicing in New York City, and the computer will generate this list from Martindale-Hubbell. You can further narrow the list by requesting firms with alumni from your own alma mater. NALPLine on Westlaw can be used in a similar manner and also contains salary, recruitment, and other information compiled by the NALP.

What Law School Offices of Career Services Do Not Offer

Just as graduates often are unaware of all the resources that their law schools offer, they are not aware of, or have misconceptions about, what a law school serving thousands of graduates cannot offer. Time and budget constraints do not allow law school career counselors to see graduates for long-term, in-depth vocational counseling. However, they can refer you to a private career counselor and work with you to find one.

Law schools similarly cannot perform the same function as headhunters; therefore, they cannot actually conduct one-on-one placements. They will provide you with a list of recruiters in your area and can help you determine if your interests will be served by consulting a headhunter. (See also Chapter 12 on using third parties in your job search.)

Who to Contact/Where to Look for Further Information

For further information or to obtain the name and address of the Director of Career Services at your law school, contact:

The National Association for Law Placement
1666 Connecticut Avenue, Suite 450
Washington, D.C. 20009
(202) 667-1666

CHAPTER 12

Using Third-Party Intermediaries

Carol M. Kanarek

When a lawyer decides that it is time to change jobs, one of his or her first thoughts probably will be: "Is there someone out there who can make the process easier, faster, and less painful?" In some cases, the answer to that question is yes, but many lawyers have serious misconceptions about the roles that various third parties—including legal search firms, career counselors, and outplacement consultants—can play in the career planning and job search process.

Legal Search Firms

Legal search firms are well known to most lawyers, yet few understand what these firms realistically can—and cannot—do for them. As of January, 1993, there were 228 legal search firms in the United States, including 64 in New York and 32 in Los Angeles. This may sound like a large number, but the reality is that these firms actually service less than 10 percent of all legal employers, and significantly less than that during difficult economic times.

Search firms are used only by those private-sector employers who are seeking lawyers who they cannot easily obtain through advertising, word of mouth, law school placement offices, and unsolicited résumés. Because there is no shortage of lawyers to fill most jobs, the vast majority of employers of lawyers—including most small law firms, many corporations, and all government agencies, academic institutions, and nonprofit organizations—do not use search firms.

Furthermore, employers generally do not use legal search firms to fill nonlegal positions, nor do they generally use them to fill positions for which no prior experience in a specific area or practice is required. Finally, legal search firms tend to have relatively few positions available for lawyers who have been out of law school for more than a few years, unless the lawyer has a large portfolio of portable business.

There are also geographic limitations. Most employers in suburban and rural areas, as well as many in smaller urban areas away from the East and West Coasts, do not use search firms.

Consequently, the ideal candidate for most legal search firms is a fairly junior associate at a large to medium-sized law firm, with excellent academic credentials, who is looking for a position practicing law in his or her current field of expertise with another law firm or, in some instances, a financial institution or corporation. Search firms do not establish these parameters; employers do. It is simply a matter of supply and demand.

So what does all this mean to you? Above all, it means that if you have tried in vain to interest legal search firms in working with you, you are certainly not alone, and you should not take it personally. At least 90 percent of all lawyers are in the same position. Second, it means that you should have a fairly clear idea of what you are looking for before you make an appointment to meet with a legal search firm. Search firms are not career counselors, and you should not forget that the only way in which they make money is by finding suitable lawyers for their employer clients.

Once you have decided that you are both qualified for and interested in the types of positions that legal search firms usually have available, you are faced with the difficult question of which firm to use. Bear in mind that not all legal search firms are headhunters (i.e., telephone solicitors). You may miss a firm that will give you a great deal of personal attention if you limit your prospective choices to those that contact you directly.

Consult a list of legal search firms so that you have some idea of the universe that you are dealing with. *The American Lawyer* includes a pullout "Directory of Legal Recruiters" in its January/February issue each year. Other legal publications also print this information periodically. If you do not have access to a directory, your law school's placement office should. The placement director also may be able to make some specific recommendations to you, as may your friends and colleagues. Many can point you in the right direction—or warn you of search firms to avoid.

In most instances, you probably will be best served by selecting a search firm in the geographic area where you intend to practice. The reason for this is simple: A search firm can develop closer relationships with local employers than it can with employers in other cities where contact is limited to mail and telephone.

When dealing with a search firm, always use your good judgment. If you feel that a search firm representative is obnoxious or pushy, the employers to which he or she wishes to submit your résumé probably will think so, too. In some instances, that can mean the difference between being granted an interview and having your résumé "circularly filed." Different styles appeal to different people, but you should always be wary of a search firm that engages in any of the following practices:

- Bait and switch. The search firm lures you in with the promise of a "dream job" and then tries to sell you on something completely different.

- "Bad-mouthing" your current employer. This is not only unprofessional but is also designed to put you in a state of mind conducive to taking the first job that comes along.
- Name-dropping ("I'm working with so-and-so"). A search firm that betrays someone else's confidence probably will not respect yours either.
- Requesting a résumé without arranging an appointment. If the search firm is not interested in meeting with you in person, how can it adequately represent you to a potential employer (and how can you decide if you want it to represent you)?

In addition, a search firm never should submit your résumé to any employer without your authorization; nor should it send your résumé to any employer from which it does not have a current job listing for someone at your level of experience in your area of practice. If a search firm representative seems to know little or nothing about the positions that allegedly are available (except that they are "great jobs"), think twice about handing over your résumé.

Not surprisingly, there is a flip side to these admonitions. Most legal search firms can lead you to positions that would be difficult or impossible to obtain otherwise; in return, you should be honest and straightforward with them. When you find a search firm that you like, it is often in your best interest to offer to work with that firm exclusively for a period of time. Many search firms will make special efforts on your behalf if they know that they are not competing with others.

As your job search progresses, you can considerably enhance your chances of success by maintaining an ongoing dialogue with your search firm. Your timetable may change; certain substantive options may begin to seem more or less attractive; you may reconsider the relative values of salary, lifestyle, and opportunity for advancement. With this information, an intelligent legal search consultant can guide you through each step of the way and help you fine-tune your approach. This assistance may include any or all of the following:

- Reviewing and, if necessary, revising your résumé to highlight the aspects of your experience that will be of greatest interest to a prospective employer. In some instances, it may be useful to prepare several versions of your résumé.
- Supplying background information on prospective employers and available positions. This should include both objective data (e.g., numbers of partners and associates in the firm and department; description of practice; salary; expected billable hours, etc.) and subjective observations.
- Suggesting effective interviewing strategies. This can be especially valuable for lawyers whose most recent job interviews were during law school, because the interviewing process generally is quite different for experienced lawyers than it is for law students.

- Helping to ease the transition to your new job. This can range from suggesting ways to deal with, and obtain references from, your current employer, to assisting in negotiating time off between jobs.

Career Counselors

Career counselors have very little in common with legal search firms, yet many lawyers mistakenly believe that they do the same things. The most fundamental difference between them is that career counselors do not provide direct access to specific jobs, while legal search firms are exclusively focused on finding lawyers to fill their employer clients' job orders. The primary role of a career counselor is to guide you through the process of career planning—including self-assessment and market assessment—with the goal of helping you identify career options that will be both satisfying and realistic. A career counselor also can assist in the job search process by providing guidance in résumé and cover letter writing, networking strategies, and interviewing techniques.

When you work with a career counselor, you are the client and you pay the fee. Consequently, you should perform the "due diligence" necessary to satisfy yourself that that counselor's approach is compatible with your particular needs and objectives. Career counselors are not employment agencies, and you always should be wary of any counseling service that lures you with vague promises of "high-level contacts" and then charges a large fee for what is essentially a mass-mailing service.

Many career counselors place a strong emphasis on interests, skills, and values clarification. These counselors may use one or more of a variety of tools, including the Myers-Briggs Type Indicator, the Strong Interest Inventory, and various other self-assessment exercises. The interpretation of these exercises may help you determine what careers and work settings are most likely to give you satisfaction. Counselors who are strongly oriented toward this aspect of the career-planning process may be particularly appropriate for lawyers who are unhappy in the practice of law but unsure about where to turn next.

A career counselor also can guide you through the process of market analysis. This is the "real-world" half of the career-planning equation, and it is very important. Without it, you might formulate a career objective that is theoretically satisfying but also totally unrealistic. The goal of market analysis is to gather as much specific information as possible about the jobs or careers that the self-analysis process identified as being potentially of interest to you, so that you can decide whether and how to pursue them.

The career counselor can show you strategies for networking and obtaining informational interviews that can help you collect this information. For this phase of the career-planning process, it can be particularly useful to work with a career counselor who has extensive experience with lawyers. In the larger cities, there are career counselors who specialize in "lawyers in transition." Your local bar association or law school placement office can help you identify counselors in your geographic area who have the background and experience that may be most useful to you.

Once the career-planning process (self-analysis plus market analysis) is completed, you might proceed directly to the job search process. In some cases, additional education or experience may be needed; in others, you may decide to stay in your current position to acquire additional skills or save some money before embarking on a new career path. When the job search does begin, however, a career counselor can provide advice regarding the most effective ways to communicate with, and sell one's credentials to, potential employers. In particular, a career counselor can help you describe your legal training and experience in a way that will be both meaningful and attractive to a nonlegal employer. Career counselors also can provide assistance with regard to myriad other matters, including difficult questions in interviews, salary negotiations, and reference checks.

Outplacement Consultants

Outplacement Consultants, long a staple in corporate America, recently have been added to the lawyer severance packages of many law firms in response to structural and economic forces that have resulted in large numbers of lawyer layoffs. An outplacement counselor performs essentially the same functions as a career counselor does, although time constraints often dictate that the focus be on rapidly securing new employment that will be consistent with the lawyer's long-term goals. The fee for the outplacement services is paid by the law firm that is asking the lawyer to leave. However, the departing lawyer should understand that the outplacement counselor is not an arm of the law firm's management.

The outplacement counselor is not involved in establishing the terms of the lawyer's severance, and conversations between the lawyer and the counselor are strictly confidential. In some instances, the lawyer may wish to have the counselor discuss a particular issue with someone at the firm, but such conversations would take place only at the lawyer's request.

Assistance typically provided by an outplacement counselor covers a range of areas, including how to analyze the needs of prospective employers; how to create a network of contacts who can provide information about the legal job market in general, as well as information about specific opportunities that may be available; how to draft résumés and cover letters; and how to interview and negotiate the terms of employment effectively.

An outplacement counselor can be of tremendous aid in navigating the uncharted waters of the legal employment world, particularly if the counselor has direct experience in the legal market. The counselor can offer information on which practice areas and types of employers are generally busy. He or she also can provide access to periodicals with relevant public-sector and private-sector job listings.

Equally important, the counselor can help the lawyer create a network of contacts and can give advice on informational interviewing and computer-assisted research. All of these can yield data about prospective employers that lawyers can use during interviews to distinguish themselves positively from other applicants.

An outplacement counselor who understands the mind-set of legal employers can help the lawyer draft customized cover letters that demonstrate an awareness of the bottom-line concerns of the law firms and companies to which the lawyer is applying. The counselor also can provide guidelines to senior associates and partners for the preparation of detailed experience summaries and practice development plans.

Effective interviewing is vital to the job change process. The outplacement counselor can help identify the probable questions and concerns that a particular employer may have regarding the lawyer's background and experience, and propose an effective strategy for addressing those issues.

A lawyer who is under time pressure to leave his or her current job is particularly vulnerable to pressure to accept a position that may not be appropriate. Unlike the lawyer's employer or a legal search firm, the outplacement counselor does not have a personal stake, financial or otherwise, in the lawyer's decision to accept or reject a particular job offer. As a third party who is both knowledgeable and unbiased, the counselor is uniquely situated to assist the lawyer in researching prospective employers and to help negotiate salary and other terms of employment.

In addition to providing an overall framework for the job search, the outplacement counselor can help the lawyer respond to the questions and crises that inevitably arise on a day-to-day basis. The counselor is someone with whom the lawyer can speak freely, without fear of personal or professional repercussions.

Conclusion

Finding a new job is seldom an easy undertaking, and the ultimate responsibility for most of the work that it entails rests with the lawyer who desires to make the move. In appropriate circumstances, however, third parties can be of significant assistance in navigating the uncharted waters of the legal employment world.

CHAPTER 13

How Bar Associations Can Help

Beth L. Kaufman[1]

For the lawyer in transition (LIT) from one job to another—even if not voluntarily—a bar association can be a useful resource. Gone are the days when bar associations were tranquil fora, at which all that occurred were debates on the great legal issues of the day. Increasingly, state and local bar associations are responding to the changing face of a profession that is ever seeking to define itself. You will find that state and local bar associations will provide you—and quite willingly—with whatever formalized services they have organized and will be open to offering others. More importantly, bar associations can provide an opportunity to meet other lawyers, to discover new areas of practice, and to take those steps that will ensure one's happiness in his or her legal career.

Bar associations may follow a multipart approach:[2]

Informational Support Groups

Designed to impart as much useful information for a job search as possible, monthly programs can be held, led by lawyers or career counselors. Such basic topics as interview techniques, networking skills, and résumé writing may be covered, often several times each year. Psychological stress—both individual and family—may be addressed in the group setting as well. Individual practice areas, how to locate jobs in them, and how to start one's own practice may be the subjects of their own programs.[3]

The workshops provide more than useful information. The greatest resource of any bar association is its members, and the workshops present the opportunity to "network" instantly with numerous attorneys.

Mentoring

The goal in mentoring is to pair a practicing lawyer with an LIT, to provide suggestions on networking, to be a sounding board for job-related questions, and just to be a friend when the stress of the search becomes overwhelming. Often, the LIT is interested in switching the area in which he or she practices, or the type of environment in which she or he practices, from, for instance, private practice to the public sector. The mentor chosen can be someone who practices in the area to which the LIT aspires.

Daylong Conference

Realizing that many LITs were unable to attend regular, in-depth monthly workshops, the association may hold a daylong conference covering many of the same areas addressed at the monthly meeting. The conference should begin with an introductory overview of job search techniques as a prelude to individual workshops, each of which usually is repeated at least twice. Four workshops can be held simultaneously, on subjects ranging from "Marketing Yourself" to "Permanent Employment" to "Temporary Employment" to "How To Use the Library To Help in a Job Search." The conference can help instill a sense of direction and confidence in the face of what generally is perceived to be a bleak market. At the Association of the Bar, the conference was titled "How To Survive the Shakeout in the Lawyer's Marketplace," and aptly so, for the conference graduated many lawyers who not only survived, but ultimately thrived, in the profession.

Emotional Support Groups

Limited to 15 or fewer participants and led by a psychologist, the groups can respond to an overwhelming need expressed by LITs just "to talk." Often, talking with others in similar situations provides the most solace and encouragement. Indeed, the groups can help all of those who participate with networking, in addition to dealing with the natural anxiety and stress a job search engenders.

Lawyer/Employment Openings Exchange

Regularly publishing a bulletin in which both employers and LITS can advertise, or something similar, is by far the vehicle of choice through which bar associations help in this area.[4] Of 33 state and local bar associations that responded to a survey conducted for the preparation of this Chapter, 13—the Connecticut Bar, Missouri Bar, Colorado Bar, Kansas Bar, Maryland State Bar, the Rhode Island Bar, the Virginia State Bar, the Washington State Bar, the Barristers Club of San Francisco, the Indianapolis Bar, the New York County Lawyers Association, the Oneida County Bar, and the Prince George County Bar Association—provided similar services. Of the 33 state and local bar associations who responded to the survey, 18 provided job-placement services, ranging from the most basic of maintaining résumés on file to actually pairing candidates with known job openings. Additionally, the Corporate Counsel Committee of the ABA-YLD regularly publishes a Job Bulletin on corporate counsel opportunities.

Volunteer Programs

To ensure that lawyers engaged in what can prove to be a long job search do not experience a decline in their considerable skills, volunteer programs should be established. Benefiting understaffed public-interest groups, the volunteer lawyers often learn new skills in areas of practice such as family law, Social-Security challenges, and housing disputes.

Conclusion

No matter how successful programs such as these may be, the attention of bar associations must turn to reducing the number of LITs by helping to ensure happy and productive job choices for law students. Bar associations are aptly suited for "networking" receptions, at which students interested in particular areas of practice have an opportunity to meet informally with lawyers practicing in the field. Students may be paired with mentors (practicing lawyers), who can assist them in deciding how to go about entering into particular fields, by showing them ways to meet other lawyers and, thus, locating possible job opportunities, and by explaining where to look for the opportunities available to students to distinguish themselves by writing, researching, or assisting in projects in the discipline. According to an ABA Young Lawyers Committee's study published in 1990, tremendous dissatisfaction among members of the profession exists, as early as one year after law school graduation. Bar associations assist students in their job choices and facilitate career decisions to add more happy, productive members to the profession.

Notes

1. The assistance of Lara T. Abbott and Darlene Keator in the preparation of this chapter is gratefully acknowledged.

2. Based on the program devised by the Association of the Bar's (City of New York) Committee on Lawyers in Transition. Originally established to assist older lawyers who wished to reduce the amount of time they devoted to the practice of law but still be valuable to the profession as teachers, mentors, and public servants, the Committee was faced immediately with a population of younger lawyers who were seeking new employment opportunities. The Committee responded quickly to fill the tremendous void that each lawyer in transition (LIT) felt, and as quickly as possible.

3. At the Association of the Bar, programs such as these were held from 6 to 8 p.m., a time that usually was free for those individuals engaged in a full-time job search. All programs were free of charge and open to all lawyers, even if they were not bar association members.

4. At the Association of the Bar, rates in its *Attorney Placement Bulletin* varied for those listing job opportunities, based on the type of employer: public-interest groups could advertise at no charge; private practitioners paid a modest fee; and an LIT paid a small fee.

PART III

Getting the Offer

CHAPTER 14

Writing an Effective Résumé

Pat Bowers Thomas

The content and presentation of a lawyer's résumé is perhaps the single most important career advancement tool. A quick glance at a résumé by an employment screener frequently determines whether a particular candidate is worthy of further evaluation and an initial interview. Therefore, you must be prepared to devote substantial thought, time, and energy to creating a résumé that distinguishes you from the crowd.

Description of a Résumé

What Is In and What Is Passé

The résumé of the 1990s is much more than a conventional skeletal chronology of data. It is a well-organized and concise, yet thorough, presentation that emphasizes a lawyer's growth and development. The language in a résumé should be meaningful to experienced lawyers and human-resources professionals. The résumé should be constructed in a format that allows readers quickly to find the information that they consider key to a specific employment slot.

A résumé should be drafted strategically, taking into consideration each potential employer's particularized criteria in conjunction with your experience and agenda. You should highlight the parallels between the two as they relate to specific accomplishments in each of your academic and professional endeavors. Effective résumés focus on the substantive nature of your practice, detailing the various types of work product produced, describing the levels of responsibility that you have achieved, and identifying your experience with specific types of clients and industries.

Different Uses of a Résumé

In this chapter, three fictitious lawyers will be discussed: Dale S. Technical, a very junior lawyer with a scientific/technical focus; John Q. Corporate, a midlevel corporate lawyer; and Sarah M. Litigator, a senior litigation lawyer. Résumés will be created for these lawyers, beginning with initial drafts and then exploring the format/style changes necessary to tailor the résumé for separate positions—one with a law firm and one with a corporation.

Even if your practice specialty is not covered in one of these examples, you should easily be able to correlate them to your substantive focus. These examples should enable you to construct résumés for all types of employment situations.

Limitations of a Résumé

Before beginning, a number of misconceptions must be dispelled.

Misconception #1: "More is better" or "less is better." While it often has been a rule of thumb that the length of a résumé should approximate one page for every seven to ten years of practice, this rule is less than helpful if your finished product does not highlight your significant accomplishments in an effective manner or if it is filled with a laundry list of every legal matter that you have touched since beginning law school. Finding the happy medium between being verbose and being laconic is a more important guideline than restricting information to one page.

Misconception #2: By carefully constructing a résumé, you can hide (1) frequent job changes, (2) lack of experience, and (3) poor academics. A lawyer's résumé should, at a minimum, contain all legal positions held since graduation from law school and most probably set forth any practice breaks or sabbaticals if they were longer than six months. Omitted legal employment information is usually uncovered—typically with less-than-favorable results.

Your résumé should be designed to put your best foot forward, proceeding toward the achievement of your short-term and long-term career goals. Therefore, it is counterproductive to inflate your experience or embellish your academics with insignificant activities. If you feel pressure to do this, then return to your career planning and redirect your efforts toward more compatible and realistic goals.

Misconception #3: A résumé should begin with an "Objective" section stating your career goals.   While there are two schools of thought on this topic, each with very plausible arguments, the information found in an objective section usually should be included in a cover letter, not in the résumé.

Misconception #4: Salary information should be included on a résumé. To avoid comparing apples to oranges, you should not include a salary history on your résumé. You may want to provide a desired salary range in your cover letter when applicable.

Misconception #5: Employers' addresses and telephone numbers should be included on each employment entry. Do not give away the store. Providing such information encourages prereferencing by a potential employer. Once an employer has interviewed you, then reference checking can begin at the appropriate and mutually agreed-on time.

Preparation of the Résumé

Evaluating Your Experiences

In earlier chapters, you have learned how to identify your career motivational attitudes, work ethics, and the current marketplace. Now you are ready to consider these elements in conjunction with your substantive experience and academic performance. Prioritize your experience, keeping in mind your career goals. Identify your detailed work product by the percentage of time you spent in a given substantive area. List levels of responsibility for each product and the types of clients for whom you produced these products.

Targeting Your Audience

Decide what experience and academic achievements should be emphasized by learning as much as possible about a particular employment opportunity. This information may be gained from friends or school alumni working for that employer, a lawyer recruiter, your law school placement office, articles in legal magazines, etc.

In analyzing a position, consider the following:

- What substantive knowledge and skills will be required? Are there any additional practice areas that will help place you in the top 10 percent of candidates?
- What productivity requirements and added levels of drive are needed to receive promotions within the organization?
- What value does the organization place on intelligence, creativity, and leadership?
- To whom will you play a supporting role? Who will be your peers? What are the profiles of these people?
- What percentage of time will you be spending interacting with people outside your legal group? Who are they?
- What oral and written skills are required?
- What is the culture and personal style of this employer and its employees? Are its lawyers known to be aggressive or reserved, formal or casual, unidimensionally focused on the practice of law or active in diverse community and family interests?

Each time you consider a different opportunity, reevaluate your résumé against that employer's acknowledged position specifications, as well as against the less obvious specifications relating to the client's culture. Then, adjust your résumé accordingly.

General Rules of Thumb

When creating your résumé, you should follow certain guidelines:

- A résumé should contain enough information to encourage a personal meeting, but not so much information that the curiosity of the reader vanishes.
- Nationally recognized employers need no introduction on a résumé; however, local or regional employers may need identifying information on the résumé when you apply for positions in other areas of the United States. Identifying factors can include size or number of lawyers, industry or practice focus, and former affiliations. For example:

    Young & Restless, Anytown, USA
    (30-lawyer litigation boutique spinoff from O'Great & Powerful in 1985)

- The body of information relating to your current position should be written in the present tense (unless you are currently unemployed). All too frequently, lawyers who are job searching have psychologically departed from their position, and this attitude is manifested by text written in the past tense for their present employment situation.
- Place related information together under one heading so that all accomplishments in one academic or employment setting are tied together. For instance, if you wrote for Law Review during law school, show this information with your law school entry. Do not place it in your publications section.
- Leave out information that is unnecessary, is assumed, or has become irrelevant. Be careful with this. For instance, it is not assumed that more senior lawyers working on complex matters perform all levels of less complex work below the experience listed.
- The telephone numbers on your résumé should place a caller in direct contact with you or allow him or her to leave a private message. Do not needlessly jeopardize your current employment situation.
- The reader of a résumé will not necessarily know the status of your present employment; therefore, mark directly on the résumé that this is a confidential submission.

The First-Draft Components

For any writer, committing pen to paper is difficult. When developing a résumé, you must remember that your first draft will be just that—a step in the process. Try to include as much information as possible, organizing each section chronologically. Then, put your first draft away for a rest and plan to evaluate it with a critical eye another day.

Education

Academic achievements and leadership qualities have long been key indicators for employers regarding potential intelligence and commitment. The competitive selection and performance standards of a highly regarded educational institution suggest greater intelligence and excellence of the applicant just by nature of the association. Moreover, some law firms give extra weight to an applicant's association with such institutions, viewing them as potential "peer breeding grounds" for future client development. Graduates from the "top 20" or first-tier law schools who achieve Order of the Coif status and become editors of their schools' Law Review continue to be coveted for their stellar academics. However, being one of the top five graduates from a midtier school may carry equal or more weight than graduating beyond the top 25 percent of the class from a first-tier school. Impressive extracurricular activities often imply productivity and commitment. Earning a degree while working or raising a family may have much the same effect, particularly if coupled with a strong record.

Begin your academic history with college, continuing through post-graduate studies. Generally, you should not include high school unless, for example, you attended a special school in Switzerland for more than a year and now are applying to an employer where that cultural and academic experience may be important.

Class standing in the top 20 percent or above should always be included in this section. Once you have become a member of the bar and practiced for 12 months, your SAT and LSAT scores can be dropped from this section.

Employment Experience

As is true with academic accomplishments, a high value is placed on prior associations with easily recognized and highly regarded employers. These employers provide a "shorthand" reference with regard to the type of training that you have received and the complexity of matters available to you at your level of practice. Less easily recognized employers can be enhanced by a short description to pique the reader's curiosity and encourage investigation regarding the value of the particular employment situation during an interview.

Within the legal community, great value is placed on job stability as well as a steady progression in level of responsibility. Employers tend to use a critical eye in this section to evaluate your level of commitment, loyalty, motivation, initiative, job performance, and intelligence. Obviously, individuals dealing with the more complex matters for their level of experience are seen as having higher potential value. Be cautious, however, not to overplay the complexities of your work at the expense of the necessary basics. Corporate employers and smaller firms become leery of candidates who perform only "headline-making" work. They often need employees who are willing to work in the trenches.

Employers appreciate detail regarding your work, including substantive expertise, client and industry interaction, roles and responsibilities, and interpersonal effectiveness. They also may gain insight into your commitment through information regarding your nonbillable legal responsibilities and management/supervisory roles. Again, remember to prioritize your experience so that you target your audience (each particular employer).

For a number of lawyers, law is a second or continued career following employment after undergraduate schooling. If this is your situation, establish separate sections on your résumé to deal with legal and nonlegal experience. Determine the amount of detail necessary regarding your nonlegal experience by evaluating its correlation to your legal employment.

Memberships, Certifications, Affiliations, and Activities

Prominently display your bar memberships. If bar admission in a particular state is considered difficult and selective, indicate the year that you passed the exam. Passing the bar on the first sitting in a state such as California, where there is no reciprocity, is considered a strong indication of intellectual achievement. Registration to practice before the U.S. Patent & Trademark Office, particularly when earned during the same year as a state bar membership, is another example of highly valued certification.

Affiliations with large organizations should be detailed to identify participation in specific sections and their committees that have easily identifiable value to your career plan. For instance, simply listing membership in the ABA is far less critical than an environmental lawyer adding: *Member, Natural Resources, Energy & Environmental Law Section: Special Committee on Environmental Crimes.* Personal-interest entries also may assist in identifying your diversifications. Entries such as *"Women's Lawyers Caucus, Secretary of Regional Activities"* and *"Member, Native American Indian Bar Association"* give the reader a more complete picture of your background and interests.

Community activities may be important to a potential employer. They can indicate diversification of interests, social responsibility, and beneficial business contacts as well as geographic ties and stability. Maturity and strong organizational skills often are inferred from significant responsibilities within these organizations.

There is much debate concerning inclusion of leisure activities and personal information. When submitting a résumé to a potential employer, determine whether inclusion of this information will indicate a cultural fit within the organization. When you do include this information, keep it short. Here are some commonly held perceptions of employers regarding certain leisure activities:

- Sports—stays fit, good health, may be a team player, competitive, self-disciplined;
- Cultural activities—diversity, intellectual breadth; and
- Travel—adaptability to different regions and cultures, curiosity.

Listing too many activities, however, may result in an employer's sensing that you lack commitment to your career.

In today's global economy, the ability to conduct business in another language often distinguishes a candidate from the pack. Many of today's employers are evaluating the international implications of their businesses. Include your language capabilities on your résumé if you have at least conversational proficiency. Be sure to list your specific proficiency in each language.

The Visual Effect

How you present your résumé is as important as the facts presented. Because you are a professional, look professional. Visually, your résumé should be clean, with easy-to-read type spotlighting important information. The page should be organized so that readers easily can find the information that you feel is key to their evaluation of your candidacy.

Remember, an individual who regularly screens numerous résumés spends approximately *five to ten seconds* glancing over each résumé. At least 80 percent of the résumés are disqualified on this first glance. Be sure you put your best foot forward, leaving a favorable impression.

Because you are initially developing a résumé that meets the overall needs of potential employers and then tailoring it for specific submission, you should access a private computer and laser printer to create your résumé. Store this information on a disc for future revisions.

Appearance

Several factors contribute to the attractiveness of a résumé. These include:

- *Quality paper*—Select a neutral (white, cream, beige, pale gray, etc.) paper in 20- to 24-pound weight with minimal grain or "tooth." This paper should feel substantial, neither heavy nor flimsy. Paper with too deep a grain or tooth tends to break up the print (broken letters) and does not fold well when placed in an envelope. Test the paper you select by printing on a sheet with a laser jet printer and folding the paper. Taking the time to test paper will yield subtle benefits in the long run. If you are submitting your information directly to an employer, purchase envelopes to match the paper.
- *Print*—Use a variety of compatible typeface styles and sizes, printing in black ink. You may choose to have a print shop typeset your résumé or use the flexibility of computer software and letter-quality printers. Many of the word-processing software programs have a variety of type fonts available. Typewriter print and dot-matrix print are not satisfactory.
- *Reproduction*—If you decide to produce a single hard copy of your résumé and photocopy originals as needed, be sure you produce clean, sharp, and evenly aligned copies. If you fax your résumé at the request of an employer, mail a hard copy on the same day as a backup. (You would be wise to consider the questionable confidentiality of faxed résumés.)

Layout

Suggestions for a suitable layout include the following:

- The text should be organized so that there are adequate margins and tabulations creating clean lines and sufficient "white" space. It should produce a visual balance, both vertically and horizontally on every page. Your name, address, and telephone information is always at the top of the first page. Second pages should be marked clearly with your name.

- Bold, underline, or italicize print to spotlight significant information and organize the page.
- Balance the length of a particular employment or academic entry against the level of experience and importance that it represents.
- Choose a layout style that assists the employer in rapidly finding your key qualifications for the position. For example, often subtle variations are better used for a corporation than for a law firm.

Organization

Decide what information should be most visible and the order in which it should be presented. Generally, very junior lawyers and new graduates provide their academic information first. As they become more senior, it often is appropriate to place legal experience as the first entry on the résumé.

You must determine how your résumé will fare in the brief-glance test. This evaluation involves critically reading it quickly left to right, top to bottom. Generally, a résumé screener spends the most time glancing from top to bottom along the left half of the résumé. Be sure the information near the end of your résumé remains interesting; otherwise, shorten your résumé.

Here are some examples of how to address employers' hiring criteria through strategic organization of information:

- Does the employer seek stability? If you are not a job-hopper, then list your employment dates first in the left-hand margin (although still in chronological order).
- Is the employer looking for identifiable training from "name" employers? Assuming you value the same employers, list them first in the left-hand margin.
- Will this employer seek a candidate who has held certain positions with increasing levels of responsibility? List your positions first followed by your employers.
- Is your overall experience most important to this employer? Summarize your experience before giving an employment history.

The Examples

These ideas now can be put to work. The three fictional lawyers have gone through a first draft and an appearance draft of their résumés. While there are numerous layouts for and organizations of résumés, these three examples provide a wealth of information and guidelines for you to compose a résumé tailored to your needs.

Dale S. Technical

Dale's search involves potential employers that will be most interested in candidates who have had specific job positions, levels of increasing responsibility, well-regarded employers, and technical knowledge. The layout and organization of the résumé shown in Figure 14.1 does not address these employer interests first, while the résumé in Figure 14.2 does.

Visually, weight has been added to the type to emphasize the most important information first. Less obvious are the changes in the headings (*Education, Other Professional Experience, and Languages*), making uniform what are similar layout functions. Additionally, the method of listing employment dates was made uniform (1987 to 1990 changed to 1987–1990). States were uniformly abbreviated rather than spelled out when identifying the location of employment. Admissions information was corrected to represent the complete and correct organizational name.

Dale worked her way through school as an engineer; therefore, she attended classes given in both the day and the night divisions. While it may be apparent to a careful reader that she worked during law school, she has given the reader a clue by adding the *Day & Night Divisions* to her law school entry. Additionally, she spent her last year of law school in Palo Alto, a hotbed of computer-related activity, where she might have studied under some important intellectual-property/patent professors. This information has been added to the law school entry to add emphasis to her computer studies and training. A sophisticated screener often will highlight such information for investigation during an interview.

Dale took the State Bar in July and the Patent Bar in August following graduation from law school. Passing both, each on the first sitting, within two months is a significant accomplishment. This accomplishment is featured in the *Admissions* section.

Information was added to the text of the current employment setting regarding the specific technical direction of Dale's practice (electronics) and the types of applications the work involves. Additionally, the work involves both domestic and foreign filings. The copy was changed to the present tense (she has not left this position). Note the change in the amount of space and information used to describe Dale's current position in relation to prior work experiences between version one and version two of her résumé. This was done to define subtly the balance between her legal and technical experience. Additionally, included in this section was Dale's work as a patent agent for the firm while in law school. This rounded out the chronology of her work experience, further solidifying a strong focus and work ethic.

Dale is a recent graduate of law school, having worked for ten years as an engineer before beginning her legal education. This experience is specifically applied in her patent practice so these prelaw employment entries have been included also.

The patent field, as in many of today's substantive practices, frequently utilizes foreign-language skills. Therefore, Dale's foreign languages are listed in anticipation of their value to a potential employer.

The work telephone number was removed as a contact point because it is not a direct dial and, therefore, not confidentially secure.

FIGURE 14.1
Dale S. Technical Résumé—Version One

DALE S. TECHNICAL
444 W. 4th Street
Midwest, IL 50505

Home (299) 555-6666
Office (299) 557-7000

EDUCATION:

The Midwest University, Chicago, IL
(Spent 3rd year at Palo Alto Law School, Silicon Valley, CA)
J.D., 1991, Top 15% (Day & Evening Divisions)
Member, Midwest Computer & High Technology Law Journal
1988–89

University of the Midwest, Duluth, Minnesota
M.S., 1981, Electrical Engineering

Polytechnic State, Milwaukee, WI
S.B., 1980, Electrical Engineering

ADMISSIONS: IL 1991
Registered to practice before the United States Patent and
Trademark Office, December 1991

LEGAL EXPERIENCE:

Prosecution, Application & Infringement,
Chicago, IL
Associate 1991 – present. Work involved patent prosecution,
validity and infringement studies, licensing and negotiation, and
client counseling.

Other Professional Experience

Magic Corporation, Chicago, IL
Engineering Manager 1987 to 1990. Managed a team of twelve
engineers involved in the development of computer–aided design
software tools. Position involved budget proposals and allocation
for the financing for the development of new applications for
company products.

EFZ Systems Company, Palo Alto, California
Design Engineer 1983 – 1987. Programmed computers to develop
tools for designing integrated circuits. Designed computer–aided
engineering software for engineering work stations.

Computer Corporation, Palo Alto, CA
Engineer 1981 – 83. Designed programs and databases.

Languages: Japanese, Chinese (Cantonese), and Russian

FIGURE 14.2

Dale S. Technical Résumé—Version Two

DALE S. TECHNICAL

444 W. 4th Street
Midwest, Illinois 50505
Home: (299) 555-6666

EDUCATION:

THE MIDWEST UNIVERSITY   1991
(Spent 3rd year at Palo Alto Law School, Silicon Valley, CA) Chicago, IL
J.D., Top 15% (Day & Evening Divisions)
Member, *Midwest Computer & High Technology Law Journal*, 1988-89

UNIVERSITY OF THE MIDWEST   1981
M.S. in Electrical Engineering   Duluth, MN

POLYTECHNIC STATE   1980
S.B. in Electrical Engineering   Milwaukee, WI

ADMISSIONS: State Bar of Illinois, 1991
Registered to practice before the United States Patent and Trademark Office, December 1991

LEGAL EXPERIENCE:

Patent Associate   1991–Present
PROSECUTION, APPLICATION & INFRINGEMENT   Chicago, IL

Preparation and prosecution of U.S. and foreign applications specializing in electronics covering computers, digital and analog circuits and systems, signal processing and architecture, semiconductors, and software architecture; validity and infringement studies; licensing and negotiation; client counseling. Clients range from independent inventors to multinational corporations.

Patent Agent   Summer 1990

OTHER PROFESSIONAL EXPERIENCE:

Engineering Manager   1987–1990
MAGIC CORPORATION   Chicago, IL

Managed a team of twelve engineers involved in the development of computer-aided design software tools. Position involved budget proposals and allocation for the financing for the development of new applications for company products.

Design Engineer   1983–1987
EFZ SYSTEMS COMPANY   Palo Alto, CA

Programmed computers to develop tools for designing integrated circuits. Designed computer-aided engineering software for engineering work stations.

Engineer   1981–1983
COMPUTER CORP   Palo Alto, CA

Designed programs and databases.

LANGUAGES: Japanese, Chinese (Cantonese), and Russian

Submitted in confidence. Do not contact present or former employers
without prior approval of Dale S. Technical

John Q. Corporate

John is a midlevel associate with stellar academics, broad corporate transactional experience, and employment stability. This very basic information is lost in his first draft (see Figure 14.3) where there is virtually no differentiation in the amount of information given between the various academic, employment, and leisure entries. In addition, the lack of dynamic format and emphasis in the type style may cause this résumé to be disqualified before it is read.

The Law Firm Résumé

Look at Figure 14.4 for a solution. John developed this résumé for potential law firm employers.

John decided that law firms would be most interested in employment stability and the "valued associate" connotation that it implies. Next, he felt that they would look for "name or selective" employers and academic institutions, followed by depth of experience in corporate practice. He chose a format that emphasized these elements in the correct proportion reflecting their priority, i.e., date, employer, experience.

With these solid credentials, John felt comfortable organizing his résumé so that his work experience came before academic achievements. He added considerable information to his law firm experience by detailing the breadth of his practice, focus specialties, levels of responsibility, types of clients, client contacts, and firm activities. He included his summer clerkship entry to underline his commitment to the firm and indicate the firm's early training and selection of John as an associate. The text was changed from the first person, because it often causes the candidate to be viewed as self-centered and questions the candidate's ability to be a team player and a *member* of an organization.

To attend undergraduate and law school, John depended on scholarships and worked odd jobs between class schedules. He bulked these work experiences under *Various Jobs*, gaining résumé space while maintaining the inference of being a hard worker, intelligent, and down to earth.

The value of John's work experiences is reinforced by his academic entries. These entries also indicate good writing skills (Law Journal) and good communication and rapport with people (being elected President of Quest Hall).

Because John did not want three short sections at the bottom of his résumé, which, perhaps, would dilute the importance of each, he chose to place his bar memberships directly above his work experience. This provides the necessary information without modifying the strength of this résumé format.

Associates know that client-development skills are an important prerequisite to making partner. John specifically included speaking before a group of potential clients in the *Activities* section to emphasize his potential talents in knowing how, where, and when to develop business.

Also included was very specific information regarding his language skills as a "plus factor" in his candidacy. His personal information was omitted because it was not essential to this law firm–oriented résumé.

FIGURE 14.3

John Q. Corporate—First-Draft Résumé

JOHN Q. CORPORATE
456 Trial Lane
Tireless, New York 12345
Home (212) 123-4567
Office (212) 765-4321

Education

Johnson High School (high honors)	1979
QSU, B.A.	1983
Stellar Law School, J.D.	1987

Employment

Tireless County Road Corporation	July – Oct 1979 Construction Worker
New York Grocery Store Clerk	Summer 1980
KHRT Radio Program Assistant Researcher	March 1983 – July 1984
Law Offices of Herman Lawyer Law Intern	Jan 1985 – June 1985
Apple, Bean, Carrot & Frye Summer Clerk	Summer 1985
O'Great & Powerful	Summer 1986

Summer associate: legal research and drafted memoranda and pleadings.

Whye, Nott, Merge & Achoir Summer associate	Summer 1986
O'Great & Powerful	Sept 1987 – present

I am an Associate practicing in the Corporate Department with an emphasis on mergers and acquisitions, securities, and general corporate law. Member of the Hiring Committee.

Personal

Born: January 1, 1962 New York Plains, NY
Single. Enjoy skiing, wines, chess, and the classics.

FIGURE 14.4
John Q. Corporate—Law Firm Résumé

JOHN Q. CORPORATE
456 Trial Lane
Tireless, New York 12345
Home (212) 123-4567
Office (212) 765-4321

Bar Member: New York (1987), District of Columbia (1988)

EXPERIENCE
Legal:

Sept 1987–
Present

O'Great & Powerful, New York, New York
Associate. Practice sixty percent of time with the Corporations Department, with an emphasis on mergers and acquisitions, securities, and general corporate law. Leading role on a variety of transactions for clients ranging from emerging companies to Fortune 250 companies. Senior associate responsible for all aspects of transactions, including drafting and negotiating documents, overseeing due diligence, and handling closings. Primary client contact for ongoing general corporate work. In addition, broad experience in financial regulatory matters, real estate loans, environmental compliance and land-use, and corporate workouts and restructurings.

Member of the firm's Associate Hiring Committee for both law school graduates and lateral associates.
(May–July 1986, *Summer Associate*)

July–Sept
1986

Whye, Nott, Merge & Achoir, Washington, D.C.
Summer Associate. Split summer clerking with the firm and current employer. Received permanent offer of employment.

May–Sept
1985

Apple, Bean, Carrot & Frye, Chicago, Illinois
Summer Clerk.

Other:

July 1979–
April 1984

Various Jobs
During undergraduate, worked in order to earn 60% of the money needed to finance QSU and first year of law school. These jobs included working as a grocery store clerk, a construction worker, and an assistant program researcher for a local radio station. Became employed full-time by the radio station to write editorials on the effect of national news items on local citizens.

EDUCATION

1987

Stellar Law School, New York, New York
Juris Doctor, Top 11% (24/200)
Publications Editor, *Stellar Corporations Law Journal*
Attorney's Scholarship 1986–1987

1983

QSU, Quest, New York
Bachelor of Arts, summa cum laude
Dual Major: English and Communications
President, Quest Hall 1981–1982

ACTIVITIES

Speaker, New York Association of General Counsel (NYGC)
    Program: "The Effect of M&A on Executive Compensation"
Member, American Bar Association Business Law Section: Subcommittee
    on Securities Regulation

LANGUAGES

Fluent French, conversational Japanese

Submitted in confidence. Do not contact present or
former employers without prior approval of J.Q. Corporate

Because John has been practicing for several years, it may be difficult to provide enough concrete examples of his responsibilities and duties to distinguish him from the top 20 percent of applicants for a position. To remedy this, an addendum was added to his résumé entitled *Representative Corporate Experience* (see Figure 14.5). This type of information can be organized chronologically or by substantive subspecialties, as in John's addendum.

In brief sentences, John has described a specific project for a client, giving the size of the deal, the type of work, his responsibilities, and the type of client. Clients may be referred to by specific name or generically. These projects are organized on one page by substantive groupings, e.g., *Securities Offerings, Mergers & Acquisitions*, and *General Corporate*.

This addendum is a very useful tool. While the basic details on your résumé may not change so rapidly, the specific projects that you work on and the level of responsibility that you have at work changes more frequently. New projects often require exploration into new legal issues and corresponding substantive work. So, this addendum becomes a simpler method of updating your résumé frequently.

It is a healthy practice to keep an up-to-date repertoire of work projects. For each project that you feel is significant (whether a favorite project or one that gave you difficulty), write out a summary of:

- The nature of the project: size, type of client, people involved on the project, etc.;
- Your role in the project: substantive responsibilities, level of autonomy, team interaction, i.e., to whom you reported and who you supervised, etc.; and
- The outcome of the project: what this project produced for the client, what could have been improved, what the project did for you.

Take these summaries and capsulize them into brief descriptions such as on John's addendum. Save your more lengthy summaries to review in preparation for interviews.

The Corporate Résumé

Figure 14.6 is an example of the way to prepare John's résumé for submission to a corporation. For corporations, managerial and interpersonal skills, business knowledge, the ability to interact effectively with nonlegal individuals, and an ability to identify with corporate goals often is as important as legal expertise. Also, they evaluate the size of the organization that has employed you and your specific team setting. Many are interested in your ability to do work as a "generalist," including the variety of your knowledge of different legal areas and your familiarity with the more mundane day-to-day legal work found in-house.

In light of these considerations, to pinpoint John's experience, information that will be important to a corporation has been "bulleted." Furthermore, John's résumé has been personalized, to a degree, for submission to corporations in the telecommunications and media industries. In determining what information to include and the order of presentation, John reviewed his law-

FIGURE 14.5

John Q. Corporate—Addendum to Law Firm Résumé

JOHN Q. CORPORATE

Representative Corporate Experience

Securities Offerings

- Participated in preparation of registration statements and other documents for public offerings of common stock and collateralized mortgage obligations for ABC Mortgage Company and its subsidiaries. Prepared stock option plans and agreements and related registration statements.

- Represented The Underwriters, Inc., in the $11 million common stock offering of Corporateronix, Inc.

Mergers & Acquisitions

- Represented Patt Industries, Inc., in its merger into a subsidiary of The Industry Corporation, a subsidiary of Major Corporation, Inc.

General Corporate

- Prepared employment and consulting agreements and negotiated shareholders' agreement and related documents for formation of joint venture for MB Corporation.

- Represented ABC Corporation in changing their state of domicile.

- Represented The Maritime Corporation in its recapitalization.

FIGURE 14.6

John Q. Corporate—Corporate Résumé

JOHN Q. CORPORATE
456 Trial Lane
Tireless, New York 12345
Home (212) 123-4567
Office (212) 765-4321

Bar Member: New York (1987), District of Columbia (1988)

EXPERIENCE
Legal:

Sept 1987
to Present
O'Great & Powerful, New York, New York
Corporate Associate at a national law firm with over 400 attorneys.

- Serve as issuers' and underwriters' counsel in public securities offerings. Responsibilities include preparing registration statements and coordinating regulatory filings.

- Frequently act as outside general counsel on wide variety of issues including general corporate, employment, real estate, environmental compliance, and land-use for the three largest subsidiaries of a national chemical company.

- Counsel clients in antitrust matters and deal with the provisions of the Robinson-Patman Act and the Clayton Act including predatory and discriminatory pricing issues and Hart-Scott-Rodino filings.

- Active in various mergers and acquisitions including serving as principal attorney for a worldwide media company in connection with asset purchase of going concern. Evaluate litigation matters as part of acquisition-related due diligence.

- Representation of three middle-market companies in workouts and restructurings.

- Senior associate responsible for overseeing junior associates on due diligence and research matters on large transactions. Personally draft and negotiate significant documents, and handle closing details.

- Administrative responsibilities for firm in the interviewing and hiring of law school graduates and lateral associates.

- *Summer Associate, May–July 1986*

July to
Sept 1986
Whye, Nott, Merge & Achoir, Washington, D.C.
Summer Associate. Split summer clerking with this firm and current employer. Received permanent offer of employment.

May to
Sept 1985
Apple, Bean, Carrot & Frye, Chicago, Illinois
Summer Clerk.

FIGURE 14.6

John Q. Corporate—Corporate Résumé, continued

JOHN Q. CORPORATE
Résumé—Page Two

Other:

July 1979 to April 1984	**Various Jobs** During undergraduate, worked in order to earn 60% of the money needed to finance QSU and first year of law school. These jobs included working as a grocery store clerk, a construction worker, and an assistant program researcher for a local radio station. Became employed full-time by the radio station to write editorials on the effect of national news items on local citizens.

EDUCATION

1987	**Stellar Law School,** New York, New York *Juris Doctor*, Top 11% (24/200) Publications Editor, *Stellar Corporations Law Journal* Attorney's Scholarship 1986–1987
1983	**QSU, Quest,** New York *Bachelor of Arts, summa cum laude* Dual Major: English and Communications President, Quest Hall 1981–82

ACTIVITIES Speaker, New York Association of General Counsel (NYGC) Program:
"The Effect of M&A on Executive Compensation"
Member, American Bar Association Business Law Section: Subcommittee
on Securities Regulation
Vice President, Big Brothers of Greater New York

LANGUAGES Fluent French, conversational Japanese

PERSONAL Single. Enjoy skiing, chess, and renovating old houses.

*Submitted in confidence. Do not contact present or
former employers without prior approval of J.Q. Corporate*

firm résumé information, addendum information, and experiences that he had thought less important given his years of practice when applying to law firms. Please note that even though there has been an information and format change on John's résumé for submission to corporations, he still may want to consider including the addendum from his law-firm résumé to further define his expertise.

John included the *Various Jobs* entry from his law-firm résumé in this corporate résumé to reveal his work experience with nonlawyers, his ability to roll up his sleeves and work hard, and his early interest in media and communications. The experience with the radio station exposed John to some of the day-to-day operations of a sector of the industry that he is seeking to join.

John added *Personal* information to highlight his "well-rounded" life-style and to point to his geographic stability. Furthermore, by stating that he is single, he hopes to imply flexibility because many positions he seeks involve significant travel. Family-oriented candidates tend to project maturity and dependability. John hopes to imply these traits by adding his participation in Big Brothers.

Sarah M. Litigator
Sarah is a seasoned litigation lawyer who has worked in a variety of settings. She has represented corporate clients in private practice, as well as having been an in-house counsel utilizing outside counsel. She has been a servicer of other lawyers' clients as well as a rainmaker. She has worked in government and has significant trial experience.

Sarah's experience presents the challenge of consolidating years of experience into a meaningful résumé. Her varied employment settings and transitions need to be shown in a fashion that leads the reader to conclude that there has been a continuity of practice and expertise that could have been gained only through such employment movement.

Figure 14.7 is Sarah's first attempt at a résumé. While it contains a lot of valuable information, it requires the reader to comb through carefully each employment description to gain a clear picture of Sarah's value. Remember, a reviewer typically spends five to ten seconds screening a résumé, even for the more senior positions.

The Law Firm Résumé
Sarah's second attempt at a résumé, with primary focus on law firm employers (Figure 14.8), summarizes her expertise in a brief opening paragraph. This legal experience is followed by her chronological employment history.

After reading an overview of her work experience, Sarah decided that potential employers would be interested in which organizations employed her, followed by specific practice experience for each employer. Although Sarah had moved in and out of the law firm environment, she was elected to partnership, an important indication of her value to the firm, and became Chair of her practice section. Therefore, Sarah included her titles immediately below the employer's identity.

FIGURE 14.7
Sarah M. Litigator—First-Draft Résumé

SARAH M. LITIGATOR

5 Beach Way
Ocean, CA 54321   (110) 543-6789

EMPLOYMENT

1984–Present

Time, Fore, Business & Strength, San Diego & Los Angeles, CA
(Small & Dynamic merged with TFB&S in June 1990)
Chair, Trial & Appellate Practice Group 1989 - Present

In 1984, joined Small & Dynamic to develop a white-collar crime trial practice as well as acting as chief trial counsel on other major complex corporate and business litigation. By 1989, had developed significant business and expanded trial practice into a group of 10 partners and 20 associates emphasizing white collar crime, labor & employment, securities, environmental, intellectual property, and insurance coverage.

Personal practice focus as first-chair litigator in white-collar crime, securities fraud (including class actions and shareholder derivative matters), directors & officers issues, and RICO as well as general litigation advice as part of a "general counsel" relationship with firm clients.

Over 20 first-chair and jury trials in both state and federal courts as well as several appellate and administrative appearances.

1980–1984

Major Corporation, Cincinnati, OH
Litigation Counsel. Responsibilities included managing litigation for the corporation and its subsidiaries, reviewing and drafting commercial contracts, and providing legal support on a wide range of marketing issues.

1978–1980

Large & Powerful, Los Angeles, CA
Associate. Business litigation experience in a variety of civil matters including RICO, contract, construction, product liability, and antitrust as well as white-collar crime. Exposure to all aspects of trial and appellate litigation. Direct contact with several major clients of the firm.

1975–1978

U.S. Attorney's Office, Los Angeles, CA
Assistant Attorney, Member, Special Prosecutions Unit

Involved in prosecution of major white-collar criminal cases, including obstruction of justice, commodities fraud, and investment frauds.

1973–1974

Honorable Charles F. Justice, III, Senior Judge,
United States Court of Appeals for the Second Circuit
Judicial Clerk.

Summer 1972

Large & Powerful, Los Angeles, CA
Law Clerk.

Summer 1971

Public Counsel, Los Angeles, CA
Law Clerk on Housing Fraud Project.

FIGURE 14.7

Sarah M. Litigator—First-Draft Résumé, continued

SARAH M. LITIGATOR
Résumé—Page Two

EDUCATION

1975	**Delaware/Washington Law School,** Washington, D.C.
	LL.M. in Securities Law

1973	**UCMB School of Law,** Sacramento, CA
	J.D., Top 20%
	Law Review Articles Editor
	Honors Moot Court Competition
	Voluntary Defenders Program

1970	**The Woman's College,** Boston, MA
	A.B., Political Science
	Phi Beta Kappa

**Graduate Institute of International Studies,
Geneva, Switzerland, 1968–1970**

ADMITTED California, 1973; New York, 1974; Ohio, 1980
United States Supreme Court
Courts of Appeal for the Federal, Second, Fifth, Seventh, and Ninth Circuits
All District Courts in California, New York, and Ohio

Submitted in confidence. Do not contact present or
former employers without prior approval of S.M. Litigator

FIGURE 14.8

Sarah M. Litigator—Law Firm Résumé

SARAH M. LITIGATOR
5 Beach Way
Ocean, California 54321
Office (110) 543-6789

LEGAL EXPERIENCE

Trial attorney with twenty years of experience focusing on civil and criminal litigation in federal, state, and appellate courts. Lead Counsel in over 40 court and jury trials involving RICO, white-collar crime, securities fraud including class actions and shareholders derivative matters, contracts, antitrust, and directors' and officers' liability issues. Have supervised up to thirty attorneys and acted as outside general counsel to clients regarding litigation advice.

EMPLOYMENT HISTORY

TIME, FORE, BUSINESS & STRENGTH; 1984–Present
Los Angeles, CA
(Small & Dynamic merged with this Firm in June 1990)
San Diego, CA

Chair, Trial & Appellate Practice Group since 1989; ***Partner*** beginning 1986.

Substantive Experience:

- White-collar crime, securities, Directors & Officers issues, and RICO for domestic and international clients ranging from middle market to Fortune 500 companies and wealthy individuals.

- Advise clients on business matters relating to contracts, agreements, and other business relationships.

- Administrative hearing experience before the Securities & Exchange Commission and Federal Trade Commission.

- Have appeared in international arbitrations and matters before the International Trade Commission.

Management Experience:

- Chair, Trial & Appellate Practice Group, 1989 to present. Established Small & Dynamic's white-collar crime practice in 1984, growing the practice into a broad-based trial practice group in Los Angeles and San Diego. Group now numbers 30 attorneys and 12 legal assistants.

- San Diego Office opening. One of three attorneys who staffed the Firm's San Diego office during its first year of operation in 1991. Responsibilities included the recruitment of attorneys and paralegals for the office.

- Partner in charge of coordinating and administering firm's basic and advanced trial and litigation training programs, 1990–present.

MAJOR CORPORATION; 1980–1984
Cincinnati, OH
($4 billion holding company involved in the manufacture and sale of financial products)

FIGURE 14.8
Sarah M. Litigator—Law Firm Résumé, continued

Sarah M. Litigator
Résumé—Page Two

Litigation Counsel. Responsibilities included managing the litigation for the corporation and its subsidiaries including first-chair responsibility for a $7 million breach-of-contract action, reviewing and drafting commercial contracts, and providing legal support on a wide range of marketing issues.

LARGE & POWERFUL; 1978–1980
Los Angeles, CA
(400-attorney international firm)

Associate in the business litigation and trial practice. Exposure to all aspects of trial and appellate litigation. Direct contact with client and responsibility for a complex litigation matter involving securities fraud for firm client, Major Corporation.

Summer Law Clerk, 1972

UNITED STATES ATTORNEY'S OFFICE; 1975–1978
Los Angeles, CA
Special Prosecutions Unit

Assistant U.S. Attorney involved in prosecution of major white-collar criminal cases, including obstruction of justice, commodities fraud, and investment frauds.

HONORABLE CHARLES F. JUSTICE, III, 1973–1974
New York, NY
Senior Judge, U.S. Court of Appeals for the Second Circuit

Judicial Clerk.

PUBLIC COUNSEL; Summer 1971
Los Angeles, CA
(Pro bono interest law firm)

Summer Intern working on housing fraud litigation.

EDUCATION

DELAWARE/WASHINGTON LAW SCHOOL, 1975
Washington, D.C.
 LL.M. in Securities Law

UCMB SCHOOL OF LAW, 1973
Los Angeles, CA
 J.D., Top 20%
 Law Review Articles Editor
 Honors Moot Court Competition
 Voluntary Defenders Program

THE WOMAN'S COLLEGE, 1970
Boston, MA
 A.B., Political Science
 Phi Beta Kappa
 President, College Debate Team

Graduate Institute of International Studies, Geneva, Switzerland, 1969-1970

FIGURE 14.8

Sarah M. Litigator—Law Firm Résumé, continued

Sarah M. Litigator
Résumé—Page Three

ADMITTED

California, 1973; New York, 1974; Ohio, 1980
United States Supreme Court
Courts of Appeal for the Federal, Second, Fifth, Seventh, and Ninth Circuit
All District Courts in California, New York, and Ohio

LANGUAGES

Fluent in French, conversational Spanish

Visually, this establishes the layout and organization of the résumé, shown in Figure 14.8. The résumé grouping titles, *Legal Experience, Employment History*, and *Education*, have been centered on the page. The employers have been made most prominent after the *Legal Experience* summary. Sarah remained at each position a respectable period of time; she wanted to provide this information without complicating the layout or confusing the priorities that she chose. These dates are less prominent when they follow the name of an employer. (Later, Sarah established a far-right column to display her ability to work in a variety of geographic locales. She felt this was a potential asset to a firm with a national client base.)

The organization and layout of the information to be contained in the description of Sarah's current employment experience is very challenging. She has both substantive and management responsibilities. She began with a smaller firm that merged into the larger entity. While her initial focus was on white-collar crime, she expanded into other areas of litigation. She established a new office for the firm, working in two of its geographic locations. She became a successful rainmaker as well as a servicer of firm clients. With her increasing levels of success and responsibility, her title changed several times. Sarah has been effective in the training of young lawyers.

The solution is to simplify the presentation of the information by using a layout that creates categories of accomplishment.

The merger is identified in conjunction with the name of the employer. Then, her experience is broken down into bulleted highlights under *Substantive Experience* and *Management Experience*. Because Sarah felt it would clutter the résumé and was better explained during an interview, she omitted her title, Of Counsel, for her first two years of employment with Time, Fore, Business & Strength.

This format successfully conveys information and leaves an overall impression of Sarah's commitment to the success of her practice and the successful growth of the firm.

Prior to joining Time, Fore, Sarah spent several years as litigation counsel for Major Corporation. For her application to law firm employers, Major Corporation was defined by giving information regarding the type of entity, its financial strength, and the nature of the products it produces. This information provides a point of reference for the potential complexities of the work Sarah performed for the corporation.

To maintain a unified format, a definition for Large & Powerful was included. The nature of Sarah's work as an associate for the firm was further clarified by emphasizing that she expanded into civil litigation after leaving the U.S. Attorney's Office. Also, a link is provided between her work with Large & Powerful as an associate and her eventual employment with Major Corporation. To clarify relationships and to give an early recognition of her potential value, her summer clerkship with Large & Powerful is included in this entry.

Judicial clerkships, particularly for a superior or Supreme Court judge, are valued by employers as indicators of intelligence, strong training on legal issues before the court, and as a strengthener of writing skills. For Sarah, her clerkship solidifies the screener's understanding of her early training and a recognition of her potential beyond her law school graduation standing.

Sarah's work at Public Counsel is included to identify her early commitment to pro bono work. The remainder of Sarah's employment and her education entries have been adjusted to comply with the layout.

Sarah spent one-and-one-half years studying abroad during college. Rather than list this schooling as a separate educational endeavor, it is included with The Woman's College because it was viewed and credited by that institution as similar to a junior year abroad.

Sarah's state bar memberships have been organized chronologically. Language proficiency can unexpectedly be viewed as a necessary asset. Sarah has maintained her conversational and written proficiency in two languages, so they are included on her résumé.

Trial lawyers often are measured by their effectiveness in court. *Recent Significant Legislation* (see Figure 14.9), an addendum to Figures 14.8 and 14.10, is developed for such an evaluation as well as for reasons similar to those discussed regarding John Q. Corporate's addendum.

This addition to Sarah's résumé is developed chronologically separated by *Federal and State Court* actions, *Arbitrations*, and *Administrative Hearings*. A very brief sketch is provided to assist in creating such a page. Each entry should include the title for the action with the side you represented, the location of the action, the substantive issues involved, the outcome of the proceedings, and whether any further action was taken.

The Corporate Résumé

Sarah may want to consider certain in-house opportunities. Figure 14.10 is a résumé designed to meet these needs. The *Legal Experience* statement was modified to help hold the interest of a corporate employer by highlighting her work experience in a variety of settings.

More detail was given to her responsibilities as Litigation Counsel for Major Corporation. This experience is delineated by bullets targeting central duties and responsibilities.

For the most part, little else has been changed on this résumé from the résumé in Figure 14.8. Many of the layout and organization choices made for her law firm résumé work well on a corporate résumé for similar reasons. Sarah has the option of including her addendum with the submission of this résumé.

The Critical Eye

Once you have printed your résumé, put it away for at least 24 hours. When you return to your résumé, review it with a critical eye:

- How clean, neat, and professional does it appear?
- What do you notice first, second, and third? Are these items correct with regard to your personal agenda and the perceived crucial elements for the potential employer?
- Does it tell what you like to do and what you know how to do?

FIGURE 14.9
Sarah M. Litigator—Addendum

SARAH M. LITIGATOR

Recent Significant Litigation

Note: <u>Double underline</u> identifies the client represented in each case.

Federal and State Court

1993   <u>Publications, Inc.</u>, v. <u>Major Corporation</u>, USDC, ND Cal (Thomas, P.)
Securities fraud, and antitrust case involving alleged Preliminary injunction sought by plaintiff denied. Currently on appeal to the Ninth Circuit.

1992   <u>Domestic Learning</u> v. The Broker-Dealer Inc.
Multi-million dollar action for breach of fiduciary duty and negligence against defendant broker. Preliminary injunction granted.

Arbitrations

1991-1992   Court appointed chair of arbitration tribunal in *In The Matter of Arbitration of The Windowpane Group, Ltd and Samont Corporation*, San Diego Superior Court No. 0597459.

Administrative Hearings

1990   Lead counsel in major Title VII administrative class action in which a federal agency was found to have intentionally discriminated against a nationwide class of upper-level gay and lesbian employees.

1992   Counsel in trial of FTC trade regulation case in the health care industry, FTC Dkt No. 9100.

FIGURE 14.10

Sarah M. Litigator—Corporate Résumé

SARAH M. LITIGATOR
5 Beach Way
Ocean, California 54321
Office (110) 543-6789

LEGAL EXPERIENCE

Civil and criminal litigation attorney with twenty years' experience working in corporate, law firm, and government settings. Lead counsel in federal, state, and appellate courts on over 40 court and jury trials including RICO, white-collar crime, securities fraud including class actions and shareholders derivative matters, contracts, antitrust, and directors' and officers' liability issues. Have supervised up to thirty attorneys and acted as outside general counsel to clients regarding litigation advice.

EMPLOYMENT HISTORY

TIME, FORE, BUSINESS & STRENGTH; 1984–Present
Los Angeles, CA
(Small & Dynamic merged with this Firm in June 1990)
San Diego, CA

Chair, Trial & Appellate Practice Group since 1989; *Partner* beginning 1986.

Substantive Experience:

- White-collar crime, securities, Directors & Officers issues and RICO for domestic and international clients ranging from middle market to Fortune 500 companies and wealthy individuals.
- Advise clients on business matters relating to contracts, agreements, and other business relationships.
- Administrative hearing experience before the Securities & Exchange Commission and Federal Trade Commission.
- Have appeared in international arbitrations and matters before the International Trade Commission.

Management Experience:

- Chair, Trial & Appellate Practice Group, 1989 to present. Established Small & Dynamic's white-collar crime practice in 1984, growing the practice into a broad-based trial practice group in Los Angeles and San Diego. Group now numbers 30 attorneys and 12 legal assistants.
- San Diego Office opening. One of three attorneys who staffed the Firm's San Diego office during its first year of operation in 1991. Responsibilities included the recruitment of attorneys and paralegals for the office.
- Partner in charge of coordinating and administering firm's basic and advanced trial and litigation training programs, 1990–present.

MAJOR CORPORATION; 1980–1984
Cincinnati, OH
($4 billion holding company involved in the manufacture and sale of financial products)

Litigation Counsel. Responsibilities included:

- Litigation Management—Managed fifty percent of the litigation for the corporation and its subsidiaries with primary responsibility for the Check Printing Division.
- Hands-on-Litigation—Lead Counsel responsibility for a $7 million breach of contract action.

FIGURE 14.10
Sarah M. Litigator—Corporate Résumé, continued

Sarah M. Litigator
Résumé—Page Two

- Commercial Contracts—Sole responsibility for reviewing and drafting commercial contracts for division of company that previously had significant litigation claims.
- Marketing—Provided legal support on a wide range of critical marketing issues.

LARGE & POWERFUL; 1978–1980
Los Angeles, CA
(400-attorney international firm)

> *Associate* in the business litigation and trial practice. Exposure to all aspects of trial and appellate litigation. Direct contact with client and responsibility for a complex litigation matter involving securities fraud for firm client, Major Corporation.
>
> *Summer Law Clerk,* 1972

UNITED STATES ATTORNEY'S OFFICE; 1975–1978
Los Angeles, CA
Special Prosecutions Unit

> *Assistant U.S. Attorney* involved in prosecution of major white-collar criminal cases, including obstruction of justice, commodities fraud, and investment frauds.

HONORABLE CHARLES F. JUSTICE, III, 1973–1974
New York, NY
Senior Judge, U.S. Court of Appeals for the Second Circuit

> *Judicial Clerk.*

PUBLIC COUNSEL; Summer 1971
Los Angeles, CA
(Pro bono interest law firm)

> *Summer Intern* working on housing fraud litigation.

EDUCATION

DELAWARE/WASHINGTON LAW SCHOOL, 1975
Washington, D.C.
LL.M. in Securities Law

UCMB SCHOOL OF LAW, 1973
Los Angeles, CA
J.D., Top 20%
Law Review Articles Editor
Honors Moot Court Competition
Voluntary Defenders Program

THE WOMAN'S COLLEGE, 1970
Boston, MA
A.B., Political Science; Phi Beta Kappa
President, College Debate Team

Graduate Institute of International Studies, Geneva, Switzerland, 1969–1970

FIGURE 14.10

Sarah M. Litigator—Corporate Résumé, continued

Sarah M. Litigator
Résumé—Page Three

ADMITTED

California, 1973; New York, 1974; Ohio, 1980
United States Supreme Court
Courts of Appeal for the Federal, Second, Fifth, Seventh, and Ninth Circuit
All District Courts in California, New York, and Ohio

LANGUAGES

Fluent in French, conversational Spanish

*Submitted in confidence. Do not contact present or
former employers without prior approval of S.M. Litigator*

- Can a screener determine how your experience is relevant to the employer?
- Does the potential employer see you as a benefit? Can the potential employer see what you have done for someone else?
- Does the potential employer have enough information to evaluate your choices and transitions?
- Can the potential employer see that you are a problem solver?
- Does the potential employer receive clues with regard to your personal style and people skills?
- Is the layout consistent?
- Are there any typographical errors?
- What is missing?

Comprehensive Addenda and the Résumé Package

Often, there is information that you feel should be included, but is too lengthy. Or you may be uncertain about its importance to an employer, but the information is important to you. Quite often, information such as speeches and publications fall into these categories. If this information is too lengthy to include on your résumé and you want to provide it to a potential employer, then create a separate page for it.

Depending on the position that you seek and the prevailing culture of that particular employer, you may want to include certain items with your résumé submission:

- School transcripts—The less experienced the lawyer, the more often these are necessary. Include them on an *initial* résumé submission only if they are an academic asset. Usually, law school transcripts are sufficient; however, undergraduate transcripts are useful if the degree earned has a direct application to your legal practice (as in B.S. Technical). Postgraduate and advanced legal degrees may have similar applications. Plan to keep an official copy of all school transcripts in a safe place where you easily can retrieve them. Today, more and more employers require your transcripts prior to processing your initial application for employment or before extending a formal offer. It often takes months to receive additional official transcripts from a school.
- Writing Samples—This is a wonderful demonstration of your written work product. While an employer may request writing samples when you submit a résumé (as in a newspaper advertisement), you may choose to submit them to emphasize experience in a particular area or offset some of your weaker credentials (for instance, they want top 10 percent and you are top 15 percent). Such submissions should be purely your own work, e.g., research, analysis, organization, and writing. If this is not the case, include a careful explanation of the contribution of others. Each submission should be no longer than 15 pages, demonstrating your clear and concise analytical thinking and your ability to communicate persuasively and effectively. All samples should be cleansed to ensure the confidentiality of the work product.

- Recommendations—If you have left a position unexpectedly, a letter of recommendation may help correct a perceived blemish on an otherwise strong résumé.

Testing Your Audience

Locate individuals who can view your résumé with a critical eye while maintaining the confidentiality of your search. A review by a third party who will not eventually be one of your search targets is an essential proofreading step. Qualified evaluators for this process may be a law school placement director, a lawyer friend who is part of the hiring team at work, a friend who works in the field that you are targeting for your search, or a lawyer recruiter. Recruiters who are members of the National Association of Legal Search Consultants (NALSC) are bound by a Code of Ethics that ensures confidentiality for you. Recruiters review and help write hundreds of résumés per month.

Provide these people with a thumbnail summary of the type of position that you are seeking. Ask them to evaluate your résumé for that purpose as well as providing you with general observations and questions arising from the résumé. Ask them to be very diligent with their critique regarding the content and visual impact of your résumé. Then, take their comments seriously and make adjustments to your résumé where necessary.

* * *

Your résumé is your ticket to an interview. It is a two-dimensional portrait of you. It is not a static career tool. Constantly revise and tailor your résumé for specific opportunities. Keep the lines of layout clean and the organization simple, yet ensure that the information is appropriately detailed. Be sure it is an exemplar of your intelligence, your contributions, and your energy. Then, be prepared to be as dynamic, organized, and informative in person when you are called for an interview.

CHAPTER 15

Cover Letters

Deborah Howard

A cover letter must be well written and attention grabbing. It is your first chance to make a favorable impression on an employer. Many employers read cover letters before they read the attached résumés. If they do not like the cover letter, they may not read any further.

A cover letter is your chance to give an employer information about who you are and what makes you special. It must help an employer realize what is unique about you so that your résumé will stand out in a large stack of other résumés. Time spent writing a quality cover letter is well worth the effort. This is especially true in a recessionary job market in which employers are bombarded with applications.

Preparation

To write a quality cover letter takes a great deal of preparation and effort. Good cover letters are the product of soul searching and thought. To be able to convince an employer that you are special and unique, you must know what it is about yourself that makes you so. You must know who you are and try to put a piece of yourself into your cover letter. You need to think about what you are looking for in a job and find a way to express that in your letter.

Self-Inventory

To figure out who you are requires that you take some time to put together an inventory of your strengths, skills, and qualities. Think about adjectives that describe you. Also think about activities that you perform well (whether they are papers you have written, cases or projects you have worked on, ideas you have developed, even sports in which you excel), experiences you have had, and specific classes in which you have excelled. Then determine what skills those activities incorporate (ability to write well, organize, be a team player, take initiative, etc.), how those experiences have affected you (i.e., you are sensitive, hardworking), and what expertise your classes represent. This exercise should serve not only to give you information about yourself that can be incorporated into a cover letter but should beef up your self-esteem and confidence as well. If you do not feel good about yourself, it is hard to convince someone else to do so.

Once you have developed your inventory list, synthesize this information into a paragraph detailing who you are and why you are special. Obviously, this paragraph will change depending on the needs of each employer.

Target List

Your next task is to develop a target list of potential employers. This too involves time and effort. Spend some time determining your interests. Knowing the area of law or practice in which you are interested in can help you to decide on the types of employers to whom you should and should not apply.

Once you are able to focus your search, it is easier to develop a target list. If you have two or more areas in which you are interested, there is nothing wrong with developing two or more different target lists.

The easiest and less effective way to develop a target list is merely to write to every job listing in your area of interest. It is necessary, however, to go beyond this. Rather than sending out cold cover letters (letters to people with whom you have no contact), it is better to send warm cover letters (letters to people suggested by other people). A letter that starts with "I am writing to you at the suggestion of Mr./Ms. So-and-So" will receive more attention and possibly better results than one that starts with "I am responding to your advertisement in the *New York Times*." The best method to develop a target list of warm letters is to network. (See Chapter 9 for more information on networking.)

Research on Employers

To write a quality cover letter, you not only have to know about yourself, you also have to know about the employer to whom you are writing. The more you know about the employer, the more personalized your cover letter will be. Employers do not react favorably to receiving a cover letter that demonstrates an applicant's ignorance about their organizations. For example, if the employer to whom you are writing is a law firm that specializes in tax litigation, a cover letter in which you discuss your experience and interest in admiralty law will make a very bad impression. Similarly, a letter to a legal-aid organization that focuses on your prosecution experience but does not mention your advocacy skills and desire to provide defendants with representation will make a less-than-favorable impression. (See Chapters 5 and 8 for more information about conducting research on employers.)

Drafting the Letter

Now that you have completed your preparation by doing a personal inventory of yourself and by conducting research to obtain information about employers, you are ready to write your letter. See Figure 15.1 for an example of a cover letter format.

FIGURE 15.1
Sample Cover Letter Format

Address
Date

Contact Name
Contact Title
Organization Name
Address

Dear Mr./Ms. _____ :

    Opening Paragraph: Statement of Objective: state why you are writing to this person/ organization.

    Qualifications and Statement of Interests Paragraph: Statement of Your Qualifications and Why You Are Interested in This Organization: state why the organization should hire you; tell the employer about you, why you are special and unique, and how you will fit the employer's needs; describe your skills, experience, qualifications, and strengths; explain what about the organization is of interest to you.

    Closing Paragraph: Closing Statement.

Sincerely,

Signature

Printed Name

Why You Are Writing to This Employer

Your opening paragraph informs the employer why you are writing to the employer's company. In the case of a warm letter, mention the name of the person who referred you to this employer. If you are responding to an advertisement, mention the advertisement and the specific position to which you are applying (an organization can be advertising for more than one position at a time).

In the next paragraph, describe your interest in the employer. No one likes to receive form letters, so you must tailor your cover letter for each employer to whom you apply. Thus, you need to be able to articulate in your cover letter why you are writing to this particular employer. This is where the research discussed previously comes into play.

To explain why you are interested in a particular employer, you need to know the kind of work the firm does. Then, state why that is of interest to you. For example, if you are interested in a firm because of its superior international law practice, mention this in your letter. An employer should not feel like just one of hundreds of employers to whom you are applying. A cover letter that sounds sincere and well thought out will always make a better impression than a rote-sounding form letter for a mass mailing.

Out-of-Town Employers

If you are writing to an out-of-town employer, let the employer know why you are interested in that particular geographic area. Let the employer know if you have any ties to that geographic area (family, bar membership, intention to take the bar). Employers are wary of interviewing someone from out of town unless it is clear that the prospective employee is serious about relocating. Be sure that you have sufficiently demonstrated that your interest in the employer's geographic area is more than a passing one.

If you plan to be in the employer's city, let the employer know when you intend to do so. Just the fact that you will be in town may lead some employers to grant you an interview.

Why the Employer Should Be Interested in You

After you have told the employer why you are interested in the firm, let the employer know why the firm should be interested in you. This is where the time you invested in your personal inventory pays off. Tell employers about yourself. Sell yourself! Point out any special qualifications, strengths, experience, or other skills that you may have and demonstrate to employers how these skills, strengths, and qualities will be of use to them.

Sell yourself to each particular employer. Try to determine what the employer values in an employee and point out how you fit the bill. If you are applying to an organization in which lawyers carry a large caseload and work under short deadlines, let the employer know that you are hardworking and can handle pressure well. If you are responding to an advertisement, do not regurgitate the wording of the advertisement, but do paraphrase the advertisement and indicate how you meet the requirements.

When writing to a small law firm, for example, you may stress your independence and your ability to take initiative and work on your own. When writing to a public-interest employer, on the other hand, you may stress your commitment to public interest and describe experiences that indicate such a commitment.

In addition to focusing on your skills, strengths, and qualities, highlight any relevant work experience and course work. Tell an employer who specializes in tax work about the A+ you received in taxation. Let an employer who specializes in environmental law know about your experience working for the Environmental Protection Agency.

Crossover Applications

A strong cover letter is especially important for lawyers attempting to cross over to a different area of practice or to a nonlegal position. In making such an application, do not forget about your transferable skills. Transferable skills are those that you have developed in one context that can be put to use in a different context, for example, skills developed in a legal setting that are applicable to a nonlegal position (or vice versa).

Do not expect an employer to look at your résumé and see the transferable skills. Use your cover letter to bring an employer's attention to these skills. If you worked as a banker before (or during) law school, highlight the skills that you developed as a banker that would be applicable in a corporate legal setting. Similarly, if you are a corporate lawyer applying for a nonlegal business position, emphasize the business skills that you have developed. Or if you are a real estate lawyer wishing to switch into the bankruptcy area, focus on the real estate financial restructurings that you have conducted. And if you have been out of work but have been active as a volunteer, discuss the projects that you have worked on and point out the skills that you have developed as a result.

What to Leave Out

Just as important as what to include in a cover letter is what you should leave out. A cover letter is not the place to bring up anything damaging or anything that weakens your application by making you appear less attractive as a candidate. For example, do not state that you are interested in working for an employer because you feel that the experience will strengthen your existing skills. Do not lead an employer to think that any of your skills need strengthening.

A cover letter is your opportunity to sell yourself and present yourself in the most positive light possible. Thus, if your law school grades were terrible, do not attempt to explain this in your cover letter. Or if you were laid off, the cover letter is not the place to bring up this fact. This kind of information, which requires explanation, is better left for an interview than a cover letter. Moreover, including such information may prevent you from getting an interview at all.

What Else to Remember

Your cover letter is the first sample of your writing that an employer sees. It, therefore, must be as well written as possible. Make sure it contains no typos or grammatical errors, nor any unrelated or inappropriate information. Write in a logical, smooth manner with appropriate transitions.

How to Address a Cover Letter

Whenever possible, address your cover letter to a specific person—the contact person listed in an advertisement, the person to whom you were referred, the hiring partner, or the recruitment coordinator.

Closing

Do not end your cover letter with a statement that indicates that you assume that you will be granted an interview. This can be viewed as presumptuous or somewhat pushy. You can accomplish the same purpose by merely stating the action you plan to take—that you will be contacting the employer in a week or so to follow up—or the action you would like the employer to take— that you look forward to hearing from the employer.

Keep Records

Always keep copies of any letter you send to an employer and review the letter before going to an interview.

CHAPTER 16

Interviewing Techniques

Michael K. Magness
Carolyn M. Wehmann

Preparing for the Interview

Successful interviewees all have one very attractive trait in common: They have spent considerable time planning their career strategy, and it shows. Lawyers are impressed by interviewees who know what they seek in a legal employer and what they want from their careers. You should follow closely the career planning steps outlined in Part I of this book. You must carefully choose how and where you will use your talents—and to what type of employer you wish to commit your energy and your future—before you interview with prospective employers.

When preparing for interviews, you should learn certain key facts: information about the employer's size, major practice areas and important current work matters, notable partners/senior lawyers and their notable achievements, and the management and training of junior lawyers. You also should try to obtain information about other employers in the same city (or practice area) that are considered "competitors." Your knowledge of each employer will be clearer if you have a sense of where it fits in the local or regional market. It also will be easier to formulate questions if you can develop a broad perspective on each of your potential employers.

Another helpful way to prepare for interviews is to search out and interview people you believe are knowledgeable about the employers with whom you plan to interview. Law school career-planning offices often have on file written statements from students or graduates describing their employment experiences. You also will find your classmates, colleagues, and law professors eager to offer their opinions on any number of "facts" about the employers that you are considering. A word of caution, however: Critical employment decisions should not be based on the advice of those notorious twins, myth and innuendo. When making a career choice, try to rule out any information that you suspect is based on hearsay, based on short-term (or no direct) work experience at the employer's office, too outdated to be relevant today, or information that is based on a single negative incident that may color the speaker's ability to offer a balanced view. Instead, to help counteract the effect of biased personal advice, you should obtain information from *as many different sources as possible,* measuring the value of each against your own criteria for evaluating each of your employment options.

Formulating questions to use in the interview is another helpful preparation exercise. You will be able to project a relaxed, confident demeanor quite naturally if you have prepared thoughtfully for your conversation with interviewers. Obviously, you will want to avoid creating the impression that you have a "canned act" to perform. Your prepared questions should be designed to elicit two kinds of information: (1) elaboration on the employer's practice, lawyers' current (and past) work matters, working style and lifestyle, and other issues that are particularly important to you in making your career choice; and (2) a variety of insights into individual lawyers' experiences that will help you predict what your own work experience might be like. In addition to your set of general interview questions, you will want to prepare questions relating specifically to each employer.

There are several other reasons for preparing your interview questions in advance. Very often, *interviewers* will not be so prepared for interviews as you will be. If the interviewer begins by asking, "What can I tell you about my firm?" you will want to have a set of questions ready to begin the interview. Occasionally, there will be awkward pauses during your interviews or you will meet interviewers with whom you find it difficult to converse. In these situations, a series of prepared questions can save the day—and spare your nerves.

You should spend a considerable amount of time thinking about the kinds of questions that *you* will be asked so that you can prepare the general answers that you will use in interviews. Not all of these questions can be listed here, but you should become comfortable discussing a whole range of facts about:

- Your past academic and work experiences;
- Your legal abilities; your career goals, and the reasons why you have made the choices you have made in your life to date (that is, what has motivated you to be successful, thus far);
- Your achievements and your failures;
- Your strong points and the areas in which you have improved; and
- The personal qualities and skills that you use to get your work done effectively.

If you take time to think about your education and work experiences in retrospect, and if you can articulate realistic career goals, your answers to interviewers' questions about your past performance will flow quite naturally. If you have formulated in advance your answers to difficult questions, it is also unlikely that you will be caught off guard by unanticipated questions or the stress questions some interviewers like to use.

The Initial Interview: Screening

The initial interview is a critical meeting. As a result of this meeting, the applicant and the employer each make a decision about whether to pursue their interests in each other. You must be ready to seize this opportunity by preparing good questions and thoughtful, honest answers to the questions that you think an interviewer may ask during an initial interview.

The initial interview is the time to ask good, to-the-point questions that will clarify specifics of the employer's practice, the work of junior lawyers, and any other information that is basic to your decision to pursue (or not pursue) your initial interest in that employer. A trained interviewer will allow you only five to ten minutes to ask questions, but inexperienced interviewers often will leave the interview—and the questioning—entirely up to you. When you have an opportunity to ask questions, *ask your specific question first*; if time permits, you also can use several of the general questions you will ask of all interviewers. Above all, your questions must be appropriate to an initial interview; they should convey your interest in, enthusiasm for, and knowledge of the employer's practice. This is not the time to ask when salary levels will be increased.

Your answers to questions, like your prepared questions, should be to the point, revealing your preparation for the interview and your enthusiasm for working with a particular employer. Articulateness is important, so pause and take time to think before you respond to important questions about your experiences and goals. Remember, the way you feel about your accomplishments will be as apparent to interviewers as the quality of those accomplishments. If you take time to prepare fully, you will be able to project a positive image of yourself in interviews instead of an unfocused or apologetic one.

Once you have prepared yourself for interviews, you will need to practice another skill: listening. Active listening means being on the alert for information you receive from the interviewer that answers your basic questions about the employer. This information will provide you with the keys to asking additional probing questions during the interview. Lazy listeners lose critical information, as well as opportunities to hear the answers to issues that are at the root of the specific questions that they have asked.

Because you can listen four times faster than a person normally speaks, you will be able to measure what the interviewer is saying against what you believe to be true about the employer, *testing your various hypotheses* about the employment situation that he or she describes. Are your basic needs for a certain type of practice, workstyle, and lifestyle likely to be met? Listen carefully, for at the end of the interview you must ask, "Does this opportunity interest me? What about this job/employer/interviewer intrigues me? Is this a place where I will feel comfortable and be free to develop to my full potential?" As you take note of (and verify) the "facts" the interviewer tells you during an initial interview, you also should *listen to the attitudes expressed* below the surface of the interviewer's "sales pitch." After the interview, you will have to ascertain what the limitations of this opportunity may be and what reservations the interviewer conveyed. By listening and carefully interjecting questions during the interview, you will be able to elicit and investigate a wide variety of facts and subjective information on which to base your decision: Should you pursue your initial interest in the employer if you are considered further?

Of course, the goal of the initial interview is to make a good—and lasting—impression. You want to be invited for another series of follow-up interviews with other lawyers at the employer's office. To make a good impression and avoid the pitfalls of initial interviews, you must prepare to take an active (but not aggressive) role in the process. What are some of these avoidable pitfalls? Here are the top five:

1. General lack of knowledge about or expressed interest in the employer;
2. Failure to convey more information than is outlined on your résumé;
3. Failure to make a lasting impression on the interviewer;
4. Lack of attention to the serious business purpose of the initial interview; and
5. Failure to demonstrate that you meet the employer's minimum standards for intellectual capability, motivation, and positive personal qualities.

The Follow-Up Interview: Choosing

Follow-up interviews provide an opportunity for you to "fine-tune" your initial decisions about suitable employers. During these follow-up interviews, you and the employer will be asking more probing questions to determine how good your mutual fit will be if an offer is made and accepted. While all of the strategies of initial interviewing also apply to the follow-up interview, some important differences do exist, both in terms of the types of questions you should prepare to ask (and be asked) and the interpersonal skills you need to use to set the tone for this kind of interview. These differences relate to the fact that the balance of power shifts toward you, the well-qualified candidate, during follow-up interviews. Up to this point, you have had to do most of the "selling"; as your interviews progress, however, you and your prospective employer are on more equal ground. If you have choices to make among employers, you will be selecting the best opportunity as well as continuing to sell yourself. Employers can be expected to do more selling than they did initially, but they also will be asking for more in-depth information to ascertain the chemistry (or fit) between them and you.

What questions are appropriate for follow-up interviews? Simply stated, ask questions about the employer's substantive practice that you wanted to ask but could not fit into your initial interview; and ask the workstyle/lifestyle questions that might be misinterpreted in an initial interview, such as how matters are staffed and how young lawyers are supervised, trained, evaluated, and otherwise developed as they progress up the ladder. Take care, though, about asking specific questions about billable hours, parenting leaves, or flextime unless these matters are critical to your selection of an employer. These questions are best discussed when an offer is in hand.

Because you will be meeting a number of additional individuals in the follow-up setting, you can feel perfectly comfortable asking the same questions of everyone you meet. The variety of their responses should paint a more accurate and intricate picture of the employer, the office environment, and the people who have chosen to work there.

There are three types of questions you can expect to answer in follow-up interviews. Unfortunately, the first type is the most often encountered and the least useful from your perspective (that is, questions that essentially duplicate the initial interview), the screening of your résumé credentials—your grades and basic work experience—that already were asked and answered during your initial interview. Too many follow-up interviewers cling to this form of questioning because they do not know what else is important—or how to get at the deeper, more subjective criteria, such as your motivation and the personal qualities and skills that indicate that you are likely to perform well on the job. Be prepared to discuss, with limitless patience, the same facts that got you through the initial interview.

The second type of question is intended to reveal the substantive knowledge, interest, and experience you have in a particular field or fields of law. You should be meeting lawyers in your area(s) of interest or practice at this follow-up stage of interviewing, and they will be curious about what your experiences have been and whether you will fit the particular need(s) that they have. This type of question offers you an opportunity (which may not have existed in the initial interview) to reveal your knowledge, experience, and intellectual qualities, and to illustrate the many, varied connections between your interests and experiences and the employer's needs. Again, it is important to prepare for these interviews. Your answers to this type of question should flow naturally. You should be comfortable fielding almost any question relating to your legal expertise and career interests.

The last types of questions deal with your motivation and personal qualities. These are questions for which you should prepare carefully. It would be unfortunate to miss getting an offer because you appeared unmotivated to do an employer's work and instead were preoccupied with a discussion of the employer's benefit plan. Often an interviewee will misjudge the level of motivation that the employer expects and will lose out because he or she seems too laid-back or too aggressive during the interview. Lawyers who use follow-up interviews effectively will spend quite a lot of time asking probing questions in this area to determine your potential fit. Your answers, therefore, must candidly articulate your strengths, thoughtfulness, and seriousness, and they should characterize you as a "good risk." You must know yourself and what you are looking for in any employer to answer these questions honestly and positively.

Good listening skills are as much in order during your follow-up interviews as they are during an initial interview. If you fail to hear what various interviewers tell you about their own original perceptions about the employer, the aspects of their practice that differed from their expectations, and what still interests them about their career, you run the risk of making a career decision based only on your *initial* impressions. Furthermore, if you find yourself talking with interviewers who are delirious with joy about their experiences working shoulder to shoulder with their comrades around the clock, and if these individuals are not much like you in a variety of subjective areas, failing to listen may mean that you will be working shoulder to shoulder with a lot of smart, motivated people you do not like very well. The bottom line is: Pay attention to what the people you will be working with say about the day-to-day work they do, their career goals, and what else they have time for in their professional lives. Listen!

In short, if you want to improve your chances of getting an offer, start out by being a prepared interviewee, then practice your interviewing skills so that your questions and answers will flow smoothly, and sell yourself by illustrating the motivation and personal qualities that will make you a desirable colleague. Be well informed about the employer and know why you have accepted the invitation for follow-up interviews. You often will be asked for those reasons. If you can, convey your commitment to your work, but balance that seriousness with a sense of humor. At the end of the interview, lawyers will ask themselves: "Is this someone I will trust to take over an assignment for me?" and "Is this someone with whom I look forward to working, on a personal level, especially in stressful situations?"

Final Tips on Interviewing Strategies

The most common reasons given by interviewers for rejecting candidates are as follows:

- The candidate did not indicate a strong interest in the employer or was not knowledgeable about the position available.
- The candidate did not make a convincing connection between his or her knowledge and experience and the employer's needs.
- The candidate was not memorable, either in terms of résumé credentials or personal presence during the interview.

If you are prepared for interviews, you should be comfortable with what you are selling. *There are no shortcuts* to taking time to assess your strengths and weaknesses, determining your needs, and planning a career strategy if you want to succeed in presenting yourself effectively during interviews.

You will occasionally encounter difficult questions during interviews. These can be divided into two categories: questions that you find difficult to answer because they probe areas about which you are uncomfortable and questions that are inappropriate (or illegal) for the purposes of an employment interview.

The answer to dealing with difficult questions is: prepare, prepare, *prepare*! You, more than anyone else, can best anticipate the employment questions that you will find difficult to answer in a positive, confident fashion. During your self-assessment, focus on the sensitive areas in your background and think about ways to cast your responses in a favorable light. The trick here is to give thoughtful, but apparently "unrehearsed" answers to difficult questions. If your answers are canned or your responses appear superficial, the interviewer may continue to question you in these sensitive areas and you may not be able to move on to a discussion of your positive selling points.

Inappropriate questions often cause the greatest amount of concern because you will be unwilling to answer these questions, but equally unwilling to forego an employment opportunity by walking out of the interview. We encourage you not to interview with "a chip on your shoulder." Often inappropriate questions indicate thoughtlessness or personal biases on the part of the interviewer, but do not necessarily reflect the views of the employer as an organization. If a question or the interview situation is blatantly discriminatory (such as sexual harassment), you may decide to excuse yourself and pursue the matter directly with the employer. In most other situations, providing a forthright answer indicates that you are aware that the question is inappropriate (or illegal) without alienating the interviewer in return. For example, you might respond to a question about your spouse's career plans by saying, "My (spouse) is willing to relocate if I decide to accept an offer of employment in (city). Is this an issue that (employer) will weigh in deciding whether to consider me further for this position?" Ultimately, you want to keep your options open and retain control of the situation. Then, if you receive an offer and are interested in the employer, you can (and should) raise the issue of inappropriate questioning at that point in the process.

Dos and Don'ts of Interviewing

To interview effectively you must:

- Prepare for the interview by assessing what the right career options are for you—fields of law, cities, and a lifestyle.
- Obtain information about the employer from as many sources as possible, including knowledgeable individuals.
- Prepare questions and answers to use in interviews.
- Be prepared to meet different types of interviewers and learn to vary your interviewing style.
- Dress and act professionally to make a positive impression.
- Take control of the interview by knowing what you want from the experience.
- Remember the differences between initial and follow-up interviews.
- Ask thoughtful questions and provide thoughtful answers.
- Listen to the interviewer and gather information.

- Make a convincing, but low-key, sales pitch to assure that the interviewer will remember you and know why you are interested in the position.
- Maintain a professional demeanor during the interview, even in the face of questions that you find inappropriate.
- Keep your career goals firmly in mind and do not be swayed by what the employer wants to sell you or by hearsay from others.
- Remember that the interview is a learning experience and a business opportunity, not a crisis situation.
- Relax and be confident: If you have done your homework, you will succeed in landing the job that will be right for you.

Successful interviewing is a skill that is developed by a combination of perception, preparation, and practice. If you can dedicate yourself to these tasks, you not only will succeed in landing a job, you will succeed in launching a productive and satisfying professional career.

CHAPTER 17

Negotiating Salary and Benefits

Laura J. Hagen

Overview

The excesses of the 1970s and 1980s are over. Law firms no longer fly neophyte lawyers first class for interviews or dole out $100 bills for "incidental" expenses. With the increased emphasis on law as a business and professional management in law firms, increasing attention is being paid to controlling costs, including salary, which is generally one of a law firm's major budget items. The recession of the late 1980s and early 1990s injected a note of reality into the recruitment process, and young lawyers should not expect to see dizzying raises in compensation or "salary wars" by firms attempting to attract the best and brightest. What is being seen in the 1990s and beyond is more differentiation in salary between the different tiers of law firms and corporations as the more profitable are able to maintain the higher salaries, while the less profitable fall behind.

Basic Compensation Schemes

This chapter deals with two major employers of lawyers—law firms and corporations. Law firms are far and away the major employer of lawyers (approximately 650,000[1] lawyers are in private practice); accordingly, this chapter focuses more on negotiating with firms. Corporations, however, increased their hiring of lawyers during the 1980s (about 70,000 lawyers are employed by corporations). This number likely will not increase tremendously, although it will certainly remain steady. The concerns in negotiating salary in each setting are different.

The trend in the 1990s within law firms will be more differentiation, both between salary levels from firm to firm and within the firms themselves as performance-based compensation systems become more the norm. In the old days, most firms categorized lawyers by law school graduating class and compensated them accordingly. The progression was "lockstep," with set raises automatically given annually with step variations between the classes. Lawyers within a class were treated equally, irrespective of the quality of their work, the number of hours they billed, or the amount of business they brought to the firm. During the years prior to admission to partnership, each class received graduated raises as successive new associates joined the firm from law school.

This description of "lockstep" no longer describes the compensation system in the majority of firms. With increased competition, many firms evaluate lawyer performance in terms of quality of work, number of hours billed, and the intangibles a lawyer brings to the table. Lawyer compensation, once immune from discussion as well as scrutiny, now is more open to negotiation.

Any lawyer moving to a firm should investigate the compensation system of the firm as it applies to partners as well as associates. At one end is the "lockstep" system mentioned previously, which rewards seniority over performance. At the other end is the "eat-what-you-kill" system, which leads lawyers to value their own billings over behavior as a "firm" and results in an entirely different atmosphere within a law firm. In many cases, an "eat-what-you-kill" system leads to a collection of individual practitioners rather than a firm that thinks like a firm.

With this change in compensation to performance-based compensation, associates are differentiated within classes. Although the compensation for the first year or two may be the same across the board, many firms now rate associates and assign salaries accordingly. Thus, there are firms with a high, low, and medium compensation designation within each class. Another trend is toward other compensation schemes, such as a base salary with a profit-sharing component or a base with a bonus to the associates depending on the performance of the associate in particular, the firm in general, or both. At the more senior levels of associate compensation, there may be a component of compensation that rewards bringing business to the firm. Another trend is the requirement that associates pay a percentage of the cost of benefits such as health care.

When negotiating your salary with a law firm, you should be aware of two components. One is the class within which you are placed. This often determines salary, or at least the range of salary that you will be able to earn. The other is the designation of years to consideration for partnership status, an area in which there is little room for negotiation for laterals. Most firms demand at least a two-year "look-and-see" period before considering a lateral for partnership. It may be in your interest to divorce the consideration of the two issues and agree to be compensated with your class of graduation, but deferred for partnership consideration to a different class. Considerations that go into this decision include the need for exposure to various partners within the firm who will be your supporters in the partnership decision, as well as the competitive composition of the classes. For example, if your class has five dead-bang winners for partnership, you may be better off agreeing to a two-year deferral.

On the corporate side, salaries are both less complicated (the cash side) and more complicated (the benefits side). They generally are set by the budget for the legal department that allows so many dollars for slots—and by the titles assigned to the slots—rather than strictly years out of law school. For example, a general counsel may have a lawyer slot at a certain range of compensation into which he or she could place a lawyer within a wide range of years of law school graduation. Corporations are far less concerned with year of graduation from law school and more concerned with substantive practice experience.

Other important distinctions are that titles can make a big difference in the way an in-house lawyer is viewed (both on the inside and from the outside) and thus should be investigated carefully. The title or rank of a position within the department may determine whether that lawyer is eligible for certain "higher level" benefits such as participation in stock options. In general, the components of corporate compensation are a base salary, with a bonus element that usually is contingent on performance of both the lawyer in particular and the corporation as a whole.

Corporate benefits often are more valuable than those provided by law firms. You should investigate the breadth of the health insurance, life insurance, retirement benefits, and miscellaneous perks (parking spaces, cars, extra vacation time) provided. The value of these benefits often can compensate for the often lower cash component of compensation offered in the corporate setting. Although corporate salaries generally are lower than those offered in firms, there are other obvious trade-offs, such as lifestyle benefits and escaping the pressure of the billable hour and the need to become a rainmaker. One should not view a corporation as a panacea, however, because elements of the same skills are required to be successful in a corporate legal department.

Additional elements of compensation within a corporate setting may include a signing bonus, which can compensate a lawyer for the shortfall in cash compensation over a period of time; relocation benefits, which can cover moving expenses and temporary living as well as the possible protection on the sale of a house. In addition, a corporation may be persuaded to pay for a lost bonus or stock options that had not vested because the timing of the move at the request of the corporation. These are not so prevalent with law firms, which tend to limit compensation to base, bonus, health and life insurance (usually contributory), and out-of-pocket moving expenses.

Preparing to Negotiate: The Rules

The cardinal rule of negotiating salary is "know thyself and thy market." Before negotiating, sit down and review your career in depth. Look at old time sheets, diaries, and reviews to refresh your memory of all the substantive areas of the law with which you have dealt. This will give you a better sense of expertise and your value to an employer. People often forget cases or projects that they worked on early in their careers and tend only to remember the recent past.

In addition to assessing your own skills, review your salary history. It is not an appropriate response to a query about your compensation to say "I don't remember, but I think . . . " Review not only your cash compensation, but also all your benefits including health insurance, life insurance, pension, and profit sharing. This will give you a range for what your skills should be worth in the market. Be sure to look at your W-2s to see what has been included. If you have stock options or unvested pension plans, look at the vesting provisions. It would be foolish to begin a job search shortly before a major vesting anniversary. You also should take into consideration the timing of your move and its effect on lost bonus or payout for work brought to the firm.

Know your market. Know how your compensation ranks vis-à-vis others within your organization. If it will appear out of line to a new employer, you should be willing to explain that it was average or high for your past employer, and you should gather information about compensation in the market that you are investigating. This information is best gathered from your peers and from secondary sources such as newspaper surveys or legal search consultants. In many cities, groups of associates compile salary surveys that can prove invaluable. When gathering salary information from others, the phrasing of the question is paramount. Do not put others on the spot by asking them how much money they make. Rather, ask them, "What would you estimate a lawyer of such and such a class with such and such skills earns in your (or another) organization?" Most people are happy to discuss compensation in generalized terms when it does not appear to be a reflection on their own compensation.

The third rule is know your employer. It will not do you any good to try to negotiate a "New York–style salary" in a law firm that has consistently been in the lower to mid range of salaries within its market. It simply will not happen. The ultimate salary is not only a reflection of the firm's desire for you, but also intrinsic factors of the firm, such as profitability. If you do not have sources within the firm, perhaps some of your classmates in other organizations have friends who will share this information with you.

Above all, know what you want. Before you go into your final set of interviews, have a clear idea of what compensation package would be acceptable to you. If there are any large clinkers (such as stock options you are about to lose and for which you would like to be compensated), be prepared to raise them at this time. Timing is of utmost importance in negotiations. Employers do not like to go down the road with a candidate and receive an ugly surprise at the end of the road when the candidate says, "and, by the way, I'd like that $100,000 bonus I'm going to lose by moving in November instead of January."

The Negotiation

Be prepared for trial balloons to be floated in the negotiation process. If you are working with a search consultant, be frank with the search consultant on what your bottom line *really* is. The consultant, who is your ally in this process, wants the transaction to be completed and can offer you helpful advice, not only as to a particular offer, but how that offer fits into the marketplace. Respond to an offer in a timely manner. Most employers understand that when the process gets to this point, everybody is serious. Do not attempt to collect offers only to bring them back to your current employer as a means of increasing your salary. If you move a negotiation to the point of receiving an offer, you should be prepared to consider this offer seriously. Most offers are made subject to references checking out, although some employers insist on checking references from former employers before proceeding. Be careful on this point. *Do not allow a prospective employer to contact your current employer until you receive an acceptable or workable offer.*

If you are dissatisfied about several elements of the offer, be prepared to sit down and discuss them. If you feel the offer is below market, say so—and present your reasons for believing so. If the employer is off the mark, he or she will appreciate being educated on this point. Remember, your negotiating power is never so high as right before you accept the offer. Presumably, the employer wants you. Once you have accepted, the power balance shifts dramatically and you are an employee. Make sure that the terms of the offer are clear and in writing. It is customary for employers to send an offer letter. If there is a contingent component of your compensation, be certain that the contingencies are spelled out. If it is a bonus, the provisions pertaining to when it is due and what factors will determine whether or what portion of the bonus you will receive should be clear. For instance, is your performance based on written reviews or the performance of the firm or company? Is it a combination of both? If you have reached an agreement consideration for partnership, be certain that this is part of the letter. This avoids possible misunderstandings later, where parties other than the one with whom you negotiated question what was promised to you.

Conclusion

Remember, you should negotiate from a position of strength, the strength that derives both from your knowledge of yourself and your skills, what you bring to the employer, as well as your knowledge of the market and how the market values your skills. Recognize that this is a business relationship and that the actual time to structure this relationship is the time period before you accept the offer. These recognitions can turn what might be an awkward and stressful situation into a rewarding experience for all concerned.

Note

1. Source: *Supplement to the Lawyers Statistical Report: The U.S. Legal Profession*, Copyright 1991; information as of 1988 reports that there are 723,189 licensed lawyers in the United States; excluding the estimated 70,000 in corporate settings mentioned later in the paragraph, the figure of approximately 650,000 is a rough estimate.

CHAPTER 18

Making the "Right" Career Decision

Robert A. Major, Jr.

You have carefully assessed your career plans and strategies. Based on that planning, you have identified what you want to do and how to go about achieving it. But how do you choose between competing opportunities that closely, though not perfectly, match your goals? What is the "right" job?

The 1990s will make the search for that fit even more challenging. With the supply of jobs decreasing, and the demand for them increasing (or remaining stable), lawyers on a job search are more likely to be forced to accept compromises. The new "buyer's market" means that the buyers (employers) will have many more applicants to choose from and inevitably will be smarter shoppers. Lawyers who become smarter job seekers will have an edge over those who believe that the 1980s never really ended.

Goals

Short-Term Goals

Making the right career choice depends heavily on defining your goals and making honest appraisals of how your job prospects meet those goals. Part I of this book details useful approaches to goal identification. Some goals are short-term. Training, for example, is an issue about which new lawyers are concerned. Dissatisfaction with training is the single biggest complaint voiced by junior lawyers. If you feel that your training has not been what it should, that will clearly be on your list of things to fix the next time around. You will know that it is not enough for a prospective employer to assure you that its training is excellent. You will want to know what constitutes the training program, how the employer tracks a lawyer's progress, how it responds to need for improvement in certain areas, and how the other junior lawyers feel about their experience in this regard.

Many job seekers are looking to do more interesting work. This is a tricky area, because so much of what lawyers do is simply not that interesting. This is especially the case with more junior lawyers, who usually are assigned the less complicated, more routine (yes, boring) tasks, such as coming up with initial drafts of contracts or pleadings, or coordinating document productions. Lawyers who are dissatisfied or bored with their work often have the lurking suspicion that they may have chosen the wrong profession; they may be right. Many lawyers are desperate to do something different, often in "exotic" fields such as entertainment or media law, or something with an international bent. While certainly there are practitioners in these specialties, the need in these fields is very infrequent and the competition is fierce. In the international area, language skills (meaning fluency, not conversational) are increasingly important.

A third short-term goal is "résumé value." Some lawyers seek a change to upgrade their résumés. They want to work for a more prestigious firm, or they want advancement in a company. Again, this is a tricky area. The reality of the 1990s is that employers are apt to be less forgiving of lawyers who do not meet their expectations. Law firms especially are finding that they no longer can carry the "late bloomers" the way that they did in the 1980s. Those who want to switch to a more prestigious law firm for no other reason than to upgrade their résumés may find themselves in the unhappy position of redoing their résumés before long. You must, therefore, analyze carefully why you want to make a change and consider the risks, and the benefits, involved. A fourth short-term goal is the desire or need to make more money. Unless the change represents a significant increase in compensation (for example, 25 percent to 30 percent), this is not a particularly good basis on which to make a move. You may be trading "down" in other areas (such as collegiality), and you might be giving up security for something far more speculative in terms of long-term advancement.

Long-Term Goals

Long-term goals, not surprisingly, provide a far better basis on which to evaluate a job opportunity.

Partnership opportunity in law firms or the equivalent advancement in other organizations. Partnership (if a law firm) or a senior position commanding responsibility and professional stature (in other organizations) is the Holy Grail of law practice. Lawyers by nature are competitors who need to feel that they are advancing toward a goal. That goal, for better or for worse, has been law firm partnership. What was seen in the late 1980s, and what the 1990s has proven, is that making partner is not for everyone. And the economic stress of the early 1990s has revealed just how deep-seated and widespread disillusionment is among partners.

Partnership, however, remains for most lawyers a greatly desired goal. Lawyers seeking new jobs must be brutally honest with themselves about just how important it is to "make" partner. If partnership is important, then the statistics each law firm compiles on how many associates make partner (and who they are) will be indispensable in deciding whether that is the place for you. If the law firm has completed an NALP form, these figures are readily available. If not, you should ask (discreetly) for them.

Corporations represent an increasingly attractive opportunity for lawyers. The 1990s have boosted the popularity of "going in-house" to unprecedented heights. The diminishing partnership "pie," the aversion to hustling for new clients, the desire for more free time, and a notion that working in a corporation will allow one to get involved in business—all these factors have lawyers in private practice polishing up their résumés. And the legal press has widely heralded the evolution of in-house legal departments from their previous "backwater" status to state-of-the-art entities that function as law firms within the corporate structure. This trend is likely to continue.

Geography.   In the seller's market years of the 1980s, lawyers were in such demand that they had the luxury of specifying where they wanted to practice geographically. Naturally, the great money and power centers—New York, Chicago, Houston, Washington, Boston, Los Angeles, and San Francisco—attracted a large percentage of new lawyers. The excitement of "big-firm" practice, fat salaries, and prestige all provided an irresistible lure to the big city. As lawyers mature, of course, their priorities change, and the new decade suggests a rather dramatic altering of priorities. There seems to be a sense among lawyers that the "big deal" does not hold the attraction it once did. Lawyers now talk about lifestyle, wanting a law firm with a culture based on something other than money, and a place where they can raise a family. Unfortunately, many of the big money centers have turned into urban battlefields where parents are uneasy rearing their children.

When assessing your long-term goals, you must choose carefully where you want to practice. The volatility of the market may preclude moving to a place where you really want to be at some later date. Do not take a "flier" in a particular city without considering the possibility that your marketability may diminish, because it is likely to do so.

Colleagues.   Interviewing in law school is rather serendipitous in terms of selecting future colleagues. Law students tend to focus on reputation and practice areas when choosing a law firm. A stint as a summer associate allows a closer look at individual lawyers (and vice versa), but the summer associate experience can differ markedly from the regular associate experience. Regardless, the shifting personnel in firms means that you never know who will be there by the time you join or make partner.

A chronic complaint among lawyers—both partners and associates—relates to interpersonal issues: "The firm isn't the one I joined when I was a summer associate." "I keep thinking, do I really want to be partners with these people?" The answer to this problem is twofold: introspection to determine just how important collegiality is to you, and research into the potential employer to find out what kind of place it is and how the lawyers and staff relate to each other.

Factors Affecting Goal Attainment

Certain overriding factors affect your selection of a job and the means to secure it. These factors are practicality, flexibility, and self-assessment.

Practicality. The 1990s mean that lawyers will have fewer choices and more compromises to make. Practicality is essential to becoming the "smart-shopper" lawyer. One aspect of this is getting a sense of what kind of practice areas are in demand and molding yourself to fit that demand. Although law is becoming increasingly specialized, there always will be certain "generic" practice areas. People always will bring lawsuits, so there always will be litigators. People always will want their business affairs negotiated and documented, so there always will be business lawyers. Certain practice areas, however, have experienced decline. Maritime law, for example, has slowed down because of containerization and other methods of transporting goods. Real estate syndications, similarly, were dramatically affected by the Tax Reform Act of 1986.

Geography is also a limiting factor. Lawyers who want to practice international law should not set their hearts on living in Dubuque. Those with fluency in Chinese, for example, are better off on the West Coast than in the Southeast. Entertainment law is centered in Los Angeles and New York, not San Francisco or Washington, D.C.

Flexibility. Lawyers should have enough variety in their skills to allow for cycles in their practice areas. In the past few years, real estate across the country has been significantly depressed, causing some anxious moments for practitioners in that field. Fortunately, most real estate lawyers had enough flexibility in their skills to respond. They became workout and restructuring lawyers. Lawyers should be careful to widen their practice to be able to embrace something else if their practice area falls into decline.

Self-Assessment. One advantage experienced lawyers have over neophytes is the fact that practicing law no longer is purely theoretical. They have come to know what they like, and do not like, about their work. For example, a common complaint from litigators is that they are tired of the constant battle of litigation and disturbed by what they see as a waste of human and economic resources. After years of warring with opposing counsel, they have turned inward and discovered that they are happiest when they are conciliators. This self-discovery often is a bit late, because—as everyone knows—"marketability" tends to narrow as one achieves seniority. Thus, it is important early on to make the critical self-assessments that should guide your career choices.

Another factor gaining importance in law firm practice is whether the lawyer is capable of attracting business, the "rainmaking" syndrome. As the economics of law firm practice increasingly emphasizes business development, lawyers will come under pressure to bring in clients. For many law firms, business development is the sine qua non of partnership. Lawyers should factor this into their self-assessments when evaluating whether a law firm is the right thing for them.

Research

Knowledge Is Power

Knowledge also is crucial to making job shoppers into *smart* job shoppers. It is an enduring curiosity that lawyers willingly commit hours to studying the most minute statutory or case law to prove a point, yet rely on instinct and superficial research when making a decision on their own choices.

The legal profession has been revolutionized in the past two decades by the amount of information available on law firms and, to a lesser extent, other employers such as corporations. *The American Lawyer, The National Law Journal,* and the local legal and popular press have unlocked what previously were the granite-like vaults closed to the public eye. Today's law firms, with their marketing directors and spokespersons, now rush to tell their story to anyone who will listen.

The story, of course, is always a mixed bag. No institution is without its problems. This is particularly true in a profession with more than its share of prima donnas. The point is not to find a flawless firm or corporation. The point is to find an employer with fewer of the qualities that you find most objectionable.

You can start with the printed materials prepared by the employer itself. These, naturally, will tell the "party line," but they are useful starting points. If the employer is a law firm and has completed an NALP form, be sure to obtain one. This form contains important data on billable hours, broken down between associates and partners; number of partners made out of possible candidates; number of laterals; compensation; pro bono policies; etc.

Law firm brochures are of limited value, although exceptions do exist. More useful are the materials prepared by individual practice groups; be sure to ask if there is one for your practice area.

Press reports and third parties are great sources of information. Be careful that information contained in press stories is current. Placement directors of local law schools and local "headhunters" usually are treasure troves of current information—if they will talk to you.

Even better are former classmates. You can identify them by comparing this year's Martindale-Hubbell with the past year's. The Bar Association will have their current addresses. Is it appropriate to ask former employees about what it is like at their former firm? Certainly. If your potential employer finds it appropriate to check your references, then you may—and should—do the same.

Making Job Selection Comport with Goals

The following exercise is a simple way to identify how different job opportunities fare in comparison with each other.

The first step in the exercise is to list all the factors that are important to you. Location, compensation, the challenge of the work, your colleagues, potential for advancement, training, and "résumé value" (or ego) may be among the factors. The second step is to rate, on a 1 to 10 scale, just how important each of the factors is to you. If you really do not care where you practice, as long as you make partner somewhere, location will score very low and potential for advancement will score very high. The third step is to rate each of your opportunities according to each category.

Are you surprised at the result? Many people end up changing the relative weights accorded each of the factors, if only by a point or two. The exercise makes them think about what is important to them, and how important. Changing the weighting also may indicate that the lawyer deep down has a "gut" favorite that should be the mathematical winner, but is not.

"Gut" feelings are important. A good way to handle the "gut" issue is to sit down with someone you really trust and who knows you very well. The best person is a friend or advisor who has no interest in the outcome other than a desire to see you happy. This person will be able to spot when you are lying to yourself, or at least shading the facts. Tell this person about the process and your options, and tell him or her honestly how you feel about the choices in front of you. Discuss the pros and cons, and pay particular attention to the grid—especially if it did not produce the desired result. You will likely hear the right answer in the discussion, or you may know it in advance and the exercise will merely confirm it.

PART IV

Career Options

CHAPTER 19

Career Options: An Overview

Robert A. Major, Jr.

An old saying advises us to "go hunting where the ducks are." When contemplating a job change, it also might be useful to identify where the jobs are and in what practice areas. You can spend a lot of time trying to find an antitrust litigation position in Boise without much luck. You might have similar problems locating that hot entertainment job in Omaha. Ultimately, when assessing your goals, you need to account for the variables of location and the demand for your practice area.

The demand for legal services is, of course, affected by general economic conditions. Long gone are the days when the practice of law was recession-proof. The result is that as different areas of the country experience different levels of economic growth and distress, your chances of landing a job may very well depend on your willingness and ability to relocate to a "hot" area.

Similarly, if you find yourself in a practice area that has experienced a slowdown (such as real estate in many parts of the country), you may be better off as a retooled workout specialist. Generally, it is not possible to market yourself to a prospective employer as a competent lawyer in a practice area that is unrelated to your prior experience, but there are many areas where skills overlap. The discussions that follow identify geographic and substantive practice area trends that may help you fine-tune your job search.

CHAPTER 20

Practice Areas

Brion A. Bickerton

Three lessons have been painfully drilled into the consciousness of lawyers in America during this past recession: First, thou shall not have undying loyalty to any employer; second, thou shall always be out looking for a better opportunity; and third, thou shall treat thy practice as a business.

Of the many issues that confront lawyers trying to come to terms with treating their practice as a business, one subject should have immediate relevance and importance to all—identifying hot and growing practice areas for the 1990s. This will be the issue for the solo practitioner in Houston, the associate in a 500 lawyer firm in New York City, and the partner in a ten-lawyer firm in St. Louis.

The need for a solo practitioner to identify a growing practice area should be self-evident. An associate in a 500-lawyer firm in New York City should give this topic great thought as well, for it may mean the difference in developing a niche at his or her firm early on and positioning himself or herself for partnership. If partnership is not a goal or becomes improbable, being in the right practice area should ease the transition into the next position. A partner in a firm should be evaluating potential growth areas of practice not only to keep his or her own practice base growing but also to target new practice areas for the firm at large.

In an increasingly crowded and competitive legal field with thousands of lawyers pumped each year into the system, many lawyers may find that their success and happiness will depend on their capacity to become experts in newly emerging fields and to capture a significant market share and a competitive lead.

The 1990s' recession debunked the theory that there is a limitless amount of legal work to be shared plentifully with the mushrooming numbers of lawyers. The number of disenfranchised partners from major firms who have been unceremoniously dumped from their firms should be testimony to the fact that the pie is not always growing. As *The American Lawyer* noted in its

June, 1993, issue, one major Chicago law firm lopped off 25 partners, including ten partners in their mid-50s or older, while another eliminated 55 non-equity partner and associate positions.

As the number of lawyers in the United States exceeds *one million* with no end in sight to the minting of law school graduates, lawyers first must become cognizant of emerging and dying areas of practice and then must plan to adjust their practices accordingly.

Predicting the Emerging Practice Areas

Practice Areas

Young lawyers in particular who have as yet been exposed to a limited number of practice areas first must identify the range of practice opportunities. The following is a comprehensive outline of current major practice areas:

Administrative
Admiralty
Advertising
Agricultural Law
Alcoholic Beverages
Alternative Dispute Resolution
Animal Law
Antitrust and Trade Regulation
Appellate Practice
Art Law
Aviation and Aerospace
Bankruptcy
Banks and Banking
   Bank Regulation
   Lending
Biotechnology
Business Law
Children
Civil Rights
Class Actions
Commercial Law
   UCC
   Secured Transactions
Commodities
Communications and Media
Computers and Software
Constitutional Law
Consumer Law
Copyrights
Criminal Law
Domestic Relations

Education
Elder Law
Election, Campaign Lobbying
Employee Benefits
Energy
Entertainment
Environmental Law
Federal Tax
Fidelity and Surety
Finance
Franchising
General Practice
Government
Health Care
Immigration
Insurance
Insurance Defense
Intellectual Property
International Law
   Customs
   Imports/Exports
   Investments
   Trade
Labor and Employment
Legal Ethics
Litigation
Medical Malpractice
Military Law
Natural Resources
Nonprofit and Charitable
   Organizations

Patents	Securities
Personal Injury	Sports
Products Liability	Taxation
Professional Liability	Telecommunications
Public Law	Trademarks
Real Estate	Transportation
Religious Institutions	Trusts and Estates
Resorts and Leisure	White-Collar Crime

Hot Practice Areas of the 1980s—A Prologue

During the 1980s, the following practices emerged as hot: environmental, real estate, corporate leverage buyouts, corporate mergers and acquisitions, syndications (real estate, equipment leasing, oil and gas), health care, employment litigation, patent litigation, and product liability (in particular, toxic torts such as asbestos and Dalkon shield litigation). Some areas deflated, such as traditional labor, Occupational Safety and Health Administration (OSHA), and antitrust. Some areas died almost as soon as they developed, such as wage and price control. Lawyers should look back at this period and evaluate the reasons for the emergence of some of these practice fields.

While the emergence or deflation of some of these practice areas was predictable, other practice areas were either negatively or positively affected by less predictable market factors or legislative changes. Anyone following the Tax Reform Act of 1986 should have moved quickly out of syndication practice. The decline of traditional labor practice was the consequence of a predictable and long-term shift in American industry from smokestack industries to high-technology and service industries that have been less susceptible to unionization.

The decline in the practice of many antitrust lawyers was to a degree the result of policy changes in the Reagan administration. While the shift in antitrust enforcement depended on a change in administration and was difficult to predict, anyone practicing in the area should have been sensitive to the fact that his or her practice area was vulnerable to such political changes.

Independent power project finance emerged as a new practice in the 1980s. The emergence of this field wholly depended on Congress passing legislation that opened up entry into the utility market. While previously the sole province of monopolistic utility companies, the power industry became the subject of extensive congressional focus. The result was the passage of a complex set of laws that allowed independent entities to develop power facilities and required the monopolistic public-utility companies to purchase power from these entities. A whole new industry was spawned, with lawyers becoming extensively involved in this statutorily created industry. Who could have predicted such developments? Anyone knowledgeable about the industry.

Predicting the Hot Practice Areas of the 1990s

The July 12, 1993, issue of *Fortune* magazine projects job growth for lawyers of 25 percent to 34 percent from 1990–2005. These jobs will likely be exceeded, however, by the number of lawyers entering the legal market. According to Steven Brill of *The American Lawyer* (June, 1993), "the marketplace for lawyer hours is bloated and in the process of being squeezed." The end result is that while opportunities are continuing to be created in the American economy, the surplus of lawyers now created and projected for the rest of the decade will have to exist in a significantly more competitive marketplace. In its broad discussion about job growth in its July 12, 1993, issue, *Fortune* magazine succinctly stated the new reality for lawyers and other professionals: "Aspiring managers and lawyers—along with those already in the workforce—will have to hone skills that set them apart from the crowd and take laser-like aim at areas where growth prospects are brightest."

How does one pinpoint growth areas of practice? Lawyers, long immune to the competitive forces that traditionally compel businesses and entrepreneurs to think strategically and plan for the future, need to step back and continually assess societal trends and technological changes affecting industry. On the required reading list should be the writings of such futurists as John Nesbitt (*Megatrends*) and Alvin Toffler. Do not ignore the larger forces that ultimately will dominate what businesses will be doing.

Some of these forces are undeniable, such as the graying of the baby-boom generation. Lawyers need to assess how such a trend will provide for growth opportunities for lawyers. Mutual fund lawyers, for example, are currently benefiting from this aging population trend. This is because the graying baby-boom generation finally is reaching a stage in life where it must start planning for retirement. In recognition of this reality, the mutual fund industry has been aggressive in capturing retirement savings. As a result, the number of funds, and the number of lawyers servicing those funds, has exploded during the past five years.

The need for the baby-boom generation to save for retirement is also because, as corporate America continues to reduce employee benefits, individuals must provide their own retirement nest eggs. This stripping away of pension benefits is itself a result of another larger trend at work—the globalization of industry. American industry has responded to the competitiveness of a wider, more unforgivable global marketplace. The graying of the baby-boom generation also is creating a demand for lawyers providing services to the elderly (Medicare, Medicaid planning, asset protection, age discrimination, health care–related problems, etc.).

Some of the areas that may be viewed as hot fields for the rest of the decade include the following:

> *Elder care.* As Ken Dychtwald points out in his book dealing with the aging of the population (*Age Wave*, Bantam Books, 1993), legal services for the elderly will explode during the 1990s. These lawyers will be assisting the elderly with protection of their assets against Medicare, dealing with nursing homes and health-care facilities, and euthanasia issues.

> *Employment law.* As *Fortune* magazine pointed out in its March, 1993, issue dealing with the "new" unemployed in America, terminations and unemployment are a permanent phenomenon of traditional corporate

America. This has resulted in significant increases in litigation for the labor force—wrongful terminations and age-discrimination complaints. All major law firms have groups of lawyers now dedicated to employment litigation cases. The newly enacted Americans with Disabilities Act is projected to greatly increase the number of job-related lawsuits. (See *Forbes*, May, 1993.)

Intellectual property. "The golden era of intellectual-property litigation was ushered in with the Reagan era when the Department of Justice reversed a long-standing policy of using antitrust laws against companies that refused to license patented technology." In its January, 1993, issue, the *Corporate Legal Counsel* assessed the great growth in patent litigation and projected continued significant activity in this area. In addition to a need for patent lawyers with litigation skills, there will be continued strong demand for lawyers conversant enough with technologies to represent companies who will continue to enter into joint ventures, research and development collaborations, and cross-licensing agreements.

Health care. According to the *Wall Street Journal* (June 1, 1993), the almost $1 trillion health-care industry in the United States has been creating 300,000 jobs per year. Managed health care and the health-care information and technology industry is expected to grow. Whether any health-care reform bill is enacted this decade, it is clear that health care will continue to be a major industry in the United States. With its range of regulations and its ability to affect all of our lives, health care promises to be an important practice area for lawyers.

International law. Large corporations are going global with a vengeance as the *Corporate Legal Times* has noted in its March, 1993, issue. While the impediment of lack of admissibility will affect American lawyers to freely market their services around the world to foreign clients, there is an emerging need for lawyers who can work in a multicultural environment. Language skills also will assume greater importance for lawyers.

Environmental law. Environmental law will continue to be a major practice area. Pollution cleanup, now estimated to be a $100-billion-a-year industry, is projected to grow to $1 trillion by the year 2000 (*Fortune*, January 15, 1993). As the United States exports not only more of its pollution technology to the rest of the world, more lawyers are assisting in the creation of more complex and broader environmental laws for other countries.

Lawyers should be evaluating carefully whether some of the following practice areas will provide much growth for the rest of this decade.

1. *Tax.* Tax practitioners, particularly in law firms, saw their practices suffer dramatically during the late 1980s and early 1990s as the number of corporate transactions tailed off.

2. *Real estate.* With the graying of the baby boomers, how many more real estate projects must be built in certain regions of the country for the next 20 years except as replacement property? Real estate development lawyers who became workout lawyers during the recession will suffer unless they develop into more general bank finance lawyers (non–real estate lending).

3. *Personal-injury litigation.* Every year new legislation is proposed limiting damage and pain and suffering claims. Eventually, some legislation will be enacted and certain practices will be affected.

In a noncompetitive environment, businesses have the luxury to keep their heads stuck in the sand and let business take care of itself. In a competitive environment, businesses always must be vigilant for market opportunities. The boom markets of the 1980s masked one trend—the rapid increase in the number of lawyers. Anyone following that trend may have predicted the competitive environment of the 1990s for lawyers.

CHAPTER 21

Geographic Areas

Northeast

New York

Carol M. Kanarek

New York, New York . . . it is still true that "the Bronx is up and the Battery's down." But aside from that, the city is a far different place for lawyers than it was only a few years ago. New York's economy—including the securities and real estate industries that generated hundreds of millions of dollars in revenue for local lawyers during the 1980s—is recovering slowly from a severe recession, but it will almost certainly peak at a level considerably below that of the 1980s' boom years. Of even greater significance to New York lawyers, however, is the fact that New York is at the center of revolutionary changes in the way in which legal services are delivered to corporate America. Companies are taking advantage of the large pool of legal talent that was unleashed by the New York law firms during the recession and are finding that they can handle a great deal of sophisticated legal work in-house. And when they need outside representation, these increasingly savvy and cost-sensitive in-house lawyers no longer are wedded to one or two large firms; instead, they turn to a broad array of firms of all sizes. The result is a legal community in a state of flux bordering on chaos, with a blurring of many of the traditional distinctions between large and small law firms.

The dominant industries and business concerns in New York include securities, banking, real estate, and insurance. Probable growth areas for the 1990s include initial public offerings; strategic business acquisitions (as opposed to the highly leveraged, and often hostile, acquisitions for purely financial reasons during the 1980s); equipment financing; international investment ventures, spurred by the privatization movement in Latin America and Europe; and both corporate and litigation work for insurance companies, brokerage firms, and investment funds. Key political, regulatory, and economic

184

issues impacting the practice of law in New York include interest rates, stock market levels, federal and state tax laws, and securities and banking regulations.

New York is home to 33 of the 100 highest-grossing law firms in the country and to more than 50 firms with more than 100 lawyers; however, the vast majority of New York's law firms employ ten or fewer lawyers. Although most small firms handle legal work for individuals and small businesses, small "boutique" firms that handle sophisticated legal work for major companies are becoming increasingly common. This is caused by market forces that are resulting in the downsizing of the very large firms; as corporations purchase outside legal services more selectively, large firms are laying off many lawyers (both associates and partners), hiring fewer new associates, and promoting fewer associates to partner. The large firms are disproportionately located in Manhattan, although a few firms of close to 100 lawyers are in Albany and Rochester. Law practices in suburban and rural New York are similar to suburban and rural law practices in other parts of the country.

Corporations, banks, and investment banks in New York have added significant numbers of lawyers—most of whom have practice experience in large New York law firms—to their legal staffs in recent years, with the result that much more legal work now is handled in-house. Because of the sizes of the legal staffs of most large corporations, it no longer is efficient to hire many more lawyers, so the employment opportunities for lawyers during the remainder of the 1990s are likely to be primarily in smaller companies, which currently have few or no in-house lawyers. A greatly increased emphasis on cost containment and supervision of outside counsel exists in New York companies of all sizes.

Most federal government agencies have offices in New York that employ lawyers, and most require prior relevant legal experience. State government jobs are located mainly in Albany, although the New York State Attorney General's Office employs 300 of its 450 lawyers in Manhattan. New York City government employs large numbers of lawyers, with more than 500 in the city's Office of the Corporation Counsel. Most federal, state, and local government jobs located in Manhattan have become extremely competitive, despite their low salaries relative to the large law firms. Positions with the U.S. attorney's office in the Southern and Eastern Districts of New York are among the most highly sought-after jobs in the United States for litigators.

Other employment opportunities for lawyers in New York include teaching and administrative positions in New York's 15 law schools; writing and editing positions with New York–based publishers of law books, legal newsletters, and many other local and national publications for lawyers (including *The New York Law Journal* and *The American Lawyer*); Legal Aid (which employs more than 1,000 lawyers in Manhattan); jobs with public interest and advocacy organizations; and nonlegal positions in corporations, banks, and investment banks.

Washington, D.C., Maryland, and Delaware

Anne Neal

WASHINGTON, D.C.

Professional opportunities abound for lawyers in Washington, D.C., a city widely recognized for its cultural and ethnic diversity, outstanding schools, and popular recreational attractions. As the nation's capital, Washington is second to none in the practice of administrative law. The federal government and its agencies continue to seek the services of qualified lawyers in such policy and regulatory areas as health care, food and drugs, and communications. The recent change in political administrations will open up many new and challenging legal positions in the city. Competition for these positions will be intense, particularly in view of the increasing number of lawyers seeking positions as a result of the national economic downturn during the past few years.

The Washington area offers unparalleled diversity in private-sector employment options for lawyers as well, including positions in local law firms, corporations, nonprofit organizations, and academia. In the past decade, many Washington law firms have broadened their historically administrative practices to include fields such as commercial and white-collar litigation and sophisticated business transactions. Washington law firms represent major international and national clients and continue to compete for local business in a region that has become the fourth largest standard metropolitan statistical area in the nation.

Washington's attraction involves more than its unique professional opportunities. The city boasts diverse communities surrounding the metropolitan area, an abundance of public and private cultural attractions, nationally recognized schools, professional sports teams, popular outdoor recreation areas, well-developed roads, a comprehensive public transportation system, and moderate, seasonal weather.

As area law firms position themselves for the next decade of legal practice in Washington, continued growth remains important. Many firms have grown either by building on existing strengths or by expanding into new, complementary practice areas as they seek to better serve key clients.

While no dramatic trends are evident among the various sizes and types of Washington area firms—local, suburban, regional, national, international, and the boutiques—there remains a healthy mix of opportunities in all such firms. National and international law firms with foreign clients affected by U.S. legislation and regulation are a growing presence in Washington. Opportunities for litigation and corporate transactions for these clients abound. Boutique law firms practicing in such specialty areas as food-and-drug regulation, intellectual property, labor, and telecommunications have maintained or expanded their practices.

Specific opportunities for lateral associates exist at all levels, particularly in such practice areas as white-collar litigation, food-and-drug regulation, environmental law, and intellectual property. Furthermore, recent reductions in the numbers of real estate and corporate associates ultimately will result in a shortage of skilled junior lawyers in these fields as the economy picks up speed.

Lateral associates seeking positions in Washington are wise to utilize the city's bountiful resources in their search. Within the legislative, executive, and judicial branches of government, there are thousands of lawyer positions. Contacting friends and acquaintances from law school and personally becoming part of the vast informal job network among the region's 35,000-plus lawyers is a good way to identify opportunities. For those with two years' or more work experience and strong academic credentials, other options are available. An efficient network of legal search consultants exists in Washington as it does in other large metropolitan areas.

The federal government has traditionally been and remains one of Washington's largest employers. Because of some reduction in the number of law firm associate positions available, the quality of job applicants for federal positions appears to have risen sharply in recent years. While law firms still recruit government lawyers to fill positions requiring specific expertise such as white-collar or environmental law, no significant increase in law firm recruiting from government agencies will occur.

In-house options are on the rise in Washington. The growth in members of the American Corporate Counsel Association's local chapter over the past decade reflects an increase in the number of corporate lawyers in Washington. Several large corporations, such as the Mobil Oil Company and General Dynamics, have relocated to Washington during the past decade. Prospects for further relocations appear good as other corporations recognize the many advantages of the region. The corporate sector will continue to add jobs to the Washington area legal community.

In summary, Washington offers diverse and challenging employment opportunities for lawyers. Many factors draw lawyers to the city—its highly educated workforce, good schools, temperate climate, midlocation along the East Coast, and proximity both to attractive recreational opportunities and to the federal government. No doubt, these factors will continue to draw legal talent to Washington, D.C., in the future as they have in the past.

MARYLAND

Baltimore's urban renewal effort in recent years, referred to regionally as the "Baltimore Renaissance," has produced one of the most inviting and stimulating downtown areas nationwide. Governmental and private sectors have worked closely together in carefully planning the city's development, and the resulting strong sense of "neighborhood" has bolstered the residents' spirits and determination. Tourism has remained strong, providing a stable economic base for countless local businesses. While private service–sector businesses employ the majority of the workforce, more than 20 percent of the workforce is employed by the government, a balance that has served to promote stability and keep Baltimore's unemployment below the national average.

Paralleling the national trend, residential and commercial real estate development has slowed dramatically in recent years. Baltimore, however, has fared better than most major metropolitan areas, and there are signs that the residential market is rebounding and commercial projects are on the rise.

Baltimore's legal community also was affected by tough economic times and the slowing of the real estate market. Large law firm salaries stabilized and some firms were forced to lay off staff and associates. In 1992, the starting salaries at major Baltimore firms ranged from the upper $30,000s to $60,000. At most firms, this did not represent an increase over 1991 salaries. Starting salaries for governmental and corporate jobs vary widely, but it is safe to assume that a move from a private firm to one of these positions will involve a $5,000 to $10,000 cut. Sadly, one of Baltimore's most well-respected large firms, Frank, Bernstein, Conaway and Goldman, could not weather the storm and dissolved. In the aftermath of the dissolution, the Baltimore legal community rallied together, and firms, large and small, stretched to make room for almost 100 lawyers affected by the breakup.

Baltimore has attracted branch offices of several major national firms. These branch offices have thrived and provide very attractive career opportunities for local lawyers. Additionally, several small and medium-sized firms with lower overhead have strengthened in recent years and have not been so significantly handicapped by economic factors as the national firms have.

During the past several years, certain practices have boomed, while others have diminished significantly. For example, bankruptcy has emerged on the scene as a hot practice area, while transactional work has slowed to a crawl. Litigation has remained a strong practice area, giving rise to several very well-respected litigation boutique firms.

Baltimore also has witnessed a recent upturn in in-house opportunities. The insurance industry, in particular, has pushed to bring an increasing amount of its legal work in-house. Nevertheless, it seems there is always a shortage of corporate opportunities relative to demand. When openings do occur, corporate recruiters are typically searching for lawyers with four to six years' experience. The majority of opportunities for lawyers in corporations occur in either litigation or corporate practice areas.

Baltimore remains an excellent choice for lawyers for both personal and professional reasons. Ideally situated geographically, Baltimore is a short day trip away from Washington, D.C., New York, the beaches, and the mountains. Baltimore firms offer a more relaxed working environment than many firms in other major metropolitan areas. Because the client base often comprises local and regional companies, a lawyer has a realistic chance of developing strong, personal client relationships. Expectations about billable hours vary from firm to firm, but generally they are not so rigid as in many other major markets. Lawyers choosing to practice in Baltimore will find a diverse and stable legal community. The reasonable cost of living, combined with the wealth of cultural activities, provide an ideal setting in which to live and work.

The practice of law in the remainder of the state of Maryland is quite different from the practice in Baltimore. Western Maryland and the Eastern

Shore offer a relaxed lifestyle and more provincial practice. The majority of lawyers have general practices either in small firms or as solo practitioners. Annapolis, the state capital, offers a thriving legislative practice and when the real estate market boomed, was home to a number of zoning and land-use lawyers.

The Maryland counties that border on Washington, D.C., offer quite varied opportunities for lawyers. Several prominent Washington firms have offices in suburban Maryland. Additionally, this area is home to several midsized firms boasting very sophisticated practices in litigation, transactional, and regulatory matters. The salary range generally is higher than in Baltimore but not often competitive with the Washington, D.C., market. Many lawyers find the ideal lifestyle in suburban Maryland. The area offers excellent schools, a stable economy, nearby cultural and recreational activities, and beautifully planned neighborhoods.

DELAWARE

Wilmington, the center of commercial activity in Delaware, offers a unique blend of practice areas. Many lawyers engage in local practice, handling the day-to-day legal needs of individuals and commercial entities. Because of the significance of Delaware law to major national corporations, however, lawyers in Wilmington are exposed to some of the most sophisticated deals on a national level. Often, this business arises as the result of referrals from major law firms throughout the country. Therefore, lawyers in Delaware are able to enjoy the lifestyle offered by a smaller metropolitan area while maintaining a challenging practice.

Economic changes have slowed the business boom enjoyed by Wilmington during the 1980s. In the past few months, however, the business community's spirits have been lifted by the movement of the headquarters of a major national company to the downtown area. Additionally, there are renewed talks of the development of a convention center, and minor league baseball and basketball have been welcomed to the area.

Perhaps one of the strongest appeals of Delaware is its location. The state offers beautiful and affordable housing with an attractive tax structure. The salary structure at the largest firms and at the branches of out-of-state firms is competitive with the Philadelphia area.

Maine, New Hampshire, and Vermont

Catherine V. Swift
Joanna Piepgrass

MAINE

Quality of life generally is agreed to be the "Maine" attraction for businesses and individuals coming to the state. A different kind of growth consciousness in Maine centers on capitalization of homegrown strengths and resources. Rather than "smokestack chasing"—luring industry and jobs from other regions—the more viable strategy for economic development has been away from Fortune 500 divisions and toward entrepreneurial, small, closely held businesses within the state.

Several positives affect Maine's economic climate, including a strong work ethic, a distinct lack of crime, few racial disharmonies, a lack of congestion, an integrated transportation network, a clean environment, good recreational opportunities, high-quality cultural opportunities, and well-functioning cities because of the population's commitment to the area.

Workers' compensation is creating difficulties in attracting and keeping businesses here, thus affecting the growth of this legal practice area. Because of the failures of Maine Savings Bank and the Bank of New England (the parent company of Maine National Bank), access to credit for small businesses has been difficult until recently. Most economists agree, however, that the biggest factors affecting Maine's overall economy are the Tax Reform Act of 1986, which deflated the real estate bubble of the 1980s, and the defense industry boom-then-bust during the Reagan years, which accounted for the largest percentage of Maine job losses during the early 1990s.

Opportunities in bankruptcy law, which accompanied the bleak economic picture of the late 1980s, generally are considered to be on the decline and are being replaced by specializations in commercial law. Health-care and environmental law are becoming the focus of several larger firms in southern Maine, along with tax specializations and labor/employment law practices. A trend is foreseen, over the next five years, in which the numerous corporations in the state initiate the hiring of in-house lawyers.

The University of Maine School of Law, located in Portland, is the only law school in the state. It has an enrollment of 270. Admission to the Maine bar is by examination only. Reciprocity allows candidates to transfer in all multistate scores. With an MBE of 155-plus, one is eligible for a two-question examination. Candidates who have been actively practicing for three-plus years are eligible for the modified Maine state examination. Fees are $250 for new graduates, $500 for lawyers admitted over one year. (Write or call for more information: Maine Bar Association, Board of Overseers, P.O. Box 1820, Augusta, ME 04332, (207) 623-1121.)

NEW HAMPSHIRE

New Hampshire saw tremendous growth throughout the entire state during the 1980s. After a period of some population migration out of the state beginning in late 1988, the total population growth has increased 10 percent from 1980 to the early 1990s. Although unemployment is currently at 8.3 percent, approximately 6,000 jobs have been created in the 1992–93 period. Permanent job losses have occurred in banking and manufacturing, for the state lost five of its seven largest banks and the cost of manufacturers' operations rose. The real estate market also is depressed because of overbuilding and excessive inventory. A list of the most influential industries and corporations in the state includes Digital, Lockheed, Raytheon, Cabletron, and General Electric. Only three or four businesses employ more than 1,000 employees.

New businesses find that power rates are high and the impact of workers' compensation is an issue. Banks generally are conservative and have limited the availability of credit and start-up loans. By the same token, regional development councils, the FDA, and the state Business Finance Authority have flourished. The overall tax structure in New Hampshire is attractive to many individuals and corporations. There is no personal income tax or state sales tax. A business profits tax is paid by a small percentage of businesses.

Law firms have consistently grown within the past two to three years. Firms located in Boston, for instance, are opening up satellite offices in New Hampshire. Manchester, the largest city in the state, is only 53 miles from Boston; it also features the lowest taxes for small businesses of any city in the United States. Law firms in the state capital, Concord, practice in the areas of government, medicine/health care, and insurance. The medical profession is a growth industry in Concord because of Concord Hospital, the largest hospital in the state. Chubb Life corporate headquarters are located in Concord as well. Small businesses, such as those involved in electronics manufacturing and printing, remain strong in this region.

There is one law school in New Hampshire. Franklin Pierce Law Center is located in Concord; it has 374 students. Admission to the New Hampshire bar is by examination only; there is no reciprocity with any other state. Examinations are administered by the state supreme court. Passing scores are 140 for the MBE and 280 overall. Third-year students, under Rule 36, can apply to "practice" under supervision of an already admitted lawyer in every court except the supreme court. Write or call for more information: New Hampshire Supreme Court, Noble Drive, Concord, NH 03301, (603) 271-2646.

VERMONT

The quality of life has been a major factor in locating businesses and residences in Vermont since the late 1960s. Supposedly, IBM is a presence in the state in part because the owner was a regular vacationer in Vermont. In fact, many owners of "nonhomegrown" businesses in the state were visitors to the state at one time or another. Despite the absence of corporate headquarters, businesses and industries maintain a strong tie to the state.

The population has grown at the rate of 1 percent to 2 percent over the past five years, with unemployment just under 7 percent in 1992. Eighty percent of businesses in Vermont employ 20 or fewer employees. Vermont has experienced moderate economic growth in recent years. Vermont strongly supports creative and expanding businesses that are environmentally sound community members. There is a vibrant, still growing, specialty food industry in the state. Ben & Jerry's Ice Cream, with 450 employees, is one of the top 25 employers. Between 1991 and 1992, this company's sales grew by 25 percent, and the company increased the number of its employees by 15 percent. Vermont is the nation's leader of captive insurance companies.

Manufacturing jobs are down over the past five years, reflecting an overall trend in the Northeast. While Vermont did not suffer numerically from defense industry losses, it was affected in percentages of supplies and vacationers from the states (specifically Massachusetts and Connecticut) that suffered more immediate decreases in terms of government contracts and jobs.

Internally generated setbacks to the state economy have resulted from factors such as environmental legislation and workers' compensation costs. Vermont was not dramatically impacted by the real estate boom seen in both Maine and New Hampshire during the 1980s. Real estate development has been slow because of the consistently shrinking household size and the lengthy review process. Vermont's environmental regulations, however, create more than enough work for lawyers specializing in this area. In fact, Vermont Law School has been ranked number one in environmental law three years in a row by the *U.S. News and World Report* survey of U.S. law schools. The law school offers a master's program in environmental law. Enrollment is 484 at Vermont Law School, located in South Royalton.

Corporate downsizing, which has produced a concomitant decrease in outside counsel lists, has had an impact on law firm practice in this state. For example, AETNA recently cut the number of law firms that it used from 12 to less than five.

Admission to the Vermont bar is by examination with a six-month internship if not admitted elsewhere; or if waiving the examination, one must have been actively practicing for five of the past ten years (unless the jurisdiction that one practices in allows the Vermont minimum of three years) with a three-month law office study. Passing scores are 135+ on the MBE and 36+ on the six-question essay portion. Fees include $15 for the examination package, $240 for filing, $600 for motion for admission, and $25 for law office study or clerkship. Vermont is one of the few states that offers a four-year law office study program in lieu of juris doctorate studies. The preceding is a simplified overview of the Vermont Board of Examiner's rules of admissions. (As the rules of admission are subject to change, write for a copy of the rules to State of Vermont, Board of Bar Examiners, 109 State Street, Montpelier, VT 05609-0702.)

Massachusetts and Rhode Island

Brion A. Bickerton

The New England economy was hit hard by the nationwide recession in the late 1980s. During this period, law firms overly dependent on the commercial real estate market faltered. As banks failed, firms either developed FDIC-related bank work, workout work, or bank-related litigation (such as lender-liability and bank-fraud suits) or suffered. Larger firms pared their ranks of associates and partners with weak practice bases.

Litigation practice boomed, a result of busted business deals, troubled banks and real estate projects, and heightened government enforcement in environmental and bank-fraud matters. Bankruptcy became the hot field. Lending lawyers became workout lawyers. As firms sought ways to develop more business, some were prompted to become more regional in nature. Massachusetts firms branched into Connecticut, Rhode Island, and New Hampshire, and Connecticut firms branched into Massachusetts.

MASSACHUSETTS

While certain engines of growth of the 1980s have been silenced—defense industry buildup, real estate, and banking—many Massachusetts industries are establishing a more sustained, though less spectacular growth pattern, including mutual funds (such as Fidelity and other funds) and the money-management industry; biotechnology; health care (including many of the country's leading teaching hospitals) and related medical technology; environmental services (encouraged by an early progreen atmosphere); and the software industry. Massachusetts's highly educated workforce and its strong university system and related research laboratories will ensure the state is at the forefront of these important growth industries.

There are approximately 41,000 lawyers in Massachusetts, practicing primarily in Boston, its surrounding suburbs, and in the smaller cities of Worcester and Springfield. The top 100 firms in Massachusetts range in size from ten lawyers to almost 300 lawyers. Because many sophisticated companies operate throughout Massachusetts, lawyers in the suburbs and outlying areas have a surprisingly sophisticated corporate client base.

Boston. Boston's law firm market is highly diverse. The larger firms range in size from 100 to 300 lawyers. Many of the firms have doubled in size since 1986. While there was once discussion nationally (in the boom days of the later 1980s) of the demise of midsized firms, there is a thriving group of midsized firms of 30 to 100 lawyers that provide a viable alternative to the larger firms. Boston is home to more than a dozen branch offices of major firms. Each year, a major out-of-state firm establishes a Boston branch office. Some of the branch offices have mushroomed in size to more than 50 lawyers.

An active and strong patent firm practice exists in Boston, based on the vibrant high-technology industry base in the area. Reflecting the diversity of the Massachusetts economy, many areas of practice remain strong—general commercial litigation, intellectual property, mutual funds, health care, environmental, and insurance litigation.

Although Boston's law schools provide ample numbers of lawyers, there still is room for lawyers from out of state. The major firms are highly selective but are interested in superior lawyers from a wide range of schools. While the hiring of lateral lawyers is widely accepted, few partner-level positions are available for lawyers without portable client bases.

The remainder of the 1990s probably will not see much demand for partner-level lawyers. Beginning associate salaries at the top Boston firms have held steady in the $66,000 to $68,000 range for the past few years and are not expected to climb much in the early 1990s. Any moderate salary increases are expected to mirror the trends nationally. First-year salaries in the smaller Boston firms range from $25,000 to $50,000.

Most larger firms have established a two-tier partnership structure featuring equity and nonequity partners. Partnership track periods are lengthening and are expected to average seven to eight years for nonequity partnerships and a further three to four years for equity partnership openings. Fewer equity partnerships will be offered during the 1990s. The average billable hours requirement is 2,000 hours per year, with a range of 1,700 to 2,600 hours. This number has been rising because firms have trimmed staff in recent difficult economic times.

Worcester.   Worcester firms vary in size from solo practitioners to firms with 65 lawyers, with several firms hovering in the 15 to 35 range. Worcester has a vibrant corporate practice bolstered by the area's historic manufacturing base, complemented recently by the establishment of a biotechnology park. Salaries start at $45,000 at the largest firms and range from the mid-$20,000s to $30,000s at most other firms for first-year lawyers. Despite the recession, legal practice has remained constant in the area.

Springfield.   The largest law firm employs 40 lawyers, two firms have 15 to 20, and thereafter, the sizes are small. Springfield previously had a strong financial-services industry, but much of that has taken a severe beating during the recession, which has adversely affected the commercial lending and real estate practice in the area. Salaries are similar to those in Worcester.

RHODE ISLAND

While Rhode Island has suffered along with the New England economy in recent times, its experience has been less severe for it was less dependent on the defense industry. The historic factors (congestion and high land values in nearby Massachusetts) that have brought a broad corporate base to Rhode Island continue as an encouragement for Massachusetts industry to relocate to Rhode Island. Rhode Island benefits from the success of Fleet Bank, which has become the powerhouse bank in New England.

Rhode Island's legal market is concentrated in Providence, an ideal location for lawyers seeking a small metropolitan setting close to Boston and New York. The top 25 law firms in Rhode Island range in size from 100 lawyers to seven lawyers. While the strongest corporate practices are located in the top ten firms, there are a wide range of firms with good commercial practices. Several Boston firms have established successful branch offices in Providence.

Because Rhode Island does not have a law school, Providence firms rely extensively on out-of-state lawyers to fill positions. Reflecting its proximity to the Boston market, the top corporate firms in Providence start associates at $55,000 to $60,000. Salaries for first-year lawyers at smaller to midsized firms scale down considerably into the $20,000s and $30,000s.

Connecticut and New Jersey

Richards Gordon

CONNECTICUT

Connecticut's economy has had a heavy impact on the legal profession as the state continues to try to rebound from the real estate woes of the late 1980s and early 1990s. Unemployment remains somewhat higher than that of the national average and is not expected to change significantly over the next few years.

Insurance companies and financial institutions, the largest employers in the Hartford area, were not spared the major real estate problems of the past few years. Companies that invested heavily in real estate were especially hard hit. One major bank that concentrated much of its portfolio in real estate did not survive and a Fortune 100 real estate company that also invested heavily in real estate has been the subject of media attention concerning its financial woes. The federal government's deregulation of the banking industry improved the outlook for Connecticut financial institutions somewhat, for out-of-state institutions have established branches or merged with Connecticut banks. Stamford Fortune 1000 companies also experienced staffing reductions because this difficult period encouraged needed cost-reduction.

Connecticut's primary legal markets are Hartford, Stamford, New Haven–Bridgeport, and the Waterbury–Danbury area. Hartford's legal market has been positively affected by the influx of out-of-state banks and bank mergers in the financial-services industry, for several out-of-state major firms from Boston and Rhode Island established satellite offices to respond to the greater regional needs of their clients. Additionally, one major Hartford firm recently announced its intent to merge with a midsized Boston firm.

Increasing emphasis is being placed on the ability of law firms to react to the wider geographical needs of their clients. Commercial lending and bankruptcy continue to be dominant practice areas because of the number of financial institutions in Hartford. Environmental and health-care practices have continued to grow at a number of firms, albeit slowly. Additionally, because of the region's real estate problems, a number of firms and corporations have added experienced real estate/workout lawyers.

Hiring at major firms over the past few years in practice areas other than those previously mentioned has been minimal. Junior associates who have been hired have included general civil and employment litigators. On the senior associate/partner level, firms have been especially attracted to lawyers with significant business, regardless of practice area. Hartford is an increasingly competitive marketplace that has a small number of major firms with more than 100 lawyers and several prominent firms of 60 to 90 lawyers. The Stamford legal market services Fortune 1000 companies concentrating in high technology, the service sector, and manufacturing.

While the largest firm employs more than 120 lawyers, a number of firms in Stamford are branch offices of major firms from Hartford, New York, and Los Angeles that employ 25 lawyers or less. With the downturn in the real estate industry, hiring at the associate level has been minimal, and some firms have implemented hiring freezes. Available positions generally have been in bankruptcy/workout, litigation, and certain specialties. Corporations in Connecticut will continue their conservative in-house counsel hiring practices in the near term. Bridgeport, New Haven, Greenwich, Fairfield, Westport, and Waterbury also have suffered with the economic slowdown, but there are signs that these legal markets may be rebounding slowly.

In general, the legal market appears to be improving modestly in Connecticut. While fewer lawyers are becoming partners at the major firms, associate hiring is improving slowly, in part because of the arrival of branch offices of several out-of-state firms. Starting salaries in 1993 at the major Hartford and New Haven firms varied from $55,000 to $60,000, with the major firms in Stamford paying slightly more. For those lawyers situated at branch offices of major out-of-state firms, first-year salaries may reach $70,000 to $72,000. At smaller firms or firms in more rural areas, salaries are lower and the range of these starting salaries is greater.

As New England eases out of its real estate woes and financial institutions ease their lending practices, more real estate and corporate positions at all levels may open up in Connecticut in the coming years. Other practice areas that individuals should consider in the next few years include litigation, bankruptcy/workout, and specialties such as intellectual property. Trust and estates lawyers are in demand whether the economy is doing poorly or not.

NEW JERSEY

New Jersey also suffered from the economic problems of the late 1980s and early 1990s. Law firms were forced to slow their normal associate hiring practices. Additionally, deferrals or rejections of partnership at the major firms became more commonplace. With improvement in the economy, New Jersey firms should accelerate their hiring practices in the next few years. Corporations may be expected to add lawyers as needed. More corporations are hiring counsel as a means of aggressively managing their outside legal costs.

Pennsylvania

Sandra G. Mannix
Susan E. Kraybill

PHILADELPHIA

Sandra G. Mannix

The phrase "Philadelphia lawyer" has two opposing definitions—an able but conservative lawyer ("a belt *and* suspenders lawyer") or one treading a thin ethical line. In truth, like other cities, large or small, Philadelphia has its share of lawyers from both groups among the approximately 19,500 lawyers in the five-county metropolitan area. More than 12,000 lawyers practice in the city, 25 percent of them female, 10 percent minority group members. But whichever definition is more accurate, the city's venerable legal history is unchallenged.

America's fifth largest city, Philadelphia is a former manufacturing center making the difficult transition to service or technology-based businesses, especially biotechnology and pharmaceuticals, while losing many other businesses to the suburbs. The city itself has 16 professional schools, 12 colleges/universities, and more than 40 hospitals. One of every eight private-sector workers in the area owes his or her job to a hospital. There are three additional law schools and dozens of other colleges, universities, and hospitals in the suburbs.

The city remains, however, the region's cultural, banking, venture capital, insurance, accounting, investment, and transportation center and is home to local, state, and federal courts, and offices and agencies that provide opportunities for public-service law employment. Recent budgetary and hiring restrictions, however, have reduced greatly the available number of such positions. In 1992, banking and manufacturing in the area were up more than 30 percent, pharmaceuticals and health care more than 20 percent, transportation 12 percent, chemicals 7 percent, and services 5 percent.

A new mayor and city administration have negotiated new union contracts to ensure municipal labor stability for several years, and a new convention center will enhance the city's active tourist and convention business. The Philadelphia Orchestra and Museum of Art are internationally respected. Many smaller museums, the Eagles, Phillies, 76ers, Flyers, and sports activities ranging from some of the nation's finest collegiate basketball and field sports to curling, cricket, and polo also attract national and international visitors.

Philadelphia has extraordinary ethnic diversity and retains several traditional, ethnic neighborhoods. The Ninth Street open-air market often is called the "Italian Market," although there are significant numbers of African-American, Asian, and Hispanic merchants. The city now has (by percentage) the largest Soviet émigré population in the United States with its newest major group of immigrants from the former Soviet Union.

More than 20 percent of America's population live within a 300-mile radius of Philadelphia. The area's 4.91 million residents enjoy a lower unemployment rate than that of the nation or state. A $1-billion renovation increased the airport's daily number of flights to 1,200, making it easier for local lawyers to conduct business throughout the world. The port of Philadelphia annually handles about 68.5 million tons of import goods and 6.3 million tons of export goods. Many larger law firms and a surprising number of smaller, specialty firms do business with companies throughout the world. A number of larger firms have European offices. Office vacancy rates are low at 11.1 percent, as is the per-square-foot cost of prime center city office space at $24.50, the lowest figure among major American cities. Suburban office space is even less expensive, averaging $15.25.

The city's hundreds of law firms, from solo practitioners to international firms with more than 700 lawyers, vary from local firms tracing their origins to the American Revolution to relatively new branches of firms with main offices located in other major cities. At least 18 firms with headquarters in Philadelphia employ more than 100 lawyers; three firms employ more than 300 lawyers. Despite recent, well-publicized reorganizations by a few major firms, most city firms appear to remain economically healthy and vigorous in their pursuit of new clients and expanded business. During the 1980s' economic boom, many larger firms moved to spacious quarters in new buildings or engaged in major redecorating projects, so the physical facilities for a significant number of firms are most attractive and highly functional, incorporating the latest technological advances in the daily practice of law.

Although the employment market for new lawyers remains tight, positions for lateral hires, particularly in specialty areas (litigation, and environmental, corporate, and intellectual property law), always can be found. Starting salaries in 1992–1993 for major firm associates averaged $63,000, with expected billable hours ranging from 1,800 to 2,100 per year. The usual partnership period is eight years. There generally is no prejudice against lateral hires in awarding partnerships.

Philadelphia's cost of living and housing prices remain relatively low for a major urban area. The average price of an eight-room, 3,200-square-foot home in one of the area's well-known suburbs is $200,000 to $300,000, half the cost of comparable San Francisco, New York, or Washington homes. More than half of the area homes are affordable for medium-income families. Excellent area public, private, and parochial schools appeal to parents. A regional transit system provides efficient public transportation from most suburban areas to the city.

An exceptionally large number of area not-for-profit institutions and corporations provide appealing law firm alternatives. In-house corporate counsel hiring competition is extremely heavy. Benefits and remuneration usually are excellent, with annual average compensation in salary and bonuses of $215,000. Extremely interesting work in the not-for-profit sector helps compensate for generally lower salaries and benefits. Environmental organizations, child-protection agencies, women's organizations, educational institutions, and other not-for-profit groups provide lawyers with emotionally rewarding and socially important work opportunities.

All major firms in the area have made significant commitments to pro bono and/or nonlegal volunteer work by their lawyers, some even requiring a certain number of hours of this work within their expected annual billable hours. The Philadelphia Bar Association's Volunteers for the Indigent Program, The Women's Law Project, Volunteer Lawyers for the Arts, and numerous other lawyer groups supply critically needed legal services to a variety of individuals and groups. And any list of the boards of directors and supporters of Philadelphia's charitable, educational, and cultural institutions shows disproportionally high representation by the city's lawyers, who are most generous with their time, money, and expertise.

Philadelphia's 25 largest firms (about 25 percent of the city's lawyers) range in size from 655 (202 in the city) to 75 (72 in Philadelphia). The largest firm grossed $220 million in 1992, with average partner profits of $355,000. Two slightly smaller firms with 315 and 342 lawyers grossed $97 million ($245,000 per partner) and $104 million ($285,000 per partner), respectively. Average billing charges among the top firms range from partners' rates of $125 to $340/hour to associates' rates of $65 to $210/hour. The number of support staff ranges from 525 for 383 lawyers to 87 for 75 lawyers. Support staff outnumber lawyers at all major firms. Most larger firms identify themselves as practicing all of the major areas of law, but about half a dozen see themselves as more highly specialized, particularly in the areas of litigation, labor, or environmental law.

Almost 7,000 lawyers actively practice in the four surrounding Pennsylvania counties. Fifteen of the city's largest firms have at least one office in these counties to serve clients who live in or have their companies in the suburbs. Several years ago, prospects for successful practice, particularly in the county seats, even for solo practitioners or small firms were good. Increased competition, especially from young lawyers entering practice, and economic downsizing make this type of practice more risky today. Lawyers considering suburban practice should examine closely their ability to generate sufficient billable hours to cover operating costs and meet their desired standards of living. Only a few suburban law firm lawyers' salaries compare to those of major firms' lawyers. Many suburban partners consider $75,000 to $80,000 a good annual salary. Unlike lawyers in major firms, however, suburban lawyers generally work from nine to five, with few or no weekend or evening hours.

While the city of Philadelphia is proud of its many national or international "firsts"—from hospital and public school to revolving door and merry-go-round—it no longer is content to look only to its history and past successes. The city of *Kitty Foyle* and *The Philadelphia Story* is now the city of *Rocky* and *thirtysomething*. The transition to new businesses, new ways of doing business, and new markets has not been and is not always easy, but there is a new sense of unity and purpose in the city, and lawyers once again are finding it a challenging and rewarding practice environment.

PITTSBURGH

Susan E. Kraybill

Pittsburgh occupies a unique place in the nation's legal climate. The combination of an East Coast business climate and midwestern lifestyle offers Pittsburgh lawyers a rewarding combination of sophisticated legal practice and quality of life. Historically, Pittsburgh's iron ore, coal, and river and rail transportation made the city the world's center of steel making. During the early 1900s, Pittsburgh was one of the industrial centers of the world, its dominance in steel and related manufacturing complemented by prominent representation in railroads, oil, glass, and paper.

Today, Pittsburgh still boasts the nation's fourth greatest number of corporate headquarters and is rated as the third best city for business. Home to USX, Westinghouse, Alcoa, PPG Industries, H. J. Heinz, Miles, Allegheny Ludlum, Kennametal, Mine Safety Appliances, Amsco International, Dravo, Calgon Carbon, L. B. Foster, Ampco-Pittsburgh, Joy Technologies, Mellon Bank, and PNC Financial, Pittsburgh enjoys a sophisticated business climate that generates interesting legal work. Pittsburgh law firms also benefit from their proximity to northwestern Pennsylvania and northern West Virginia, headquarters for numerous significant coal, oil, and steel companies such as

Quaker State Corporation and Weirton Steel, the nation's largest employee-owned company.

It is not surprising, therefore, that Pittsburgh has one lawyer for every 250 people—perhaps the highest ratio in the country after Washington, D.C. The two largest law firms headquartered in Pittsburgh each employ approximately 200 lawyers in Pittsburgh and 350 nationwide. Two others employ more than 150 locally and more than 200 nationally. Eight more firms employ 50 to 100 lawyers, and 14 firms employ 25 to 50. Six Pittsburgh firms appear in *Of Counsel* magazine's *1992 Guide to the 500 Largest Law Firms* (May 4–18, 1992). One ranked as the tenth fastest-growing firm in the country from 1991 to 1992, and, virtually unique among the major cities, *none* of them declined in size during that period.

At the large firms, starting salaries averaged $65,000 in 1992 and thus were comparable to other major U.S. cities, with the exception of New York, Los Angeles, and Washington, D.C. Large firms require 1,800 to 2,000 billable hours per year and offer a partnership track of eight to 12 years. Billing rates are comparable to other major cities such as Washington, D.C., Boston, and Los Angeles.

Pittsburgh is justifiably known as a hardworking, honest town with old-fashioned family values. In 1985, it was named the Most Liveable City in the United States by the *Places Rated Almanac* (and still third most liveable in the 1989 study) and in 1991, the safest city in the United States with a population of more than one million. It is notable that many who seek fame and fortune elsewhere return quickly to Pittsburgh when the time comes to raise children.

A number of resources are available to job seekers in this region. The Allegheny County Bar Association has a placement office, as do both the University of Pittsburgh Law School and Duquesne University Law School. The local recruiters can be found listed in the directories of legal recruiters published by the National Association of Legal Search Consultants, *The American Lawyer*, and *The National Law Journal*. The Sunday edition of the *Pittsburgh Post-Gazette* and the daily *Pittsburgh Legal Journal* carry advertisements for legal positions. The *Pittsburgh Business Times* publishes the *Book of Lists*, which ranks the 25 largest local employers in a wide variety of industries. Martindale-Hubbell and *The Law and Business Directory of Corporate Counsel* (published by Prentice Hall) are still the most complete directories for law firms and corporations. For those who want current information about an employer (other than what is available in an annual report), the Carnegie Business Library in downtown Pittsburgh keeps a clipping file made up of news items about local employers. The Carnegie also has computerized lists of companies that can be searched by industry, size, etc.

If you live in Pittsburgh and are trying to find a job locally, you have a distinct advantage over people who must relocate to the area. Employers prefer not to relocate outsiders for two reasons: the expense and the possibility that the new hire will not stay and will at some point want to return to his or her hometown. If you are not from Pittsburgh, be prepared to answer the question, "Why would you relocate here?" If you have family here or close by, be absolutely sure to mention that to the prospective employer.

Once you have identified a position for which you are qualified, the first test, and the test toughest to gauge, is "the fit." Employers look for employees whose personalities, personal chemistry, ambition, and aggressiveness blend with others in the organization. The Pittsburgh style tends to be more Midwest than East Coast, and what is accepted in New York as confident and aggressive may be perceived in Pittsburgh as arrogant and abrasive. You are not off the hook either, California; the laid-back, go-with-the-flow approach could be viewed by the sons and daughters of the hardworking steelworkers as not industrious enough. Ability, enthusiasm, and a cooperative team spirit will score lots of points in Pittsburgh.

Southeast

Lee Ann Bellon

Atlanta, Georgia, will host the 1996 Summer Olympics; North Carolina's research triangle is nationally recognized for its growth in high-technology companies; Florida continues to be the destination of choice for many from colder climates; and the president of the United States hails from Little Rock, Arkansas. These are just a few of the developments that have led to the perception that the Southeast is one of the hottest employment markets in the country. In fact, during the height of the recession, a number of lawyers were so convinced that the Southeast was the land of opportunity that they packed up their families and moved to the region with nary a job prospect to their name. Unfortunately, some of them were sorely disappointed.

While the Southeast is a thriving region and new opportunities do exist, obstacles must be overcome in making a successful transition to the region. First, job opportunities are concentrated in a few metropolitan areas. Many smaller communities continue to lag in both lateral hiring and compensation. Second, a number of previously prosperous southeastern cities were hit hard by the oil crisis and the recent recession, resulting in anemic growth in locations such as Birmingham and New Orleans. Third, law firms prefer to hire lawyers who have some significant ties to the region. Many have relocated families from other areas of the country only to discover that the regional differences were too strong or home was too far away for the family to adjust. Finally, entrance to the bar of many southeastern states may present the most significant obstacle. Many southeastern bar associations offer limited reciprocity and have an expensive and time-consuming application process and strict bar rules, making it difficult for employers to hire lawyers who have not passed the state's bar examination. Therefore, before deciding to relocate to the Southeast, it is important to clearly understand what the state bar rules are, where growth has already occurred, and which practice areas have current and future potential.

For instance, while Atlanta has earned national recognition and is continuing its development as an international city, overly enthusiastic real estate development in the 1980s has led to an abundance of vacant office space in the 1990s. While construction of large, multiuse developments has slowed significantly, strip shopping center developments, fast-food companies, and large outlet stores continue to be built. There is fierce competition for the existing deals, however, and construction lawyers are struggling. On the other hand, in south Florida, the devastation caused by Hurricane Andrew and the recovery efforts required undoubtedly will lead to a huge demand for lawyers with those skills.

As previously noted, most southeastern states have one or two metropolitan centers in which legal activity and hiring is concentrated. Tennessee, Kentucky, Georgia, South Carolina, and Arkansas are all examples of this. The exception is Florida, which has at least seven major business centers and numerous emerging areas of activity. As a result, Florida currently boasts an extensive network of state firms with branch offices in Jacksonville, Gainesville, Tampa, Orlando, Fort Lauderdale, Miami, and West Palm Beach. While a number of Florida firms do have offices in the state's capital, Tallahassee, they tend to be relatively small and focus on legislative or government practices.

Florida is also home to more branch offices of national law firms than any other southeastern state. National firms have been attracted to this state because of its phenomenal growth over the past few years. While Florida continues to lead the region as home to the largest number of national law firms, Atlanta, Georgia, is providing some competition, having welcomed at least four new national law firms in as many years. Some of this influx is the direct result of corporations moving into the area. If a major client picks up and relocates its home office, the prudent law firm will follow. Other national firms are recognizing that to have a national practice, a southeastern presence is required. Atlanta presents a cosmopolitan environment that is open and accepting. North Carolina may well become the next state to see a significant influx of national firm activity.

North Carolina escaped the recession relatively unscathed, is the home of a growing number of large corporations, and is beginning to replace Florida as the region's most desirable location.

It is interesting to note that the national law firms that have been the most successful in the Southeast are those who have made extensive use of local talent, either merging with existing firms or handpicking specialists with local ties. The success of their efforts can be attributed to the recognition that while the Southeast is becoming increasingly eclectic, it is crucial to understand the network or relationships and traditions that make the region unique.

Corporate opportunities continue to grow in the Southeast as it becomes home to an increasingly varied number of industries. Historically, the region has been known for its agricultural, mining, and textile roots. Manufacturing as well as service industries, however, continue to be drawn to the area by its pleasant climate, its reasonable cost of living, and the availability of a high-quality workforce. Even the entertainment industry is making its way south, taking advantage of the area's hospitality, beautiful filming location, and well-trained local talent. Despite the growing opportunities, lawyers interested in seeking in-house legal positions should be prepared to face tremendous competition because these positions are considered highly desirable. A word to the wise for lawyers in any region of the country—corporations can be as volatile as law firms. Do your homework.

Many lawyers are lured to the Southeast by the dream of a more affordable and slower-paced lifestyle. Is the cost of living in the Southeast lower than in other metropolitan areas in other regions of the country? Probably. Is the practice of law more low keyed and less stressful? Probably not. Southeastern employers are feeling the pressures of increasing overhead and intensified competition just like their counterparts in other regions of the country are. In addition, they sense opportunity and are eager to take advantage of it. As a result, it is more and more common to see associates required to maintain increasingly high billable hours. The Southeast no longer can afford the aura of gentility if it means being less competitive in the work marketplace. Nonetheless, southern hospitality still exists and many find the region a pleasant place to do business.

What about money and partnership opportunities? Miami, Atlanta, and Richmond continue to be the highest-paying cities in the Southeast with 1993 starting salaries ranging from $52,000 to $65,000. The starting salary range in Charlotte is $48,000 to $53,000, while beginning lawyers earn between $45,000 and $50,000 in Nashville and Memphis. Salaries tend to drop as much as $10,000 outside the major metropolitan areas. Salaries consistently increase between $2,000 and $5,000 a year for more senior associates, with only a few of the larger firms offering significant bonus programs. Of course, in some cases, modest salaries are counterbalanced by lower real estate costs. However, one of the mysteries of the region is why starting salaries continue to lag in North Carolina's research triangle, despite significantly inflated real estate, which resulted from the influx of executives of high-tech companies.

Partnership has become increasingly elusive in the cities with the most competitive compensation plans. Lawyers in Atlanta and Miami who become partners within eight years can count themselves fortunate. Many firms have multitiered partnerships with an increasing number offering permanent associate status to lawyers with technical capabilities but lacking partnership capabilities. National law firms with branch offices in the region are complicating the issue. Lawyers who practice in the branch office often find it difficult to earn the support of management committees located in a distant city. Given the difficulty of achieving partnership, an ironic trend is emerging as a growing number of lawyers are seeking to avoid equity partnership status to avoid becoming personally liable for their law firms' financial commitments.

In summary, the Southeast is like most other regions of the country. It possesses unique opportunities and has much to offer both personally and professionally. Those lawyers who hope to make the Southeast their home will be faced with special challenges. Careful research, however, combined with a well-thought-out job search plan, can lead to discovering an opportunity with potential for future growth and long-term success.

Midwest

Gary A. D'Alessio

The midwestern-based law firm, in-house corporate, government, and non-profit organization opportunities reflect the diversified economy in the region. Although fewer jobs probably will exist in the future in the transportation, steel, defense, and retail industries, more openings will arise in the environmental services and in the computer/high-technology and health-care/pharmaceutical fields. Hot areas of practice over the next ten years will be environmental, intellectual property (especially biotechnology), employment (discrimination, employee benefits, and wrongful discharge), health care, and litigation.

More than one-fifth of the country's 500 largest law firms are located in the Midwest and 53 of these have their homes or branch offices in Chicago, the service center of the Midwest. These larger firms will continue to grow at the expense of many smaller general practice firms. In today's increasingly competitive market for legal services, the smaller firms often lack the necessary resources to effectively maintain or significantly develop clients and business. Consequently, an increasingly number of these firms will either dissolve or merge their practices with larger firms. A viable alternative, however, is the "boutique," a firm specializing in one or two closely related practices such as intellectual property, litigation, or employment law and employee benefits.

Another trend in the Midwest, particularly in the larger and medium-sized firms, is the implementation of two- (or more) tiered partnerships and the initiation of new lawyer categories. The multitiered partnerships have lengthened the track to equity/income partner to eight to ten years (versus six to eight years for a one-tier partnership). In addition to the standard partner and associate classifications, firms have created the following new categories: nonequity/nonincome/nonparticipating/nonshareholder partner; provisional partner; counsel/special counsel; senior lawyer/permanent associate; staff lawyer; and part-time lawyer. These alternatives have been formed for several reasons: (1) to keep competent lawyers who will not be promoted either to partner or to the equity/income/participating/shareholder level of partner; (2) to use as a step to partnership for laterals already at or near the partner level; (3) to accommodate lawyers who choose more flexible lifestyles and prefer to work fewer hours or not develop clients; and (4) to cost-effectively staff for certain practice areas where clients will not pay higher rates. Fortunately, these additional classifications will result in more flexibility and job opportunities for lawyers.

The compensation range at midwestern firms varies greatly depending on their size and location. In 1993, large Chicago-based firms typically compensated entry-level associates at a $70,000 base salary. The starting salary at medium-sized firms generally falls within the $50,000 to $70,000 range and for smaller firms, between $30,000 and $50,000. The key criteria for determining associate compensation, however, is not a firm's size. This primarily depends on the nature of the firm's client base, the type of practice, the lawyer's billable hourly rates, and the required billable hours (which range from 1,600 to 2,400). The differential in starting salaries in smaller cities in Illinois and at other midwestern firms tends to be 20 percent to 30 percent less than the previously mentioned salaries. Firms increase associates' salaries during their first few years of practice by typically using either a "lockstep" approach (each associate within the same J.D. class year receives the same raise) or a "merit" system (raises differ based on various factors including billable hours, work performance, client and business development, and overall contribution to the firm).

The cost of living in the Midwest generally is less expensive than most East Coast and West Coast cities. The Midwest also has a reputation for offering people a friendly atmosphere that is ideal for family living. Naturally, these factors appeal to many lawyers who want to relocate here. When lateral lawyers are hired in the Midwest, however, most firms prefer lawyers, particularly litigators, who already are admitted to or can waive into their state bar. Employers feel more comfortable when the lawyer is entrenched in the local community and less likely to relocate. Therefore, experienced lawyers relocating from other states to the Midwest are generally at a disadvantage unless local qualified candidates cannot be identified for a position.

The corporate, government, and nonprofit organization employment sectors in the Midwest also offer lawyers many viable alternatives to law firm practice. The trend in a majority of the corporations is to bring more work in-house and expand their legal departments. This anticipated growth, however, will be slow. The numerous opportunities in the public sector with nonprofit organizations and government agencies at the county, state, and federal levels are drawing renewed interest from lawyers in private practice. These positions, though, are subject to funding reductions and increased competition for limited resources.

Examples of the diverse governmental agencies that hire lawyers include the following:

- United States Attorney
- Environmental Protection Agency
- Equal Employment Opportunity Commission
- Federal Deposit Insurance Corporation
- Immigration and Naturalization Service
- Internal Revenue Service
- Department of Justice
- National Labor Relations Board
- Office of the Public Guardian
- State's Attorney

Representative nonprofit organizations include the following:

- John D. and Catherine T. MacArthur Foundation (Illinois)
- Mayo Foundation (Minnesota)
- UAW (Michigan)
- American Bar Association (Illinois)

- American Medical Association (Illinois)
- National Association of Insurance Commissioners (Missouri)

There are numerous types of nonlaw firm employers of lawyers in the Midwest. The following list is representative of only a few of these: accounting firms, advertising agencies, airlines, associations, banks/savings and loan associations/multibank holding companies, benefits consultants, colleges/ universities, construction contractors, credit unions, executive and legal recruiters, foundations/charitable organizations, health-care institutions/ HMOs/hospitals/medical PPOs, labor unions, management consultants, museums, pension funds, professional societies, public-relations firms, religious organizations, trade associations, travel agencies, and venture capital firms. Pertinent information regarding many of these organizations is contained in the following publications:

- *Crain's Chicago Business, Crain's Cleveland Business,* and *Crain's Detroit Business* annual *Top Business Lists,* Crain Communications, Inc.;
- *Law & Business Directory of Corporate Counsel,* Prentice Hall Law & Business, Englewood Cliffs, NJ;
- *The Greater Chicago Job Bank 1993, The Detroit Job Bank 1993, The Minneapolis-St. Paul Job Bank 1993, The Ohio Job Bank 1993* and *The St. Louis Job Bank 1993,* Bob Adams, Inc., Holbrook, MA;
- *Jobs '93,* Kathryn and Ross Petras, Fireside–Simon & Schuster, Inc., New York, NY;
- *Chicago & Illinois Job Seekers SourceBook,* Donald D. Walker & Valerie A. Shipe, Net-Research, Bolingbrook, IL;
- *Doing Business in Chicago,* Jeffrey P. Levine, Business One Irwin, Homewood, IL;
- *First Chicago Guide, A Scholl Corporate Guide 1992–93,* Scholl Communications Incorporated, Deerfield, IL;
- *How To Get a Job in Chicago,* Thomas M. Camden and Susan Schwartz, Surrey Books, Chicago, IL;
- *The Corporate Report Fact Book 1993* (covers Minnesota, Montana, North Dakota, South Dakota, and parts of Michigan and Wisconsin), MCP, Inc., Publishers, Minneapolis, MN;
- *Corporate Report Minnesota,* a subsidiary of MCP Publishing Co., Minneapolis, MN;
- *Financial Briefs of Michigan Corporations* and *Financial Briefs of Wisconsin Corporations,* Robert W. Baird & Co. Inc., Milwaukee, WI;
- *Northern Great Lakes Job Seekers SourceBook* (covers Michigan, Minnesota, and Wisconsin), Donald D. Walker & Valerie A. Shipe, Net-Research, Bolingbrook, IL;
- *Ohio Valley Job Seekers SourceBook* (covers Indiana, Kentucky, Ohio, and Western Pennsylvania), Donald D. Walker & Valerie A. Shipe, Net-Research, Bolingbrook, IL;
- *Plains States Job Seekers SourceBook* (covers Iowa, Kansas, Nebraska, North Dakota, and South Dakota), Donald D. Walker & Valerie A. Shipe, Net-Research, Bolingbrook, IL; and

- *Southern States Job Seekers SourceBook* (includes Missouri), Donald D. Walker & Valerie A. Shipe, Net-Research, Bolingbrook, IL.

The Midwest legal community will continue to change and grow during the 1990s. Many firms have opened branch offices in this region, especially in Chicago (more than 20 firms), to service existing and newly developed clients located here. There also are many public, closely held, and privately held companies doing business or relocating their offices here. In conclusion, a demand for qualified lawyers in the diverse Midwest market still exists.

Those lawyers most likely to succeed in securing a job in the Midwest will be admitted to the bar in the state where they desire to practice. Therefore, you should position yourself accordingly to demonstrate the added value of hiring you versus a local lawyer. If not bar-admitted, you should complete the necessary application process for that state's bar examination and note this on your résumé as "Sitting for the (insert specific month and state) bar examination." It is essential to review the numerous local, regional, and national legal and general business publications that advertise legal jobs and discuss the legal and business community in a particular city or state. You also should fully utilize the wealth of information (e.g., lateral job listings, reference materials, law firm practice area descriptions, and alumni contact lists of fellow graduates presently employed in the Midwest) readily available to you at your law school's placement office. It also is advisable to contact one or more legal search firms based in the geographic area where you intend to practice. Recruiters typically have insightful information about the legal market and know about more current job openings with local employers. If you follow a well-conceived plan of action and utilize the previously mentioned multiple resources, you will have a competitive edge in finding the right job in the Midwest.

Texas

James M. Wilson, Jr.

In the words of Dizzy Dean, Texans believe that they already have "slud" as far as they can go, and optimism is in the air. True, Texas no longer owns its own banks, savings and loans, or much of its commercial real estate; Houston's air carrier just emerged from bankruptcy; and Dallas's air carrier is losing money. But one thing is clear—Texans have managed to consolidate most of the country's energy businesses in their state (including the burgeoning foreign business), while at the same time diversifying the state's economy, even if not so completely as would be desired. There is a refreshing vitality and entrepreneurial spirit in the state that is infectious. The subject of oil prices often is conspicuously absent from cocktail chatter and is being replaced with discussions about biotechnology, computers, software, information systems, and health care.

Houston probably is perceived as leading the recovery, largely as a result of having been hit harder, having bottomed out earlier, and having sustained a longer recovery. In addition, Houston's prospects are enhanced by the perception that it is a large international city, while Dallas is thought of as a regional metropolitan area whose economy depends on defense, distribution, and nonheavy manufacturing. Most other areas in Texas continue to have soft economies, with the possible exception of Austin, where early diversification in high technology and related businesses seems to have helped. The feeling in Texas is that while the current rebound probably will not surge with the same force as previous oil-led recoveries, the state nevertheless will emerge healthier and with a stronger base of jobs.

Despite the current optimism for the state's economy, the Texas legal community has been devastated by the bust and still is reeling from the decline in demand for legal services. There have been massive layoffs, critical defections, dissolutions and rumored dissolutions, rampant price competition, and widespread frustration about the diminishing supply of work and the abundance of hungry lawyers. Although there was an upswing in litigation and bankruptcy work, much of the state's average, nonpremium transactional work disappeared, along with its transactional lawyers. Some transactional work is slowly reappearing—the premium work never really left—but most lawyers in Texas have resigned themselves to the realization that law practice in Texas probably will never again boom as it did in the heady days of the early 1980s.

Houston and Dallas

In 1993, there were slightly more than 56,000 lawyers in Texas. Harris County, Houston's home, has more than 15,000 lawyers, the largest concentration of lawyers in the state. Dallas County is second, with more than 11,000 lawyers, and Austin's Travis County is third, with approximately 5,000. Bexar County, home of San Antonio, is fourth with under 4,000 lawyers, and Fort Worth's Tarrant County is fifth with almost 3,000 lawyers. Thus, the two dominant metropolitan areas, Houston and Dallas–Fort Worth, are home to more than half the lawyers in Texas, with Austin and San Antonio accounting for another 15 percent of the state's lawyers.

Although Houston and Dallas–Fort Worth have approximately the same concentration of lawyers, the cities' large law firms have evolved much differently. In Houston, the three largest law firms employ approximately 1,600 lawyers firmwide, while the three largest Dallas law firms employ less than 900 lawyers firmwide. The 15 largest Houston firms employ approximately 2,900 lawyers, and the 15 largest Dallas firms employ approximately 2,800 lawyers. The difference is that all 15 Dallas firms employ more than 100 lawyers, while only eight of the 15 largest Houston firms employ more than 100 lawyers. Another interesting comparison is the number of local lawyers practicing in each of the cities' three largest firms. In Houston, the three largest firms employ almost 1,000 lawyers practicing in Houston, while the three largest Dallas firms employ less than half that number of Dallas practitioners. It is easy to see that the greatest concentration of size in the large Houston firms is in the three-to-five largest firms, while concentration in Dallas is much more diffuse.

These statistics show the natural, free-market type of growth that has characterized Dallas and that contrasts sharply with Houston. In Dallas, banks and other businesses historically were less closely tied to their law firms, preferring instead to spread their legal work among several firms. As a result, these clients tended to have less institutional loyalty to Dallas firms and were more inclined to transfer business to other firms, including new firms established by defecting partners. This may explain why lateral movement always has been more prevalent in Dallas than in Houston: Dallas lawyers' entrepreneurial spirit often was rewarded by clients eager to move their business. After 20 or more years of volatility in the legal industry, lateral movement in Dallas continues to be as brisk as ever.

Houston, on the other hand, probably is like no other metropolitan area in the United States today. The largest Houston firms, with their great relative size and prominence, historically acted as somewhat of an oligopoly. They so dominated the premium law business in Houston that their sheer bulk and stature acted as a barrier to entry by non-Houston competitors and as a competitive barrier to smaller indigenous firms. These large law firms have historically been tied to, affiliated with, and in some cases founded by their clients and experienced significant, sustained growth for decades, in tandem with the phenomenal growth of those clients. The result was that these firms themselves developed an institutional character, and their relationships with their historic clients persisted, although in some cases more as a product of inertia than of carefully evaluated business reasons. Because of these strong law firm/client relationships, there never has been much opportunity for lateral movement among the big Houston firms. Certainly, partners never expected to transport business if they did move. Therefore, except to the extent that firms hired associates during the associate boom of the 1980s, lateral movement in Houston never was much of a mainstream event.

That no longer is the case in Houston, whose legal industry is currently in the midst of an episodic transformation of great proportion. The first episode was the downsizing that began in 1990 and is largely completed now, in which Houston law firms lost anywhere from 10 percent to 20 percent of their lawyer personnel firmwide. Although downsizing was happening elsewhere, including in Dallas, the cessation or reversal of growth in the Houston firms was, and is, big news. It is the first real evidence that these firms are not invincible. The second episode was the general realization by a handful of practitioners in big Houston firms that there was life on the outside and that they actually could take business with them if they defected. Thus died perhaps the strongest myth (the glue that held these large firms together): the dogma that lawyers could not leave and expect to take institutional clients. In its place a new idea cropped up: "Clients hire lawyers, not law firms." Amazingly, some of these large law firm partners began proving that it could be done. Although the first wave has been primarily comprised of litigators—who probably are best suited to boutique practice—it is highly likely that others will follow, which will further accelerate the process of change. The third episode has been the incursion of out-of-town firms. Branch offices of

Dallas firms, with some exceptions, have been no match for indigenous Houston firms and have failed to compete effectively on any large scale. There have been, however, one or more examples of out-of-state firms that have seized premium business, and the rumors are rampant about other national firms that have their sights set on Houston. The spread of prominent branch offices in Houston will likely have a considerable impact on the large Houston firms, who certainly will continue to prosper, but will be forced to redefine their roles in Houston and look to other markets for additional strength. As the Houston legal market gradually is transformed, it probably will begin to look more and more like other metropolitan areas, such as Dallas, where free market forces are at work and fewer barriers to entry, and where major national firms have been able to establish branch offices and capture a substantial share of the premium business.

BRANCH OFFICES IN TEXAS

Branch offices have contributed more to job creation in the Texas legal marketplace than any other factor. Dallas at one time enjoyed a reputation as the branch office capital of Texas, but Houston is catching up quickly. In 1990, Dallas had approximately 25 branch offices of out-of-town firms, employing more than 400 lawyers. In 1993, there were a total of 32 branch offices in Dallas with more than 700 lawyers. Although branch office growth has been respectable in Dallas, with a net gain of seven offices and almost a doubling of lawyers working in branch offices, recent gains in Houston have been truly spectacular. In 1990, Houston had 11 branch offices of out-of-town firms, with slightly more than 100 lawyers. In 1993, there were a total of 32 branch offices—the same number as in Dallas—with almost 500 lawyers. Therefore, the number of branch offices in Houston has almost tripled, and the number of lawyers working in branch offices has been multiplied by a factor of almost five.

Even though the surge in the development of branch offices in Houston lagged behind Dallas by seven or eight years, Houston has made up much of that ground in the past few years. The real difference between Houston and Dallas is that because Dallas branch offices have had longer to grow, some of these offices have become very large, with the largest four branches in Dallas being roughly twice the size of each of their four counterpart branches in Houston.

Houston firms also have managed to maintain more of a national and international presence. Houston firms have a total of 16 branch offices in New York, Washington, D.C., Los Angeles, and London, while Dallas firms have approximately one-half that number, with far fewer lawyers practicing in those locations. Houston firms certainly have taken the lead in establishing New York branch offices. Three large Houston firms became bold enough to take the big step of establishing branch offices in New York. It is too early to say whether these ventures will be successful.

LAW AS BUSINESS

Twenty years ago a starting lawyer in Texas would have been lucky to earn $7,500 per year; in 1993, the average starting salary in both Dallas and Houston was approximately $54,000, with approximately $9,000 in additional bonuses. Salary levels for Texas associates have historically been pushed upward in proportion to across-the-board increases in other cities. Merit-based benefits have resulted from the increasing need of Texas firms to reward associates who make the largest contributions to firm profitability. As a result of these types of programs, significant compensation disparities exist among law firms in Texas. For example, with respect to the 1992 salary year, the lowest total compensation amount paid by a major Texas firm or branch office for 1987 graduates was approximately $75,000, while the highest amount was approximately $145,000, a whopping difference. The average amount paid to 1987 graduates was between $85,000 and $90,000.

Partnership opportunities are evolving in Texas as they are elsewhere. Partnership tracks have been extended to as much as nine years in some large firms, and prospects for partnership generally are not so good across the board as they were several years ago. According to a joke making the rounds, a large law firm associate has a better chance of surviving an airline crash than making partner! When coupled with the decreased hiring of law school graduates, it is clear that the prospects for lawyer employment in Texas are not nearly so good as they used to be. In essence, law firms now take the view that they overhired and overpromoted in the 1980s, and they do not intend to make that mistake again. Some law firms have instituted programs of non-equity partnership, two-tiered partnerships, and senior associate positions to enhance their flexibility in dealing with lawyer employment issues. Recent law school graduates should think very carefully about their career paths to mitigate some of the supply-and-demand problems that they will encounter in the legal marketplace today. One good idea is to choose a practice area that has growth potential. Labor, health care, and environmental law continue to be areas of practice that are attracting much attention. In addition, many firms are beginning to focus more in the area of intellectual property law and patent litigation. While the job market in Texas is certainly not so hospitable as it once was, opportunities do exist, especially with branch offices and boutiques, for highly qualified candidates. The important thing to remember in searching for a job is that there really only has to be one job opportunity, as long as it is the right one.

Rocky Mountain Region

Colorado

Irene Honey
Rita D. Zaslowsky

Colorado is a unique state where one can find rustic, rural ambience as well as high-rise, high-technology, sophisticated urban landscapes. The state's appeal is enhanced by the ability of the Colorado economy to consistently outperform the national economy.

During the early 1970s, baby boomers demonstrated their mobility and love affair with the mountains by flocking to Colorado. The population grew a phenomenal 31 percent, almost three times the national growth rate. Employment growth during this time reached 10.4 percent. These factors spurred a building bonanza. In 1972, 65,700 building permits, a record high, were issued for new homes. The boom continued through 1981 because of the policies and market realities encouraging the growth of another leading industry—energy. Employment during the energy boom grew by 8.7 percent. The Denver skyline became an architectural playground as one imposing skyscraper after another was erected.

When oil prices began to slide in 1981, the go-go days came to a grinding halt and Colorado entered a severe recession that was not duplicated on a national level. Overall, 30,400 jobs were lost. Construction and mining industries lost almost 40 percent of their employment base, and service industries, developed to support the infrastructure of mining, oil and gas, real estate and construction, suffered as well. Colorado's unprecedented levels of bankruptcies and foreclosures made national headlines.

Colorado's economy was insulated somewhat from the negative effects of the 1990s' national recession because its earlier recession already had forced a dramatic reduction in excesses. This fact apparently created a perception of job availability and quality of life in Colorado. The 1990s thus far have been marked by robust "in-migration," particularly from California, Texas, Arizona, and Nevada. In 1991, Colorado's population experienced its strongest growth since 1983 (2 percent). The trend continued through 1992 and softened slightly in 1993 and 1994.

Not all new inhabitants are finding jobs. In fact, it has been difficult for many to gain employment, particularly at previous salary levels. During 1991–92, 5,562 more unemployed people moved into Colorado than left it. Sadly, the Colorado Coalition for the Homeless reported an 88.5 percent increase in homeless families between April of 1990 and October of 1992.[1] The unemployment rate in 1992 increased one percentage point over 1991. According to the Colorado Legislative Council, employment growth in 1993 was around 2 percent. Similar growth was predicted for 1994. It is anticipated that this economic softening will result from the closure of Lowry Air Force Base, defense cuts, completion of the new Denver International Airport (9,000 workers), completion of a federal prison in Florence, Colorado (1,200 workers), and continuing layoffs at the Rocky Flats weapons plant. These cautionary economic flags will contribute to continued conservative hiring practices in the legal market. Other factors impacting Colorado's economic future include a recently enacted state constitutional amendment that restricts state taxation and expenditure levels. While it is unclear exactly what effect these factors will have on the state's long-term economic future, the repercussions may be significant, for state and local budget growth may be curtailed.

The legal market reflects the competitive nature of the market at large. Selection and retention criteria remain extremely tight, particularly in light of the influx of new residents. Legal employers are far less tolerant of mediocrity or lengthy learning curves. According to 1992 year-end Colorado supreme court data, 15,586 lawyers maintain an active practice status (an additional 4,175 are inactive); 72 percent of practitioners (11,224) are in the narrow

Pueblo to Fort Collins front range corridor; of this, 59 percent (or 6,613) of practitioners are located in Denver County. According to 1990 U.S. Census figures, the state's population is 3,294,394; there is one lawyer for every 211 people in the state. The state supreme court reports that the high volume of requests for reciprocal admission to the bar now are taking up to a year to process—a sure indication of lawyer in-migration. In the eyes of beleaguered job-hunting lawyers, the market appears quite saturated.

The Colorado legal market is largely comprised of small firms. Of the 25 largest firms, only nine employ 50 or more lawyers and only three employ 100 or more lawyers. Most firms hire when a specific need arises and will focus their efforts on applicants admitted to the Colorado bar and with local attachments to the area. Networking is the best job-hunting strategy.

Salary surveys indicate that Denver salaries generally are higher than elsewhere in Colorado. "The Denver Almanac" in *The Denver Business Journal* recently published a salary report indicating that the average Denver metropolitan 1992–93 lawyer wage was approximately $58,760 annually. Starting salaries averaged approximately $40,000 and have not shown significant growth in the past year.[2] Conservative hiring practices are expected to continue until the national recessionary economy shows marked improvement. At a time when law firms predict limited hiring needs, most firms report an overabundance of highly qualified applicants. Consistent with in-migration trends, firms statewide have reported an increasing number of out-of-state applicants.

There is always room for outstanding talent, but the job hunter must demonstrate this quickly and decisively. For those unable to do so, the likelihood of rewarding employment leading to career satisfaction may be slim.

Wyoming, Montana, and Idaho

Debra J. Madsen

The economic climate in the mountain states of Wyoming, Montana, and Idaho is mixed. Idaho has rebounded from the difficult economic times of the mid-1980s while Montana and Wyoming are struggling with the recessionary times of the 1990s. As a result, Idaho is experiencing an influx of experienced lawyers who are looking to relocate within the state. The number of experienced lawyers looking to relocate to Montana and Wyoming does not appear to be on the rise.

No one industry is particularly dominant in the mountain states. Each state depends, to varying degrees, on businesses related to either the extraction and exploitation or the conservation of its vast natural resources. Obviously, lawyers with an expertise in natural resources or environmental law will have greater opportunities in these states.

In-house counsel opportunities are limited. Although several national corporations have offices in Wyoming and Montana, very few employ lawyers in those offices. With a few exceptions, most local businesses do not have in-house counsel. The in-house counsel opportunities are more numerous in

Idaho, with major employers such as Boise Cascade, Morris Knudsen, and Hewlett-Packard employing in-house counsel within the state. Openings in these legal offices are rare, for turnover generally is low.

Law firms in the mountain states are predominantly small to medium in size. In Idaho, the largest firm employs 43 lawyers; in Montana, 53 lawyers; and in Wyoming, 20 lawyers. These firms are the aberration, however. Most are small general practice firms in rural areas. Hiring, therefore, is very sporadic. One area of concern for experienced lawyers considering a move to a small firm in these states will be salary. Before embarking on an exhaustive job search, an experienced lawyer should make inquiries regarding salaries within a particular community. Starting salaries for a new law graduate average between $24,000 and $30,000. Lawyers from large metropolitan areas with more than three to four years' experience may find the low salaries prohibitive.

The state attorney general's offices are centralized, with hiring through one main office. The attorney general's offices in these states are experiencing a large increase in applications from experienced lawyers. Experienced lawyers should keep their résumés on file with these offices, for a position is filled as a vacancy occurs. Opportunities at the county level generally are considered entry-level positions and usually are filled by recent law graduates. Federal job opportunities generally are limited to the U.S. attorney's office within each state.

Experienced lawyers considering a move to the mountain states should begin their job searches with visits to the state and should plan to spend a great deal of time making personal contacts. Because of the small size of the firms in these states, hiring is very sporadic and highly depends on the right "fit." Firms do not regularly hire and applicants must be willing to keep knocking on the door until an opening materializes.

Utah

Kathy D. Pullins

Utah, with a population of less than two million, has long been known for its scenic national parks and abundant recreational activities. While defense cutbacks have affected certain Utah employers, a significant number of businesses in other industries have recently located to the state. During the past decade, high-technology enterprises in particular have experienced significant growth. After California's Silicone Valley and North Carolina's Research Triangle, Utah's Provo-Orem area has become the nation's third largest setting of computer-related industries. Affordable housing, low taxes, a reasonable cost of living, a young workforce, and low crime rates make Utah a very attractive place to live and work.

Current Utah bar statistics list more than 4,000 active lawyers in the state, with the vast majority of them (more than 3,500) practicing in the four most densely populated north-central counties. Salt Lake City is the capital and legal center of the state, with ten firms of 30 or more lawyers. In 1993, the average entry-level salary ranged from just over $34,000 at a small firm (2 to 15 lawyers) to $48,000 at the largest firms. The average annual billable hours are listed in a recent bar survey as between 1,800 and 1,850.

Applicants seeking legal employment in Utah should tap the resources of the two law schools in-state at Brigham Young University (BYU) and the University of Utah. Each school publishes monthly listings of lawyer job notices in newsletter form that may be subscribed to by contacting the career services offices. BYU also offers a 24-hour job hotline (1-801-378-3595). In addition, the *Utah Bar Journal* lists "Lawyer Positions Available" in its classified section.

Southwest

Phyllis Hawkins

For those searching for a more relaxed lifestyle situated in a mild climate with plenty of recreational opportunities, the southwestern United States offers a great attraction. Most of the Southwest, especially Arizona, experienced tremendous growth during the 1980s. Unfortunately, because the economically paired industries such as real estate, oil and gas, and tourism are the predominant forces in the Southwest, this area experienced an early and, in some cases, a lasting downturn because of the recession. Layoffs, firm closings, and a general stagnation in hiring have become prevalent. Like most other areas of the country, the Southwest is saturated with an overabundance of lawyers. Positions that do open up generally are filled locally. Most firms are unwilling to pay for flybacks, moving costs, and bar-related expenses for new lawyers. Relocating, though difficult, is not impossible and the first step is to target a location.

Arizona

Arizona is one of the fastest growing states in the country—boasting warm, dry weather in the desert areas and snow-capped mountains in its higher elevations. Most of Arizona is forested with great expanses of breathtaking scenery. The Arizona economy is expected to make some gains during the 1990s, but without the wild growth expectations of the preceding decade. The predominant industry is tourism, followed by real estate, copper mining, and high technology. A number of companies have located their corporate headquarters in Phoenix during the past few years with indications of more to come. Tax credits and favorable regulations have helped make Arizona an attractive location for new businesses.

The vast majority of the population of Arizona is clustered in two areas—Phoenix and Tucson. Phoenix and the surrounding suburbs are known as "the Valley of the Sun." This area has a population of more than two million and the amenities of most cosmopolitan cities. Phoenix also boasts more than 200 golf courses. Tucson is a much smaller city with more of the demeanor of a small college town. (The University of Arizona is located there and is the city's driving force.)

Most of Arizona's lawyers and legal positions are in Phoenix and most positions are in law firms. Currently, there are approximately 7,300 lawyers in Maricopa County. Approximately seven law firms in Phoenix employ 75 or more lawyers and, in most cases, have branch offices in Tucson. Arizona's largest firm has well over 150 lawyers. While the larger firms generally offer both litigation and transactional services, transactional work has seen a marked decline over the past few years. Most opportunities today are found in litigation.

A number of national law firms have branch offices in Phoenix. Most are based in the Midwest and service major clients in the area. Many of the national firms have been joined by local talent with their own clients, thus making an increasing impact on the local legal community.

In 1993, starting salaries for the larger Phoenix firms ranged from the mid-$50,000s to the low $60,000s. There is a wide diversity in compensation for lateral hires. Most firms have eliminated incremental "steps" but retain some set guidelines for incoming laterals—often based on what they are currently paying lawyers at a similar level. Billable hours average 2,000 annually in most firms, and partnership tracks are from six to nine years. Tiered partnerships are commonplace.

While many corporations have headquarters in Phoenix, in-house opportunities have remained few. Many Arizona corporations are smaller and have either no in-house counsel or only one. The few large corporations that do have larger staffs tend to have low turnover and a wealth of local talent to select from for the few positions that do become available.

With more than 200 lawyers on staff, one of the larger local employers of lawyers in Phoenix is the Arizona Attorney General's Office. In addition, the United States Attorney has offices in both Phoenix and Tucson. Both cities have good-sized county attorney offices and most positions are in litigation.

New Mexico

The good news/bad news for New Mexico is that the general economic climate rarely changes: It is never very high or very low and tends to remain fairly static. Compared to the rest of the country, however, the general economy is not strong. Its main industries are oil, gas, mining, agriculture, and defense contracting. New Mexico enjoys a good labor force with wages in the midrange.

New Mexico recently crossed the line between supply and demand of lawyers, and it has become increasingly difficult for lawyers to find jobs. Most new or incoming lawyers tend to cluster as solo practitioners or go to the smaller firms outside the major metropolitan areas.

The largest city in New Mexico is Albuquerque with a current population of 380,000. There are three firms with 50 or more lawyers in Albuquerque, six to eight firms are in the 30- to 50-lawyer range, and the remaining firms employ less than 30 lawyers.

Santa Fe, with a population of 93,000, has approximately 40 to 50 law firms, most with ten or fewer lawyers. The largest firm has approximately 40 lawyers. In addition, the cost of living in Santa Fe is extremely high.

There is not a lot of industry in New Mexico. The largest employers are the state and federal governments. Government-operated laboratories at Los Alamos and Sandia employ lawyers who specialize predominantly in government contracts, and corporate and employment law.

The legal market is not so good in the major metropolitan areas as it is in the rural parts of the state. Most legal needs tend to be in smaller towns. The New Mexico bar admits 300 to 400 new lawyers each year, with about 100 graduating from the law school at the University of New Mexico. In 1993, starting salaries among major firms in the area were $40,000 to $50,000.

Nevada

Nevada is one of the few states whose economy has remained strong even during periods of recession. Business and industry are encouraged to locate in Nevada primarily because of the absence of corporate and personal income taxes. Revenues from gaming provide the bulk of state funds, and the cost of living in Nevada generally is lower than in most parts of the country. These factors, combined with an abundance of sunshine and recreational activities, have helped Nevada maintain a vigorous rate of growth. Paradoxically, Nevada remains one of the least densely populated states, averaging only nine persons per square mile. Almost 60 percent of the state's population is clustered in the Las Vegas valley.

By far the biggest industry in Nevada is tourism. Almost one-half of all jobs are service-oriented, while nearly one in three is directly related to hotels, gaming, and recreation. Construction, both residential and commercial, are strong as well.

Law firms in Nevada tend to be smaller in size, with only two or three employing 40 or more lawyers. In 1993, starting salaries were in the $45,000 to $50,000 range. Partnership tracks are in the six- to eight-year range.

Gaming law is a high-demand specialty. Because Nevada has no law school, most lawyers receive on-the-job training in this field.

In-house corporate opportunities are relatively low, with most positions provided by the hotel chains. Environmental law is the predominant specialty of lawyers with governmental agencies who regulate Nevada's oil, gas, and mining and nuclear waste dumps. Most of the rural areas are serviced by lawyers who grew up there.

Oklahoma

The general economic climate in Oklahoma is improving gradually after a long slide down. The oil and gas industries are critical to Oklahoma's economy, and even the hint of an issue that might impact the oil business can make or break Oklahoma's economic condition. Agriculture, Oklahoma's other predominant industry, has remained steady.

Regulatory matters that arise in Oklahoma have had a favorable impact on opportunities for lawyers. Environmental litigation involving giant pollution cases is increasingly common. Other specialties most in demand in Oklahoma are bankruptcy and general litigation, real estate, tax, and health-care law.

Law firms are hiring on a limited basis. While the demand remains low, a cautious optimism is developing. Many firms went through a tremendous boom and now are taking a cautious approach to hiring. Oklahoma's legal market is extremely saturated. Unfortunately, with three law schools in the state, many new lawyers cannot find jobs at all. What legal opportunities are present are found in Oklahoma City and Tulsa.

The largest firm in Oklahoma currently is Crowe & Dunlevy with more than 100 lawyers and offices in both Oklahoma City and Tulsa. Three other firms range in size from approximately 40 to 70 lawyers. Starting salaries in 1993 were in the neighborhood of $46,500 to $56,000. Most firms, especially those in Tulsa, have a lockstep compensation system. Years to partnership are in the six-year range.

More in-house lawyers are being hired than in the past. Individuals with experience in the oil and gas industry are most in demand. Because of the oversaturated market, governmental agencies have been able to be more selective about hiring.

How to Get a Job in the Southwest

For lawyers in the 1990s who want to move to the Southwest, by far the greatest obstacle is competition from local lawyers. Local lawyers have the dual advantages of bar admission and presence. Taking the bar examination and becoming admitted in a state *before* looking for a position, and then arranging in advance for a trip to the area, levels the playing field tremendously. It also sends a signal to a prospective employer that you are truly serious about relocating to that area.

Pacific Northwest

Carol Richardson

The Pacific Northwest has diversified significantly from its once primary dependence on the mature industries of timber and aerospace. Agriculture and the marine and fishing industries continue to play a large role in the region's economic base. The region is home to The Boeing Company, the world's largest aerospace business, as well as Microsoft, the world's leading producer of software. More than 1,500 other software companies are located in the Pacific Northwest, including Nintendo, the computer-game giant, and Aldus, whose Pagemaker revolutionized desktop publishing. Seattle is a national leader in the biotechnology field and home to nearly 50 biotech companies, including the Immunex Corporation, maker of the Leukine cancer treatment drug. Only two other cities, Boston and Los Angeles, boast as many biotech companies.

The Pacific Northwest is poised to take advantage of its internationally strategic location. The free trade agreement between the United States and Canada signed in 1988 has resulted in a significant increase in cross-border business. Supposedly, the North American Free Trade Agreement will greatly increase trade in goods, services, and investments between the Pacific Northwest and Mexico.

Increased environmental regulation and enforcement will have a significant impact on jobs and growth throughout the Pacific Northwest as the battle continues between the preservation of land resources and the harvest of timber. The Endangered Species Act will continue to increase regulation of private lands as well. Clean water and air will remain ongoing problems in the face of continued growth. The federal government's regulation of prices, irrigation, water, and pesticides will have an impact on the predominantly agricultural areas. As expansion continues in the Pacific Rim, Seattle is poised to be the international city of tomorrow. Only Los Angeles and San Diego are larger ports. The combined ports of Seattle and Tacoma, however, are larger than Los Angeles. Transportation will be significantly affected by land-use law, bond issues, and commercial financing.

The lawyer population in the Pacific Northwest varies greatly from state to state. Alaska has 2,200 lawyers; Washington, 15,600; and Oregon, 8,600. Seattle has seven large firms with from 100 to 200 lawyers, Portland has five large firms with from 75 to 165 lawyers, and Anchorage has one large firm with 50 lawyers and four firms with from 20 to 25 lawyers. As might be expected, the rural areas in eastern Oregon and Washington are home to many solo practitioners and smaller firms with from 3 to 40 lawyers.

Lawyers practicing in the largest metropolitan areas of the Pacific Northwest earn salaries generally 20 percent to 30 percent lower than in other U.S. urban areas. Salaries in the rural areas of the Pacific Northwest generally are even lower, although Alaska tends to maintain a similar salary structure statewide.

Hiring authorities want candidates to have strong ties such as family, friends, or school connections to the Pacific Northwest. Because of the region's unique climate, employers seek reasonable assurance that candidates are committed to the area as well as to the employment opportunity.

Corporate counsel positions are limited in the Pacific Northwest, with fewer than 400 companies throughout the region maintaining an in-house legal staff. There are a few large corporate legal departments, but, generally, the Pacific Northwest is home to corporate subsidiaries with small legal staffs. Legal opportunities in the corporate arena are extremely limited and competition is keen for a few choice positions.

Law firm growth was significant in the 1980s, for partners changed firms for the first time and laterals moved from other parts of the country in search of quality-of-life improvement over the personal and professional demands of larger metropolitan practices. The 1990s thus far have been marked by a virtual standstill in firm expansion, with emphasis on efficiency and strategic planning. As the economy strengthens during this decade, the Pacific Northwest will be positioned to take advantage of opportunities in international trade and high technology as it maintains its diverse economic base.

California

Randi G. Frisch

In the middle to late 1980s, California law firms experienced intensive growth. Japanese, Korean, and other Pacific Rim–based investors generated a tremendous amount of business for law firms, particularly in the Los Angeles and San Francisco regions. There was an increased demand for legal services in the areas of international finance, real estate, and mergers and acquisitions. The dynamic high-technology field required intellectual property lawyers. The defense industry, located primarily in southern California, was booming because of the substantial increase in military spending. Drawn in part by the burgeoning California economy and expanding Pacific Rim markets, out-of-state law firms from New York, Washington, D.C., Chicago, and other major cities established branch offices. As a result, the demand for high-quality attorneys exceeded the supply.

In recent years, the California legal market has experienced a pendulum swing. The lawyer job pool has decreased significantly as a result of the recession. Cutbacks in the defense industry have led to layoffs in southern California's aerospace industry. The global recession has resulted in fewer Pacific Rim–generated and other foreign-generated investments. Because a greater number of firms have competed for a diminished amount of legal work, many firms have been forced to lay off lawyers.

Nevertheless, there is optimism in the legal community. Many firms have responded to the economic challenges of recent years by downsizing, improving internal management, and increasing efficiency. There is a greater emphasis on long-term health as opposed to short-term inflated profits. Slow growth and selective hiring are the current practices for many firms.

Lawyers interested in California are well advised to focus on its growth industries. High-technology companies in the Silicon Valley are flourishing and new growth is anticipated in view of the Clinton administration's commitment to the development of high-technology products, the environment, and transportation systems. This trend could result in an increased demand for lawyers in the fields of intellectual property, litigation, venture capital, and other types of corporate finance.

The corporate area has demonstrated renewed vigor. The May 3, 1993, issue of *California Law Business* reports that the number of public offerings of California companies is on the rise. Ninety-four California companies went public in 1992. Projections for 1993 indicated further increased activity. A significant number of the California-based startup companies that completed initial public offerings are in the health-care, biotechnology, pharmaceutical, and computer fields.

There is an increased need for environmental lawyers to advise clients regarding laws such as California's Proposition 65 and federal environmental regulations. The implementation and enforcement of federal laws pertaining to hazardous waste and other environmental concerns also has produced a great deal of environmental-related litigation.

Commercial litigation practice is consistently active. Because many insurance companies are located in California, developments in insurance defense and coverage matters have created a steady source of business for many firms. The recessionary times have further resulted in an increased number of business-related disputes.

Health care is another area of steady growth. Many biotechnical firms, pharmaceutical companies, hospitals, and health maintenance organizations are located in California. Even during the height of the recession, health-care firms reported a consistent flow of business. The proposed revamping of the nation's health-care policies will be reflected in the demand for health-care lawyers.

Other practice fields hit hard by the recession are rebounding. San Francisco and Los Angeles are major banking centers. Financial institutions provide a source of legal work concerning interstate banking regulatory matters and litigation pertaining to lender liability, fraud, and Resolution Trust Corporation issues. Proposed legislation involving the expansion of the role of financial institutions in investment markets could further stimulate the financial-institution field and result in greater demand for legal services.

Although real estate development work has been radically reduced, real estate departments in many firms have shifted from handling purchases and sales and other developer work to concentrating on loan workouts, real estate finance projects, and leasing matters. Many economists agree that the California real estate market has bottomed out and is due for expansion.

The entertainment industry is of major economic significance to California, specifically to southern California. A number of firms specialize in representing studios and talent. Entertainment law can be transactional in nature or focus on litigation. Transactional practice may include negotiating and drafting contracts or registering copyrights and trademarks. Litigation encompasses copyright infringement, libel and slander, and other entertainment-related issues. Although the entertainment field is particularly competitive, legal departments in studios and some firms have openings for entry-level candidates.

Corporate legal departments are expanding. In an effort to cut costs, an increasing number of companies are retaining work in-house. In-house legal positions may involve monitoring outside counsel as well as assuming "hands-on" responsibility for entire litigation matters or transactions. Generally speaking, in-house positions require a minimum of four years' experience. Corporate salaries can be significantly lower than law firm compensation packages; in-house counsel positions, however, often provide an attractive lifestyle alternative. Because most companies do not require lawyers to keep time sheets, many lawyers find that the absence of billing pressures results in a more relaxed working environment.

With a greater number of lawyers competing for fewer positions, lawyers must be aggressive and open-minded when seeking employment. When choosing a specialty, keep in mind that demand has consistently been highest for junior litigators. Certain areas, such as environmental or health-care practice, have been targeted for growth; because specialty practice is confining, however, lawyers must select areas that will be personally rewarding.

Utilize law school placement centers. Some placement centers have reciprocity with other out-of-state law schools. Organizations such as the ABA, the California State Bar Association, and smaller local professional associations hold regular general as well as specialty section meetings. These gatherings provide excellent opportunities to meet prospective employers. Be persistent in applying for a position. If rejected because no position is available, recontact the firm monthly.

Associates who realize that they do not want to remain in their current position long-term should bear in mind that demand is highest and there is a maximum number of opportunities for lawyers with one to four years' experience. Firms find it less costly to hire junior associates and can better integrate them into the firm without threatening other associates. Commencing a job search early in one's career can bring optimum results.

Lateral movement among partners has increased significantly. Partners are sought after to start new departments or to supplement a firm's client base. Many firms will not consider lateral partner applicants unless the applicant controls a portable book of business equal to a minimum of $500,000 in annual collections. Often, lateral partners are regarded as "of counsel" for one or two years, before becoming equity partners. This enables the firm and the lawyer to evaluate whether the employment relationship is mutually rewarding.

Long-term partnership potential should be examined before joining a firm. Partnership prospects are changing within California firms. Until recently, associates in most California firms could expect a six-and-one-half- to seven-year partnership track compared to an eight- or nine-year track for New York firms. Today, associates no longer can assume that they will automatically be admitted as partners after seven years of dedicated service. Difficult economic times have resulted in fewer available partnership positions. Some firms have an "up-or-out" policy, requiring those who do not make partner to leave. Others offer alternatives such as "special-counsel" or "permanent-associate" status that enables lawyers to remain with the firm after partnership decisions are made. An increasing number of associates who have no desire to assume law firm liabilities or management responsibilities are voluntarily choosing such nonpartnership tracks.

Law school graduates should consider practicing with a nonprofit, government agency or other public interest–oriented law firm or organization. These organizations provide excellent opportunities to contribute to the community while gaining experience and training. California has numerous public interest forums. For instance, the State Bar of California recently established the Legal Corps that, through fellowship or loan-deferment programs, enables new admittees and more seasoned lawyers to provide legal services to the indigent while further developing legal skills. In addition, the State Bar of California organizes preventative law and educational clinics to service low-income members of the community.

Many California law schools support public-interest law centers. For example, the Western Law Center for Disability Rights at Loyola Law School in Los Angeles is a nonprofit, public-interest law center specializing in disability-related civil-rights issues. Bet Tzedek Legal Services in Los Angeles provides free legal assistance to low-income people. Bet Tzedek services include handling landlord-tenant disputes, bankruptcy matters, and consumer-fraud complaints. Finally, Public Counsel, considered the largest pro bono law firm nationally, provides a wide variety of legal services to those in need.

California is evolving economically and socially. Consequently, California law firms are in the process of developing and present many new opportunities. Although the market is competitive, with perseverance and flexibility, a lawyer should be able to find a job that is rewarding.

Hawaii

Margaret Masunaga

The legal community in Hawaii consists of 3,594 active lawyers[3] practicing on the islands of Hawaii (the Big Island), Kauai, Maui, Molokai, and Oahu. Of that number, 3,030 lawyers practice on Oahu, where Honolulu is located. The highest starting salary in Hawaii during 1992–1993 for a lawyer out of law school was $55,000. The cost of housing is the highest on Oahu and averages $358,000. Housing in Hilo (east Hawaii on the Big Island) is considered "reasonable" at $160,000 for a three-bedroom house on a 10,000-square-foot lot.

Hawaii law firms range in size from solo practitioners to firms with 96 lawyers. The four largest law firms with more than 75 lawyers examine many factors in recruiting, including education, experience, and potential business contacts. Salaries for associates are the same in Honolulu and on the neighbor island branch offices. Billable hours range from 1,800 to 2,500 hours per year.

Most, if not all, government lawyers are appointed by either the governor, mayor, or prosecutor of that particular county, state public defender, or the state attorney general. The majority of governmental legal positions are found in Honolulu, the state capital and location of the only federal court in the state. Available governmental legal positions include deputy prosecuting lawyers and public defenders, deputy attorney generals and deputy corporation counsels on all islands, and administrative hearings officer and the legislature in Honolulu. There also are judicial clerkships available (usually limited to one year after law school) for the Hawaii supreme court justices, appellate judges, and circuit court judges.

Many lawyers in Hawaii limit their areas of practice. While large firms offer a full range of legal services, in the rural areas of Oahu, Hawaii, Maui, Molokai, and Kauai, most lawyers are general practitioners or specialize in areas such as bankruptcy, family, personal injury, or business law. Other opportunities for lawyers include in-house counsel positions with corporations and teaching positions at the University of Hawaii law school.

Hawaii's population is racially diverse and includes Native Hawaiians, Japanese-Americans, Caucasians, Filipino-Americans, Chinese-Americans, and Portuguese-Americans. Because no majority racial group exists in Hawaii, racial tensions are not so prevalent as on the mainland. Individual economic circumstances often dictate whether persons will seek the advice of counsel.

Residents tend to be close-knit in rural areas and "fitting in" as a "local" in the community takes time. Word travels fast and lawyers who use questionable tactics in their practices without extending professional courtesy to other lawyers will find that their reputations suffer among their peers.

Generally speaking, Hawaii is a great place to practice law. While the cost of living is high and billable hour requirements rival the mainland, lawyers in Hawaii wake up to beautiful blue skies, green mountains, 70-degree temperatures, and a view of the ocean from their offices and homes.

Notes

1. *Focus Colorado: Economy and Revenue Forecast, 1993–1994* (Denver: Colorado Legislative Council Staff Report, December, 1992), 35.

2. "The Denver Almanac" in *The Denver Business Journal* (November 27–December 3, 1992), 4.

3. This statistic, provided by the Hawaii State Bar Association on March 2, 1993, does not include active lawyers licensed to practice in Hawaii but living elsewhere.

CHAPTER 22

Law Firms

Sandra O'Briant

Law firm archetypes always have followed these general lines: Large law firms are competitive, impersonal, high paying, prestigious, and hours intensive with limited opportunity for client contact and real responsibility for challenging case matters. Smaller law firms frequently are thought of as collegial, family oriented, low paying, and mentor accessible, with reasonable hours, added responsibility and client contact, and greater opportunity for partnership.

Although every archetype may contain a basic grain of truth, in the final analysis, these descriptions are just broad generalizations. There are small firms with firm cultures that appear to be directly transplanted from the big firm paradigm. There are large firms that have responded to the recruiting wars of the 1980s by designing practice groups to offer more training and responsibility for associates. In evaluating the variable of law firm size when considering a job change, remember that appearances may be deceiving and further investigation may be required. The legal community continues to reverberate from the impact of the ongoing recession and other economic stresses. These "other" economic stresses must be identified, because they underscore some basic distinctions between different-sized law firms.

Large Law Firms

For instance, much media attention was focused on the large firm associate pay hikes in the middle to late 1980s. The competitive nature of recruiting by firms for the top graduates of the top law schools was the reason for these salary increases. Certainly, business was booming for many of these firms and it required the labor of the best and the brightest lawyers, but what was the true cost of this competition and who paid for it? For example, during this salary war, many small to midsized law firms struggled to stay afloat as large firms cherry-picked their top talent.

225

The outcome of the pay wars of the 1980s also involved brutally long hours and a long wait for partnership or, alternatively, the elimination of the partnership option for many lawyers by the creation of "special-counsel" designations. In addition, the salary increases led to an increase in billable rates for associates passed directly on to the clients.

It quickly became apparent to many that it might become commercially impractical to use associates. Indeed, at present, many large law firms have turned their attention to premium billing by partners and senior associates and have placed decreased emphasis on hiring and training new lawyers.

Traditionally, the "finders, minders, and grinders" of the lawyer working force all had an equal chance at the ultimate payoff—partnership. Partnership status was a virtual guarantee of employment until retirement. Associates paid their dues by putting in long hours and, once made partner, actual billable time went down while attention was focused on developing new business, community affairs, firm administration, and mentoring more junior lawyers in the firm. Today, however, partners are working harder than ever. Partners with no significant client bases of their own must strive to keep their billable hours high and may be less likely to delegate work to associates.

The rising demands on partners are caused in large part by increasingly sophisticated clientele. Corporate clients are watching the bottom line, demanding detailed budgets and negotiating for pared-down legal bills after the work is completed. Additionally, they have dramatically stated their unwillingness to foot the bill for training junior associates.

Recognizing this situation, many entrepreneurial large firm lawyers have taken their institutional client bases and started their own firms, utilizing lateral recruits with big firm training. Eschewing law school hiring, they neither have the time nor the inclination to train raw recruits.

Often, clients themselves encourage partner defections from major firms. The impetus could be conflicts among clients of the firm, client preferences regarding lawyer staffing of matters, client demands for flexible billing rates, or the opportunity to participate with clients in certain business transactions that otherwise might not be allowed in a more institutional law firm. Such partners tend to bill numerous hours themselves and are involved in virtually every deal and case matter. Many clients believe that they receive more personal attention from these lawyers than from larger law firms.

Small Law Firms

Many small law firms have thus weathered the recession well and perhaps more profitably than their larger competitors. With less overhead and leanly staffed cases, boutique law firms in major geographic areas with diverse client bases generally have not found it necessary to lay off lawyers. Other small firms with one or two major clients or those that concentrate in a single practice area such as real estate, however, have a much greater potential to be adversely affected by any significant economic downturn.

Many small firms that are competing with larger law firms for the same talent are willing to pay competitively with a commensurate expectation of billable hours. As matters are staffed leanly, associates in smaller firms can expect more responsibility, more visibility, and early hands-on training.

Small firms prefer to hire lawyers who can handle cases with a minimum of supervision, thus creating ample room for the demonstration of partnership potential. However, it is difficult to determine whether the partnership track is any easier at smaller firms. The primary variable affecting small firm partnership growth is the size of the client base and the relative size of the partnership profit slices. The same considerations exist in a large law firm context; however, it often is easier to make partner in the earlier years of a newer law firm.

On the other hand, there are small firms that were started by big firm expatriates who merely wanted greater control of their clients and a bigger and faster share of the revenue generated by these clients. Because the individuals starting these firms may be more interested in satisfying their short-term needs than in creating a long-term entity, partnership potential in such firms is generally unclear.

Law Firm Culture

Law firms are in many ways like families because each individual is unique and the amalgam of personalities is complex. Nevertheless, they reflect a distinct culture. Each firm is different in its workstyle, the types of clients it wants to serve, incentives offered to lawyers, and the firm's long-term goals. Firm culture is a consequence of the manner in which hiring and management decisions are made, and how such decisions are communicated to lawyers within the firm and the outside community. Seniority or meritocracy systems are relevant, and even size and decor of offices can indicate the firm's personality.

Firm culture comfort depends on an individual's workstyle, lifestyle requirements, and career objectives. Most large law firms employ an established method of training and promoting lawyers, which can be determined through some research. Before choosing a law firm, go beyond the firm résumé and the lawyers you met on the interviews set up by the law firm and consider contacting other lawyers at the firm who attended your law school and college.

Small law firms may simultaneously present greater risk and potential for greater gain. Try to get a sense of the relationship between specific partners and key clients and speak to former and present associates regarding their experiences at the firm. Ask partners to explain proposed growth strategies for the firm and their anticipated roles in firm development. Generally, when key rainmakers reach the age of 55, they may prefer to be nestled comfortably within the confines of a giant where the risk is spread among many lawyers, rather than remain part of a small firm, responsible for yet another office lease and other management burdens.

Larger law firms are frequently in better financial positions to address quality-of-life issues such as maternity and paternity leave. While smaller law firms may try to keep pace, the impact of functioning with fewer lawyers is often a hardship for them and may create unspoken pressure on those on leave to return to work earlier than desired. Such pressure very often is self-imposed, whether at a large or small firm, but the implication may be more manifest in a smaller firm.

Firms of all sizes generally promote pro bono work on a lawyer's own time. Some larger firms offer encouragement through such incentives as crediting a small percentage of pro bono time to total billable time. When interviewing, consider asking partners how they spend their spare time and the extent of firm members' involvement in community services and pro bono activities. If the opportunity arises in a more casual context, ask what time people tend to arrive in the morning and what time they leave and whether everyone is inclined to come in on Saturday mornings.

Many large law firms are attempting to attract recruits and reduce attrition by providing associates with additional responsibility. For example, some large law firms known for megacases staffed to the hilt routinely bring in modest-sized matters to educate their junior associates. Large law firms also frequently sponsor in-house seminars and usually are very generous regarding attendance at worthwhile legal seminars.

With the intense pace, work load, and emphasis on profitability greater than ever for both partners and associates, many nonpartners in law firms have begun to take a long, hard look at how the lives of partners are really constituted, and, in many cases, the view is daunting. "Virtually all the midlevel and senior partners have had at least one divorce," according to one associate, "because they are never home." Another remarks that the junior partners in his firm "don't have lives. They work as hard as I do and assume more of the financial risk." To paraphrase Freud, what does an associate want?

In a 1983 survey of lawyer attitudes toward changing jobs, associate lawyers at all levels and in all areas of practice, including those who had been hired out of law school and those who had been hired laterally, were interviewed.

When asked what attracted them to their present firms and what they would look for in a new firm, the following areas were rated highest: client base/practice, responsibility, training, partnership, and people. Reputation of firm, size, location, money, and growth/stability issues came in much lower on the scale. If the survey was conducted today, responses probably would be much the same, with added consideration given to hours and stability of the firm.

When considering the attributes described previously that most concern lawyers when considering a job change, "client base/practice" always has ranked at or near the top, as well it should, because level of responsibility, potential for client contact, opportunity for partnership, and even stability derive in some measure from it.

Much has been written about quality-of-life issues and the growing emphasis on longer hours. As noted previously, the salary wars of the 1980s were at least partially responsible for the rise in billable-hours expectations. Profit-margin expectations and leveraging already are undergoing changes in many law firms. It is unlikely, however, that a drastic drop in billable-hours requirements will occur in the 1990s. Fewer partners will be made in the future and more new categories of lawyer-employee will be created. This trend is perhaps the only way to address quality-of-life issues and maintain a competent workforce.

Opportunities Available

Opportunities exist at both large and small law firms. Evaluating these opportunities requires a careful examination of where you are in the evolution of your legal career and where the law firm is in its development. In general, a large law firm can be a good place to get some decent basic training, but do not count on very much one-on-one. Your stay at a big firm also packs a tremendous punch in terms of résumé power and is never ignored by future employers. You may even find the pace and the people to your liking and appreciate the alternative career paths being developed within the framework of your traditional large law firm.

If you are looking for a faster track, then look for a boutique law firm with institutional clients and an entrepreneurial flair. Check the goals of the major rainmakers and their reputations as managers and mentors. Be aware of what opportunities may exist for you to develop your own client base.

Where is the midsized law firm in this analysis of law firms? Dead center with the pluses and minuses associated with their larger and smaller competitors. If you are considering such a law firm, the same inquiries described previously pertain.

In the final analysis, your long-term job security lies in your own skill and your ability to develop and maintain relationships within your law firm and with clients. Not everyone will develop star rainmaking powers, but in the marketplace of the 1990s, lawyers will have to pay increasing attention to building a network of contacts. "Networking Skills 101" is not presently offered in most law schools, but it should be.

CHAPTER 23

Solo Practitioners

Donna M. Ballman

When I was 15, I had two dreams. The first I had no doubt about: I would have my own law practice by the time I was 30. The second was more wishful thinking: I would become a pilot. At the end of 1989, right after I turned 30, I began making both dreams come true. Call me wild. This is the story of my progress in both adventures.

Fear of Flying

I actually began my flying lessons several months before I opened my practice. I was bored with the same old routine in my firm and thought I needed some excitement. My life was stable and I was making more money than I knew what to do with, so I thought, why not?

My first lesson gave me little chance to be afraid. It was in the air, with me in the pilot's seat. Actually, it is amazingly like driver's education. Your instructor is seated to your right and has an identical set of controls. I had white knuckles, but it was comforting knowing that someone else was in control. After I got over my initial shock, I began to look around and realize some of the exhilaration of soaring slightly below the clouds. I did not actually believe in my heart then that I had the courage to go it alone.

Fear of Fleeing

Shortly after I began my lessons, things started happening at my Miami law firm that made me examine the relative comfort of my existence. A big client left and refused to pay a large hunk of fees. Half of the partners had broken off the year before, and many associates were leaving. The firm dropped from 25 lawyers when I started to ten. The litigation department, to which I belonged, dropped from 13 to four lawyers. The firm lost two other steady clients within a very short period of time.

230

When I began to confess my worries to my best friend, who had started her own practice with a partner three years ago, she started putting a bug in my ear: The tenant in the office space she sublet with her partner was about to move. They needed a new tenant. The terms could be flexible. They would refer all of their litigation to me. At first I balked. I was not ready. I had only graduated from the University of Miami School of Law three years before. It was comforting knowing that someone else was in control. I gave in to the school of thought that a young lawyer had to "apprentice" for other lawyers, develop his or her own sturdy client base, and become well known in the community before he or she could go solo. I knew people who had gone out on their own, but surely they were suicidal daredevils.

I began a somewhat frantic search for another job. After all, I was an experienced commercial litigator. Surely someone would snap me up. I did not believe then that I had the experience, the clients, or the courage to go it alone.

Stalls in the Air

The worst part about my first set of flying lessons was practicing stalls. Stalls are maneuvers that basically require you to point the airplane as straight up toward the clouds as possible until the plane stalls and starts dropping rapidly. These maneuvers prepare you for making mistakes while landing or taking off. If you point the plane's nose up too high then, the plane will stall and you will not have time to think about what to do. You have to know it instinctively.

I could not get stalls right for anything. There was nothing in the world, other than the physical strength of my instructor, that could get me to point the plane up far enough to actually get it to stall. I knew in my heart that I would drop from the sky like a rock.

I only got over it by having a ground school lesson on aerodynamics. Only after my instructor proved to me beyond a doubt that the plane could not smack into the ground from 2,000 feet up without defying natural laws was I able to get over my fear. The next time I went up, I performed my stalls without a fight.

Stalls on the Ground

The worst part about looking for a job was trying to be patient. It was the end of the calendar year and interviews were coming slowly. Nobody wants to hire anyone in November or December. I thought I had all the time in the world, but frustration was setting in. As a new law school graduate, in the top 10 percent and with law review on my résumé, the large firms wanted me, but I did not want them. Now that I had decided that my best, most stable bet was with the large firms, they did not want me. Nobody goes from small to large. Small is better was the common wisdom.

Somehow, I could not seem to get my interviews right. The large firms all seemed the same. I kept thinking that I would be going from bad to worse. Was I really that bad off? Our end-of-the-year bonuses were withheld, first "just until the beginning of January," then indefinitely. The partners, who never had gotten along well, began sniping in front of the associates. Staff started being laid off. Still, my friend was having a hard time convincing me to go solo. I had no clients that I thought would come with me. Surely, I never would be able to bring in clients like my boss, the amazing rainmaker. I was no daredevil.

I only started to become convinced when my friend and her partner mentioned that a client of theirs had a possible litigation matter. Would I at least have lunch with them? We had a pleasant lunch and I discussed the client's problem with him. We hit it off well. What would it take to get me to handle the case, he inquired. My friends were pleased. They had proven to me beyond a doubt that I could get clients. I went to lunch with the next potential client without a fight.

Touch and Goes—Preparing to Solo

Once you show that you know your stalls, you have to learn to take off and land before you can solo. The practice exercise is called "touch and goes," which is just like it sounds. You take off and land over and over until you get it right. You can solo when you do it completely without help and without scaring the instructor.

I took it very slowly. I only could go to lessons once a week at best, so it was taking a long time to get it right. I enjoyed working the radio, but the instructor was too comforting and too "there" for me to not rely on her. So I took off and landed over and over again for weeks, until it was comfortable.

Touch and Go—Preparing to Solo

The Florida bar does not have any prerequisites for going solo. There is no comfortable period of practice beforehand. The only person you scare is yourself. I went to the library, got all the books, and did the calculations. How much my expenses would be, how much I would need to survive, and how much I would need to bill to pay overhead and survive. It turned out that if I used my reasonable associate's hourly rate (at that time it was $125/hour) for the first year, I only would have to bill and collect four hours a day.

I gave my firm six weeks' notice and began working three jobs. I began to wrap up my old practice, set up a new one, and do my own secretarial work for the new practice. I had to do everything at once. It had to be right the first time or else. I bought computers and programs, got supplies at a going-out-of-business sale, and borrowed and bought some furniture. I hired a part-time free-lance secretary who would start in a few weeks. I started doing work for my new clients. It was nerve-wracking and there was no one to rely on but myself.

Solo Practice

I soloed in my law practice before I soloed flying. I held my open house on March 1, which was a whopping success. I invited all the lawyers,

Top Ten Things to Do When Forming Your Firm That You May Not Think About

1. Decide on your firm's form. Will you incorporate? Form a partnership? Be a sole proprietor?
2. File your articles of incorporation or partnership documents with the proper authorities in your state.
3. Obtain your occupational licenses.
4. Get your bank account. Decide what accounts you will need. You will need an operating account. You also may need trust accounts or other special accounts depending on the nature of your practice.
5. Reread the ethical rules for your state. Check up on advertising, trust accounts, conflicts of interest, and other restrictions that your old firm took care of for you.
6. Buy a computer. Get one that you will be able to use yourself. I *love* my Macintosh because it is intuitive to use. My secretaries have universally hated it because they were used to IBM. WordPerfect on Windows and on the Mac are virtually identical, so the differences are beginning to disappear. Most legal programs still are available only in DOS, but some enlightened software companies are developing some great Mac programs. Consider what programs you will likely need. Your state bar association may have an organization that advises solo and small practitioners on computer programs for lawyers. Call them. Contact a local computer store or a consultant to have him or her demonstrate programs designed for lawyers. Time and billing, accounting, and word processing probably are essential. Consider hooking up to computerized research services, such as ABANet.
7. Make sure you understand all of the tax rules. Consider payroll, unemployment, intangible property, sales or services, and other taxes that you may be subject to as a business. Your local offices of the Department of Labor and the Internal Revenue Service can send you publications on whatever topics you need. Hire an accountant or bookkeeper unless your field is tax law. My accountant has been worth his weight in gold.
8. Find office space. Consider your needs. If you need to do research almost every day, you probably will need a law library. Find office space that already has one or consider whether your office space has room for one. Check out space-sharing with law firms and executive suites that may provide receptionist and secretarial services. If you decide to practice from home, consider whether clients will need to visit your office and the security problems that may result. Look carefully at the home office tax rules. Talk to other lawyers who have home offices and ask them about advantages, disadvantages, and advice.
9. Announce your opening. Send press releases and announcements to anyone who publishes notices about lawyers or law offices, such as bar publications. Hold an open house for potential clients and friends. Make sure people know you exist.
10. Get insurance. Make sure your health, life, disability, and other insurance needs are taken care of. Obtain COBRA coverage from your previous employer if you can. Consider group plans that are available through bar and other associations. Remember ERISA requirements if you have employees.

businesspeople, politicians, and friends I knew. Most of them came. My free-lance secretary started working part-time that same day. Being an employer changed my perspective on life. I took back almost everything I ever said about my former bosses. Suddenly, I had no runners, copy people, paralegals, or any of the other services I was used to. I bought a billing program and an accounting program for my computer to manage my administrative duties.

Just as everyone had told me, the clients came somehow, mostly through other female lawyers who were delighted that I had "broken free." I started to market my practice with some limited success by joining organizations and networking, writing articles, and with a brief stint with direct mail. I had no trouble billing my four hours a day, except that administrative duties took up much of the rest of my time.

I was free. I could come and go as I pleased, work the way I had always wanted, and abide by no rules but my own. In many ways, I was more stressed, but it was a *good* stress that came from being in control of my own life.

Solo Flying

My first solo flight came about two months into my new practice. My instructor asked me if I could come during the week because the airport was less crowded. I could, much to my own amazement, because there was nobody to tell me that I could not. It was clear when I went up; my first touch and go was fine. Then came the traffic and the cloud. I had to continue downwind of the airport because traffic was coming. The air traffic controller would tell me when to turn. I kept going, further and further, until I no longer could see the airport. A rain cloud was ahead and I must have veered to the left a little. Finally, air traffic control authorized me to turn. I turned toward the airport. All I could see was my rain cloud.

I figured that the airport was somewhere ahead of me, so I went forward. When I finally saw a runway, I headed for it. Then I realized it was the wrong runway. I quickly turned and somehow got to the proper runway and landed. I had made it. It had been stressful, but now that I had passed the point of no return, it seemed easy.

What It Is Like to Go for It

People always ask me, "What is it like to be on your own?" I tell them it is scary and exhilarating and tedious and exhausting all at the same time. It is scary because you have to be totally self-reliant and confident, and sometimes you have moments of fear and doubt. You wake up at four in the morning and think that you have missed that big hearing or deadline, just like the old law school nightmares of missing an exam. If you go out on your own right out of school, you have to have the self-confidence of Superman or Superwoman, because you still are learning the ropes. I waited until I had some experience and felt confident in my area of practice, which is what I would recommend to people who are thinking about soloing.

As a solo, you have to be extra careful "calendaring," and if you are sick on the day of a hearing, you have to hope for some understanding from opposing counsel and the judge. You do not always get that understanding, either. I remember one case where I called the judge's office, too sick to come to the hearing. I asked to appear telephonically or to reschedule. The judge allowed neither. I asked opposing counsel to call me and reschedule. He went in ex parte and got the order he sought. Of course, I sought a rehearing and got it, but I had a bitter day of panic in the interim while being too sick to do anything about it.

Solo practice is exhilarating because your victories are your own. When I won my first solo jury trial, the victory was all that much sweeter knowing it was mine alone. The clients thank *you*, not the partner in charge of you. They then recommend you to their friends, the highest compliment of all. And when you get that new client, nothing can compare to the feeling that it was *your* hard work and success that brought him or her through the door.

The tedium in soloing comes from performing the boring administrative tasks that you must do to keep the firm functioning. Billing, accounting, government forms, reports, and all the things you may have depended on your office manager for, now fall on you. On the brighter side, however, you know you will perform these tasks correctly the *first* time, unlike being in a large firm where you are truly at the mercy of support staff.

Soloing is exhausting because you work all day and still have to market (networking, always turning out quality work, more networking) and do all the other things to keep the firm going, and still have a life on the outside. My free time is spent in politics, my first love. However, I have managed to connect my profession and my avocation by advising campaigns on election law. I volunteered as Florida legal counsel for the Clinton for President Campaign and currently serve as general counsel for the local political party. I have turned my avocation into a profession by writing a book on election law and acting as counsel to candidates on various legal issues. The point is that you can do what you love and make money if you are creative about it.

People say it is daring to go out on your own. I say it is daring to rely on a firm for your living in these days of economic recession and hardship. I know too many young lawyers who were thrown out of their jobs without warning. The best person to rely on is yourself.

Beyond Solo—Time to Expand

Now that my practice is three years old, I am starting to feel restless. There is only so far you can go in your practice as a solo practitioner. The time has come for me to think about expanding beyond solo. How do you know when that time has come?

The first and most important reason to expand is when you begin to turn down too many cases. My choice was to handle litigation only, but I have a tremendous amount of real estate, probate, transactional, and divorce work that I refer out to other lawyers. This work could be kept in-house if I had partners to whom I could refer the work.

Second, the thing that I find most frustrating about solo practice is vacations. Every time I take a vacation, I lose a case that could otherwise have been mine had there been someone to handle the matter while I was away. Plus, there is no one to cover for me during emergencies. Many judges and opposing counsel have tried to prevent me from taking any vacations. I never have had a vacation as a solo practitioner that I have not had to *fight* to take, whether by motions for continuance, motions for protective order, or some other means to stop cases from proceeding in my absence. If I had a partner, he or she could cover for me while I was away.

3. What relationship are you to have with the client? Are you in charge of the case or is the referring lawyer? Are you allowed to communicate directly with the client? (Do not laugh. I know of one lawyer who swears to me that in one situation that was referred to him, the referring lawyer would not let him communicate with the client except through the referring lawyer.) How much control does the referring lawyer want to have over the client and you?
4. If the client asks you to refer him or her to another lawyer on an unrelated matter, will the referring lawyer expect you to send the client back to him or her for the reference?
5. What about new matters? Will you owe the referring lawyer a referral fee on them? Do you need to ask the referring lawyer's permission to take a new matter from the client?

How do you bill clients and actually get them to pay you?

1. Itemize your time. Get a computer program to generate your bills or you will go crazy at billing time.
2. Attach copies of everything you have filed or responded to on the client's behalf that month. That way the client will not ask what you spent all that time doing. I never have had a client complain about one penny of any bill I have sent when I have done this.
3. Have a signed retainer agreement. Make the client agree to pay interest for late payments. Include a provision that entitles you to an award of lawyer's fees and costs if you have to sue the client over the agreement.
4. Return clients' telephone calls. Answer their questions. You are a service person. Give them the service they want and deserve.
5. If they do not pay, stop work as much as you can. Withdraw if you must. Do not become an indentured servant, which is what happens when you wait until the date of trial and the judge will not let you withdraw.

What do you do during periods when business is slow?

1. This will happen periodically. Do not panic.
2. Write an article on a topic in your area of practice. Write a book. Join an organization. In other words, do something useful and creative that may generate some business and will keep you from twiddling your thumbs.
3. Tell your friends. They may think you are too busy to take on new work. They may be able to refer some work to you.
4. Play a video game. Learn how to fly. Have some fun with your free time while you can. The work will come.

Right now, I am talking to another lawyer who also has a solo practice. We are looking over the possibility of forming a firm and seeking out a third partner. Who is she? She is the lawyer to whom I refer the bulk of my non-litigation business. She is the person whose work I trust and who feels the same kinds of growing pains that I feel. There is work that we could seek out but are not seeking because we are unable to take on any more than we have. When you reach the point that you avoid potential new clients, something has to give. You must either expand or stagnate where you are.

I am just as afraid of expanding as I was of soloing. I am comfortable again, and it is hard to move on even though it could benefit me. I need to regain the nerve that I had when I started soloing. I have to give up some of the control I have learned to love. I think it may be worth it. The problem is finding partners whose practices and personalities are compatible. I am still looking for that third partner to make it work.

A few months ago, I met with the founding partner of Florida's largest law firm. I asked him how he did it. It turns out that he started with a three-lawyer firm and ended up with more than 200 lawyers. He told me how he did it, and I plan to use him as a model. What was his secret? I will tell you when my firm grows to more than 100 lawyers.

Conclusion—Go for It

My point is that in any endeavor, there is a first time. The first step is always the hardest. In flying, I had a truly hair-raising experience that first solo flight. I had to develop the confidence to know I would be OK up there; otherwise, my instructor always would have to be by my side.

Down here on the ground it is really the same. It would have been easy to stay in the cozy cocoon of a law firm. A partner always would have been at my side. I would not have had to learn the ins and outs of the administrative side of the practice. It is maddening and frustrating, but the hardest part is that first solo.

The thing you must do is think it out carefully, plan your first steps, then jump. And if you become so busy that you turn down work and stop seeking out clients, know when it is time to stop soloing. The key to success is overcoming that initial fear. I hope all of you budding soloists find out what it is like to be so busy that you turn down work. Trust me—as impossible as it seems, it happens to even the most tentative soloists.

CHAPTER 24

Corporations

Gwen Baumann Harrell

For a lawyer considering a career change, a corporation often appears as an attractive place to start. For years, in-house counsel often were not viewed as "real" lawyers or top-notch legal minds. As business competition has changed in the past decade, however, so has management's view of the role a lawyer can play on the management team. For reasons of both cost-efficiency and crisis prevention (as opposed to damage control), corporate legal departments have gone through a major metamorphosis. Business and legal management now are trying to create the most productive, cost-effective legal environment in which a corporation can operate.

Along with the changes in the roles and duties of in-house counsel have come changes in the milieu in which they work. Once considered cushy, Monday-through-Friday, nine-to-five jobs, with steady salaries, good benefits, bonuses, and job security, corporate counsel positions have become at least as—if not more—competitive as positions with law firms.

Professional mobility is another area of change. Historically, in-house counsel positions were viewed as final steps on the road to retirement. Until recently, few in-house lawyers left the business environment to return to traditional areas of practice. Such mobility, however, is increasing dramatically in the 1990s. As certain corporations downsize their legal departments for economic reasons, outside law firms are employing former in-house counsel to work closely with specific corporate clients. Law firms also appreciate the attractiveness of hiring lawyers who have worked for corporations, understand the corporate environment, and know how to speak the language of business management. Other in-house lawyers leave their jobs to set up their own practices, focusing on a specific area of corporate or business law.

Before beginning a corporate job search, a lawyer should investigate the corporation, its industry, and its internal legal structure. There are many ways of finding and getting the job of in-house counsel. While the best way to secure a position may be to move from an existing outside counsel relationship to an in-house counsel position, because of the diversity of legal departments, this is not the only way to find a job. Development of an area of expertise pertinent to the corporation's business is a plus, as is a lawyer's prelegal background. Management often will consider new and unique proposals of ways in which a lawyer can assist the corporation. The key to the corporate job search is to be thorough, creative, and persistent.

The Legal Department of the 1990s

There is no "standard" for in-house legal departments. Nor are there clear trends on where the legal departments of the 1990s are heading. Following the economic boom and crash of the 1980s, many corporations have been rethinking *all* of their internal strategies, which has led some corporations to downsize their legal departments to cut costs. Other corporations are expanding their in-house departments to cut outside counsel costs.

The variety of in-house legal departments is wide and divergent. Working for a corporation may entail serving as the only in-house lawyer or as a litigation specialist in the patent section of a multisection law department. The atmosphere of the corporate legal department also may be vastly different from that of a law firm. Remember, in-house counsel function in a business, rather than a legal, environment. They often work directly for business personnel and are required to operate structurally as businesspeople. Rather than analyzing a variety of legal issues and theories, in-house counsel often are expected to gather, analyze, and report factual data; propose one best way to handle a potential or actual problem; and focus on the economics of any proposed action. As well, a corporate lawyer usually functions in a certain area of trade or business. The lawyer, therefore, is expected to stay abreast of developments in the industry, be familiar with industry technology and terminology, and be able to add an additional business perspective to a nonlegal issue as part of a management team.

Another critical aspect of in-house counsel's work is the relationship with outside counsel. In-house counsel are in the unique position of employing, directing, supervising, and controlling the costs of outside lawyers handling legal matters. While this can create a novel working relationship, it often places in-house counsel in the unusual and sometimes difficult role of being both the client and cocounsel in the relationship with outside counsel. While the majority of in-house lawyers worked as corporate generalists in the past, most in-house counsel today are specialists. Depending on the size of the corporation and the industry in which it operates, corporate legal departments may have one lawyer or an entire section specializing in areas such as labor/employment law, environmental law, patent/trademark, real estate, litigation, securities, tax, commercial law, franchising, public utilities, etc. The variety is endless and the opportunities for a lawyer well versed in one of these areas of the law may be great.

The Corporate Environment

The Business Workplace

The most conspicuous contrast between working at a law firm versus a corporation will be the ambience of the workplace—both physically and intellectually. The in-house lawyer generally will work at the site of the business headquarters. This can mean a corporation's headquarters or a regional office site. It may be an atmosphere like that of many law firms, a mobile building sitting adjacent to a manufacturing plant, or anything in between. While most in-house lawyers work in corporate headquarters and wear standard business attire, others work in casual attire and may be going in and out of warehouses and physical plants. The point is that the in-house lawyer is working for a business and must be able to converse with the businesspeople in *their* environment and in their language.

Corporate lawyers often must integrate their offices into the administrative systems of the business. This may mean reporting directly to a nonlawyer—sometimes on legal issues. Depending on the corporation, there may be very specific organizational charts detailing exactly who reports to whom and who may (or may not) have access to whom. If the "chain of command" is not followed to the letter in some corporations, the lawyer may learn a quick lesson in office politics.

Another rude awakening may come in the attitude of nonlegal staff to the in-house lawyer. Lawyers are viewed as "necessary evils" in many corporations and are seen by the businesspeople as the nay sayers who prevent them from making the big sale or who cause delays in a project because of compliance with legalities. Conversely, if the in-house lawyer proves responsive and interested in making things happen, the businesspeople may openly embrace the lawyer. The bottom line *is* the bottom line: The business exists to make money. If the lawyer can save more money than he or she costs, then the lawyer will be viewed as part of the team.

The Legal Department

Another major difference between working in a law department and in a law firm is the client base. As corporate counsel, the client is the corporation. The corporation is to be distinguished from corporate officers, directors, and employees. While all of those individuals may be working for the corporation, at times some or all of them may be in conflict with the corporation for a variety of reasons. The critical thing to understand is that the corporation and its people are different legal entities and that the lawyer/client relationship may not be so easy to identify as it is when a lawyer is outside counsel.

Another difference between a law firm and a legal department may be time reporting. It is relatively rare for an in-house lawyer to "bill" the corporate client for hours worked on a specific legal matter. While in some corporate legal departments there is no time-reporting requirement, such freedom is becoming a thing of the past. While hours may not be "billed," however, they often are reported, and these reporting requirements may range from daily reports on how much time was spent working on which project, to weekly or monthly reports itemizing time by project. Because of budgets for different departments, the procedures will vary, but some type of time reporting now is the norm in legal departments across the country. In a 1993 survey taken of members of the ABA-YLD Corporate Counsel Committee, 33 percent of those in-house lawyers responding reported that they work 40 hours per week or less. Thirty-one percent reported working 45 to 50 hours, and 36 percent said they work 50 hours or more. For the purposes of this survey, "work" was defined as "billable" work only and excluded time spent on pro bono, civic, or bar activities.

A corporate lawyer also may be surprised at the resistance received when proposing to be active in local bar groups or pro bono work. Unless a true business advantage can be shown for such work, many corporations will not allow it during business hours and may even frown on it after hours. Other corporations, however, see community and bar association involvement as a plus. If such work is personally important, the lawyer should specifically inquire into the corporation's policies during the interview process (and possibly bargain for such permission).

Of course, for many lawyers, the reward comes with the paycheck. In the 1993 Corporate Counsel Committee survey, 44 percent of in-house counsel responding reported a base annual salary between $25,001 and $50,000. Forty-four percent were making between $50,001 and $75,000, while 12 percent were making more than $75,000 per year. Of the 41 corporate lawyers responding to the survey, 52 percent received no bonuses, while 48 percent received bonuses ranging from $500 to $32,000 per year. These lawyers, however, were under the age of 36, and most had been practicing fewer than eight years. Employee benefits reported, however, exceeded standard benefits. Of those responding, 90 percent received health/medical coverage and reimbursement for bar dues and continuing legal education seminars. Approximately three-fourths were provided with dental, disability, retirement, and life insurance policies at no cost to themselves. One-half of those surveyed also received dependent health insurance and profit-sharing benefits, and one in four had an automobile allowance and health-club or private-club membership. More than 18 percent benefited from paid parental leave, and 12 percent were provided with child care (on-site or reimbursement). In addition to working fewer hours than most young law firm associates, 43 percent of those surveyed reported receiving ten vacation days per year, 12 percent reported 12 to 14 days, 31 percent had 15 days of vacation, and 12 percent had 19 to 21 days off annually. Generous sick leave also was noted by 34 percent, who had no limit on sick time; 15 percent reported six to 13 weeks of sick leave annually.

Working with Outside Counsel

Switching roles from outside counsel to in-house counsel can be a dramatic transition. Because the corporate lawyer is often the only contact outside counsel has with a corporation, the relationship roles can be cloudy. Is the in-house lawyer the client or co-counsel? If the in-house counsel is directing and supervising legal work, and reviewing and approving (or questioning) bills, there is control that is inconsistent with a typical co-counsel relationship. On the other hand, if the relationship is to be a successful one, both in-house and outside counsel must work together to serve the corporate client in the most effective and economical manner. Accordingly, the in-house lawyer often must specifically assign and delegate work to outside counsel, monitor its progress, and "ride herd" on the costs incurred.

Selecting a Career as In-House Counsel

Having considered one's suitability to a job as in-house counsel, one also should consider short-term and long-term career goals. Depending on the corporation, the salary and benefits may be comparable to or better than those at law firms. If your professional goals include obtaining a top legal position with a corporation, you should consider how a particular corporate job could help qualify you for a senior position. If you hope to find a corporation where you can work up to a general-counsel slot, consider the age and experience of those lawyers already holding positions as assistant general counsel. Legal specialties also are important. If your goal is to be general counsel of a Fortune 500 service-industry corporation, starting out in the government-regulation department of a manufacturing company may not be the best idea. The key is to think like business management when planning a career within a business.

Researching the Market

Before preparing your résumé, your should explore several matters. Are you licensed in the state in which the corporate legal department is located? Although many states do not require that an in-house lawyer not practicing in state court be licensed in that particular state, some states do. More states are requiring some type of state bar license, either a limited authorization to practice for in-house lawyers or full admission to the state bar. If the latter is required, consider what will be necessary to obtain such a license.

Geographic preferences also should be considered. Do you want to limit your search to the metropolitan area in which you live? To the state? If so, you may be limiting your prospects. Are you willing to relocate? Whether you believe this is important or not, a prospective corporate employer will. With the large number of qualified lawyers on the market, corporations are very interested in finding someone who wants to be where they are and who will be interested in staying with them or in moving to other corporate locations.

Consider the industry as well. The corporate environment is vastly different in service versus manufacturing industries. Think about what type of atmosphere you are most comfortable in. Are you more content working with sales and marketing people or with technical people? While you may have both within one corporation, look at the background of management. If you are used to an expense account, elaborate offices, and working by gut instinct and individual creativity, avoid a company run by engineers who want facts and figures and who have spartan, but practical, offices. If you value your private time away from the office, avoid a company that requires evening and weekend social activities and pushes your community involvement. The key to your success within the corporate environment is that you become a part of the team. If the style of the team is vastly different from your style, eventually either you will be unhappy at your job or corporate managers will be unhappy with you. Finding a good match of business and personal styles, however, can lead to an immensely happy and productive career.

Beginning Your Search

There are a variety of ways to approach a corporate job search. Most experts will tell you that the best way to find a corporate job is by using normal business strategies, i.e., networking. To the extent you have existing business or personal relationships with corporate executives, you should use these to inquire into possible openings or to make general inquiry about in-house counsel jobs. Many corporations approach existing outside counsel when considering adding legal staff. Having enjoyed a successful working relationship and already knowing about the corporate client's business and legal problems certainly work in a lawyer's favor when an opening becomes available. Although this is the easiest way to find an in-house position, there are other ways, also.

Consider attending meetings of or joining a local or national corporate counsel group. Attending seminars aimed at in-house counsel also can be advantageous. Not only will you have the opportunity to learn about legal matters that are of interest to in-house counsel, but you may have the opportunity to meet some general counsel, inquire into the corporate legal department atmosphere, and do a little networking at the same time. Some local and the national corporate counsel organizations, such as the American Corporate Counsel Association (ACCA), based in Washington, D.C., may be able to assist you in your job search. ACCA has a résumé bank available to members and nonmembers for a fee.

Publications targeting corporate counsel, such as *Business Law Today* and the *American Corporate Counsel Association Journal*, can offer ideas, as well as being good sources of classified advertisements for in-house counsel positions. *The National Law Journal* and *The American Lawyer* also feature periodic sections aimed at in-house counsel. General business publications, such as the *Wall Street Journal*, are alternative sources of information about possible structural changes within corporations that may include their legal departments. The classified sections of such publications also include listings for in-house counsel positions. The larger the data base from which you draw, the greater are your chances of finding out about corporations or positions that you are well suited for.

Other sources include the legal and executive search firms. Although "headhunters" are more likely to be interested in you if they are making the call, it does not hurt to contact one or two to inquire into the overall job market and into your suitability for positions that they are seeking to fill. It is *not* advisable, however, to contact a large number of such search firms, for you may "oversaturate" yourself.

Although professionals in the search business are unenthusiastic about the last search option—the "blind search"—you may want to consider it. By thoroughly researching corporations in which you are interested and sending in a résumé, you may find a job that becomes available earlier than a corporation contemplated or one that is created especially for you. Often corporate officers spend months contemplating adding a new person to fill an uncreated position, but they are in no rush to get the search started. If they find a candidate who fits the anticipated position, however, they are spurred into creating the position rather than risk losing a good candidate. Similarly, general counsel may be considering restructuring the legal department, but have not yet presented any recommendations to management. Your résumé could be the one that catches their eye, leads to a general interview, and then to the creation of a new position to match your experience and qualifications. Statistics show that roughly 25 percent of positions filled are created to fit the qualifications of a specific individual.

The Hiring Process

Once in the door, the candidate may face a variety of hurdles before getting the offer. These may include multiple interviews and, often, a variety of tests. Initial interviews are for the most part conducted by in-house human-resources personnel or executive search firms. If the candidate passes this screening, an interview with the legal hiring authority normally will occur.

Depending on the policies of the corporation, a candidate who advances through this phase will often undergo a battery of personality, intellectual, and management-style tests. Assuming the outcome of such tests is favorable, count on *at least* one more round of interviews with some level of business management. Corporations are very careful about their legal staff and want their lawyers to fit the management style of the corporation, as well as being technically proficient. As a final step, be prepared to submit to drug testing, for many corporations require this of *all* employees as a precondition to employment.

Negotiating the Offer

If you are offered the job, consider whether you want to accept it immediately or if you want to negotiate for better terms. Normally, salary and benefits are discussed during the interview process so that both parties have an understanding about these matters by the time the offer is made. If the salary is not what you expected, you may want to negotiate for a review and possible increase after an initial trial period, such as 90 days or six months. You also should consider the value of the benefits that the corporation offers that you have not had before. Bonuses based on company profits or success rather than on *your* performance must be carefully evaluated. Ask how often bonuses have been paid in the past two to three years and in what percentage. You may find that they are not so great a benefit as you had anticipated or you may find that they make the difference between a salary that is acceptable and one that is not.

Finally, consider whether you want to negotiate for nonpecuniary benefits. Do you want a particular job title? Do you want to work nonstandard hours to accommodate certain family obligations? What about pro bono work? Would extra vacation days make the offer more attractive? If you have made it through the long interview process and have been offered the position, chances are that the corporation values you and may be willing to make accommodations to get you and keep you happy.

Conclusion

A position as in-house counsel often is one of the most coveted of any legal position. The merging of the business and legal professions can be very fulfilling to the right lawyer. The professional environment, salary, benefits, and working hours may be more flexible and may provide the atmosphere in which a lawyer can prosper. Such a position also may be a stepping-stone to other employment later in the lawyer's career. By taking a closer look at this career option, one may find that being a lawyer takes on a whole new meaning.

CHAPTER 25

Government: Federal Agencies

Marilyn Tucker[1]

The federal government employs approximately 24,000 lawyers, as well as many others with law degrees who work in law-related or nonlegal positions. Nearly 45 percent of these lawyers are concentrated in the Washington, D.C., area. Nationally, women account for 33 percent of federal lawyers, which represents an increase of approximately 6 percent over the past five years. During that same time period, however, the percentage of women in federal legal positions in the nation's capital declined from 42 percent to the current 35 percent.

Economic and political factors govern the number of lawyers hired annually by the federal government. During the 1991 fiscal year, the most recent year for which this information is available, there were 1,654 new full-time permanent lawyer hires, according to the Statistical Analysis and Services Division of the Office of Personnel Management (OPM). At the present time, lawyer hiring is at a very slow pace as a result of extensive freezes and cutbacks and because current economic conditions reduce employee turnover at all levels. Nonetheless, lawyers always are being hired somewhere in the government, even while a freeze is on and cutbacks are occurring.

An understanding of the employment patterns of federal lawyers, and which agencies provide the most likely opportunities for experienced lawyer applicants, will make the job-hunting task less daunting. According to Linda A. Cinciotta, Director, Office of Attorney Personnel Management (OAPM), Department of Justice, of the total number of lawyers employed by the federal government, about one-third work at the Department of Justice. Other federal lawyers work for approximately 64 different agencies. The top ten agencies employ almost 20,000, and only 25 agencies have more than 100 lawyers on staff. A list of the 25 agencies that employ 100 or more lawyers appears at the end of this chapter.

Lawyers, as part of the Excepted Service, are not rated by the OPM; rather, the recruiting and hiring of lawyers is handled by individual federal agencies. Because the OPM does not supervise lawyer hiring, the bureaucratic red tape of the OPM rating process is eliminated; this also means, however, that there is no central information source on lawyer job vacancies. Consequently, a decision to seek legal employment with the federal government means checking with each agency of interest to determine current needs and procedures. Often applicants have difficulty obtaining such information, and while the process can be overwhelming and frustrating, understanding that lawyer hiring is decentralized and a matter of agency policy should help in recognizing the need to be assertive in seeking federal legal opportunities.

Advertising of Lawyer Positions

The OPM's lack of involvement in lawyer hiring also means that lawyer job openings do not have to be advertised; individual agencies have authority to hire without justifying their selection to an outside oversight agency. Government agencies with large lawyer populations have separate offices for lawyer personnel recruitment; most of these offices, however, are more involved in entry-level rather than experienced lawyer hiring.

Although not required to do so, some agencies regularly advertise lawyer openings, while others advertise only when they are seeking very specialized and difficult-to-find experience. In some agencies, when an opening becomes available, employees within the immediate division, as well as within other divisions of the same agency, are made aware of the opening. Also, some agencies mail job announcements to those federal agencies on their employee-service mailing list.

A small number of federal agencies use vacancy announcements to advertise lawyer openings. Because vacancy announcements are used infrequently for advertising legal positions, many applicants overlook this valuable information source. Agencies that do use vacancy announcements, such as the Commodity Futures Trading Commission, post these announcements in their own personnel offices and send them to other agencies and to law school career-services offices. All legal positions have a "905" occupational code designating a "lawyer" position—one in which the individual has a lawyer-client relationship with the agency. This code, which appears on the vacancy announcement, is reserved for lawyer positions. Jobs that directly draw on legal skills, but that have been classified as law related, will not have a "905" occupational code.

Vacancy announcements also give the position title, location of the job, opening and closing dates for accepting applications, qualifications desired and required, and a position description. The position description section is highly detailed and as a result, it is the most helpful part of a vacancy announcement. Job seekers are able to use the specifics of the job description in tailoring a résumé, completing a Standard Form 171, and in planning an interview strategy. Do not overlook vacancy announcements when seeking government legal employment.

Positions that are publicly advertised usually appear in the *National and Federal Legal Employment Report* or in the *Federal Career Opportunities Bulletin*, which is more general and not exclusively for legal positions. The Federal Bar Association publishes the *Lawyer's Job Bulletin Board*, another source used by agencies to list lawyer positions. If very specialized experience is sought, positions are likely to be advertised in trade publications whose readers are prospective applicants and in periodicals such as the *Legal Times* and *The National Law Journal*. The *Wall Street Journal* and some law school alumni job bulletins also are good sources for job announcements. Additionally, the Interagency Attorney Personnel Group, a group of lawyers and lawyer personnel recruiters representing approximately 40 agencies, is basically a forum to discuss rules and regulations affecting lawyers; however, hiring trends can be announced at these meetings and, therefore, hiring officials from one agency may be aware of recruitment efforts at other agencies.

If lawyer positions do not have to be advertised and only a small portion of lawyer job listings reach the public, how can you as a job seeker expect to get into the federal government?

Target Your Federal Job Search

The first thing you will need to do is to narrow down "the federal government." Begin by reading about and understanding the nature of the legal work performed by each of the various agencies. Do not assume that general knowledge provides enough information about the agencies to enable you to skip the research step. Too often, opportunities are overlooked because job seekers take this attitude. Many job seekers, for example, believe that all positions with the Internal Revenue Service (IRS) require a background in tax. Although this certainly is true for most of the IRS divisions, one does not need a tax background to work in the Disclosure, Litigation, Criminal Tax, or General Legal Services divisions. It is important, therefore, to do the background reading and not assume that the name of an agency provides all of the required information. Lawyers, as job seekers, frequently base major career decisions on "hunches" and "assumptions." You would not advise a client to make important decisions without facts, and this decision is at least as important to you and your long-term career satisfaction.

Begin by reviewing the *U.S. Government Manual* for a broad overview of each federal agency and its mission. Read *Federal Careers for Attorneys* and *Now Hiring* to learn about legal positions in the federal sector. Then refer to *The Federal Legal Directory*'s excellent "Topical Index." The index simplifies the task of identifying which agencies and specific divisions within agencies to consider if interested in a particular content area. For example, the civil-rights topic refers the reader to approximately 27 different divisions or sections of federal agencies that deal in some way with civil-rights issues. These four volumes should provide enough background for you to eliminate some agencies and determine which others are of interest. You then will be ready to develop a list of "target" agencies. You may even want to develop two lists—those agencies that are likely to be interested in your background and those for which you would like to work but have no obvious match.

While focusing on agencies in which you have a particular interest because of the content of the work performed, think also about geography. Although nearly half, approximately 10,600, of all federal lawyer positions are in the Washington, D.C., area, there are more than 30 federal agencies with regional, district, or field offices that have legal staffs. The staffs of regional offices are small and as a result, it can be more difficult to obtain a legal position with a satellite office. Nevertheless, if your primary goal is to get a job with a specific agency, either because you have expertise you want to build on or because you are determined to develop the expertise in a specific field, it certainly is worth considering several locations. A number of publications will be helpful in identifying possibilities outside of the Washington area. One excellent resource mentioned previously, *Federal Careers for Attorneys*, provides a geographical listing of federal agencies in each state that have legal staffs. Other publications do not limit their information to agencies with legal staffs; however, these resources are helpful information sources when considering federal employment. The *Federal Regional Yellow Book*, for example, is a semiannual publication covering federal government offices outside of Washington. Two other resources for identifying nationwide possibilities are the *Federal Yellow Book* and the *Federal Personnel Office Directory*, which identifies the federal hiring offices throughout the country. While incomplete, the list that follows is intended to give you an idea of agencies with satellite offices:

> Department of Agriculture
> Department of Transportation
> Environmental Protection Agency
> Equal Employment Opportunity Commission
> Federal Deposit Insurance Corporation
> Postal Service
> Securities and Exchange Commission

Once you have narrowed your initial search to a few agencies, check to see if those agencies publish a brochure for prospective lawyers. Recruitment brochures, though generally written specifically for new lawyers, contain information that is relevant to all lawyer applicants. Reading the brochures will help you determine to which sections, departments, or divisions of the agency you want to direct your application. Otherwise, when you do not indicate a preference, those individuals screening résumés will decide for you where to direct your application. The choice should be yours; it is, after all, your career.

Law-Related Positions

Many government jobs do not require a law degree, but frequently are filled by persons with such a degree. *Federal Law-Related Careers* defines a "law-related career" as one in which "[a] law degree, legal training, or knowledge of one or more areas of law is directly applicable to the work involved" and, in fact, "the job description [may require] the incumbent to utilize certain legal skills."

This publication contains an excellent chart showing federal law–related careers according to legal fields of interest. A job seeker can use this chart to identify positions closely related to a particular legal background or interest. For example, a job seeker interested in international trade would be directed to seven different law-related positions, while the applicant interested in civil rights would find that there are six different types of law-related positions.

Federal Law-Related Careers currently lists more than 80 such positions. As the issues of the day change, however, and new areas become increasingly important, additional law-related opportunities are created to deal with these concerns.

Law-related positions, unlike lawyer positions, do not have "905" occupational codes; each law-related position has a different code. Lawyers working in law-related positions frequently have sought to have their positions reclassified. Reclassifying a position, particularly attempting to have a law-related position designated as a "905" classification, is an extremely difficult, if not impossible, task even when the job draws directly on legal skills. Job seekers should not accept a law-related position with the expectation that once in the job, they may be able to arrange for such a reclassification.

Unlike lawyer, lawyer-adviser, or law clerk jobs, law-related positions are not Excepted Service; they are part of the competitive OPM process and, thus, to qualify, applicants must be listed on the appropriate register. For law-related positions, the Standard Form 171 takes on a whole different meaning; it is extremely important. Every phrase and clause, every function performed, every class attended helps to add to the rating score and makes the applicant more competitive.

The inclusion of law-related positions in the OPM rating process does offer the advantage of centralized job vacancy information sources. Job seekers can find advertised openings in the biweekly publication *Federal Career Opportunities*. Additionally, a wide range of recorded federal job information, including current employment opportunities and special programs, is available by calling (202) 606-2700 in the Washington, D.C., area, or (912) 757-3000 in all other areas of the country. In Washington, a Telephone Device for the Deaf (TDD) can be accessed at (202) 606-0591. Contact local State Employment Services for the TDD numbers in other regions of the country.

A sampling of positions follows that will give you an idea of the variety and types of positions that are classified as law-related:

Civil-Rights Analyst	Financial-Institutions Examiner
Contract-Termination Specialist	Foreign-Affairs Officer
Copyright Examiner	Hearings-and-Appeals Officer
Court Administrator	Insurance Examiner
Criminal Investigator	Intelligence Analyst
Employee-Relations Specialist	Internal Revenue Officer/Agent
Estate Tax Examiner	International Trade Specialist

Labor-Management Relations	Unemployment Compensation
Examiner	Examiner
Mediator	Veterans-Claims Examiner
Passport and Visa Examiner	Wage-and-Hour Compliance
Procurement Analyst	Specialist

For a complete listing of law-related positions, use the *Federal Law-Related Careers* and *The Paralegal's Guide to U.S. Government Jobs.*

Where the Jobs Are and Will Be

As a job hunter, you must recognize and be aware of market trends. What are the current issues, hot new areas, and trends affecting American business and, therefore, lawyer hiring? Where is legal work growing and where is deregulation causing it to diminish? An excellent source is the front page of each month's *National and Federal Legal Employment Report*, which deals with current trends. Regularly reading business periodicals such as the *Wall Street Journal* or scanning the *Index to Business Periodicals* will help you keep current.

In recent years, specialties that have been growing and showing evidence of continued activity are financial services, international trade, and law enforcement—including immigration and drug enforcement. Recent legislation and current events also lead job seekers to consider the food- and transportation-related agencies. How does this translate into federal hiring possibilities? Although an opening may not exist at any given moment, agencies involved in these areas are likely to be experiencing growth over the long term, and they are good bets for those seeking legal employment with the federal government. As one issue is resolved, another surfaces, and with it the need for more personnel to staff, direct, and implement programs, the law, and its regulations. Predicting where the jobs are likely to be is a matter of understanding current national priorities.

Moving In and Then Moving Out

Although individuals who come to the federal government as laterals, having previously practiced, are likely to remain in the government employ, it is worth making career decisions with an eye toward flexibility. It is easier to move from private practice to agency practice because there is virtually no aspect of the private sector that does not exist in the federal government—although the opposite is not true. (Those agencies with private-practice counterparts are more likely to have a continuous need for applicants as people move in and out.) Therefore, to increase your long-term marketability when seeking government employment, do so with the prospect that you eventually may leave and go into the private sector. Keep several issues in mind as you consider the multitude of federal legal opportunities. Know which substantive areas have a counterpart in the private sector and thus are more marketable. Know which of the divisions in what agencies provide that experience—the division frequently plays a greater role in future transferability than the agency itself.

Be very discreet in asking questions about marketability. Any individual knowledgeable about a particular specialty field, whether inside or outside the federal government, will know which divisions provide sought-after experience. Recognize that some agencies, for example, the IRS in the tax area, the Department of Justice in the litigation field, and the Comptroller of the Currency in the banking area, are "training grounds" for the private bar. Mobility is afforded to those who practice with those agencies whether they begin there directly after law school or move there later in their careers. By the same token, regardless of the prestige of working in the Solicitor General's Office, if an individual's experience is overwhelmingly appellate, it will not be easy to translate that into the private-practice world. Many agencies are engaged in fields that are not practiced by the private bar. Although their areas of specialization are extremely interesting, understand transferability ahead of time and make decisions regarding employment with all available information, including future prospects. Do not find out after the fact that your assumptions were inaccurate.

Also, most agencies have lawyers handling "housekeeping matters" such as equal opportunity, contracts, conflicts of interest, Freedom of Information Act (FOIA), torts, property, work related to the Federal Advisory Commission's Act, Sunshine Act, and Administrative Procedures Act. Although the name of the office handling these matters varies, the content areas may be pursued in any agency, but are not easily transferable to the private sector.

The Job of Getting a Job in the Federal Government

Different Agency Patterns

In many agencies, lawyer hiring occurs through the general counsel's office; occasionally, as with the Securities and Exchange Commission (SEC), it may be through the personnel office. To determine which of these patterns exists, and therefore to whom to send a résumé, use *Now Hiring*. That publication designates by agency a lawyer, general counsel, personnel officer, or a lawyer recruitment coordinator. Where a title is listed without a name, make a telephone call or several calls to the general counsel's office or the personnel office or use the *Federal Yellow Book* to obtain the correct name rather than addressing your correspondence to the personnel office. When you have identified the correct person, send a résumé and a well-written cover letter to the office listed in *Now Hiring* even if the job has not been advertised. Do not stop with a résumé to the central location suggested. You must send a résumé to each of the legal divisions in which you have an interest, or if you are uncertain about which division or have no preference, send the résumé to all of the divisions within the agency staffed by lawyers. Send multiple résumés to different divisions of a single agency. A breakdown of divisions is provided in *Federal Careers for Attorneys* and *Now Hiring*.

In addition to sending a résumé to the designated individual, you should spend time finding lawyers within each of the divisions of interest to you to whom you can direct a résumé. These lawyers, while probably unknown to you, will be individuals to whom you have been referred through a mutual friend or acquaintance. The "insider" lawyer probably is not involved in hiring and may not be aware of openings with the division or within the larger agency. This individual's ability to be of assistance is based on being an insider. Consequently, this person will know the power structure within the division, will know to whom to direct your résumé, and can provide the name of an individual whom you should contact.

At the time you apply, it generally is not necessary to submit a Standard Form 171. Lawyers, and those who hire lawyers, usually rely on the résumé; a 171 generally is completed after the fact to conform with government regulations. Because it is rarely necessary to begin the process with the 171, do not wait until that form is complete to apply for an opening; you will, however, need to complete the 171 at some point. Agencies that have their own forms and 171 supplements routinely send those forms to applicants from whom they receive résumés.

Because each agency handles recruitment in its own manner, it is very difficult to describe the general process in great detail. When résumés are received, they may be automatically circulated to the division requested by the applicant or the one deemed appropriate by the reviewer, or they may be kept on file until a division requests résumés. Agencies keep résumés on file for varying lengths of time, generally three months to one year. After that time, if you wish to remain an active applicant, you should inform the agency in writing and send another résumé with the written request.

An Aggressive Approach

Regardless of which divisions receive your résumé, your job search has only just begun. Too many job seekers send a résumé and then wait—and the longer one is out of law school, the less likely this approach will work. If you are serious about finding a position with a federal agency, you cannot afford to stop after the résumé is in the mail. Each agency receives an overwhelming number of applications. The personnel officer in an agency with a small legal staff mentioned that the agency receives approximately 50 to 150 unsolicited résumés monthly from experienced lawyers. If that is the case in agencies with small legal staffs, imagine the number of résumés received by the large agencies, and you will understand why you cannot afford to sit back and wait.

Another reason to avoid a passive approach is the tendency of everyone who has an opening to spread the word aggressively among professional colleagues involved in the same specialty area. "My top-notch litigator is accepting a position in private practice. Do you know anyone with a few years of litigation experience?" Additionally, everyone who receives a continuous flow of résumés realizes that there is no systematic, guaranteed way to find the best employee, nor is there a way to interview all of the applicants with promise. Consequently, the personal-recommendation route has huge advantages for those doing the hiring.

It is not surprising, therefore, that people coming into the government, as well as people leaving the government, continue relationships with their private-sector counterparts and serve each other as unofficial hiring sources. A Federal Communications Commission (FCC) lawyer mentioned that excolleagues, now in private practice, call him whenever their firm needs a communications lawyer. This process is not limited to the FCC. It cuts across agencies and is unrelated to specialties; it takes place on a regular and continuing basis. Even when there is no direct private-practice counterpart, hiring lawyers prefer to use recommendations from colleagues as a way to screen the pool of applicants they will interview. One young government lawyer indicated that when an opening occurred in his division, he solicited candidate recommendations from both a judge he had appeared before and a law school professor with whom he had worked. The position was advertised, but those who actually were interviewed were recommended either by the judge or the professor.

In addition to their private-practice counterparts and professional colleagues, government-hiring people recruit experienced lawyers from client agencies. It is usual for applicants, for example, to the Environment and Natural Resources Division of the Department of Justice to come from the Environmental Protection Agency (EPA) and the Department of Interior, or for Criminal Division applicants to be sought from state and local district attorney offices. As an experienced lawyer, it is important to understand these "feeder" relationships and accordingly plan a realistic strategy. You cannot rely on being at the right place at the right time or being selected from a huge field of applicants based on your paper credentials. A small percentage of job seekers find opportunities in that way, but the majority do not. You must be willing to conduct an aggressive campaign.

If you do have contacts in an agency of interest, call the individual you know, even if it has been many years since you have seen or spoken to each other. You might say something like, "It has been a long time since I have seen you, and I understand that you have been at Housing and Urban Development [HUD] for five years. Currently, I'm at a crossroads in my career. I am contemplating seeking a position in the government [or switching agencies], but I have not yet made any decisions. I'm calling you now because you obviously know a great deal about the agency, and I would value your opinion. Would you be willing to spend 15 to 20 minutes with me?"

If you do not know anyone in the agency of interest, your first job will be to find an intermediary, someone who does know a lawyer on the inside. Two items should be remembered here: First, your intermediary/colleague does not have to be a lawyer to lead you to an inside government lawyer. Second, the lawyers to whom you are referred by the intermediary do not have to be branch or section chiefs, or individuals with hiring authority, or even lawyers in the same department. If they practice law with the agency, if they are staff lawyers, they still can direct you to the appropriate sources, albeit less directly. Once you have found people who know lawyers inside, get started by using the name of your acquaintance. You might say, "Hello, Mr. Smith. My name is John Tailor. I'm a friend of Chris Potter's, and I got your name from

Chris. I seem to be at a crossroads in my career and am contemplating several different types of career moves. One possibility is to move into the federal sector [or to transfer agencies]. Based on what I have learned about you from Chris, I would value your opinion and your experience. Would you be willing to spend 15 to 20 minutes with me?" (See Chapter 10 for a discussion of informational interviewing.)

Frequently, job hunters do not use their contacts. They assume that their own contacts, and those to whom they have been referred, can do nothing to help because they are not responsible for hiring, high enough in the pecking order, in the right division, or likely to put themselves out for another applicant. Making such assumptions will have a detrimental effect on the job search process. Regardless of the size of the agency's legal staff and the turnover, personal contacts are important; they are invaluable. From conversations with several FCC lawyers, for example, it appears that everyone knows each other. Therefore, a comment from a lawyer that he or she has met you and that you seem bright, articulate, and well qualified should be very helpful in giving you an edge over faceless applicants whose résumés sit piled on an interviewer's desk.

Be prepared for the job search to take six to nine months or longer. The actual length of time, of course, depends on many factors. Some of these factors are out of your control, such as the economy and the hiring goals of the agencies that you have targeted. Your qualifications, level of job-seeking activity, and luck also affect the time it will take. A longtime government lawyer who regularly writes articles on federal opportunities said that even in a good job market, it will take a "hotshot" applicant at least two to three months to get into the government.

In recent years, there has been a marked increase in experienced lawyer hiring. This trend always has existed in agencies recruiting litigators and in those agencies, such as the FCC, whose staff consists of a very high percentage of lawyers. Today, however, this trend is more widespread; lateral hiring is taking place in greater numbers at many federal agencies.

Lawyers at all experience levels apply and accept employment with the federal government. While it is true that the largest percentage of experienced lawyers seeking government employment do so with two to six years of experience, seasoned lawyer applicants cover the whole spectrum in terms of years in practice and in background. They come with one to 20-plus years of experience from all legal settings, including private law firms, corporate counsel, local government, and solo practice. Successful applicants also include those who have taught in law schools and never have practiced.

Several years ago, the NALP updated and published the results of a survey originally conducted by the OAPM of the Department of Justice. In that survey of government agencies and their hiring needs, the following agencies indicated an expectation to do more lateral than new graduate hiring:

Department of Energy—Office of the General Counsel
Department of Justice—U.S. Attorney's Offices
Department of Transportation—Federal Railroad Administration

Department of Defense
General Services Administration
Overseas Private Investment Corporation
International Trade Commission
National Transportation Safety Board
Peace Corps
Selective Service System
Smithsonian Institution

Although there is no hiring season for experienced lawyers, some agencies indicate that spring may be a good time for lawyers moving in laterally. Would-be government lawyers should recognize that hiring officials in those agencies that annually seek out large numbers of new law school graduates are busy with recruits from August through December. Therefore, at those agencies, the process for experienced lawyer hiring may be longer and slower in the fall. Also, if the target agency has a peak season, like the IRS, recruiting and hiring will not be a top priority for a period of several weeks or months. Other agencies may have their own informal scheduling issues related to seasonally heavy work loads.

Compensation

Experienced lawyers generally begin federal service at the GS-13 ($47,920) level, although this varies not only with the agency but occasionally with the division (the Enforcement Division of the SEC begins people at a GS-12) and also with the number of years and type of experience. Some laterals come in at a GS-14 ($56,627) or GS-15 ($66,609) level, but this certainly is not the norm.

Salary has long been a factor for those considering federal government positions. The dramatic gap between private and public salaries often is compounded by the high cost of living in Washington, D.C., where most federal lawyers are based. Within grades, however, there is some flexibility if an agency can justify that the potential hire's expertise or credentials warrant a special circumstance. Some agencies have fairly rapid grade promotion ladders, so that salary can increase significantly in a short period of time. Nonetheless, regardless of in-grade flexibility and promotion schedules, the monetary differential has been a factor to consider. This extends beyond the General Schedule (GS) level into the Senior Executive Service (SES), where the pay cap is approximately $115,700.

During the summer of 1986, private-practice salaries escalated and compensation became an issue of great concern among those charged with finding good legal talent for the federal government. As a result of the recent economic downturn and the unprecedented layoffs of lawyers at all experience levels, federal pay scales, which remain much lower than private-sector compensation, now play a far less significant role in the government's ability to attract extraordinary legal talent. At every level, the current business slowdown, combined with an increasingly vocal commitment to a balanced lifestyle, have reduced earlier concerns about salary differentials.

Career Advancement

Moving from a GS-13, where most experienced lawyers begin, to a GS-14 is a matter of time in grade. In many agencies, the number of GS-15 positions are limited and most require supervisory or management duties. A lawyer who wants to be a strict practitioner and not handle the administrative matters may have difficulty securing a nonsupervisory GS-15 position. The pyramid is clearly very wide at the bottom and narrow at the top. If you are in an office with more qualified people than top slots, you may get stymied at the GS-14 nonmanagement level. If that happens, what can you do? The answer is that except for being patient and making your commitment to the agency known, there is very little that can be done. A lateral move to a regional office generally is not the solution; it is difficult to transfer into those offices at high grades. Nor is a move to another office within the agency a viable option because they, too, have their own people in line. In many agencies, there are a limited number of GS-15 positions, and the branch chief and section chiefs in these positions generally are career people not likely to be moving on. Nonetheless, although there are ceilings on the number of positions, ambitious individuals who plan to stay in the federal government employ and who make that known eventually do get into supervisory positions.

Beyond the GS-15 are the SES positions that are compensated at levels above the grade schedules. Each agency establishes the technical qualifications for its SES positions, and there are government-wide managerial qualifications, known as "executive competency review factors," which are listed in each issue of the *National and Federal Legal Employment Report*. SES positions, such as technical adviser, division director, etc., are extremely competitive, and many people find that leaving the government and then returning makes them more competitive for these prestigious appointments.

Advantages of Federal Legal Practice

There are numerous advantages to practicing law for the federal government. In addition to having the opportunity to be involved in making national policy decisions, government lawyers are given responsibility at a very early stage. As a result, those lawyers coming into the government with several years of experience have immediate opportunities to work on significant issues and to litigate. Frequently, individuals coming into the federal government having practiced for just a few years are dealing with law firm counterparts at the partnership level.

Private practitioners must continuously compete for new clients. This constant pressure to get and then to keep clients is not for everyone. Practicing law for a federal agency where there is a "captive client" frees lawyers of this concern and allows them to concentrate on solving legal issues rather than on wooing prospects.

Because government lawyers are not competing for clients or attempting to make a profit for the organization, they also are freed of billable-hour pressures and the extraordinarily long days that often result. There is great variation from agency to agency, but as a general rule, government lawyers work more reasonable hours—another advantage of federal employment. An individual who wants to pursue outside interests will find government practice more in tune with personal needs.

Another advantage of federal practice is the marketability of the experience. Those who leave the federal practice go not only to private law firms but also to financial institutions, associations, Capitol Hill, and academia. Career mobility from the government depends on how much experience one has and by which agency(ies) one has been employed. Some agencies are clearly revolving doors, while others provide little transferability. Lawyers who enter the government already having practiced for a number of years are less likely to move around; they often stay and become the career lawyers. However, those who want to leave government should do so before they have practiced in that setting for too many years. It is difficult to move with more than four or five years' experience.

Experienced lawyers change jobs, among other reasons, in order to move into a different specialty. Changing specialties is not easy to do under any circumstances, but many lawyers have found federal agencies far more receptive than private employers. For those who want to move out of a content area that they dislike or is defunct, for those who want to move into the private sector but whose credentials are a drawback, the federal government often provides a credible interim move from which they later are able to achieve their ultimate goals. One government lawyer with five years of experience wanted to achieve two goals—to change from energy to another specialty area and also to move into the private sector. She was unsuccessful in finding a private-sector nonenergy position. Although she was unable to achieve both goals simultaneously, however, she did find an agency that was willing to hire her in a totally different content area. If she later decides to leave the second agency, and her new specialty is one that is marketable, the new content area may provide another opportunity to move into the private sector and achieve her second goal.

Interim moves into the federal sector as a way to change content specialties or as a way to fill a content gap before moving into private practice, while not without risk, have worked for many ambitious career-changing lawyers. The federal government provides the credibility and the opportunity that is otherwise difficult to attain.

Finally, if a lawyer's career gets off track for some reason, accepting a position with the federal government can be a face-saving way to get back on track. Occasionally, lawyers who have been denied partnership in a private firm will take this route.

Clearly, the motivation of experienced lawyers to find a government position or to switch agencies is related to the previously mentioned advantages—a desire to change content specialties, get a career back on track, have time for other interests, or to escape the intense pressures of private practice.

The major disadvantage to being a government lawyer is perhaps compensation. Another issue that concerns many experienced lawyers is the time commitment required by a number of the federal agencies. Those commitments, which ask that new hires remain with the agency for three or four years, are considered necessary because of the magnitude of the cases and the need to rely on experienced counsel. Some agencies require that new hires sign a commitment, and other agencies appear to treat the issues more informally. Before accepting an offer with a federal agency, applicants should know whether a commitment is required and for how long a time period.

In addition to this commitment to remain with an agency for a specified time period, there now is another time issue—the five-year rule that does not permit an individual to appear before an agency with which he or she was previously associated. This new Clinton ruling is keeping many excellent lawyers from accepting high-ranking government appointments. These individuals are anxious to make a contribution within the administration, but when they leave after four or five years, they do not want to wait another five years to pursue their personal and professional goals.

Other disadvantages are the negative perception of a "government lawyer," the lack of support staff and services that make the practice of law easier, and the levels of bureaucracy and "red tape," which cause everything to move very slowly. Despite the previously mentioned drawbacks, career government lawyers experience a very high degree of career satisfaction, camaraderie, and work autonomy.

As mentioned at the beginning of this chapter, the process of obtaining a legal position in the federal sector can be an overwhelming and frustrating experience. However, armed with the information provided in this chapter, the knowledge of the agencies likely to be hiring experienced lawyers, recognition of the need to conduct an aggressive campaign, and a sense of humor, you are ready to begin the search. Career satisfaction awaits you.

Capitol Hill

Lawyers are found in many different jobs on Capitol Hill but generally are employed either as House or Senate committee staff or on the personal staff of a member of Congress. Lawyers also work for the Democratic or Republican National Committees and the Congressional Research Service. Although lawyers occupy a myriad of different positions on the Hill, no standard criteria or written guidelines make a law degree a requirement for obtaining a position. Nonetheless, those who have law degrees find them very helpful during the job search and definite advantages once in the job. They are able to better understand the legislative language, recognize essential issues, write effectively, and develop persuasive arguments. In theory, a J.D. is not a requirement; in practice, however, especially on a committee staff, a law degree has become essential.

Lawyer Positions on the Hill

Responsibilities differ for personal staff lawyers, usually called legislative assistants/directors, and committee staff lawyers who most frequently are called legislative counsel or associate/assistant counsel. The constant is that

Hill lawyers do not practice law in the traditional sense; rather, they draft and then negotiate final provisions of the law. Typical duties involve advising members on legislative proposals, preparing memos on particular matters, developing policy positions and legislative initiatives, writing position papers and speeches, negotiating questionable provisions, overseeing agency activities, dealing with constituents and the press, and handling a variety of administrative matters.

Personal staff lawyers are generalists; they focus on a wide variety of issues. They regularly work with local politics and constituents. Their duties vary depending not only on the position and level of activity of the particular congressional person with whom they work, but also on that individual's issues of interest. Because these positions usually are less well defined, the quality of experience that a personal staff lawyer has varies widely and depends on the chemistry that develops between the lawyer and the member.

Unlike personal staff lawyers, those on a committee staff need substantive knowledge in a particular issue area. As a result, lawyer graduates who are successful in obtaining a committee staff position often are individuals who had developed a content expertise prior to attending law school. Otherwise, lawyer graduates, whose goals are to obtain committee positions, often go first to another employer (i.e., a federal agency), develop an expertise, and then pursue Hill employment. Committee staff lawyers are more autonomous and more involved in policy and getting legislation passed than are their personal staff lawyer colleagues.

The administrative assistant position, the highest position in a member's office, often requires extensive experience. These individuals, as their title implies, handle major administrative matters, such as developing annual operating goals, hiring staff, and preparing budgets. As such, these positions may hold less interest for lawyer applicants, although there are certainly many Hill administrative assistants who have a law degree.

Because of the political nature of Hill work, certain personality characteristics and skills are valuable. Staff members must act proactively to accomplish their agendas, while simultaneously reacting to the agendas of others. Consequently, those who are successful possess an extraordinarily unique combination of interpersonal skills that make them good negotiators and consensus builders. And while it sounds contradictory, the most successful Hill professionals tend to be aggressive and tenacious. The environment is fast-paced and demanding; therefore, lawyers work quickly and often at a hectic pace with little time to attend to details. Those who enjoy Hill work and find the pace energizing have a genuine fondness for strategy and policy.

Job Search Techniques

There is no central placement authority or formal structure in the hiring of committee staff and even less structure to hiring for the personal staffs of congressional people. Rather, each office/committee/subcommittee has individual hiring authority. Each can set its own hiring requirements, salary, and conditions of employment and does not have to justify selections or adhere to equal-opportunity dicta. As a result, obtaining a position on the Hill not only requires a great deal of effort and persistence but often seems overwhelming to job hunters.

It is very unusual to get an interview on Capitol Hill through the passive résumé mailing approach, and while many job hunters are adverse to developing contacts and networking, this is an indispensable part of securing a position on the Hill. Networking is not only the most effective way of finding a Hill job, it actually may be the only way to be successful. Job hunters must use whatever contacts they have or can develop. For this reason, campaign work has long been a favored method for making initial contacts because it frequently puts workers in contact with individuals who know the ins and outs of getting Hill positions.

The most valuable contacts are with individuals who have political connections, those who currently are employed on the Hill, or with those who recently worked on the Hill. Beyond these direct contacts, however, job hunters must be willing to start the networking process on a more remote level— with non-Hill contacts, such as members of various interest groups, who are likely to be able to connect them with someone on the Hill. It is necessary to utilize every professional, educational, social, and political contact available, including one's own congressional person. Additionally, Hill job seekers should contact both their law schools and undergraduate school alumni offices for names of graduates on the Hill.

Committee staff positions go to those with previously established content knowledge. Prior to beginning the search, job seekers with a developed expertise should target the committee staffs where that knowledge could be useful. This can be accomplished by checking the *Congressional Directory* to determine the content specialty of the various committees. Often the scope of a committee's work is not evident from the name, and, therefore, it is very important to look beyond the title when using the directory. It also is worth remembering that most committees have both a majority and a minority staff, organized by political party affiliation.

Although a majority of the committees hire lawyers, certain staffs are considered to be among the most likely to employ legal personnel. The following list, while not a complete list of committees that hire lawyers, may be regarded as a beginning step in the research process. In the House of Representatives this list includes Armed Services, Education and Labor, Energy and Commerce, Government Operations, Interior and Insular Affairs, Judiciary, Merchant Marine and Fisheries, Public Works and Transportation, Small Business, and Ways and Means. In the Senate, the list includes the Judiciary and the Labor and Human Resources Committees, and the Select Committee on Ethics.

Job candidates who may be seeking a position on a member's personal staff should target specific members. The targets would be those individuals with whom the job seeker shares some common interest or background. Thus, the targeting criteria may be based on party affiliation or mutual interests as noted by the member's committee assignments. Additionally, consider geography when creating a target group. Individuals in a position to make hiring decisions frequently seek out applicants who have geographic ties to the member's state or district. Undoubtedly, such applicants have an inherent advantage in the Capitol Hill job market.

Those interested in a member's personal staff can develop their target group by checking the *Almanac of American Politics* and *Politics in America* to learn about the members, how they vote on key issues, and their states or districts. Just as one might have done as a prospective judicial clerk, it is worth checking into a member's style and reputation. The working relationship between the member and the personal staff lawyer greatly influences how enjoyable the term of employment will be and how much the lawyer will learn while on the Hill. Choosing to work for someone who takes a visible position on issues and who is actively involved in the legislative process might increase both job satisfaction and personal growth.

When the appropriate committees or members have been targeted, applicants then should identify the staff members who would be involved in the hiring process. The situation varies between offices, but generally it is appropriate to contact the Chief Counsel or Minority Counsel on Senate committees, the Chief Counsel, Minority Counsel, or Staff Director on House committees, and the Administrative Assistant or Legislative Director on the personal staffs of members. The names and titles of staff may be found in the *Congressional Yellow Book* and the *Congressional Staff Directory*. Because job seekers should not leave a stone unturned, the résumé and other application materials should be directed to these traditional hiring officials. Simultaneously, however, the job-seeking applicant should be heavily involved in the networking process and identifying connections to the members of committees that they have targeted.

Although one is unlikely to find a Hill position without networking, there are several publications that contain Capitol Hill job listings. Occasionally, positions are advertised in the *National and Federal Legal Employment Report*, in *Opportunities in Public Affairs*, and in law school placement offices.

Both House and Senate Placement Offices act as employment referral services for members, committees, and administrative offices. Job seekers may complete application forms that will be sent to those offices that have requested assistance in filling positions matching their qualifications. The Senate Placement Office does offer a telephone job line—(202) 228-5627.

The Democratic Study Group, another source of available positions, publishes vacancies in congressional offices and updates the list each Tuesday. These job listings may be obtained only at the House Placement Office, House Annex II; they cannot be mailed to job seekers nor are they available through a telephone listing service. Opportunities advertised through the Democratic Study Group's weekly publication range from entry-level positions to top policy jobs.

Every two years, when a large number of positions turn over on Capitol Hill, a special employment office is established for new Senate members. This temporary employment office receives résumés for new members and functions alongside of, but independently from, the traditional Senate Placement Office.

These job listing services do not include every vacancy available on Capitol Hill; they list only those openings in offices that have requested publication. Most vacancies on Capitol Hill never are advertised. It is helpful for job seekers to review such publications regularly, but the majority of these listings are for support positions. Consequently, lawyers making a transition to the Hill cannot view these tools as a substitute for networking or for making direct contact with the administrative assistants in hundreds of elected representatives' offices and with the staff directors of the full committee and subcommittees. Once you have secured an interview, you must be well prepared and be able to convey your interest and enthusiasm to the interviewer. To ensure that you are well informed the day of the interview, consider the following ideas. Read the *Almanac of the Unelected* to learn about the backgrounds of select committee staff members. Be familiar with the jurisdiction of the committee or subcommittee and knowledgeable about the member's state or district. As stated previously, this information can be found in the *Congressional Directory* and the *Almanac of American Politics*. Second, learn about the issues currently before the committee, subcommittee, or member. Both the *National Journal* and the *Congressional Quarterly Weekly Report* contain well-written reports on the key legislation currently facing Congress.

Applicants interviewing for committee positions should learn about the member who chairs that committee. Similarly, those who are seeking positions on a personal staff should investigate that member's committee assignments.

Locating Hill employment is time-consuming and requires a great deal of legwork and persistence, all of which makes long-distance job hunting extremely difficult. In fact, because most congressional offices receive thousands of résumés, it is highly unlikely for an out-of-town job seeker, unless well connected, to obtain a Hill position without coming to Washington for an extended stay. Not only does getting a job on the Hill require continuous effort, but it can be frustrating to novices because of the all-to-familiar "Catch 22": Applicants with previous Hill experience are preferred. Some job-seeking lawyers have gained Hill experience during their undergraduate summers, others worked on the Hill during law school, and still others worked with a Hill staffer on a pro bono case or another matter. It is unclear why such short-term experience is so sought after; perhaps it is merely a screening device, given the volume of applications received.

Specific times to anticipate vacancies on the Hill include the period directly following an election when new members are building their staffs or possibly in September when Congress begins. Frequently, there is a staff turnover in August, and because Congress is not in session, staffers often have time to talk and be sources of information and advice. Expect the competition to be intense because many others also will be looking at these times.

Advantages and Disadvantages

Work on the Hill generally is very exciting, and one certainly has the opportunity to impact national decisions and influence the direction of legislation. You are called on to develop new ideas to implement a member's goals, translate those ideas into legislation, and build the political support necessary to implement the ideas. Hill positions offer a great deal of variety, independence, and the opportunity to work with extremely interesting people.

Another advantage is the marketability afforded Hill lawyers. When staffers decide to leave, there are a number of different places where those with law degrees find employment; a lawyer's particular marketability, however, depends greatly on the type of work performed while on the Hill. Law firms hire Hill-experienced lawyers when they are interested both in the applicant's contacts and Hill "know-how," as well as in the specific content expertise. Also, lawyer-trained staffers find positions with the administration, public-interest organizations, and trade associations. This marketability, however, generally is limited to the greater Washington area and may not be so valued in other locales.

Long hours and low pay are two of the most frequently mentioned disadvantages. Salaries for individuals with a J.D. cover an amazingly wide range. Because there are no guidelines, some members pay whatever the market will bear; therefore, a Hill lawyer may earn as little as $14,000 to $19,000. According to a report by the Congressional Management Foundation, Capitol Hill employees earn less and receive fewer guaranteed benefits than federal executive branch employees.

As reported in the *Federal Employees New Digest* of December 14, 1992, "the average salary of employees of House members' personal staff is about $33,000, roughly the same as federal employees nationally. But the Washington-based congressional staffers make about $8,000 less on average than federal workers in the capital area, where the average federal salary is nearly $45,000. And unlike the executive branch where pay and benefits are standardized by law, congressional staff pay and benefits vary according to the individual member."

On the House side, committee members can make $100,000, especially those on the committees that pay the highest salaries, including Appropriations, Energy, Commerce, and Ways and Means. Personal staff lawyers without much experience could earn about $30,000. Committee positions, which require some Hill experience, pay more. Previous agency or law firm experience also is helpful. Allowances may be made for special expertise. On the Senate side, committee staff lawyers may earn between $90,000 and $100,000.

Two publications enable the public to locate precise salary information for the staffs of particular members or committees. The *Report of the Clerk of the House*, published quarterly, and the *Report of the Secretary of the Senate*, published semiannually, itemize personnel expense accounts in each office. Salary figures are identified both by the staff person's name and title. To find these publications, contact libraries that have government document collections or call the House and/or Senate Document Rooms through the congressional switchboard at (202) 224-3121.

Lack of job security is another disadvantage associated with Hill positions. Jobs are at the whim of the committee chair and/or the election process. The highly charged political atmosphere can be another frustrating reality when it leads to "politics over substance." One can work exhaustively on an issue and lose because of unrelated political issues that have nothing to do with the merits of a particular case. Additionally, although the daily pace may be fast, actual bills, legislation, and preliminary negotiations tend to move very slowly because of the bureaucracy and red tape associated with government practice.

Finally, working on the Hill requires the ability to work under pressure. The process of getting a bill on the floor and having it reflect your member's interest or a committee's goals can be very stressful. You are expected to know everything in the bill plus every amendment on the floor. In meetings you will be responsible for having all of the appropriate documents ready. When something happens on the floor, you will need to know about it and make a quick decision about whether to notify the member of what took place on the floor or whether to get him or her onto the floor as soon as possible. This often requires having a television monitor on at all times, even when trying to concentrate on drafting other documents.

These disadvantages, while real, are clearly overshadowed by the positive aspects of being employed on the Hill. There are many more qualified job seekers than available openings, and there always are lawyers who are willing to give up very large salaries to be involved on Capitol Hill.

Job-seeking lawyers who want the challenge, excitement, and enjoyment of a career on Capitol Hill, and who are determined to achieve their "goals," succeed in finding a position. It requires an undaunted commitment to the job of finding a job; it takes persistence, persistence, and more persistence. Nonetheless, those who do persevere have been successful. Now it is your turn.[2]

Federal Government Agencies Employing 100+ Lawyers[3]

Department of Justice (8,283)
Defense Agencies (4,210)
   Department of the Army
   Department of the Air Force
   Department of the Navy
   Defense Logistics Agency
   Marine Corps
Department of the Treasury (1,890)
Environmental Protection Agency (1,000)
Securities and Exchange Commission (900)
Federal Deposit Insurance Corporation (870)
National Labor Relations Board (600)
Department of Labor (558)
Department of Health and Human Services (550)
Department of Transportation (531)
Federal Trade Commission (475)
Equal Opportunity Employment Commission (450)
Department of Energy (301)
Small Business Administration (300)

Department of Interior (274)
Department of Agriculture (243)
Department of Commerce (225)
Commodity Futures Trading Commission (200)
General Accounting Office (165)
Postal Service (160)
Department of State (160)
Department of Housing and Urban Development (150)
Merit Systems Protection Board (130)
Library of Congress (100)
Federal Labor Relations Authority (100)

Notes

1. The author was assisted by Margaret Prinzing in preparing this chapter.

2. For individuals seeking jobs in local or state governments, contact should be made with the particular agency or entity for the local or state government. Job opportunities will vary widely, depending upon the locality or state.

3. This list was prepared for a presentation entitled, "Government Employment Opportunities" given by Linda A. Cinciotta, Director, OAPM, Department of Justice, at the NALP's Regional Conference, Albuquerque, New Mexico, February, 1993.

CHAPTER 26

Government:
U.S. Attorneys' Offices

Mary Anne Hoopes[1]

The 94 U.S. attorneys' offices employ more than half of the lawyers working for the U.S. Department of Justice. Assistant U.S. attorneys (AUSAs) prosecute federal criminal offenses ranging from relatively minor violations to major commercial conspiracies and transnational crimes. They also represent the United States in connection with civil matters, defending prominent government programs and policy initiatives as well as handling constitutional claims, financial-institution fraud, civil-rights cases, and other matters. In 1993, there were approximately 4,700 AUSAs throughout the United States, Puerto Rico, the Virgin Islands, and the Pacific protectorates. This chapter discusses the procedure for obtaining a position as an AUSA.

Appointment of AUSAs

U.S. attorneys are appointed by the president and confirmed by the Senate; a U.S. attorney serves a four-year term. AUSAs, however, are nonpolitical Excepted-Service employees like other federal lawyers, and are not subject to removal for reasons of political affiliation. Newly appointed U.S. attorneys may choose their own managerial and supervisory staffs and usually do so from among AUSAs in the district.

Several factors have combined to make the competition for AUSA positions more fierce than was previously the case. The exciting and challenging nature of the work in the U.S. attorneys' offices continues to attract numerous highly qualified applicants for available positions. In addition, the downturn in hiring by private law firms has sharply reduced the number of AUSAs taking positions in the private sector. In fact, the nationwide turnover rate for AUSAs in 1992 was less than 5 percent.

Legal appointment authority for AUSAs nationwide resides with the attorney general and is delegated to the OAPM in Washington. At present, recruitment and selection of candidates for these positions occurs at the local level within each individual U.S. attorney's office. The Department of Justice intends to implement a centralized clearinghouse for information on AUSA positions in late 1993. Until the new clearinghouse is in place, experienced lawyers interested in obtaining employment as AUSAs must contact the specific office(s) in which they wish to work. Contacts and addresses for each office are contained in *Legal Activities*, a recruitment and informational publication of the Department of Justice. This publication and additional information may be obtained by calling the 24-hour information and message service at (202) 514-3396.

AUSAs, like other federal lawyers, are exempt from the competitive process applicable to other civil-service employees. Each U.S. attorney, therefore, is free to establish individualized screening and hiring processes. In smaller offices, low turnover rates may leave no openings for extended periods of time. Even when a lawyer does depart, vacancies may be filled by transfer from another U.S. attorney's office or from one of the litigation divisions of the Justice Department.

Vacancies

Vacancies occur with regularity in larger offices, and as a result, a structured screening process exists. For example, the Southern District of New York, whose staff of 185 lawyers makes it one of the largest U.S. attorney's offices in the country, projects that it will have 25 to 30 lawyer vacancies each year. Consequently, the Southern District has a ready pool of candidates to fill positions as they become available. Applications are accepted at any time throughout the year, and the district imposes no standing requirements other than requiring each candidate to have at least two years' legal experience. The Southern District of New York also has developed its own application form and requires a résumé, a completed background inquiry form, a certificate of good standing with the bar, a law school transcript, writing samples, and letters of recommendation.

Application Review

Completed applications are reviewed by two AUSAs, one from the Civil Division and one from the Criminal Division. Successful candidates then are called in for an initial interview with another AUSA and, in turn, may be asked to return for "Wednesday-night rounds," during which they will be interviewed by four senior AUSAs. Following these interviews, a standing committee determines which candidates will be invited to meet the U.S. attorney and the executive staff for final selection.

Candidates who are selected by the U.S. attorney at the conclusion of the process are so advised and are asked to submit extensive background information to prepare for review by the Executive Office for U.S. Attorneys and the OAPM. Many other candidates to whom offers are not extended are encouraged to reapply after obtaining further experience.

An appointment request package for a prospective AUSA must include a résumé and an SF 171, a completed security form (SF 86), a preemployment inquiry form, confidentiality waivers, a set of fingerprints, and the results of contacts with the candidate's former employers. If preliminary review of these materials discloses no derogatory information, then the lawyer may be offered a 14-month temporary appointment to allow actual employment pending completion of a full-field background investigation. Every candidate who accepts a position with the Department of Justice is required to pass a drug test prior to entering on duty.

During the background investigation, Federal Bureau of Investigation agents interview the candidate's personal associates, classmates, neighbors, landlords, and former employers regarding the candidate's suitability for employment as an AUSA. Military, police, tax, and credit records regarding the candidate also are reviewed. Any history of drug or alcohol use is explored. Candidates are expected to be completely honest about these matters, and any dishonesty during the application process is viewed as disqualifying.

Once the background investigation is completed and any questionable information explained, a final suitability determination can be made and permanent appointments offered to successful candidates.

While time-consuming, the appointment process is well worth the effort. Many lawyers who have served as AUSAs find it to be the most stimulating, challenging, and rewarding period of their legal careers. In addition to its inherent satisfaction, litigation on behalf of the government offers unsurpassed preparation for legal positions in other federal agencies, as well as other legal careers.

Note

1. The views expressed in this chapter are solely those of the author and do not necessarily represent the views of the U.S. Justice Department or the U.S. Attorneys' Offices.

CHAPTER 27

The Judicial Branch

The Honorable Rebecca A. Albrecht

From time to time, almost every law student and lawyer considers the possibility of a career on the bench. But is that really a calling for you? And if it is, what should you do to best assure success in seeking and maintaining the office? The purpose of this chapter is to give you some answers to these questions.

Who Should Become a Judge?

With the exception of some limited jurisdiction courts, most courts require that their judges be lawyers. At the trial level, most judges come from the ranks of lawyers who have practiced in that court. The appellate courts attract some judges from the trial bench, law professors, and other lawyers who have developed their legal writing skills.

An experienced litigator brings to the trial bench a knowledge of the courtroom and advocacy that cannot be learned in a classroom. Well-regarded, experienced lawyers are invaluable assets to any trial bench. Lawyers tired of being lawyers, however, soon will tire of being judges. If you are burned out with lawyering, you should consider a completely different career such as sky diving or food handling—a burned-out lawyer can only be a jaded, bitter judge.

What Skills Should a Judge Have?

The skills necessary to be an effective advocate and those necessary for an effective judge are fundamentally different.

Having spent an entire career presenting only one side of the issue, and presenting the strongest case possible for a client, the new judge suddenly finds that he or she is called on to review impartially a set of facts presented and to apply those facts to the broad base of law applicable to the facts. That type of balanced thinking does not come easily to an entrenched advocate for one side or the other.

Obviously, the basic requirement for an effective judge is the ability to make decisions and the desire to do so. This requirement does not seem to be a difficult criteria to meet, but for many lawyers it is not an easy thing to do. A judge must be able to make a decision and move on. As a judge, you are responsible for making decisions about other people's lives and property. This responsibility is awesome, but one that a judge may make four or five or more times a day. If you are a person who makes a decision and then revisits that decision for weeks, serving as a judge will be very stressful for you.

A judge's role is not to frame the issues of the case, but, rather, based on the presentation of the issues by the lawyers, to analyze the pleadings filed and to challenge the law cited when necessary.

A new judge must learn to sit quietly during a lawyer's presentation of the case. A few thoughtful questions from a judge may help to clarify an issue or move a case forward, but a judge cannot become the examiner. Many judges find it very difficult to set aside their former roles as advocates. If your blood still rises when an objection is not made, the key line of questioning is overlooked, or a witness is dancing around a question, perhaps you need a few more years at the bar before you take the quieter courtroom role on the bench.

In many jurisdictions, the modern trial judge is called on to be an active participant in the movement of cases through the courts. Through trial management and pretrial conferences, the "managerial" judge is expected to take control of the pace of litigation.

With the increasing costs of litigation, the courts and their judges are being called on to participate in alternative means of dispute resolution. Judges, acting in the capacities of arbitrators or mediators, are adding innovative settlement techniques, including minitrials and advisory jury trials to traditional judicial skills.

What Are the "Costs" of a Judicial Career?

In many states, the courts are chronically underfunded. The reasons for underfunding of state courts are as varied as the states, but the effects on the courts are similar nationwide. Courts are being called on to do more and more with less and less. As a result, courts are turning trailers into courtrooms, trimming budgets, and even cutting the number of civil trials.

For a lawyer from a successful law practice, the reality of working for an underfunded bureaucracy may be a difficult adjustment. Nationwide, judges generally earn less per year than associates entering large law firms. An individual considering becoming a judge must carefully consider the needs and expectations of his or her family. Many judges find that the demands of a growing family cannot be met on current judicial salaries and for that reason alone leave the bench.

Staff salaries lag even further behind that of the judges, so finding and keeping qualified personnel is another problem for the judiciary.

Litigators, by nature, tend to be a gregarious group of people. The opportunity to interact with peers and clients is an important outlet for many lawyers. A judge must act to assure his or her ability to remain impartial and, even more difficult, to maintain the appearance of impartiality. Participation in certain partisan or agenda-based organizations may have to be limited or terminated. This does not mean that a judge must live in isolation; indeed, many judges are active in a variety of organizations, but the judge always must be aware of the effect that his or her participation may have on the appearance of impartiality.

Advantages of Being a Judge

With so many negatives, why would anyone want this job?

In the judiciary, a person has the opportunity to make a difference. For a child in a dependency case, the judge can help assure a bright and promising future. For a partner in an unhappy marriage, the judge can offer hope and a new life. In his or her rulings, the judge can assure that justice is served. Not often, but on occasion, long after the case is concluded, the judge will hear from one of the parties that the judge's decision made a positive difference.

For those judges who leave the bench, the experience can be an aid to greater success in a legal career or as a stepping-stone to "higher" political office.

There is, for a judge, a sense of control and independence that cannot be achieved in other areas of the law. As a judge, you are not subject to billing sheets or billing discussions. If you choose to write an opinion in a particular case, the time you spend on that opinion is up to you. You are not limited in your research and writing to those cases and articles that support a client's particular requirements. You are granted the power, indeed, are required, to look at an issue impartially and make decisions for other people when they cannot or will not.

The Judicial Selection Process

The State Court System

Judges in the state court systems are selected in a number of ways. They may be selected through contested elections, appointed by the chief executive, or first appointed and than retained through an election process. You will need to determine which system is in place in your jurisdiction. In Arizona, for example, a number of different processes are utilized. Court of appeals judges, supreme court justices, and superior court (trial-level) judges in the two most populous counties are first appointed by the governor and then periodically run for retention. In the remaining counties, the superior court judges run for election in contested elections.

The merit-selection process utilized in Arizona sometimes is referred to as the Missouri Plan, because Missouri was the first state to utilize this system for the selection of judges. When a vacancy is announced, all qualified persons are invited by public notice to apply. The application does inquire into political affiliation. After a review of the applications, a commission appointed by the governor, comprised of lawyers and nonlawyers, interviews some, or all, of the applicants. The commissioners then recommend three to five persons to the governor for each vacancy. The governor may, but need not, interview the candidates. Judges, once appointed, are subject to a nonpartisan retention election. The judge does not "run" against an opponent, but rather "against his or her record." A simple majority of the votes cast will retain a judge in office.

In a number of states, the governor appoints judges, again subject to retention, but without the intervening step of a commission recommendation. In those states, party affiliation, political connections, and name recognition, as well as professional competence, will help assure an appointment to the court.

Most state courts have quasi-judicial positions that are filled by the courts themselves. These positions frequently are seen as first steps toward judicial office. These commissioners, referees, or special masters, as they are variously called, preside over a limited range of matters, generally uncontested, or as referred to them by the judges. You should contact your local court to determine what process is used to select persons for these positions.

Administrative law judges may be found in a number of state agencies. These judges usually are not a part of the judicial branch of government, but are attached to an agency in the executive branch of government. A lawyer who specializes in administrative practice may find the position of an administrative law judge open to him or her. Administrative law positions generally are not seen as avenues to positions on a general jurisdiction bench.

Not strictly a part of the state court system are the municipal court judges. These judges usually are appointed by the city council or mayor. Municipal courts generally are not seen as avenues to the general jurisdiction court.

The Federal System

Judges of the district, circuit court of appeals, and Supreme Court, or Article III judges, are nominated by the president and confirmed by the Senate. Article III judges, once appointed, have life tenure. Names of persons to consider as judges of the district courts are submitted to the president by the senior senator of the state of the president's political party. The recommendation of the senators for district court appointments is given great weight. It is up to each senator how he or she obtains names of potential appointees. Many senators have their own judicial screening committee that seeks out potential nominees. The process from the screening committee to the nomination is political in nature. Qualifications are not irrelevant; a good reputation in the legal and civic community is important, but having once determined that a candidate meets the minimum requirements, political considerations take over. A person generally needs to have similar political views to that of the senator and the president; however, some senators occasionally recommend members of a different political party.

At the circuit-court level, the appointments generally rotate geographically through the circuit. For both circuit court and supreme court nominations, however, the preference of the president's staff generally is given greater weight than in the district court process.

All names of proposed federal court nominees are submitted to the ABA's Standing Committee of Federal Judiciary. The committee completes a background check on the person's professional qualifications. The ABA then gives the nominee a rating of "exceptionally well qualified," "well qualified," "qualified," or "not qualified." According to the ABA, a person should be admitted to practice for at least 12 years before a "qualified" rating would be given. This submission to the ABA is not required by the Constitution, but is a part of the appointment process by tradition.

Bankruptcy judges are appointed by the circuit courts of appeals. These judges are Article I judges and are appointed for 14 years. They may be reappointed for additional 14-year terms. Bankruptcy judges handle only bankruptcy and related cases. They are considered a part of the district courts in which they serve. Each vacancy is widely advertised. An extensive application is required of each candidate for bankruptcy judge; however, no political affiliation questions are asked. Each application is screened by a bench/bar committee in the circuit and the top candidates' names are sent to the circuit court for the final decision. A strong background in all areas of bankruptcy practice is considered an excellent factor in appointment as a bankruptcy judge. The appointments are strictly merit appointments, and persons with strong credentials in areas other than in bankruptcy law will be given consideration as well. In many circuits, appointment to the bankruptcy court can lead to a nomination to the district or circuit court. Generally, a minimum of seven to ten years of legal experience is necessary for consideration.

Magistrates in the federal system are appointed by the district judges for the district in which they serve. All of the decisions of a magistrate are subject to a de novo review by the district court. In most districts, a minimum of five years' legal experience is necessary.

As in state government, the federal government uses administrative law judges to adjudicate matters in many of its agencies. Some of these positions are handled through the OPM in Washington, D.C.; others are handled through the agencies. In both instances, the vacancies are advertised either in the legal press or in the *Federal Register*.

Becoming a Judge

The route every person took to the bench is different. There are some things that you can do, however, to help yourself along the way. A strong academic background and a clerkship with a judge in the court in which you are interested certainly will be pluses. If you are interested in becoming an administrative law judge or in a bankruptcy court position, specialization in those areas of law will be invaluable.

A reputation in the community for fairness is probably the most important asset that you can bring to the pursuit of a judicial appointment. This type of reputation can be developed through your activities in the community and through the bar associations. A recognized community leader has the advantage of name recognition as well as an acknowledged commitment to the improvement of the community. Service as a judge pro tem, or as an arbitrator or mediator, not only can help you decide if the judiciary is a career for you, but can help you develop the reputation for fair, thoughtful decision making.

Every judicial selection process has some element of politics in it. You, and the persons supporting you, must have strong, positive connections with the person(s) or commission making the appointment decisions. Strong letters of support from well-recognized and well-respected members of the legal and civil community can be extremely helpful in an appointment process.

Finally, you must be in the right place at the right time. Do not be discouraged if your first, second, or third foray into the selection process is unsuccessful. If you are convinced that you want to be a judge, and that you will be a good judge, eventually you will succeed in achieving your goal.

CHAPTER 28

Judicial Clerkships

Sheila Anderson

Shortly after graduating from law school in May of 1989, I received an offer from a Philadelphia court of common pleas judge to serve as her law clerk beginning in August of 1989. I was elated, for clerking was and always had been my number-one choice for employment directly out of law school. I accepted the judge's offer, very excited to launch my legal career in this manner.

I remember telling my family shortly thereafter of my clerkship offer. For the most part, they seemed pleased. It was my aunt, however, who softly said, "So, you're going to be a law clerk? That's nice, sweetie. I guess you have to start *somewhere*. . . . Maybe next year you'll be able to get a *real* legal job perhaps?" I knew that my aunt, like most laypeople, believed that a "law clerk" position was probably a clerical position. Even now, I still believe the title can be somewhat misleading—or at least, may seem to minimize the duties and responsibilities delegated to a judicial law clerk. However, if you are at a point in your development as a lawyer where you are about to launch your legal career, or are already in the workforce and want to try something new, a judicial clerkship experience is an employment option that should *not* be overlooked. In fact, for numerous reasons, a clerkship experience is an option that should rank among the top three of your employment choices.

What Are Law Clerks and What Do They Do?

A law clerk, simply stated, is the judge's chosen judicial assistant who performs legal research, advises the judge of legal issues, drafts decisions, including memoranda of law, and most important, published court opinions. There really is nothing mystical about it; these duties constitute the bulk of what a judicial law clerk will be asked to perform during his or her 12- to 24-month experience. Unlike legal research performed while in law school, however, a clerkship permits you to perform research on real issues that are not easily answered. In this regard, the thoroughness of your research is critical and in almost every instance, creates an opportunity for you, the judge, and fellow law clerks to discuss the law, its applicability (or inapplicability), and (if your clerkship is at the appellate level) whether the law should be changed. Knowing that the research you perform will provide the foundation for the legal opinion of the judge for whom you work can be extremely rewarding.

Obtaining a Clerkship

How do you go about obtaining a clerkship? How do you apply? Which judge should you clerk for?

Typically, the application process for a judicial clerkship begins with a résumé, a well-written cover letter, a transcript of your grades, references, and in some instances, an unedited writing sample. The latter three of these components, taken in conjunction with your interview, however, are of immeasurable importance. First, law school grades generally are held in the highest regard by most judges because judges almost uniformly believe that the better you have performed in law school, the better you will be able to perform legal research, spot issues, and discuss them. In fact, most judges prefer applicants who have somehow demonstrated academic excellence by either ranking at the top percentage level of their class or by participating on Law Review or moot court. Secondly, solid references are important, because the judge probably never has heard of you and will want to know what others think of your character. A judge will need to know how you are perceived by former professors and employers, your level of intellect and your demonstrated ability to articulate, your commitment and conscientiousness, and your ability to perform a task to completion. Finally, an unedited writing sample gives the judge an indication of your ability to analyze a legal issue, while at the same time providing the judge with a taste of your writing style and your ability to convey thoughts clearly. This is of paramount importance, for the scholarly writing that ultimately becomes the Opinion of the Court (or of the particular judge) will in all likelihood begin with a law clerk's draft.

Determining which judge to clerk for should be a well-thought-out decision. (Remember, you will be working very closely with this individual for at least 12 months.) You may want to first decide which level of the court system is most attractive to you. For instance, if you think you might enjoy observing courtroom procedure, jury and nonjury trials, and learning the nuts-and-bolts of motions practice and other aspects of litigation from a fairly innocuous position, you should consider seriously a trial-court clerkship. If, instead, the scholarly aspects of reviewing appellate briefs, assessing the merits of appellate arguments, and addressing more complicated legal issues seem more attractive, then definitely consider an appellate-level clerkship. Next, consult the placement office of your law school/alma mater. Oftentimes, judges will inform a particular law school that they are seeking applications for the upcoming year and will provide a description of the type of clerkship experience the applicant can expect, as well as the qualifications and background that the judge is seeking in prospective law clerks. Finally, it is also a good idea to speak with local lawyers and law professors about the particular judge. This is key. Give credence to the opinions of those who have either worked with or argued before the particular judge you are considering. In all likelihood, you will find their opinions invaluable. A judge may have stellar credentials, sound great on paper, and offer exactly the type of clerkship experience that you are seeking. However, it would, indeed, be tragic for your judicial clerkship to end up as miserable a union as Peg and Al Bundy's marriage.

In deciding when to apply for a clerkship, an applicant should keep in mind that the competition for these coveted positions has increased dramatically over the past several years, particularly among graduating law students. Although the number of applicants for a particular judge or level of clerkship undoubtedly will be influenced by the court's location (i.e., large city versus rural area) as well as the judge's fame and/or popularity, as a general rule, an applicant would be well advised to make his or her interest in a clerkship known to the judge at *least* eight months before the onset of the clerkship. With federal clerkships, where the competition is even fiercer, applicants now are submitting résumés almost 24 months in advance of the clerkship. Consequently, if you are considering a job change and you think, even remotely, that you may want to clerk for a particular judge, send in that résumé immediately—"Better safe than sorry."

Preparing for the Interview

At this point in your career, job interviews should be a fairly familiar ritual. To maximize your success when interviewing for a judicial clerkship, however, the following tips should prove helpful:

- Where possible, check Lexis and/or Westlaw to compile a list of opinions that have been authored by the judge you are considering. By retrieving copies of the judge's opinions, you not only become familiar with his or her style of writing, but, if time allows, this gives you an additional topic of discussion that centers on the judge. Your endeavor to learn as much as possible about the judge before the interview will be immediately apparent and will definitely speak to your level of interest and resourcefulness.

- As much as possible, try not to be intimidated by the judge's mere presence. This may sound like corny advice, but you would be surprised how many lawyers become timid in the presence of "the judiciary." As you sit there wondering how to articulate impressive information about your background, remember, this deal works both ways: Judges need judicial law clerks just as much as law clerks need the employment. And because this union lasts anywhere from 12 to 24 months, a judge will want to see what type of person you are during the interview. Certainly resist any urges to kick off your shoes or slap the judge on the back in jest, but do let the judge see your winning personality—including your sense of humor (if you have one).

- Last but not least, be sure to send the judge a thank-you letter thanking him or her for affording you the opportunity to interview. As with most thank-you notes to prospective employers, be sure to indicate why you remain interested in this clerkship opportunity. And, of course, highlight once again your ability to meet the responsibilities that will be assigned to you if you are the successful candidate.

Taking the Good with the Bad: The Judicial Clerkship "Cost-Benefit" Analysis

As with any job opportunity, there are some disadvantages to clerking. Although these disadvantages are minor, it is best to discuss the "negatives" associated with a clerkship experience.

As a judicial law clerk, you are required to maintain a strict level of confidentiality about the cases or issues that have been assigned to you for review and research. Although a law clerk is free to discuss these issues with the judge and other fellow law clerks who work with you, the circle of lawyers among whom you may speak freely is somewhat small. In fact, unless your judge has given you express permission to speak with a lawyer (either as an administrative function or otherwise), discussions between law clerks and outside lawyers generally are discouraged—in some cases, absolutely prohibited. If you are the type of individual who enjoys the comfort of being able to discuss your work with numerous lawyers (as in a megasized law firm), you may perceive this limitation as a negative. You simply will not enjoy this luxury with a clerkship.

Second, salaries for judicial law clerks tend to be much lower than those offered at law firms or even other areas of government. Generally speaking, clerkship salaries may range from as low as $18,000 per year to a high of $35,000. For most lawyers, especially those with enormous student-loan indebtedness, the meager salary offered to law clerks means definite sacrifices; "creature comforts" (such as new cars, vacations, etc.) may need to be placed on hold for the next 12 to 24 months. To some, this may be a very unattractive feature, because delayed gratification will definitely be the name of the game.

Nevertheless, even in light of this "negative" backdrop, practically every lawyer who has ever clerked for a judge will readily admit that it was one of the highlights of his or her legal career, and that if the lawyer had to do it over again, he or she still would opt to clerk. Individual opinions vary as to why a clerkship is considered to be such a positive experience, but here are a few reasons that keep popping up among those who have clerked:

- If the match with your judge is a good one, you have truly hit the jackpot. For the remainder of your legal career you will have not just a "former employer," but a trusted mentor who may be able to guide you and offer "words of wisdom" as you develop as a lawyer. Becoming a good lawyer is truly a maturation process, and who better to counsel you in that development than an individual who has developed beyond the lawyer stage to become a member of the judiciary.

- Judicial clerkships generally are held in very high regard within the legal profession. Overall, the presumption is that if you can draft opinions for a judge, your legal research and legal writing skills are, in all likelihood, quite good. Of course, the judge for whom you have clerked generally will be able to verify this.
- The time commitment required of judicial law clerks usually is very reasonable. Typically, law clerks work 40 hours per week; rarely (if ever) are law clerks required to work burdensome hours, which means that a law clerk can "have a life"! Clerking is definitely conducive to having a social and family life. In fact, for the lawyer who may be thinking about starting a family, a clerkship typically provides you with a reasonable schedule that will permit you to spend more time with your spouse and/or children. You may not have much money, but if you can afford the pay cut for a year or two, the other benefits to you and your family may be priceless.

Clerking is never, ever, a waste of time. Whether a clerkship opportunity is your first step or a transitional move, most former law clerks will agree that the benefits are far reaching. Your legal writing and analytical skills are honed to a degree that will be an asset to you no matter what you decide to do next. Make no mistake, a clerkship experience is well worth the sacrifice.

CHAPTER 29

Legal Aid, Legal Services, and Public-Interest Organizations

Lisa Tessler
Jane Thieberger

The decision to make a transition into the public-interest sector is a challenging and difficult one. Like most sectors of the legal profession, the market for public interest–law positions has been reduced considerably in recent years, because of the cutbacks in federal funding for civil legal services. The need for these services, however, has increased, and despite the limited options available, the desire to make a contribution to this sector remains strong among law graduates.

Before embarking on a job change, law graduates considering a move into the public-interest sector should be aware of certain aspects of the job search that are unique to this area. First, the hiring criteria established by employers are somewhat different from those valued by private-sector employers. While strong academic credentials are highly desirable, employers place an equally high value on factors such as (1) clinical law courses or externship experiences; (2) strong trial and oral advocacy skills; (3) prior and current volunteer, extracurricular, and pro bono activities; (4) the ability to relate well to diverse individuals and constituencies, with backgrounds that may differ dramatically from one's own; (5) familiarity with more than one language, particularly Spanish; and (6) the ability to function effectively in a variety of "nonlawyer" roles, such as lobbyist, community organizer, public speaker, fund raiser, and administrator, to name a few.

Marketability in the nonprofit sector is enhanced greatly by the ability to establish personal and professional contacts within the public-interest community. In many cases, these contacts may date back to law school, at which time you may have worked part-time or during the summer, or through ongoing involvement in volunteer pro bono and community organizing activities, bar associations, alumni associations, and on boards of not-for-profit organizations. The public-interest community in a particular geographic location is often a tight network, and employers are more likely to take a chance on someone whose presence in the community has been visible and with whose work they are familiar.

Salaries in the public-interest sector are typically lower than in any other sector of the legal profession. To survive, one must possess a flexible attitude and a willingness to change jobs more regularly than the average lawyer. Many entry-level positions in public-interest organizations are obtained through fellowships lasting one or two years, with no guarantees of a permanent position thereafter. Two excellent guides to current fellowship opportunities include the Yale Law School *Fellowship Opportunities Guide 1993–1994* (Yale Law School Career Development Office, 127 Wall Street, New Haven, CT 06520, (203) 432-1676) and *The NAPIL Post-Graduate Fellowships Guide 1992–1993* (National Association for Public Interest Law, 1118 22nd Street, N.W., Third Floor, Washington, D.C., (202) 466-3686). NAPIL also publishes *The NAPIL Guide to Public Interest Career Resources 1993*. In making a move from one organization to another, experienced lawyers may not be credited fully with the years of experience they had in other positions, both in terms of title and salary. Opportunities for mobility within an organization may be quite limited, as senior or managing lawyer positions are few in number and less likely to open up on a regular basis. Moreover, obtaining information about available public-interest positions can be particularly difficult, for they are not widely advertised and rarely handled by legal search firms.

Given such high stakes, what are the factors that motivate experienced lawyers to move into the public-interest sector? The incentives probably are as varied as the individuals themselves. For most, there is a strong desire to serve the interest of underrepresented groups who cannot afford private counsel, both on the individual and policy level. For lawyers who do criminal defense work, there is a sense of providing satisfaction to all clients, regardless of the accusation. On a less altruistic level, public-interest lawyers experience a greater degree of autonomy and decision-making ability at their jobs than their private-sector counterparts do. At the outset, one assumes a great deal more responsibility, often handling one's own cases from start to finish. Upon specializing in a particular area, one's work within the organization may become highly visible to the community at large, adding to the personal satisfaction derived from the work. Public-interest lawyers also report having more control over their caseloads and more freedom to determine what evening and weekend hours they will work.

Many lawyers in the public-interest sector place a high value on workplace environment and quality-of-life factors. Their organizations tend to have a more informal, nonhierarchical atmosphere. Peer camaraderie is another plus in offices where lawyers often share social values and political interests. Dress codes and social mores are more relaxed and less rigid, and a high value is placed on pursuing interests outside the law. For the purposes of this book, this chapter will cover five categories of public-interest legal employers: (1) legal aid, (2) legal services, (3) public-defender offices, (4) public-interest law centers, and (5) public-interest law firms. Although the strategies for finding jobs in these offices are relatively similar, the skills and experience desired by these employers vary significantly, as do the funding sources that keep these offices afloat.

Legal Aid

The Legal Aid Society is a private, nonprofit legal-services agency dedicated since 1876 to providing quality legal representation to New Yorkers who cannot afford to pay a lawyer. The Legal Aid Society, governed by a board of directors, has a full-time staff of 1,100 lawyers who provide legal assistance to approximately 300,000 people a year in all courts in New York City, including state and federal appellate courts and the U.S. Supreme Court. Its main address is The Legal Aid Society, Administrative Office, 15 Park Row, 22nd floor, New York, New York 10038, (212) 577-3300. Ten years ago, the Legal Aid Society consisted of 732 lawyers, so this organization has increased its lawyer hiring by 33 percent in the past decade. The Criminal Defense Division, with 680 lawyers, accounts for more than half of the lawyers there. While the Criminal Division, Juvenile Rights Division, and the Criminal Appeals Bureau as well as certain special projects are supported by government funds, the Civil Division is supported primarily by contributions from law firms, foundations, and individuals. The Volunteer Division is supported by a combination of government and private funds.

The society is well known for providing excellent training opportunities for its lawyers, both on an initial and on an ongoing basis. Early on, new lawyers at The Legal Aid Society receive trial experience and courtroom experience that they would not receive at law firms. They have extensive client contact. In addition, there is supervision and extensive training to help new lawyers with their cases. Lawyers hired by The Legal Aid Society come from law schools throughout the country. Most begin at the entry level, while others join the society's staff after initial experience in private firms, government agencies, clerkships, and other public-interest organizations. Most of the lawyers in the Civil Division and Criminal Division come to the society right out of law school. In the past few years, however, the Criminal Division began hiring laterals. In 1992–1993, the Criminal Division received a total of 2,400 applications, 400 of which were from admitted lawyers. A total of 30 lawyers, including new graduates, were hired to start in September of 1993. While the salary for a new graduate after admission to the bar is $32,284, the salary at The Legal Aid Society for a lawyer five years after graduation is $46,230.

The Criminal Appeals Bureau recruits lawyers from a number of other sectors. Of the 105 lawyers on staff in 1992–1993, 23 percent came from private law firms, 10 percent from judicial clerkships, and 7 percent from other government and public-interest organizations. Appellate work, like law school, is a highly academic, intellectual practice, involving research, writing, and issue spotting. Because legal writing is the most highly prized skill, lawyers who have honed this skill in whatever settings are highly valued in the lateral hiring process at the Bureau.

The Juvenile Rights Division of The Legal Aid Society is smaller and more specialized, and unlike the other divisions, only recruits candidates who are admitted to the bar. Here, experienced lawyers clearly have an edge. Similarly, the Volunteer Division is staffed primarily by experienced lawyers who oversee the work of volunteer lawyers and paralegals from private law firms and corporate law departments. The Federal Defender Division mainly hires admitted lawyers with experience.

Legal Services

The Legal Services Corporation (LSC), a federal agency funded by congressional allocations, was established in 1974. LSC currently supports the work of more than 323 offices nationwide and hires lawyers to provide free civil legal services to those who cannot afford private counsel. Although it has repeatedly come under attack during the past 13 years and during the early 1990s, LSC has managed to survive amidst cutbacks in both funding and hiring. While staffing is tight, positions do open up in offices nationwide for entry-level as well as experienced lawyer positions. Experience in housing, consumer, family, government benefits, and welfare law are highly desirable.

Promotional opportunities within legal-services offices vary from office to office. Staff lawyers move up to become unit or project directors, directors of litigation, and managing lawyers within their organizations. Most middle-management positions require staff lawyer experience in legal services, although occasionally lawyers are hired from the outside to assume these jobs. Those interested in LSC may contact the agency at 750 First Street, N.E., Washington, D.C. 20002, (202) 336-8800. To obtain a directory of LSC-funded programs, contact Sylvia Spate in the LSC book division at (202) 336-8906.

Public-Defender Offices

Public-defender offices, established by state and local governments to provide criminal-defense services to clients unable to afford private counsel, offer unique opportunities for lawyers to get experience defending clients in court. Staff lawyers experience the challenge of taking on a great deal of responsibility at an early stage in their careers, handling extensive client contact, trying cases, and grappling with complex constitutional issues. Lawyers typically start out handling misdemeanor cases and then move up within three years to try felonies. Some lawyers may be considered for supervisory and administrative positions. Without prior experience, most lawyers who make a move to a public-defender's office are not likely to go directly into the felony division without first mastering their trial skills at the misdemeanor level.

Public-defender offices mostly hire lawyers who are directly out of law school, but because there is a considerable amount of turnover, positions at the higher levels do open up regularly. Experience in criminal law obviously is most helpful, with courtroom experience a plus. Lawyers from private practice, academia, clerkships, and the government have joined the ranks of these offices in significant numbers during recent years.

Public-Interest Law Centers

The work of public-interest organizations or law centers differs somewhat from that of legal aid, legal services, and public-defender organizations. The range of issues handled by these groups is wide and the expertise required is great. Public-interest law centers tend to focus on policy-oriented cases, where a decision will have an impact on large numbers of people and/or achieve a major law reform objective. These programs generally will select cases with consequences that extend well beyond the particular litigants. The work of lawyers in these organizations is largely supported through fund-raising efforts by sponsoring organizations and through grants and foundations.

Positions within these organizations are scarce and competition is keen. Experienced lawyers are strongly preferred, particularly those with strong backgrounds in litigation and demonstrated commitments to special issues or interests. Many organizations seek strong law school credentials, such as high grades, academic honors, and journal experience.

Many public-interest law centers in the United States offer one- to two-year fellowships that enable job changers to enter into a particular area of public-interest law. A list of those fellowships is provided in the Appendix to this book. The bulk of these programs are in Washington, D.C., New York, and California. Most have early application deadlines (i.e., September–November of the year preceding the fall that the fellowship begins). Salaries vary greatly, ranging from $24,000 to approximately $33,000 per year. Several of these programs are affiliated with the clinical programs at major law schools in the country and offer LL.M. degrees on their completion. For example, Georgetown University Law Center sponsors six fellowships of this kind, all of which provide an excellent foundation for entry into public-interest and clinical-law teaching positions afterward.

While fellowships at public-interest law centers provide excellent exposure to the work of a particular organization, they are not designed to serve as entry-level positions into that organization. If a position opens up, the fellow may be considered a serious candidate for that slot. In any event, although the fellowship does not offer much in the way of job security, it does provide a "feather in one's cap" for entry into similar privately funded organizations.

Another option experienced lawyers may want to consider is creating their own public-interest law project. Several foundations have been established at law schools throughout the country to provide support for innovative projects that benefit underrepresented individuals and groups. Candidates apply for funding in the form of a grant request or proposal. Project grants are typically of one year's duration and provide modest stipends.

For lawyers interested in making a more dramatic shift in their work lives, there are occasional opportunities for talented administrators within some of the larger, more well-established public-interest organizations. Many of the executive directors, development directors, human-resource managers, and other administrators on staff at these organizations are lawyers. Higher-level administrative positions provide a chance to utilize skills in management, fund-raising and grants administration, lobbying, recruitment, public relations, public speaking, as well as in law, making the work more diverse and challenging. People with these kinds of qualifications are highly sought after by public-interest organizations.

Public-Interest Law Firms

The last category of employment to be included in this chapter is the small private firms that devote a significant portion of their practice to noncommercial areas of the law, such as constitutional, civil rights, consumer, environmental, labor (union side), workers' compensation, plaintiff's tort cases, tenants' rights, and immigration and family law. Lawyers with experience are strongly preferred for associate positions in these firms. The founders of these firms are themselves, for the most part, former legal-aid/legal-services lawyers, public defenders, and disillusioned commercial law firm lawyers. Openings for these positions are few and rather competitive, for they offer an ideal combination of a public interest–type practice in a private-sector environment. Because many of these are fairly new firms, they can offer more possibilities for making partner at an earlier stage, but also might run the risk of having a shorter life span. Many public-interest law firms could not survive in this day and age without also taking on a substantial amount of general and commercial practice.

Locating public-interest law firms is much easier now that the Martindale-Hubbell law directory is available on-line on Lexis. Computer searches can be done on Lexis to identify firms by practice areas. Similar research can be done on Westlaw with the new West Legal Directory, which lists about 600,000 lawyers.

The employment outlook for lawyers of color and women in the public-interest sector is very favorable. On the whole, public-interest offices strive for diversity in the staffing of their offices and seek individuals who can relate well to their client population. Public-interest employers often are well represented at minority recruiting conferences, and they request applications from candidates of color at law schools on a regular basis. Most position descriptions reflect an organization's commitment to affirmative action in their hiring practices, and many require candidates to be bilingual.

Some public-interest organizations offer flextime and part-time opportunities for lawyers with children. Job sharing is more common in public-defender and legal-services offices than in private law firms. Most lawyers agree that appellate work lends itself best to a part-time schedule.

Salaries

Perhaps the most significant and obvious drawback of public-interest employment is salary. As the NALP Class of 1992 Survey demonstrates, public-interest lawyers are clearly the lowest paid graduates at the entry level. The mean salary level for this group was $27,500 per year in 1992 compared with $42,600 for all graduates. The 1992 national median salary for all entry-level jobs in public interest was $26,000, while the median for all employment categories was $36,000.

Legal-services positions vary in the compensation they offer, with jobs in the larger cities offering the highest salaries. Generally speaking, starting lawyer salaries in legal services range from $19,200 to $32,500, with a median of $24,800. Lawyers with experience receive a salary from $31,500 to $60,000. Salaries are determined on the basis of the year of graduation from law school. Legal Aid pays slightly better with starting salaries in the low $30,000s.

Salaries in public-defender offices parallel those in legal services and vary significantly from one geographic location to another. Public-defender salaries for entry-level lawyers in 1992 ranged from $22,000 to $42,000.

Public-interest organizations cannot be easily characterized in terms of salary. The Public Interest Research Groups (PIRGs) offer the lowest salaries, starting as low as $18,000 per year (Douglas Phelps, Esq., Chair, Public Interest Research Groups, 29 Temple Place, Boston, MA 02111). Public-interest law centers pay significantly better, ranging from $20,000 to $50,000 per year for entry-level lawyers in the class of 1992, with a median salary of $28,000. Fellowships range from $20,000 to $30,000; those affiliated with law school clinical programs granting an LL.M. degree on completion pay about $26,500.

Public-interest law firms are likely to offer the most lucrative opportunities, with starting salaries from the high $20,000s to more than $50,000, with significant increases from year to year. Those with a highly successful commercial practice may more closely parallel law firms in their salary structures.

Finding a Public-Interest Job

The public-interest job search is by far one of the most difficult and frustrating of all legal job searches. Positions open up infrequently, politics and budget influence the hiring in existing programs, and it is difficult to find discernible areas of significant growth as one can more readily find in the private sector. Offices that have positions available advertise on a limited basis. How does one find out about openings and what are the best resources available?

One of the best ways to begin is to inquire whether you can receive your law school's career planning and placement office alumni job newsletter that regularly advertises positions. Many law schools have designated full-time public-interest career counselors and some even have established Public-Interest Law Centers. Most law school career resource libraries contain commercially prepared newsletters that post job listings in the public-interest field. They include: *The National and Federal Legal Employment Report*, *Community Jobs*, *The Public-Interest Clearinghouse Newsletter*, and others. One important "must-have" resource book is the Harvard Law School's *Public Interest Job Search Guide*. (The book is available through the Public Interest Advising Office at Harvard Law School, Pound Hall 328, Cambridge, MA 02138, and costs $15 for public-interest lawyers and $35 for lawyers in private practice.) This book contains a valuable directory of public-interest employers as well as a public-interest fellowship directory and resource bibliography.

Consider joining professional organizations, including the National Legal Aid and Defender Association (1625 K Street, N.W., Suite 800, Washington, D.C. 20006, (202) 452-0620), which publishes an annual booklet of member organizations. Individual lawyer dues are $60 per year, which entitle the member to receive the directory. The National Lawyers Guild, which has a 1993–1994 membership directory as well, is another possible group that can produce job leads and important contacts (National Lawyers Guild National Office, 55 Avenue of the Americas, New York, New York 10011, (212) 966-5000). Many organizations provide publications that advertise job listings and sponsor conferences that offer opportunities for building a network of contacts. Being affiliated with law school alumni associations and revitalizing relationships with law school faculty members, especially those in the clinical programs, can be helpful ways of learning about opportunities firsthand. Volunteering with offices can be another excellent way of learning about openings.

While the public-interest job search can be time-consuming, and sometimes frustrating, the process of learning about the range of options available to you can be very exciting and well worth the time and energy that you put into a search.

Landing the job that you really want, and one that fulfills personal and societal needs, requires perseverance but also creates the potential for tremendous professional satisfaction.

CHAPTER 30

Teaching Law

Gary A. Munneke

Law teaching is a career that offers special challenges and unique rewards. Virtually every lawyer retains in his or her mind images of law professors and law school. Individually and collectively, law school teachers have a profound effect on their students' perceptions of the legal system, approaches to analytical problems, and attitudes about clients, the law, and life. Whether they terrorized, bored, challenged, or nurtured students, law school teachers certainly molded their students.

Given the powerful influence that law school teachers can exert on their students, those who choose this career path assume a weighty responsibility. They bear the burden of instilling professional values and imparting legal knowledge to succeeding generations of lawyers. In a changing and uncertain professional environment, this responsibility is even heavier.

A law school is in one sense a highly specialized law firm. The tenured faculty are the partners; the nontenured faculty, the associates. The dean is the managing partner who oversees a large support staff. A law school engages in a very specialized type of practice: education. Its clients are the students, and fees are collected in the form of tuition. Because of the school's specialized mission, its offices contain unusually large conference rooms called classrooms and an extremely large library. This analogy may be helpful to someone from practice considering a career in teaching.

Opportunities in Teaching

Traditional tenure track positions are the most desirable and sought-after opportunities in legal education. A tenured faculty member is somewhat like a federal judge who sits for life unless impeached or retired. The tenure system assures contract renewal to professors who have passed successfully through a period of review, generally from three to six years. Unlike an employee at will or even a law firm partner, a tenured professor cannot be dismissed without cause.

At most schools, the tenure review process is designed to weed out those who just want an easy job; rather, the emphasis is on identifying lawyers who have a long-term commitment to scholarship, teaching, and public service. To attain tenure, a candidate must demonstrate excellence in writing; in service to the school, community and profession; and in the classroom. Professors considered for tenure are evaluated with the same rigorous level of scrutiny that is applied to associates being considered for law firm partnership.

All law schools provide some form of clinical education program. Clinical education and other skills training courses have evolved over the years in response to charges that the traditional Socratic legal education was incomplete. Although clinical and skills programs have blossomed since the late 1970s, many schools have been slow to accord clinical educators with the recognition that they deserve, and some even exclude clinicians from tenure track positions. Nevertheless, clinical education has made great progress and at most schools has become a firmly entrenched part of the curriculum.

In recent years, an increasing number of law schools have applied their resources to hiring full-time, frequently tenure track teachers in other lawyering skills areas such as legal research and writing, trial and appellate advocacy, client interviewing and counseling, negotiation, law practice management, and mediation. In the past, many of these skills, if taught at all, were assigned to a part-time teacher.

Law schools also offer administrative opportunities that do not include teaching. These nonteaching positions include assistant and associate deans, placement and admissions directors, financial-aid officers, comptrollers, recruiters, development officers, registrars, and assistant librarians.

Such administrative positions, however, are not likely to lead to teaching opportunities. The better career path for the lawyer/administrator is to advance through the ranks of university administration or laterally to other law schools into more responsible administrative positions. A few career administrators have become successful deans, although most deans come from the academic ranks.

One exception to this rule involves head librarians at law schools, who also are tenured faculty members who often carry a teaching load in addition to their administrative responsibilities. Thus, the field of law librarianship may prove to be an avenue to teaching status for individuals qualified in both law and library science.

Many women who want both career and family are attracted to law teaching because of the flexibility of scheduling, liberal sabbatical policies, and open attitudes about working mothers. Consequently, the number of women entering the law teaching profession has risen dramatically over the past 20 years.

On the other hand, the number of minorities engaged in law school teaching is very small. Despite an increase in the percentage of minority law students and lawyers, racial and ethnic diversity remains an issue for many law school faculties.

For anyone who is determined to teach but unable to find a job because of the competition, many opportunities exist outside of law school. Universi-

ties, colleges, community colleges, and even secondary schools often hire lawyers to teach certain law-related courses, such as business law, legal history,
legal philosophy, criminal justice, real estate, and tax. Positions also are available in such places as paralegal programs and law-enforcement training insti-
tutes. Lawyers who simply want to teach regardless of the venue should
consider lecturing in CLE programs, public education, or client seminars.
These activities may provide an outlet for some inner desire to teach without
necessitating a career change.

Adjunct or part-time teaching positions also provide excellent opportunities for many practitioners, although they are unlikely to lead to full-time
employment in a law school. Adjunct professors usually are respected practitioners who teach one course at a law school in an area of special expertise.
Compensation for adjunct positions, however, may be one-tenth of full-time
salaries or less.

Work

Lawyers teaching in a law school typically carry a class load of two or three
courses per semester depending on such factors as number of hours per week
the class meets, class size, level of individual student contact, number of sections of the same course, and whether the course is a new preparation. A
teacher carrying a six-hour load must spend considerably more time than that
in preparation, particularly if this is the first time that he or she has taught the
class. At the end of the term, the teacher must spend a significant amount of
time grading exams or papers. Most law professors consider this task the
most onerous aspect of teaching.

In addition to teaching, faculty members are expected to engage in research and writing in areas related to their professional expertise. In fact, at
almost all law schools, there is a publication requirement for tenure. Anyone
considering a career in law teaching should be admonished: The adage "publish or perish" is not an empty phrase. If you do not enjoy research, and do
not like to write, do not choose this career path. While some schools may be
liberal in what they consider scholarly or acceptable writing, most expect
untenured professors to produce a series of traditional Law Review articles
during their probationary period.

Effective professors spend a large portion of their time working with
students outside of class. Following almost every class, some students come
by their teacher's office with questions. Faculty members direct students' research for papers; they help students clerking with law firms to handle cases;
they advise moot court teams, law journals, and other student organizations;
they attend banquets, receptions, picnics, and social events when invited. This
aspect of teaching can be rewarding and fun, but it cuts into the time available
for pursuits such as research and writing.

Every faculty member assumes various administrative responsibilities,
such as law school and university committees. Just as a lawyer in a law firm
may be required to serve on administrative committees, law professors frequently are expected to participate in the governance of the institution.

Moreover, law professors are expected to engage in work outside of the law school. Such external activities not only increase the visibility and reputation of the law school itself, but keep the academician in touch with realities and trends in the real world. Some professors handle pro bono cases in areas of their expertise. Some work with law firms on a consulting basis. Others become active in local, state, and national bar association activities and CLE programs. Still others participate in the political process in some way.

Qualifications

Over the years, law professors have been drawn from a narrow range of candidates. The typical law professor studied law at a prestigious national law school where he or she ranked at the top of the class and often served as a Law Review editor. After graduation, this future professor clerked for a high-ranking judge and perhaps worked in a large law firm for a couple of years.

The traditional teaching career path from Law Review to law clerk to teacher demanded that candidates have strong academic credentials, either good grades from a leading school or superior grades from a good school. Even the best students from less prestigious institutions often found few doors open to them. One survey showed that 50 percent of all law teachers graduated from seven law schools and many of the rest from a handful of others. Thus, the law school attended may present an insurmountable barrier for many aspiring teachers.

Although the range of schools from which law teachers are recruited seems to be broadening, and practice experience is becoming more important than a judicial clerkship, the emphasis on grades has not waned, but has increased with the level of competition for available positions. If you are thinking about law teaching, you should discuss candidly with one or more law professors who you know what your prospects for getting a job will be.

Some aspiring teachers, who discover that their paper qualifications do not give them the appeal that they need to land a position, may earn a graduate law degree, or LL.M., from a school more prestigious than the one where they received a J.D. Some of these LL.M. programs are promoted as preparation for teaching, while others may be associated with a particular field of law. Generally, schools place their LL.M. students in teaching positions at a success rate commensurate with the prestige of the school.

Many schools utilize practicing lawyers as first-year writing instructors, sometimes in conjunction with an LL.M. program. Although some law schools may hire tenure track faculty from the ranks of these instructors, such a bootstrap approach is frequently not a viable one. On the other hand, schools that maintain a permanent writing faculty may recruit writing teachers from the ranks of such programs.

Another career path is to attain recognition as a leading practitioner in a specialized area of law. Many law schools have begun to seek out teachers with practice experience. These schools conclude that three to six years of practice with a good firm not only gives candidates substantial expertise, but also establishes solid work values and habits. Those who follow this path frequently have developed a specialty or expertise that proves to be marketable to law schools.

Judicial clerkships, particularly at the federal appellate level, remain an important training ground for law teachers. Even though many law schools today expect teaching applicants to have some practice experience, clerking is almost never a detriment and may significantly improve the candidate's marketability. Many law graduates these days go to work for a firm after clerking and before applying for teaching positions. Some individuals are doing the reverse, clerking for a judge after a stint at a law firm.

Pay and Benefits

No one goes into teaching for the money. Most individuals with the credentials to be hired by a law school could make more money in the private practice of law. A 1992 survey by the Society of American Law Teachers (SALT) disclosed that starting salaries for law teachers, while above the national median of $40,000 for law school graduates, were significantly below the $85,000 paid to new associates in large New York firms. Although salaries for teachers vary according to the location and resources of the school, as well as the academic rank of the professor, the SALT survey reported a range of median salaries (by school) between $39,796 and $81,450 for assistant professors, $41,900 and $87,550 for associate professors, and $54,300 and $122,500 for full professors. Salary increases are typically 3 percent to 6 percent per year. These figures may be competitive with lawyers' incomes generally, but they certainly are far below the seven figure incomes that top the profession or the high six-figures earned by many law firm partners.

Low salaries are ameliorated in several ways. First, there are nonmonetary rewards associated with ego gratification and personal satisfaction. Law schools frequently offer liberal leave and sabbatical policies that simply do not exist in private practice. In addition, schools generally have long holiday breaks during the school year.

More importantly, base salaries can be somewhat deceiving. Teaching contracts are normally for ten months, giving teachers two months during which they can vacation, teach summer school, or write. Law schools usually offer supplemental pay for summer teaching or research. Many schools have chairs and professorships—trust funds donated by alumni and other benefactors—that supplement the salary of professors to whom they are awarded. As a rule, the more prestigious schools have more such endowed positions. Most schools also have a good benefit package, including a tax-deferred annuity/retirement program.

Opportunities to earn outside income are not to be ignored. Because many professors write casebooks and other publications, the prospect of receiving royalty income is very real. It also may be possible to handle a small number of fee-generating cases while teaching or to engage in consulting on a part-time basis.

In short, while it is unlikely that an individual will get rich teaching in a law school, it is possible to attain a very comfortable standard of living. The nonmonetary rewards combine with real income to provide a quality of life difficult to match in any other area of practice.

Finding a Job

Full-time law school teaching openings are limited. Of 176 ABA-approved law schools, there may be as few as one or two openings per school each year. Academic appointments run for an academic year beginning in August or September, so the heaviest interviewing season is typically from January through March or April. Some positions may be filled before or after this time, depending on the needs of the school, but most offers are made during the spring.

Every school has a hiring or appointments committee charged with soliciting and reviewing résumés, conducting interviews, and evaluating candidates. Hiring decisions normally are made by the entire faculty, although the dean may be empowered to make one-year appointments or visitorships. Schools frequently advertise in the *Chronicle of Higher Education,* a weekly educational paper, the *New York Times* classified advertisements, local newspapers, and other journals. Schools have not begun to use headhunters.

The Association of American Law Schools (AALS) maintains a register of candidates and conducts an annual recruiting fair attended by most schools that is held around December 1 in Washington, D.C. Anyone interested in teaching should utilize these AALS services and may contact the AALS at 1201 Connecticut Ave. N.W., Suite 800, Washington, D.C., 20036-2605. Many applicants also write directly to an appointments committee, dean, or faculty member whom they know. Some may schedule informal meetings outside the formal hiring process. Those who are fortunate enough to have attended a law school with a substantial number of graduates engaged in law school teaching may be able to utilize that network. Some may get a better audience at their own law school than elsewhere, although schools differ widely regarding their willingness to hire their own graduates.

Throughout the 1990s, competition for positions is expected to be fierce. Law firm layoffs and early retirements, dissatisfaction with law practice generally, and an influx of highly qualified recent graduates guarantee that the schools will find themselves in a buyer's market for the foreseeable future. Some law schools have discussed reducing the size of their student bodies, which would limit opportunities further. And because the studies of law school teachers suggest that most are happy where they are and not contemplating retirement any time soon, openings related to attrition will not increase appreciably for a number of years.

Conclusion

Law school teachers lead comfortable lives. They maintain status and respect in the community and enjoy a highly flexible schedule with very little supervision or external control. Institutional politics can be bitter and petty, but probably no more so than in any other organization of 30 to 50 lawyers. On balance, for those who possess the qualifications, determination, and good luck to find a position in legal education, a career in teaching can be highly satisfying.

Who among us has not speculated about what we would do if given the opportunity to step on to the podium and teach a law school class? For some of us, that fantasy comes true. For those who do enter law teaching, the questions should be: How can I be like the teacher I admired most? How do I avoid becoming the one I enjoyed least? How do I give my students the type of legal education they deserve?

CHAPTER 31

Part-time, Temporary, and Contract Employment

Shelley L. Wallace

The common availability of part-time, temporary, and contract opportunities within the field of law is a fairly recent and growing phenomenon. Reflecting firmly established trends in workforce demographics and sweeping changes in corporate philosophy, the number of these opportunities will continue to expand throughout the 1990s and beyond. By the year 2000, most lawyers will have considered the pursuit of such an option or will have found themselves in a position to offer such an opportunity to others.

Overview

Economic and societal forces converged in the late 1980s to create many different groups of lawyers who would form a highly qualified and experienced applicant pool for temporary and part-time work. Simultaneously, market forces influenced law firms and corporate law departments to explore alternatives to more traditional hiring and retention methods. This candidate pool includes:

- Corporate counsel who had been caught in the frenzy of merger, acquisition, relocation, or dissolution of their corporations and who found it difficult to find comparable positions within the corporate community.
- Associates and partners who quietly were asked to leave their law firms for economic reasons when the recession reduced the number of paying clients at the firm.
- Women lawyers who have formed the next largest class of qualified candidates seeking part-time or temporary work arrangements. By the end of the 1980s, law schools had graduated record numbers of women into the workforce who found the traditional legal career path at odds with child rearing.

297

Not coincidentally, during the middle to late 1980s, a new commercial enterprise also emerged to match the needs of these able and deserving candidates with those of legal organizations: the temporary lawyer placement agency. Emerging in different regions of the country, and with different motivations and perspectives, the agencies' message found an eager audience, especially among prospective applicants. Gradually, the advocacy of alternative working arrangements by these temporary services encouraged trial of the concept by a growing number of corporations and law firms and served to move such options into the mainstream of legal staffing.

Alternative Working Arrangements Defined

Encompassing many different work arrangements in a variety of legal settings, these temporary and part-time opportunities are characterized principally by the absence of a traditional employee-employer relationship. Thus, the lawyer acts as an independent provider, serving at the will of the client, and generally without recourse to benefits, bonuses, sick pay, vacation pay, or personal days. As with most consultants or outside counsel, these lawyers are paid a set fee for hours worked. Frequently, this remuneration is greater than a comparably experienced lawyer receives in a full-time permanent position.

A law firm or corporation—the "client"—may engage the lawyer's services directly or through an agency that specializes in these types of arrangements. The client can decide to pay hourly fees directly or have them paid by the agency. Assignments can last for any length of time—from a few hours to a few years—and can entail any area of the law, from the most routine to the most complex. The client can require that the work be conducted on its own premises, at the lawyer's home or office, at some distant location, or at any combination of these locations.

The length of a temporary assignment is determined exclusively by the client. Though clients usually provide a general estimate of the time required for the job's completion, they retain the right to terminate the project and position at any time and for any reason. Similarly, the client can stipulate to both the number of days to be worked per week and the number of hours to be worked per day. These standards, and the fees to be paid, are negotiated before the assignment begins by the candidate or by an agency acting as an intermediary for that purpose.

Temporary and part-time assignments also can include job sharing—when two lawyers work together closely to fulfill the responsibilities of one full-time position. Job-sharing arrangements often evolve into permanent part-time positions for one or both of the job sharers. In such an event, hourly payment usually is abandoned in favor of fixed salaries, set to reflect the anticipated number of hours or days to be worked. These positions frequently entitle their holders to certain company or firm-paid benefits.

Contract employment implies that the terms and conditions of the assignment are agreed to and affirmed in writing before the assignment begins.

At the end of the term, at their mutual consent, the parties can renegotiate these terms and conditions.

The Marketplace

Corporate Law Departments

With no end in sight to the fierce competition throughout the global marketplace, corporations have been compelled to rethink virtually every aspect of their operation. Responsiveness is the modern imperative. Success will derive from the ability to turn on a dime, to pursue emerging opportunities, and to get to the market faster with products and services that anticipate rather than react to buyers' needs. To accomplish this, the organization must be structured to allow rapid response to every contingency. A small group of highly competent managers and task specialists will be found at its core. Each member of this "nucleus" will be charged with the responsibility of building, training, sizing, and deploying staffs as conditions dictate. To the extent that such conditions change, so, too, will the character and composition of these staffs. As a consequence of this new corporate profile, a worker's livelihood and security will reside in his or her abilities and distinctive competence. These workers will be employed with increasing frequency by specialized leased labor pools to which corporate management will turn to meet current staffing requirements.

Legal departments within these "nucleus" organizations will face a very specific challenge. On the one hand, fewer permanent staff resources will be available to deal with an ever-expanding workload. On the other hand, departments will be pressed by senior management to hold the line on outside counsel fees. As elsewhere throughout the corporation, when significant gaps emerge between varying work demands and the capacity of permanent staff resources to meet those demands, general counsel will have to resort to new and creative approaches to hiring and utilizing legal professionals.

For the able and experienced lawyers open to these new conditions, flexibility will be key. Today, in one company, the premium may be on lawyers with extensive environmental or employment expertise; in another company, the needs may center on health care or finance. Opportunities will be arising constantly for qualified candidates willing to get the job done and move on to the next. In some cases, this may mean assignments measured in weeks. In others, terms may stretch to several months and even years.

Law Firms

As mentioned previously, the influx of women lawyers has served to expand and legitimize part-time alternatives within the law firm sector. Recognizing the value of retaining women lawyers who had been trained by the departments and now were producing an excellent work product, most major law firms established policies addressing part-time partnership, full-time requirements prior to partnership consideration, how much part-time work is allocated toward partnership track, etc. Different tiers of partnership, permanent associates, and job sharing of files all may be seen as products of women advocating change within their law firms.

With respect to temporary lawyer employment, concerns about quality work product, conflicts of interest, and confidentiality have tended to discourage the practice, especially in large firms. In 1988, however, some of those concerns were swept away by the opinion of the Ethics Committee of the ABA. The ABA stated in Formal Opinion 88-356, dated December 16, 1988, that the use of temporary lawyers was "an efficient and cost-effective way" for law firms and corporations to "manage their work flow and deployment of resources."

More recently, downsizing has left some firms either with a lack of depth and substance in certain specialized areas or without the staff to handle large, unexpected projects. Here, the high caliber of the temporary lawyer applicant pool has played a part in reassuring partners of the quality of their work product and encouraged partners to look much more carefully at the temporary employment alternative.

Smaller law firms, which typically do not have the resources to maintain a permanent staff to cope with peak work periods, present the greatest number of opportunities for temporary and part-time assignments. Given their client base, which usually is less corporate and more focused on a general practice—personal injury, negligence, family, and real estate law, etc.—these law firms tend to be less demanding about the credentials and experience required of the temporary lawyer. At the same time, many of these firms are employing temporary lawyers as a means of serving those client needs that fall outside the expertise of the partners and full-time associates. The end result is improved service and an enhanced client relationship.

Alternative Work Arrangements: Circumstances and Opportunities

Though this marketplace is still in its formative stages, many ground rules have evolved, for buyers and sellers alike, that are likely to prevail for some time to come. The following address the alternative working arrangement options that currently attend a variety of legal career situations:

1. *Entry-level, newly graduated lawyers:* Unfortunately, inexperienced lawyers will have few prospects for meaningful and well-paying temporary work. Smaller law firms probably will be the sources of those prospects that do exist. Unfortunately, most résumés are rejected by these firms on the assumption that the new lawyer is seeking only a permanent position. To counter this, the cover letter and résumé should reflect a desire for an alternative work arrangement. A personal presentation showing what can be provided to the firm at any level and an eager desire to work on a trial basis may be appealing to the overworked practitioner.

2. *Top-performing senior associates just turned down for partnership:* Besides being stunned by the announcement, these senior associates now are facing career decisions of great importance. Faith in the law firm en-

vironment is shaken, and there is curiosity about opportunities in corporate legal departments. Most associates also are aware that there are few permanent opportunities within this segment, and, frankly, unsure whether this is the career path to follow. A temporary position within a corporate setting will allow a lawyer to assess his or her aptitude for such a career path and may even engender an offer of permanent employment.

3. *Associates who do not want to pursue a full-time career at law or who have decided to open their own practices:* Evaluations at the law firm by the partners indicate that these associates are excellent lawyers; however, they have decided that they do not want to become a partner at a large law firm because they want to have their own solo practices or they have too many outside interests to devote and dedicate themselves to full-time careers.

    Instead, with years of experience under their belts, these associates have decided that this is the time to take the plunge and pursue opportunities as legislative assistant, lobbyist, author, real estate developer, musician, entrepreneur, or talk-show host.

    In any event, income still is needed to meet mortgage payments while their law practices are taking off. Or these lawyers want to keep their legal skills sharp in case their entrepreneurial dreams do not come true. Temporary assignments in specific areas of expertise probably will be available in both the law firm and corporate sectors.

4. *Senior corporate counsel (eight-plus years) who are displaced by merger, acquisition, or reorganization:* The hierarchical nature of the law firm makes it very difficult to return to the larger law firm environment in a permanent position. Although a senior counsel may be willing to assume an associate's position, the other associates may feel threatened by his or her greater experience and maturity. Partners do not want to create an uncomfortable situation for their associates who expect to advance each year toward partnership. Partners also prefer to work with associates who have recently graduated from law school, believing that their way of training is the best.

    These days, the only senior lawyers of interest to law firms are those who can bring business to the firm. If these lawyers do not fit within this category, temporary assignments may offer a number of benefits. Besides providing a substantial hourly wage, the law firm and its partners may well present a route of access to corporate clients who are seeking to build or enlarge in-house legal departments.

5. *Women associates at major law firms or within corporate legal departments:* These women lawyers would like to remain at the firm or within the legal department but also would like more time with their families. If other women associates at the firm or department are currently working on a part-time basis, it would be best to inquire about their situation to determine whether that is a viable option. Before approaching the partners or supervising counsel, have a clear idea about the number of days per week and hours per day to be worked. Options include

working a few full days or only part of the day five days a week. Some women with school-age children prefer working daily until the children come home from school in the late afternoon. Some firms consider a working schedule of nine to five, five days a week, a part-time position within the firm. If there are no other women working part-time, a woman lawyer may want to make a more formal presentation to the partnership or department by gathering articles and information to support an economic argument for the position. Women associates also may want to consult their local women's bar organizations to determine whether surveys have been issued to the various firms or departments within their areas. Most salary arrangements are a prorated portion of the full-time salary and benefits often are negotiated as part of the arrangement.

Bear in mind that it is much easier to secure a permanent part-time position with the current employer where the partners or counsel are familiar with the women associates' work. If the evaluations have been good and the lawyer is held in high regard by the firm or department, there is a better chance of being retained. Also understand that there are both advantages and disadvantages to a prospective part-time status. On the negative side, many associates find themselves in the position of being expected to discharge full-time responsibilities for part-time salary. By and large, though, the permanent part-time option offers an optimum solution: ongoing compensation and benefits, the potential for entering the partnership or advancing up the corporate ladder, and a more balanced lifestyle.

6. *Retired, "golden handshake" lawyers:* These lawyers have the most knowledge and experience, but as a group are very difficult to place. Most law firm and corporate clients prefer junior associates or those in the 10- to 15-year range for temporary assignment. Unfortunately, there is an industry bias against senior lawyers on the part of supervising lawyers who suspect that the senior lawyers will be reluctant to take orders and directions from young, less experienced superiors. Similarly, they imagine that senior lawyers will not do "grunt" work. Unless an agency or other referral source is acting on their behalf, and serving to dispel these stereotypes, chances of these senior lawyers landing temporary assignments will be meager.

Pursuing the Opportunity

As with any career decision, the pursuit of a temporary assignment should be grounded in an honest assessment of each lawyer's situation and prospects in light of the credentials, experience, and performance. Take the time to define the ideal situation: the setting, the hours to be worked, the experience the lawyer wishes to gain. If that ideal is not dramatically different than the current reality, and there is strong evidence that the lawyer will be retained and advanced in the current position, a change may not be in his or her best interests. If, on the other hand, such security is lacking, or if the lawyer's working conditions are incompatible with certain personal needs or aspirations, an alternative arrangement may be in order.

The approaches available in the pursuit of temporary or other alternative employment opportunities are much the same as one might employ in a permanent job search: Do it yourself or do it with the help of an agency. In fact, enterprising applicants who are willing and able to do the extensive brainwork and legwork that are required to uncover needs can land assignments. In most cases, the effort usually exceeds the reward. The truth is that very few corporations and law firms advertise temporary openings. Those that do tend to be barraged by résumés, the overwhelming majority of which are either wholly inappropriate to the need or come from permanent job seekers who see it as a means of getting their foot in the door. With barely enough time to fulfill the professional responsibilities of their jobs, most corporate counsel and hiring partners quickly tire of the burdensome and usually unproductive interviewing process. Because such assignments reflect immediate needs, in the absence of an immediately acceptable candidate, in most cases the search is abandoned.

The "immediate-need" factor works just as strongly against the practice of distributing unsolicited résumés as part of a job search strategy. Yes, it is conceivable that the receipt of one's résumé could coincide with the identification of an appropriate project or task. Unfortunately, most such résumés never reach the right decision maker at the right time and are rarely retained for future reference.

As a practical matter, most lawyers who currently are employed do not have the time or resources to explore the job market for continuing opportunities. Today's temporary legal placement agencies, which are typically managed and staffed by lawyers, are in the day-to-day business of finding and filling temporary job openings through routine interaction with the area's hiring partners and administrative general counsel. The best are equipped with sophisticated computerized systems to match prospective employers and applicants. They provide ongoing access to the marketplace and the expertise to help applicants translate access into employment.

For information on agencies within local markets, check local legal trade publications, bar magazines and journals, or the classified sections of major daily newspapers. Friends and fellow staff members can be good sources of insight into the local agency's capabilities, professionalism, and customer service. Every lawyer has the right to expect the utmost in confidentiality and the certainty that his or her résumé will be sent to prospective employers only with expressed permission. These qualities and operating policies may best be assessed through inquiries into the experience of others. Several long-established agencies do have very similar standards, but with new firms emerging with great frequency, it is only prudent to know as much about the people an applicant will be dealing with before beginning the process.

When working with most agencies, the lawyer applicant will be required to send a résumé and a cover letter before any communication is received. If the résumé is selected, the lawyer will be called for an interview. During the interview process, the applicant will be asked to fill out a variety of forms regarding legal experience, references, type of work hours and setting desired, financial needs in terms of hourly rate, travel preferences, etc. References will be checked, as well as bar, graduation, and law school attendance.

Permission will be requested to send the résumé to the client. If the client is interested in meeting the applicant, the agency will assist in arranging interviews. Sometimes the agency will have the lawyer report to the client immediately to begin work. The temporary lawyer will be responsible for sending a time card, signed by the client, to the agency before receiving payment by the agency.

As an independent contractor, the temporary lawyer will be responsible for his or her own taxes, health insurance, other benefits, etc. Malpractice coverage is not provided by the agency, or the law firm or corporation. Most lawyers, however, do not seek this insurance if they are working under the supervision of other lawyers within a law department or firm. Temporary lawyers who are litigating on behalf of the client or those temporary lawyers involved in complex securities work are advised to seek their own coverage.

In terms of compensation, hourly rates vary by geographic region and tend to reflect a combination of the lawyer's experience, area of specialization, and the complexity of the assignment. At present, lawyers are receiving from $30 per hour for routine work to upwards of $125 per hour for highly specialized and sophisticated assignments. Even a brief stint as a temporary lawyer can be highly lucrative.

The Alternative Career Path

The following list of practical dos and don'ts can be very helpful in assisting a lawyer during this career transition:

1. *Dealing with the agency:* To get the most from a temporary agency, understand that the agency is dealing with a large, changing roster of candidates and the constantly changing needs of its clients. As a result, qualifications or expertise not in demand today may be just what is required tomorrow. The point is to keep your profile high and take every opportunity to make an impression that will differentiate you from your counterparts. To accomplish this:

   - Call the agency periodically to update your résumé or discuss upcoming opportunities.
   - Ask to meet all of the lawyer personnel who may be involved in your placement.
   - Be forthcoming about references and reasons for job changes. The more the agency knows about you, the more information it will have at its disposal to argue on your behalf to the client.
   - Request that your résumé remain on active status regardless of how long the job search continues. (A rule of thumb in this business is that it could take a minimum of one month for each $10,000 of salary before a position of choice is secured; in this recession you could double that time comfortably.)

2. *Maintaining flexibility:* Be flexible and open to new situations. Your idea about part-time work may be very different from the client's notion of temporary or part-time work. A great opportunity could be two full days a week with a prestigious company. You should actively consider this position if there may appear to be possibilities of further employment. Also, a short-term assignment often is better than no assignment and can lead to other opportunities. Some lawyers were offered permanent placement positions while on short-term or menial assignments. One lawyer accepted a temporary paralegal position and did such a great job that the company offered her a permanent counsel position within the company. Particularly be flexible about:

- Working part-time for two clients at the same time, thus maximizing your opportunities from one or both of them.
- Rearranging your schedule if you are a solo practitioner to accommodate one big corporate client.
- Your pride. So many lawyers do not register for temporary positions or accept them because they think that the positions are beneath them. You should be informed about all opportunities and then make a decision. You cannot assess what you do not know.
- Rewriting your résumé, if requested by the agency, to emphasize your experience in a particular area of law or to highlight a particular credential.

3. *Listening to your placement director or counselor:* You might be the most knowledgeable, substantive lawyer on earth, but you probably know precious little about the placement process, particularly the temporary employment field. If you are told to spend more time on-site by the lawyer placement director, do so. Visibility is important to future work opportunities.

    If the placement director tells you to mingle and mix if possible with the other lawyers, listen to this advice. Because relationships and friendships are great sources for learning about opportunities within the company, do make a sincere, not a phony, effort to learn about your colleagues. In other words, come out of your office, make lunch dates, take time to smile and be cordial to everyone you come in contact with, especially the support staff; one of the best supporters on your behalf could be a well-regarded secretary, clerk, or paralegal.

4. *Fulfilling the assignment:* First and foremost, clients are interested in your completing the task as accurately and quickly as possible. If they believe you are lobbying for a permanent position among the other counsel, you will be perceived as not focused on the task at hand. You also run the risk of becoming embroiled in a political situation by crossing departmental lines. In one incident, a temporary lawyer was dismissed when he asked another department head for additional work. It so happened that the "client" was an underling to the other department head and he was affronted that the temporary lawyer would go over his head. Now, this is not always the case, and there

are times when bringing up your availability will lead to new assignments, but you must first assess your work environment regarding alliances, departmental lines, and hierarchical positions. Always include your agency in your planned actions. Often, the agency's knowledge of the department or experience in this area is invaluable.

5. *Working "temp" but wanting "perm":* If you are concerned that a temporary assignment may limit your ability to accept a permanent position should it arise while you are on assignment, there are tips you should know that could permit you to accept both opportunities:

  - First, be realistic about your permanent "irons in the fire." If you are on a third interview and selected as one of the finalists for a permanent position, do not accept a temporary position. If you back out at the last minute after you have been put forward for the temporary spot, the agency and the client will not think very highly of your character. Although you may not care, you must remember what a small world this is becoming and what appears secure and guaranteed one moment is subject to dissolution and acquisition the next.
  - Be candid at every step of the process with the temporary agency. Together you can assess the course of action to undertake. The agency can request an initial time commitment from the client. If you are just beginning a job search, a two-month assignment will hardly interfere and could present other opportunities. Also, if an unexpected offer does arise, the agency can arrange for you to train your replacement, minimizing the lag time and the client's ire.

6. *Making the most of every assignment:* Regardless of your long-term expectations or aspirations, your interests always will be best served by approaching even the most humble assignment with the utmost in energy, interest, and professionalism. Here are some rules to live by:

  - Treat the opportunity of the temporary assignment as you would any other permanent offer.
  - Send thank-you notes after the interview process, but make sure you proofread them. A client was all set to hire a temporary lawyer until the thank-you note arrived with typographical errors.
  - Act professionally at all times while on an assignment.
  - Minimize personal calls and absences.
  - Keep the confidences of every lawyer within the department and certainly those of your immediate supervisor.
  - Stay away from all politics and taking sides.
  - Analyze the working environment and conform. If the client is an early riser and starts work at 7:30, you should be there.
  - Always search for ways to create a great impression. Attitude is key. If the client does not want a dissertation paper on every issue, but wants you to approach the caseload more like a business lawyer than a fourth-year associate, do so. Learn to handle the matter in the client's manner.

CHAPTER 32

Nontraditional Careers for Lawyers[1]

Deborah L. Arron

What else can we as lawyers do with our extensive education and professional experience besides practicing law?

The short and honest answer is: *Anything we want to do.*

A law degree and subsequent professional experience are valuable credentials in a competitive job market. But most of us are not ready to admit that reality. Instead, we sabotage our potential by asking questions such as:

- How can I earn as much (or more) money?
- Am I qualified for anything else?
- Who else hires lawyers?
- What nontraditional jobs have other lawyers taken?

Contrary to popular opinion, we actually create more opportunities than we miss by carefully narrowing our occupational focus to something that excites us. "People don't care how much you know until they know how much you care," says David Maister, a Boston-area management consultant. "Enthusiasm and the hard work it inspires count for more than an extra piece of ability."

Or in the words of the late publisher Malcolm Forbes, "The only [career] advice of any value is to do what turns you on."

Why Change Careers?

Each of us could pinpoint a different reason for wanting to leave the profession. We may be tired of the overly adversarial posture of our opponents; we may be frustrated by the high cost of running an office and growing pressure to get and keep clients; or we may be losing the struggle to balance the demands of our personal and professional lives. For some of us, a desire for creative expression, or a need to contribute to society in a more positive way, is the trigger. Others simply yearn for a change of environment or pace.

Some of us can think of as many reasons to leave the profession as to stay. But consider whether one of these statements is motivating your thoughts of change:

- *I cannot find a job practicing law.*
- *I am not earning enough money.*
- *I am looking for less demanding work.*
- *I am burned out.*
- *I want new challenges.*

None of them are good foundations for a career change. If they sound familiar to you, first take steps to meet your needs within the profession.

A transition also is better delayed if any of these circumstances apply:

- You have been disenchanted with law less than three years and are not strongly drawn to an alternative career.
- You are not sure what type of field attracts you, and you are holding a job that provides enough flexibility or financial security to concentrate on self-assessment.
- You have not explored how to generate greater satisfaction in the legal profession, or you have not tried to implement the solutions that you have pondered.
- You do not have sufficient financial resources to support yourself (and your family) for the six months to two years it can take to switch from law into another field.
- You are undergoing a marital separation or divorce, grieving a recent death, experiencing serious health problems, or feeling great strain from some other personal matter.

If you have done all you can to find satisfaction within the law and you are prepared for the emotional and financial trauma a career change can bring, then evaluate whether your desire to leave the law is grounded in one of four sound reasons to change careers:

1. You are dissatisfied with the practice of law and strongly drawn to a new career.
2. You have reached the end of your career path in law and are unlikely to experience any further growth in the profession.
3. You never had the opportunity to pursue another career, and you now wish to act on that long-suppressed desire.
4. You have experienced a significant shift in your life interests, goals, or values that has ended your interest or belief in the law, and you wish to express your newfound ideals and objectives in another field.

Keys to Success in Making a Career Change

The first time that I questioned my choice of law as a career was in 1979. "I don't want to be a lawyer anymore," I confided to a colleague over dinner. I felt as if I had confessed treason. My friend insisted that I was perfectly suited to the profession and that it would be a *terrible* mistake even to think about another career. Thoroughly chastised, I continued to practice for another six years, but I could not shake my doubts. Eventually, I began a one-year sabbatical—from which I never have returned.

My own path away from law clearly taught me three lessons:

1. Our identification as "lawyer" is an extremely difficult bond to break.
2. To avoid debilitating feelings of guilt and shame, we should do everything we can to find satisfaction within the profession before leaving the practice of law.
3. The key to moving from law into another field is to find a new career direction from within, rather than expecting the marketplace to provide a direction.

Finding a New Career Direction

This last point cannot be emphasized strongly enough: We must define the specifics of the environment and the type of work that will suit us *before* exploring the marketplace, rather than looking to the marketplace to determine what type of work we can get.

This critical discovery only develops through rigorous introspection, and adds an extra step to what most of us wish could be an even speedier process. But, in any competitive job market, those who refuse to engage in the introspective process are at a distinct disadvantage. Those who are willing to take anything they can usually do not convey the passion and enthusiasm that result in employment. It is also difficult to persist through the disappointment and rejection that accompany every career transition if we're not sure that this is something we really want.

The self-assessment process does not have to cost a lot of money or take a lot of time. You will quickly get to the bottom of your needs if you consider these three questions:

1. Who am I?
2. What do I want?
3. What am I willing to give up to get what I want?

The question "Who am I?" is not meant to be an existential, spiritual inquiry into the meaning of life. Instead, it calls for a careful definition of your unique preferences and strengths.

Research confirms that we tend to enjoy work that draws on our natural aptitudes, those skills that come most readily to us. Some of us, though, feel guilty about engaging in tasks that come too easily. We believe that we always should be struggling to feel truly valuable. On the other hand, avoiding certain tasks or frequently putting them off may signal a career that needs changing. The following stories should illustrate this idea.

A small firm practitioner for 15 years, John spent most of his time meeting and talking with others. He loved to empathize with his clients and brainstorm solutions to their problems. In the meantime, files stacked up on his desk, begging for completion, especially when the matter involved a lot of details, rules, or complex documentation. When John realized that his procrastination was not a personal failing, but an indication of his preference to work with others in a fast-paced environment, he closed his law practice. He now sells law firm software for a company large enough to provide substantial support and follow-up.

This objective (or left-brained) assessment of our strengths, values, interests, and preferences must be combined with a right-brained, more illogical inquiry: What do I want?

Barbara tried general practice, and both criminal prosecution and defense, in her eight-year legal career. When she realized that the practice of law was not bringing her the satisfaction that she wanted, she read self-help books, attended career-planning seminars and workshops, and penned endless lists of likes and dislikes. Eventually, she identified two skills that gave her enormous satisfaction—research and mediation. Yet, she was not attracted to any of the careers that matched those talents.

At one seminar, she heard this quotation from David Maister, a Boston-area management consultant:

> The keys to what you really want are the things you don't like to admit: "I don't like to admit it, but I need to be the center of attention." Okay, find a job that will let you show off. "I don't like to admit it, but I really want to be rich." Fine, go out and make lots of money. *Play to your evil secrets; don't suppress them.*

At first, Barbara resisted the concept, because her "evil secret" was that she was not interested in a career at all. She would rather work on well-defined, short-term projects in a variety of fields. Once she accepted the truth, she generated a series of temporary and diverse assignments: a research project for a mediation practitioner; designing a plan for coordinating solid-waste and recycling contracts; reviewing municipal codes for statutory and constitutional inconsistencies; and filling in for a hearing examiner on maternity leave.

Only after we've considered who we are and what we want is it time to turn to the third question, What am I willing to give up to get what I want?

Gordon, with nearly 20 years of law practice behind him, hated his work but confided in a group workshop that something was preventing him from leaving the law. He told the group that he promised to put his sons through college, and the only way that he could meet that commitment was to maintain the status quo. When someone in the workshop asked whether he had shared his dilemma with his sons, Gordon looked shocked. "I can't do that," he said. He had given his word, and that was that.

The next week, he returned to the workshop with a lighter spirit. He related how he had confided his conflict to his eldest son and was astonished by his response. His son *urged* him to quit. His son said that he admired his father for putting himself through college and wanted the same opportunity to prove himself. More importantly, he missed the supportive, fun-loving father he had before Gordon's depression set in. Shortly thereafter, Gordon withdrew from his partnership. Now, he supports his family—and his interest in fiction writing—by driving a city bus.

Transferable Skills Analysis

Our work as lawyers helps us develop and perfect a wide variety of skills used and valued in other environments: for example, negotiation; gathering, analyzing, and organizing data; simplifying complex concepts; oral and written communication; and interviewing. Many of us, however, get so used to thinking in technical terms—taking depositions, writing briefs, filing motions —that we are unable to see the relationship between our legal experience and the demands of other fields. When we try to market ourselves to nonlegal employers as former civil litigators, or we describe our extensive "discovery" experience, nonlegal employers have no idea what skills we used in our work.

Some of us figure the solution is to try to find employers who already recognize the relationship between our legal backgrounds and their nonlegal positions. We ask which employers like to hire lawyers in nonlegal positions, or better yet, which headhunters are able to market lawyers into alternative careers. *There are no such employers or headhunters.* It is our responsibility, and our responsibility alone, to understand and communicate the transferability of our background and experience.

The good news is that once we finish the self-assessment process—especially answering the question, Who am I?—it is much easier to articulate our strengths and qualifications in terms a nonlegal employer will understand. For help in coming up with names of skills, see the "Dictionary of Skill Synonyms or Related Words" contained in Richard Bolles's well-known career-planning book, *What Color Is Your Parachute?*

Representative Alternative Career Choices

So, what can we do with our law degrees and legal experience besides practicing law? Truly, the options are almost unlimited. For inspiration, here are some of the ways that other lawyers have made use of their legal backgrounds, with more common career choices. Again, please keep in mind that just knowing what positions *other* lawyers have found or created will not lead *you* into a new career.

Working Within the Legal Profession as a Nonpractitioner

The rapid growth of the profession and the corresponding increase in law firm size have provided tremendous opportunities for the nonpracticing lawyer.

In some law firms, former practitioners with business skills have created niches for themselves as managers and office administrators. Those with marketing instincts have taken positions as client-services or marketing directors. To pursue interests in education, training, and human resources, still others now serve as directors of professional development or associate recruiting.

More lawyers practicing law, combined with added regulation such as specialization and mandatory continuing education requirements, also have led to growth in bar association services: legal education, lawyer assistance, mentoring, public affairs, and lobbying. Many of these programs are managed and staffed by former practitioners.

Providing Products or Services to the Legal Profession

In 1988, the *New York Times* called legal publishing a "new growth industry." Some former practitioners have taken advantage of this explosion by publishing, writing for, and distributing newsletters and journals catering to legal specialties. Conventional legal publishers and legal research services also hire former practitioners in departments as diverse as sales, management, marketing, training, and acquisitions.

An entire industry of service providers to the profession has developed, many of them founded, operated, or staffed by former colleagues. Any edition of *California Lawyer* or the *ABA Journal* will offer dozens of examples: computer software vendors, contract lawyer placement agencies, and management consultants, among many others.

We also have witnessed dramatic growth in the mediation field. Former practicing lawyers act as mediators and participate in the training, marketing, and administration of mediation services.

Using Legal Knowledge

As the law has become more complex, the demand for lawyers to act as interpreters for nonpractitioners has grown. Some lawyers find positions with corporations or the government in which their familiarity with the law is used on a daily basis. Tom, a sixth-year associate in a large law firm, serves as a good example.

When Tom was told that he never would be a partner, his immediate reaction was to interview—unsuccessfully—with two other insurance defense law firms and one insurance company. Those rejections forced him into self-assessment. By enrolling in a career evaluation workshop, and working with a career counselor, he discovered that the training field was better suited to his talents and interests.

Within six weeks after he focused his job search, Tom secured a position as a training administrator with an aircraft manufacturer. In his current job, he sees that federal and state health, safety, and environmental regulations are being met by the company's numerous training departments. Besides his ability to understand the intent of the regulations, he uses the skills that he developed in his trial practice to organize the materials that he presents to training consortiums and to mediate discussions among groups of people with vastly different opinions and agendas.

Lawyers also have designed products and services that explain legalities and provide easier access to the lay public. Examples include do-it-yourself divorce and estate-planning books and software programs; seminars that explain the defamation laws to journalists; and intellectual property protection system design.

Using Legal Skills

Corporations, nonprofit organizations, and federal, state, and local governments employ many former practicing lawyers in nonlegal positions. Examples include labor-relations manager, employee ombudsman, lobbyist, dispute-resolution expert, public-affairs representative, Equal Employment Opportunity Commission or other compliance officer, technical writer, and development or planned-giving specialist.

Mark spent six years working for a Manhattan insurance defense firm, and one year as a lawyer in city government, when he accepted a planned-giving position in the development office of New York University. He now designs testamentary plans that maximize benefits to both the donor and the beneficiary. Although Mark had no experience in estate planning before this job, he impressed his new employers with his ability to learn what was needed, a skill he developed when handling a wide variety of court cases.

Starting Over Completely

It is hard to imagine a career that would not use any of the background that we develop as lawyers. Those who return to school to become high school teachers make use of the insight, self-discipline, and knowledge that they developed as lawyers. Even a couple of Pacific Northwest entrepreneurs who decided to lead mountain treks using llamas called on their legal experience to navigate the licensing process.

Those lawyers who move the farthest from the profession, though, seem to gravitate toward the following fields and positions:

- Real estate—development, property management, construction, remodeling, and interior decoration;
- Communication (newspapers, magazines, television, radio, public relations)—publishing, editing, writing, reporting, producing, and public speaking;
- Entrepreneurial ventures;
- Teaching; and
- Counseling.

Obviously, a wide range of opportunities is available for law school graduates. *Please do not limit yourself to considering only these jobs.*

Heading Back to School

On the theory that specialized education translates into good jobs, we often are inclined to look at earning another degree as the answer to our career dilemma. The problem with this approach is that education only provides a knowledge base; when we have earned the degree, we still have to find a job.

The good news is that a law degree provides enough education to qualify us for employment in almost any field of interest.

Consider teaching and counseling for example. It is true that conventional jobs in those fields—public school instructor or clinical psychologist—demand rigid educational qualifications to pass licensing requirements. But we can teach or counsel with no more background than our law degrees, legal experience, and other "life credits."

In the counseling area, the Oregon State Bar's Attorney Assistance Program is staffed solely by former practicing lawyers, rather than licensed therapists, to manage and facilitate their peer counseling programs. As for teaching, lawyers work as paralegal instructors and teach law-related courses such as political science, criminal justice, sports management, and business law in colleges across the country. In fact, more than 1,000 of these teachers have formed the American Business Law Association.

The first issue to explore, then, is what practical advantages we think the educational investment will yield. To find out, we must research answers to these questions:

- How much will it cost?
- How long will it take?
- How much more money or opportunity will it yield?
- What positions could I obtain without earning another degree or certificate?
- How long will it take me to work my way up to the level that I hope to attain by earning the extra credential?

You may want to return to school even if a cost-benefit analysis does not justify the additional investment. It may be that conventional employment suits you better. Or your subjective motivations—a yearning for the student lifestyle, a love of learning, a need for a break from wage earning—may outweigh any financial considerations.

Getting the Job

For the career-changing lawyer, the job search requires some special considerations.

First of all, we are totally on our own. Because of the economics of the headhunting business, *there are no executive search consultants anywhere in the United States who place lawyers in nonlegal positions.*

Second, our résumés, much more than the résumés of those with backgrounds directly related to the open position, must read like persuasive briefs. They cannot establish that we have excelled as lawyers. They must prove that we are eager and able to perform that specific job. As a result, we cannot rely on the chronological format commonly prepared by lawyers.

A *chronological* résumé, which offers our employment background, education, and other relevant experience in order of date, never is effective for career changers. Its sole purpose is to demonstrate suitability for another similar position or one that is a step up the same ladder. Instead, draft a functional or targeted résumé, perhaps buttressed by a chronological overview of employment and volunteer background.

No matter how well we craft our résumés, though, we are likely to be confronted with the question, perhaps unspoken, Why do you want to leave the profession? Many members of the general public regard law as a glamorous field that they might have pursued if they felt they had the talent and persistence. To some, only a "loser" lawyer would consider a position outside of the profession. Each of us must come up with our own heartfelt answer to counter that perception.

As stated previously, the desire to earn a larger or more regular income is insufficient justification for a career change and certainly will not persuade a potential employer. This is why it is so important to clarify our motivations for leaving the law and to be able to illustrate our justifications with specific examples from our past experiences, both professional and volunteer.

Many employers also will assume that our salary demands will be excessive. Alison anticipated that objection when she lobbied to obtain a position as director of career services of a Texas law school. Before the issue was raised, she explained that she recently had moved to a less-costly residence and paid off all of her debts to prepare herself to take a job that she knew she would enjoy, but that would result in a substantial pay cut.

Nonlegal employers might hold negative stereotypes about lawyers as well. According to the *New York Times*, some human-resources personnel automatically typecast lawyers as "narrow-minded, confrontational, and unimaginative." If we think the interviewer might share those prejudices but is not voicing them, we should raise the issue ourselves and then explain why those stereotypes do not apply to us. For example, in anticipating a belief that lawyers are too confrontational to be good team players, we might say:

> You might believe that with my law background I'm not a team player. My experience shows that not to be true. In my position as volunteer coordinator of the hospital fund-raising project, I managed a team of 20 men and women. All but one of them worked with me on the project from start to finish, and we raised 20 percent more money than in any previous year.

On the other hand, if a stereotype does apply, we shouldn't argue that it does not. (If we are suspected of being contentious and confrontational, we will only prove the point!) Instead, we can show how that characteristic strengthens our credentials. Or we might be better off looking for work in an area where those traits are desired.

Stepping Out of the Profession

The transition into another career rarely occurs rapidly. Gail's story should illustrate this.

In 1988, Gail realized that civil litigation, and probably the practice of law itself, was not for her. She quickly enrolled in a self-assessment program and discovered that her interests, skills, values, and workplace preferences translated into a job in sports management or promotion. Gail was a good athlete and had some experience with amateur sports organizations. Even so, it took a year of research and national networking to land a position 2,000 miles away from her home. Gail now works in the NCAA Championships Department, supervising their awards program.

Gail's story is typical of the time it takes to find a job outside the profession. It is unusual because she was offered her new job while still actively practicing law in the same law firm. It is a rare lawyer who manages this type of career change. More commonly, a transitional period or "halfway-house" job intervenes. The following anecdotes illustrate five typical transitions.

Career-Planning Sabbatical

A 1991 law school graduate, Bill started his career by working in a small corporate law firm, first on a contract basis and then as an associate. After nine months, he knew he was not in the right place. In May of 1992, he quit his job to attend an international law conference in Australia. When he returned a month later, he knew that he did not want to go back to corporate law but did not know what else he could do. Rather than taking up his former employer on an offer to return to his job, he devoted his time to self-assessment.

Within a few months, he had "cleared away enough goo" in his head to develop a picture of his preferred next step: a job in international affairs or human rights. He told everyone he knew of his desire. By August, he had obtained a position as the Director of Policy and Legislative Affairs for the Foundation for International Cooperation and Development, a nonprofit organization that sponsors and promotes conferences and symposiums to address the economic and political issues caused by the breakup of the Soviet Union. His duties include gathering and disbursing information, writing letters and promotional materials, summarizing the information he gathers into educational packages, and helping to coordinate the international conferences sponsored by the foundation.

Volunteering

Nancy worked as a public defender for several years and grew tired of the one-on-one helper role. After engaging in self-assessment and some research, Nancy pinpointed waste management as an area with great social utility and with less of the futility she felt as a public defender.

She then set out to learn more about current issues in waste management, volunteering for a citizen's recycling group. That experience gave her the background to land a one-year consulting position as a recycling coordinator. A few months later, while reading an industry publication, she noticed an announcement for a supervisory position in another state. She now oversees about ten different waste-reduction and recycling projects.

Creating a Position

With 15 years of legal experience, the last eight as senior law department manager and assistant general counsel for a health insurance company, Michael wanted "to be more in the happiness business." Through a sustained self-assessment process, he mapped out four major professional interests: hospital-service providers, in-house legal, community service, and education. Then he began to network.

In the course of his networking, he came in contact with the president of a progressive community hospital. First, he studied the hospital's operations. Then, he began a dialogue with the senior staff about what they saw to be the hospital's needs. Within a few months, he had created a new position for himself as assistant to the president. He now counsels the hospital staff on risk management; advises on governmental, legislative, and regulatory issues; serves as employee ombudsman and advocate; and maintains the hospital's not-for-profit status through community-needs assessment and by recommending community service projects.

Building a Business

Earl and Kate, marriage and law partners, spent more than a year developing their home-based business in ceramic Christmas tree ornaments while operating their bankruptcy law practice. In Earl's words:

> I cut out every ounce of deadweight in my practice. Every minute at the office was productive so I had big blocks of time to devote to the ornaments. It got to the point where I was working at the law office only as long as the parking meter would last—120 minutes at a time. I went in and moved through my work as fast as I could. By the fall, it looked like the business would fly. We packed up the office and left.

Often, the transition combines two or more of these interim steps. For example, Michael worked on a temporary part-time basis with the health insurance company while he engaged in self-assessment. When he was certain that he did not want to continue in that job, he supported his family with contract legal work while he was searching.

Nancy, a partner in a commercial law firm, had volunteered for years in the human-services area while practicing law. It was not until she resigned her partnership and started a career change sabbatical, though, that she was able to focus on human services as her new career. Through networking, she obtained two part-time, temporary positions: one planning a human-services project as a city employee; the other working with a human-services consulting company. Both led to offers of full-time work.

Accept the Possibility of Failure

Many lawyers have moved from law into another career. They came from widely different backgrounds and chose equally diverse second careers, but they approached their transitions in the same way:

- They first figured out what they wanted to do and then researched the market to find a place to do it.
- They overcame their fear of the unknown and took the risk of failing.

To develop the courage to follow in their footsteps, find your own answer to the question: *What do I want to do with my law degree?*

Note

1. Adapted from *What Can You Do with a Law Degree?: A Lawyer's Guide to Career Alternatives Inside, Outside and Around the Law* (Niche Press, 1992) and *Running from the Law: Why Good Lawyers Are Getting Out of the Legal Profession* (Ten Speed Press, 1991), both by Deborah Arron.

APPENDIX

List of Fellowships

ACLU—William J. Brennan First Amendment Fellowship
ACLU—Brumbaugh Fellowship
ACLU—Marvin M. Karpatkin Fellowship
ACLU—Kennedy/Coleman Fellowship
ACLU—National Prison Project Fellowship
ACLU—Sherwood Shafer Fellowship
ACLU—George Slaff Fellowship
AMA Medical Ethics and Health Policy Fellowship
Amnesty International—Ralph J. Bunche Fellowships
Charles Bannerman Memorial Fellowships
Berkeley Law Foundation
Bet Tzedek Public Interest Law Fellowships
Ruth Chance Law Fellowship
Child Care Law Fellowship
College of Public Interest Law Fellowship
Columbia Public Interest Law Foundation
Community Law Center Attorney Internships
Congressional Fellowships on Women and Public Policy
Consumers Union Economic Justice Fellowship
Coro Foundation Fellows in Public Affairs
Harry H. Dow Memorial Legal Assistance Fund Fellowship
Echoing Green Public Service Fellowships
Family Law Advocacy Training Program
Georgetown University Law Center—Appellate Litigation Clinical
    Fellowships
Georgetown University Law Center—Center for Applied Legal Studies
    Fellowship
Georgetown University Law Center—Harrison Institute for Public Law
    Fellowships
Georgetown University Law Center—Institute for Public Representation
    Fellowships

Georgetown University Law Center—E. Barrett Prettyman/Stuart Stiller
      Fellowship
Georgetown University Law Center—Street Law Fellowship
John J. Gibbons Fellowship in Public Interest and Constitutional Law
      at Crummy, Del Deo, Dolan, Griffinger & Vecchione
Hall & Phillips Fellowships
Earl Johnson Community Lawyer Fellowships
Litt, Marquez and Fajardo Fellowship
Loyola University School of Law—Public Law Center Fellowships
Massachusetts Legal Assistance Corporation Minority Fellowships
Ralph C. Menapace Fellowship in Urban Land Use Law
Minnesota Lawyers International Human Rights Committee Fellowship
NAPIL Fellowships for Equal Justice
National Consumer Law Center Fellowships
National Puerto Rican Coalition, Inc.—Phillip Morris Public Policy
      Fellowship
National Veterans Legal Services Project—Dean K. Phillips Fellowship
Natural Heritage Institute Environmental Fellowship
Natural Resources Defense Council Fellowship
New York IOLA Legal Services Fellowships
New York University Public Interest Law Foundation
Northwestern School of Law—Natural Resources Law Fellowships
The Public Advocates Fellowship
PIRG Fellowships Nationwide
Reporters Committee Fellowship Program
Orville Schell Fellowships in International Human Rights
Shute, Mihaly & Weinberger Fellowships
Sierra Club Legal Defense Fund Fellowships
Skadden Fellowships
Southern Poverty Law Center Fellowship
Stanford Law School Graduate Fellowship Program for Aspiring
      Law Teachers
Stanford Public Interest Law Foundation
Student Press Law Center Fellowship
Tulane School of Law—Environmental Law Fellowships
Félix Velarde-Muñoz Graduate Internship
Howard C. Westwood Fellowships at Covington & Burling
University of Wisconsin School of Law—William H. Hastie Fellowship
University of Wisconsin School of Law—Program in Family Policy
Women's Law and Public Policy Fellowships
World Wildlife Fund Research Fellowship
Yale Initiative for Public Interest Law

R E S O U R C E   L I S T

Career-Planning Information

Altman, Mary Ann, *Life After Law—Second Careers for Lawyers*. Washington, DC: The Wayne Smith Company, Inc., 1991.

Anderson, Evelyn, and Elaine Dushoff, *Legal Careers—Choices and Options*, Vol. II. Washington, DC: NALP, 1984.

Anderson, Nancy, *Work with Passion*. New York: Carroll & Graf, 1984.

Arron, Deborah L., *Running from the Law: Why Good Lawyers Are Getting Out of the Legal Profession*. Seattle, WA: Niche Press, 1992.

Arron, Deborah L., *What Can You Do with a Law Degree?: A Lawyer's Guide to Career Alternatives Inside, Outside, and Around the Law*. National Association for Law Placement, Seattle, WA: Niche Press, 1989.

Barber, Professor David H., *Surviving Your Role as a Lawyer*. Dillon, CO: Spectra Publishing Co., Inc., 1987.

Bell, Susan J., *Full Disclosure: Do You Really Want to Be a Lawyer?* Princeton, NJ: Peterson's Guides, 1989.

Bellon, Lee Ann, "Coping with Job-Loss Trauma," *The National Law Journal* (November, 1990).

Bellon, Lee Ann, "Firms Need to Regroup for 1992," *The National Law Journal* (December 30, 1991).

Bellon, Lee Ann, "Recruiting Requires Joint Effort," *The National Law Journal* (March 26, 1990).

Bellon, Lee Ann, and Kathryn C. Alexander, "Scaling Down—Need Seen for Project Attorneys," *The National Law Journal* (December 31, 1990).

Bellon, Lee Ann, and Tamara Hampton, "Minimizing Trauma of Terminations," *The National Law Journal* (August 27, 1990).

Bennett, Hal Z., and Susan J. Sparrow, *Follow Your Bliss*. New York: Avon Books, 1990.

Bodner, Joanne, and Venda Raye-Johnson, *Staying Up When Your Job Pulls You Down*. New York: Perigee Books, Division of The Putnam Publishing Group, 1991.

Bolles, Richard, *How to Find Your Mission in Life*. Berkeley, CA: Ten Speed Press, 1991.

Bolles, Richard N., *The Three Boxes of Life and How to Get Out of Them*. Berkeley, CA: Ten Speed Press, 1987.

Bolles, Richard N., *What Color Is Your Parachute?* Berkeley, CA: Ten Speed Press, 1987.

Bridges, William, *Transitions: Making Sense of Life's Changes*. Reading, MA: Addison-Wesley, 1980.

Byers, Samuelson, and Gordon Williamson, *Lawyers in Transition: Planning a Life in the Law*. Natick, MA: The Barkley Company, Inc., 1988.

Caple, John, *Careercycles*. Englewood Cliffs, NJ: Prentice Hall, Inc., 1983.

Career Associates, *Career Choices for Undergraduates Considering Law*. New York: Walker and Company, 1985.

Couric, Emily, *Women Lawyers' Perspectives on Success*. Clifton, NJ: Prentice Hall Law & Business, 1984.

Crystal, John C., and Richard N. Bolles, *Where Do I Go From Here with the Rest of My Life?* Berkeley, CA: Ten Speed Press, 1974.

Csikszentmihalyi, Mihaly, *Flow: The Psychology of Optimal Experience*. New York: Harper Perennial, 1990.

Curran, Barbara A., *The Lawyer Statistical Report: A Statistical Profile of the United States Legal Profession in the 1980s*. Chicago: American Bar Foundation, 1985.

Dail, Hilda Lee, *The Lotus and the Pool: How to Create Your Own Career*. Boston, MA: Shambhala, 1983.

DeBold, Elizabeth, Ed., *Legal Career Planning Strategies to Plan and Live a Life in the Law*. Chicago, IL: Samuelson Associates, 1989.

Figler, Howard, *The Complete Job-Search Handbook*. New York: Holt, Rinehart & Winston, 1979.

Flood, John A., *The Legal Profession in the United States*, 3rd Ed. Chicago: American Bar Foundation, 1985.

Ford, George, and Gordon Lippit, *Creating Your Future: A Guide to Personal Goal Setting*. San Diego, CA: University Associates, 1988.

Frank, Steven J., *Learning the Law—Success in Law School and Beyond*. New York: Citadel Press, 1992.

Freund, James C., *Lawyering—A Realistic Approach to Legal Practice*. New York: Law Journal Seminars Press Inc., 1979.

Gibaldi, Carmine, and Thom McCarthy, *Self-Directed Career Planning Workbook*. New York: McGraw-Hill, 1993.

Granfield, Robert, *Making Elite Lawyers—Visions of Law at Harvard and Beyond*. New York: Routledge, 1992.

Haldane, Bernard, *Career Satisfaction and Success—How to Know and Manage Your Strengths*. Seattle, WA: Wellness Behavior, 1988.

Hirsch, Ronald L., "Are You on Target?", *Barrister* (Winter 1985), 17–20.

Hirsch, Sandra, and Jean Kummerow, *Life Types*. New York: Warner Books, 1989.

Hollander, Dory, *Doom Loop System: A Step-by-Step Guide to Career Mastery*. New York: Viking Penguin, 1991.

Jackson, Tom, *Guerilla Tactics in the New Job Market*. New York: Bantam, 1991.

John-Roger and Peter McWilliams, *Do It! Let's Get Off Our Buts*. Los Angeles, CA: Prelude Press, 1991.

Killoughey, D. M., Ed., *Breaking Traditions: Work Alternatives for Lawyers*. Chicago: Section of Law Practice Management, American Bar Association, 1993.

Kroeger, Otto, and Janet Thuesen, *Type Talk*. New York: Delacorte Press, 1988.

Lawrence, Gordon D., *People Types and Tiger Stripes*, 2nd Ed. Gainesville, FL: CAPT, Inc., 1982.

The Lawyer's Almanac, 8th Ed. New York: Prentice Hall Law & Business, 1988.

Lipman, Burton E., *Professional Job Search Program: How to Market Yourself*. New York: John Wiley & Sons, 1983.

Magness, Michael K., with Howard I. Bernstein, "How to Build Your Career," *Barrister* (Spring 1984), 35.

McCormack, Mark H., *What I Should Have Learned at Yale Law School—The Terrible Truth About Lawyers*. New York: Aron Books, 1987.

Moll, Richard W., *The Lure of the Law—Why People Become Lawyers, and What the Profession Does to Them*. New York: Penguin Books, 1990.

Munneke, Gary, *Opportunities in Law Careers*. Chicago: National Textbook Co., 1986.

Myers, Isabel B., with Peter B. Myers, *Gifts Differing*. Palo Alto, CA: Consulting Psychologists Press, Inc., 1980.

National Association for Law Placement, *Employment Report and Salary Survey*. Washington, DC: NALP, published annually.

Pearson, Carol, *Awakening the Heroes Within: Twelve Archetypes to Help Us Find Ourselves and Transform Our World*. New York: HarperCollins, 1991.

Pearson, Carol S., *The Hero Within*. New York: HarperCollins, 1986.

Peck, M. Scott, M.D., *The Road Less Traveled*. New York: A Touchstone Book, Division of Simon & Schuster Trade, 1978.

Pilder, Richard J., and William F. Pilder, *How to Find Your Life's Work*. New York: Prentice Hall, 1981.

Raelin, Joseph A., *The Salaried Professional: How to Make the Most of Your Career*. New York: Praeger Publishers, 1984.

Richard, L. R., "Lawyer Dissatisfaction Rising, but Many Alternatives Exist," *Pennsylvania Law Journal-Reporter* (November 5, 1990), 4, 8.

Richard, L. R., "Personality Styles of U.S. Lawyers: New Findings," *ABA Journal* (July 1993), 4–14.

Richard, L. R., "Resolving for New Year to Effectively Plan Career," *Pennsylvania Law Journal-Reporter* (January 21, 1991), 4.

Richard, L. R., "Understanding Lawyers' Personalities," *The Pennsylvania Lawyer* (1992; 14:2), 22–26, 32.

Rodin, Robert J., *Full Potential: Your Career and Life Planning Workbook*. New York: McGraw-Hill, 1983.

Scheele, Adele, *Skills for Success*. New York: Ballantine, 1979.

Schein, Edgar H., *Career Anchors: Discover Your Real Values*. San Diego, CA: University Associates, 1985.

Schwartz, Laurens R., *What You Aren't Supposed to Know About the Legal Profession—An Exposé of Lawyers, Law Schools, Judges, and More*. New York: Shapolsky Publishers, Inc., 1991.

Sher, Barbara, *Wishcraft: How to Get What You Really Want*. New York: Ballantine Books, Division of Random House, 1979.

Sinetar, Marsha, *Do What You Love, the Money Will Follow*. Mahwah, NJ: Paulist Press, 1987.

Sinetar, Marsha, *Living Happily Ever After*. New York: Dell Doubleday, 1990.

Snelling, Robert O., *The Right Job: How to Get the Job That's Right for You*. New York: Penguin, 1993.

Stephan, Naomi, *Finding Your Life Mission*. Walpole, NH: Stillpoint Publisher, 1989.

Studner, Peter K., *Super Job Search: The Complete Manual for Job Seekers and Career Changers*. Los Angeles: Jamenair, 1993.

Sturman, Gerald M., *If You Knew Who You Were, You Could Be Who You Are!* Woodstock, NY: Bierman House, 1989.

Tieger, Paul D., and Barbara Barron-Tieger, *Do What You Are: Discover the Perfect Career for You Through the Secrets of Personality Type*. Boston: Little Brown and Company, 1992.

Utley, Frances, and Gary Munneke, *From Law Student to Lawyer*. Chicago: Career Series, American Bar Association, 1984.

Vogt, Leona M., *From Law School to Career: Where Do Graduates Go and What Do They Do?* Cambridge, MA: Harvard Law School, 1986.

Wasserman, Steven, and J. W. O'Brien, Eds., *Law and Legal Information Directory*, 4th Ed. Detroit, MI: Gale Research Co., 1986.

Wayne, Ellen, and Betsy McCombs, *Legal Careers—Choices and Options*, Vol. I. Washington, DC: NALP, 1983.

Wendleton, Kate, *Through the Brick Wall: How to Job Hunt in a Tight Market*. New York: Villard, 1992.

Woodman, Marion, *Addiction to Perfection*. Toronto, Ontario: Inner City Books, 1982.

Zemans, Frances Kahn, and Victor G. Rosenblum, *The Making of a Public Profession*. Chicago: American Bar Foundation, 1981.

Job Finding Information

Brennan, Lawrence D., Stanley Strand, and Edward Gruber, *Resumes for Better Jobs*. New York: Monarch Press, 1981.

Carey, Williams T., *Law Students: How to Get a Job When There Aren't Any*. Durham, NC: Carolina Academic Press, 1986.

Dickhut, Harold W., *Professional Resume & Job Search Guide*. Englewood Cliffs, NJ: Prentice Hall, 1981.

Feferman, Richard N., *Building Your Firm with Associates: A Guide for Hiring and Managing New Attorneys*. Chicago: Section of Economics of Law Practice, American Bar Association, 1988.

Good, C. Edward, *Does Your Resume Wear Blue Jeans? The Book on Resume Preparation*. Charlottesville, VA: Word Store, 1985.

Kanter, Arnold B., *Kanter on Hiring: A Lawyer's Guide to Lawyer Hiring*. Chicago: Lawletters, Inc., 1983.

Komar, John K., *Resume Builder*. Chicago: Follett Publishing Company, 1980.

Lathrop, Richard, *Who's Hiring Who*. Berkeley, CA: Ten Speed Press, 1977.

Lewis, Adele, *How to Write Better Resumes.* Woodbury, NY: Barron's Educational Series, Inc., 1983.

Magness, Michael K., "The Art of Effective Interviewing," *National Law Journal* (October 11, 1982), 15.

Medley, Anthony H., *Sweaty Palms: The Neglected Art of Being Interviewed.* Belmont, CA: Lifetime Learning Publications, 1978.

Miller, Saul, *After Law School? Finding a Job in a Tight Market.* Boston: Little, Brown and Company, 1978.

Pell, Arthur R., *How to Sell Yourself on an Interview.* New York: Monarch Press, 1982.

Provost, Maureen, *Charting Your Course: Identifying Your Success Patterns and Career Preferences.* New York: Fordham University School of Law, 1987.

Ryan, Joseph, *Stating Your Case: How to Interview for a Job as a Lawyer.* St. Paul, MN: West Publishing Co., 1982.

White, Christine, and Abbie Willard Thorner, *Managing the Recruitment Process.* New York: Law of Business, Inc., 1982.

Career Choice Information

Private Practice (General)

American Lawyer. New York: American Lawyer Media, published monthly.

American Lawyer Guide to Leading Law Firms. New York: Am-Law Publishing Corp., 1983.

Directory of Legal Employers. Washington, DC: National Association for Law Placement, published annually.

Flying Solo, A Survival Guide for the Solo Lawyer, 2nd Ed. Chicago: Section of Law Practice Management, American Bar Association, 1994.

Foonberg, Jay, *How to Start and Build a Law Practice,* 3rd Ed. Chicago: ABA Career Series, American Bar Association, 1991.

Martindale-Hubbell Law Directory. Summit, NJ: Martindale-Hubbell, Inc., published annually.

The National Law Journal. New York: New York Law Publishing Co., published weekly.

National Law Journal Directory of the Legal Profession. New York: New York Law Publishing Co., 1984.

Singer, Gerald M., *How to Go Directly into Solo Practice (Without Missing a Byte).* New York: Lawyers Co-operative Publishing Co., 1986.

Stevens, Mark, *Power of Attorney: The Rise of the Giant Law Firms.* New York: McGraw-Hill Book Co., 1987.

Government Agency Information

Almanac of American Politics. Washington, DC: National Law Journal, 1987.

Almanac of American Politics. Washington, DC: National Law Journal, 1992.

The Almanac of the Unelected. Washington, DC: The Almanac of the Unelected, 1993.

Braddock's Federal-State-Local Government Directory. Washington, DC: Braddock's Publications, Inc., 1984.

Braddock's Federal-State-Local Government Directory. Alexandria, VA: Braddock Communications, 1990.

Brownson, Anna L., *Congressional Staff Directory*. Mt. Vernon, VA: Staff Directories, Ltd., 1992.

Brownson, Anna L., *Judicial Staff Directory*. Mt. Vernon, VA: Staff Directories, Ltd., 1992.

Brownson, Charles B., and Anna Brownson, *Congressional Staff Directory*. Mt. Vernon, VA: Congressional Staff Directory, Ltd., 1988.

Brownson, Charles B., and Anna Brownson, *Judicial Staff Directory*. Mt. Vernon, VA: Congressional Staff Directory, Ltd., 1988.

Congressional Directory. Washington, DC: Joint Committee on Printing (Congress), 1993.

Congressional Yellow Pages. Washington, DC: Monitor Publishing Co., 1987.

Congressional Yellow Book. Washington, DC: Monitor Publishing Company, 1992.

Directory and Profile of Federal Legal Offices. Washington, DC: Federal Legal Council, 1982.

DumBaugh, Kerry, and Gary Serota, *Capitol Jobs: An Insider's Guide to Finding a Job in Congress*. Washington, DC: Tilden Press, June, 1983, 1986.

DuChez, Jo-Anne, Ed., *The National Directory of State Agencies*. Bethesda, MD: NSA Directories, 1987.

DuChez, Jo-Anne, Ed., *The National Directory of State Agencies*. Bethesda, MD: Cambridge Information Group Directories, Inc., 1989.

National and Federal Legal Employment Report, *Landing a Legal Job*, Revised Ed. Washington, DC: Federal Reports, Inc., 1987.

National and Federal Legal Employment Report, *1988–89 Federal Personnel Office Directory*. Washington, DC: Federal Reports, Inc., 1989.

Federal and State Judicial Clerkship Directory. Washington, DC: NALP, 1987.

Federal Careers for Attorneys. Washington, DC: Federal Reports, Inc., 1991.

Federal Judiciary Almanac. New York: John Wiley & Sons, 1987.

Federal Law-Related Careers. Washington, DC: Federal Reports, Inc., 1991.

Federal Legal Directory. Phoenix, AZ: The Oryx Press, 1990.

Federal Personnel Office Directory. Washington, DC: Federal Reports, Inc., 1990–1991.

Federal Regional Yellow Book. Washington, DC: Monitor Publishing Company, 1993.

Federal Regulatory Directory. Washington, DC: Congressional Quarterly, Inc., 1988.

Federal Regulatory Directory. Washington, DC: Congressional Quarterly, Inc., 1990.

Federal Reports, Inc., *The National and Federal Legal Employment Report*. Washington, DC: monthly newsletter.

Federal Research Service, Inc., *Federal Career Opportunities*. Vienna, VA: bi-weekly.

Federal-State Court Directory. Washington, DC: Want Publishing Company, 1987.

Federal Yellow Book. Washington, DC: Monitor Publishing Company, 1993.

"1992 Guide to Legal Washington," *The Washington Lawyer*, DC Bar Association, Washington, D.C. (July/August 1992).

Hermann, Richard L., and Linda P. Sutherland, *110 Biggest Mistakes Job Hunters Make (And How to Avoid Them)*. Washington, DC: Federal Reports, Inc., 1993.

Lawyer's Job Bulletin Board. Federal Bar Association, 1815 H Street, N.W., Suite 408, Washington, DC (subscription series).

National Directory of Prosecuting Attorneys. Alexandria, VA: National District Attorneys Association, 1986.

The National Directory of State Agencies. Bethesda, MD: National Standards Association, 1987.

171 Reference Book. Washington, DC: Workbooks, Inc., 1984.

Opportunities in Public Affairs. Washington, DC: The Brubach Corporation (subscription series).

The Paralegal's Guide to U.S. Government Jobs. Washington, DC: Federal Reports, Inc., 1993.

Politics in America. Washington, DC: Congressional Quarterly, Inc., 1993–1994.

Shapiro, Norman H., *How to Find a Job on Capitol Hill*. Chicago: University of Chicago Law School Record, 1981.

State Elective Officials and the Legislatures. Washington, DC: The Council of State Governments, 1987.

State Elective Officials and the Legislatures. Lexington, KY: The Council of State Governments, 1991–1992.

State Information Book. Washington, DC: Potomac Books, 1987.

Thorner, Abbie, *Now Hiring: Government Jobs for Lawyers*. Chicago: Law Student Division, American Bar Association, 1987, 1990.

U.S. Court Directory. Washington, DC: The Administrative Office of the U.S. Courts, 1987.

U.S. Government Manual. Washington, DC: U.S. Government Printing Office, 1987–1988, 1992–1993.

Washington Information Directory. Washington, DC: Congressional Quarterly, Inc., 1987, 1992–1993.

Public Interest

Anzalone, Joan, Ed., *Good Works: A Guide to Careers in Social Change*, 3rd Ed. New York: Dembner Books, 1985.

Balancing the Scales of Justice: Financing Public Interest Law in America. Washington, DC: The Council for Public Interest Law, 1976.

Bergner, Douglas J., *Public Interest Profiles*, 5th Ed. Washington, DC: Foundation for Public Affairs, 1986–1987.

Brown, Burnett, Lolita Plank, and Lynne Plank, *Annotated Bibliography of Public Interest Placement Resources*. Washington, DC: National Association for Public Interest Law (NAPIL), 1988.

Clearinghouse Review. Chicago, IL: National Clearinghouse for Legal Services, Inc., published monthly.

Conservation Directory. Washington, DC: National Wildlife Federation, 1983.

DeBroff, Stacy M., *The Public Interest Job Search Guide: Harvard Law School's Handbook Employer Directory.* Cambridge, MA: Harvard Law School, 1992.

The Directory of Legal Aid and Defender Offices. Washington, DC: National Legal Aid and Defender Association, 1987–1988.

Fox, Ronald, W., Ed., *The Public Interest Directory, A Law Student's Guide on How and Where to Find Public Interest/Human Services Jobs.* Cambridge, MA: Harvard Law School, Placement Office, 1986.

Fellowship Opportunities Guide 1993–1994. New Haven, CT: Yale Law School Career Development Office, July, 1993.

Hughes, Kathleen, *Good Works: A Guide to Social Change Careers.* Washington, DC: Center for Study of Responsive Law, 1983.

Kaiser, Geoffrey, and Barbara Mule, *The Public Interest Handbook: A Guide to Legal Careers in Public Interest.* West Cornwall, CT: Locust Hill Press, 1987.

Konen, James S., *How Can You Defend Those People? The Making of a Criminal Lawyer.* New York: McGraw-Hill, 1983.

Law Firms & Pro Bono 1992/1993. Washington, DC: National Association for Public Interest Law, 1992–1993.

Legal Services Corporation Program Directory. Washington, DC: Legal Services Corporation, 1984.

McAdams, Terry W., *Careers in the Nonprofit Sector: Doing Well by Doing Good.* Washington, DC: The Tact Group, 1986.

Mental and Developmental Disabilities Directory of Legal Advocates. Chicago: Commission on the Mentally Disabled, American Bar Association, 1983.

The NAPIL Connection. Washington, DC: National Association for Public Interest Law, July, 1992.

The NAPIL Guide to Public Interest Career Resources 1992/1993. Washington, DC: National Association for Public Interest Law, 1992–1993.

The NAPIL Post-Graduate Fellowships Guide 1992–1993. Washington, DC: National Association for Public Interest Law, 1992–1993.

National Lawyers Guild National Referral Directory. New York: National Lawyers Guild National Office, 1986.

Public Interest Private Practice—A Directory of Progressive Private Law Firms in Northern California. San Francisco, CA: Public Interest Clearinghouse, 1993.

Public Interest Profiles, 5th Ed. Washington, DC: Foundation for Public Affairs, 1986–1987.

Renz, Loren, Ed., *The Foundation Directory,* 11th Ed. New York: The Foundation Center, 1987.

Wiseberg, Laurie S., and Hazel Sirett, *North American Human Rights Directory,* 3rd Ed. Cambridge, MA: Human Rights Internet, 1984.

Corporations

ACCA Docket. Washington, DC: American Corporate Counsel Association, published quarterly.

American Bank Directory, Vols. I and II. Norcross, GA: McFadden Business Publications, 1987.

The Corporate Counsellor. New York: Leader Publications (The New York Law Publishing Co.).

Directory of Corporate Counsel. Clifton, NJ: Law & Business, Inc., Prentice Hall Law & Business, 1988–1989.

Langer, Steven, *Compensation of Attorneys (Non-Law Firms)*, 8th Ed. Crete, IL: Abbott, Langer & Associates, 1986.

Parker, Penny, Ed., *Legal Careers in Business*, Vol. III. Washington, DC: National Association for Law Placement, 1984.

Standard and Poor's Register of Corporations. New York: Standard and Poor, 1986.

Stevens, Mark, *The Big Eight*. New York: Collier Books, Macmillan Publishing Co., 1981.

Specific Areas of Practice (Legal and Nonlegal)

Altman & Weil, Inc., *Compensation Plans for Lawyers and Their Staffs—Salaries, Bonuses, and Profit-Sharing*. Chicago: Section of Economics of Law Practice, American Bar Association, 1986.

Arts Law in Theory and Practice. Washington, DC: Washington Area Lawyers for the Arts, Inc., 1985.

Attorneys & Agents Registered to Practice Before the U.S. Patent and Trademark Office. Washington, DC: U.S. Department of Commerce, 1987.

Berry, C. S., "Temporary Lawyers: The Do's and Don'ts." Special Section: Law Office Management, *New York Law Journal* (April 17, 1989), 201.

Best's Directory of Recommended Insurance Attorneys. Oldwick, NJ: A. M. Best Company, 1987.

Cherovsky, E., "The Use of Temporary Lawyers Is on the Rise in Many Firms," Special Section on Recruitment, *New York Law Journal* (March 4, 1991), 205.

Couric, E., "Contract Attorneys," *Student Lawyer* (September 1988), 21–27.

Davis, Anthony E., and Jeffrey Glen, *The Law and Ethics of Partner Movement: An Overview*. Washington, DC: NALSC, 1992.

Directory of Law Teachers. Washington, DC: Association of American Law Schools, 1987.

Evers, M., "A Non-Traditional View on Job Search Strategies," *Chicago Bar Association Record* (January 1993), 30.

Fleming, P. E., and L. Friedman, "Evaluating Temporary Lawyers; Careful Screening Yields Rewards," *New York Law Journal* (April 15, 1991), 13:18(2).

Gottschalk, Jack A., and Robert J. Small, *Managing a Law Firm for Survival*. Philadelphia, PA: American Law Institute—American Bar Association, 1992.

Greene, Robert Michael, *Making Partner—A Guide for Law Firm Associates*. Chicago: Section of Law Practice Management, American Bar Association, 1992.

Gruber, Katherine, Ed., *Encyclopedia of Associations*, 21st Ed. Detroit, MI: Gale Research, Co., 1987.

Guiley, Rosemary, *Career Opportunities for Writers*. New York: Facts on File Publications, 1985.

Heintz, Bruce D., and Nancy Markham-Bugbee, *Two-Tier Partnerships and Other Alternatives: Five Approaches*. Chicago: Section of Economics of Law Practice, American Bar Association, 1986.

Katz, Judith A., *The Ad Game*. New York: Barnes & Noble Books, 1984.

Kelly, Robert E., *Consulting: The Complete Guide to a Profitable Career*. New York: Charles Scribner's Sons, 1981.

Knowles, D., and P. S. Knowles, "One Family's Experience," *Oregon State Bar Bulletin* (February/March 1993), 31–33.

Kocher, Eric, *International Jobs: Where They Are, How to Get Them*. Boston: Addison-Wesley Publishing Co., 1984.

Lavins, D. L., "Staffing Document Productions with Temporary Assistants," *New York Law Journal* (November 3, 1986).

Law & Business Directory of Bankruptcy Attorneys. Englewood Cliffs, NJ: Prentice Hall Law & Business, 1993.

Law & Business Directory of Entertainment and Sports Attorneys/Agents. Englewood Cliffs, NJ: Prentice Hall Law & Business, 1993.

Law & Business Directory of Environmental Attorneys. Englewood Cliffs, NJ: Prentice Hall Law & Business, 1993.

Law & Business Directory of Intellectual Property Attorneys. Englewood Cliffs, NJ: Prentice Hall Law & Business, 1993.

Law and Business Directory of Litigation Attorneys. Englewood Cliffs, NJ: Prentice Hall Law & Business, 1993.

LoPucki, Lynn M., *Directory of Bankruptcy Attorneys*. Englewood Cliffs, NJ: Prentice Hall, 1988.

Lubofsky, M. "The Pros and Cons of Temporary Work," *Massachusetts Lawyers Weekly* (June 22, 1992).

Lubofsky, M. "Time to Kiss Hourly Rates Goodbye" (Special Supplement), *Massachusetts Lawyers Weekly* (December 14, 1992).

Luney, Percy R. Jr., *Careers in Natural Resources and Environmental Law*. Chicago: American Bar Association, Career Series, 1987.

Magness, Michael K., and Carolyn M. Wehmann, Eds., *Your New Lawyer—The Legal Employer's Complete Guide to Recruitment, Development, and Management*, 2nd Ed. Chicago: Section of Law Practice Management, American Bar Association, 1992.

Malone, Gerry, and Howard Mudrick, *Anatomy of a Law Firm Merger—How to Make or Break the Deal*. Chicago: Section of Law Practice Management, American Bar Association, 1992.

Marcotte, P., "Temporary Lawyer Firms Get O.K.," *ABA Journal* (March 1989).

Moberly, R. B., "Temporary, Part-Time, and Other Atypical Employment Relationships in the United States," *Labor Law Journal* (November 1987), 38.

The National Job Bank, 4th Ed. Boston: Bob Adams, Inc., 1987.

Pashker, Marti, and S. Peter Valiunas, *Money Jobs*. New York: Crown Publishing Inc., 1984.

Powell, K., "Alternative Work Schedules," *Oregon State Bar Bulletin* (February/March 1992).

Russell, John J., Ed., *Directory of National Trade and Professional Associations of the United States*, 23rd Ed. Washington, DC: Columbia Books, 1988.

Scheffey, T., "In House," *The Connecticut Law Tribune* (November 2, 1992).

Scogland, W. L., and K. P. Hacket, "Employee Leasing Comes to the Legal Profession," *Illinois Bar Journal* (November 1991), 80:577(2).

Utley, Frances, with Gary A. Munneke, *Nonlegal Careers for Lawyers in the Private Sector*, 2nd Ed. Chicago: American Bar Association, Career Series, 1984.

Walker, E., and R. Webster, "Contract Attorneys Can Be Useful in Many Situations," *Los Angeles Daily Journal* (May 11, 1992), 105:12(1).

Wayne, Ellen, *Careers in Labor Law*. Chicago: American Bar Association, Career Series, 1985.

Wayne, Ellen, and Betsy McCombs, *Graduate Law Study Programs*. Boston: Joint Committee on Law Study Programs, 1986.

Williams, John W., *Career Preparation and Opportunities in International Law*. Chicago: Section of International Law Practice, American Bar Association, 1984.

Miscellaneous

Brown, Ronald L., *Juris–Jacular: An Anthology of Modern American Legal Humor*. Littleton, CO: Fred B. Rothman, & Co., 1988.

Hay, Peter, *The Book of Legal Anecdotes*. New York: Facts on File Publications, 1989.

James, Simon, and Stebbings, Chantal, *A Dictionary of Legal Quotations*. New York: Macmillan Publishing Company, 1987.

Kanter, Arnold B., *Advanced Law Firm Mismanagement from the Offices of Fairweather, Winters & Sommers*. North Haven, CT: Catbird Press, 1993.

Magness, Michael K., "Bullet-Proofing Your Firm: Why You Should Integrate Associates," *Lawyer Hiring and Training Report* (April 1989), 2.

Magness, Michael K., "Dealing with the Dog Days: Staying in the Law Business Is Serious Business," *Lawyer Hiring and Training Report* (August 1991), 2.

Magness, Michael K., "Reaping What They've Sown: Firms Struggle with Yesterday's Mistakes," *Lawyer Hiring and Training Report* (March 1993), 2.

Magness, Michael K., "The Problem with Recruiting," *National Law Journal* (August 23, 1982), 14.

Magness, Michael K., and Carolyn M. Wehmann, "Extending Effective Interviewing Beyond Campus: Tips on Conducting Callbacks," *National Law Journal* (September 1, 1986), 14.

Magness, Michael K., and Carolyn M. Wehmann, Eds., *Your New Lawyer: The Legal Employer's Complete Guide to Recruitment, Development and Management*. Chicago: American Bar Association, August, 1992.

Magness, Michael K., with Peter N. Kutulakis, "A Guide to Lawyer Recruiting," *The Pennsylvania Lawyer* (December 1987), 26.

Magness, Michael K., with Peter N. Kutulakis, "Campus Recruiting by Non-Attorneys," *National Law Journal* (April 28, 1986), 16.

Magness, Michael K., with Peter N. Kutulakis, "Getting Value from Campus Visits," *National Law Journal* (December 23, 1985), 14.

Magness, Michael K., and Carolyn M. Wehmann, *Attracting Law Students You Want to Hire*. New York: Magness & Wehmann Management Consultants, Seminar handbook, March, 1989.

Magness, Michael K., and Carolyn M. Wehmann, *Boosting Your Sign-Ups on Campus: Marketing and Summer Program Strategies*. New York: Magness & Wehmann Management Consultants, Seminar handbook, February, 1990.

Magness, Michael K., and Carolyn M. Wehmann, *Interviewing Skills for Lawyers*. New York: Magness & Wehmann Management Consultants, Seminar handbook, 1990.

Magness, Michael K., and Carolyn M. Wehmann, *Marketing Your Firm to Law Students More Effectively*. New York: Magness & Wehmann Management Consultants, Seminar handbook, March, 1988.

Magness, Michael K., and Carolyn M. Wehmann, *Maximizing the Return from Your Summer Program*. New York: Magness & Wehmann Management Consultants, Seminar handbook, March, 1988.

Magness, Michael K., and Carolyn M. Wehmann, *Reducing the High Costs of Lateral Hiring*. New York: Magness & Wehmann Management Consultants, Seminar handbook, March, 1989.

Schrager, David, and Elizabeth Frost, *The Quotable Lawyer*. New York: Facts on File Publications, 1986.

Wehmann, Carolyn M., "Beating the Odds with First-Years," *National Law Journal* (August 24, 1992), 27–29.

Wehmann, Carolyn M., "Better Preparation Helps a Firm Take the Guesswork Out of Recruiting," *New York Law Journal* (September 12, 1992), S9–S10.

Wehmann, Carolyn M., "Downsized Firms May Still Recruit Inefficiently," *New York Law Journal* (November 23, 1992), 7.

Wehmann, Carolyn M., "Evaluation Checklist Helps Rate Candidates," *New York Law Journal* (November 13, 1989), 35.

Wehmann, Carolyn M., "Getting the Best—In a Buyer's Market," *Lawyer Hiring and Training Report* (June 1992), 2.

Wehmann, Carolyn M., "How Does a Firm Change an Apathetic Attitude Toward Recruiting?" *Lawyer Hiring and Training Report* (May 1989), 4.

Wehmann, Carolyn M., "In Slow Economy, Firms Use 'Down-Time' to Reshape Goals," *New York Law Journal* (April 15, 1991), 42.

Wehmann, Carolyn M., "Planning Ahead Pays Off for Interviewers," *National Law Journal* (December 16, 1991), S4–S5.

Wehmann, Carolyn M., "Recruiting More Effectively," *National Law Journal* (January 25, 1988), 21.

Wehmann, Carolyn M., "Welcome to the 1990s—And the Lifestyle Generation," *Lawyer Hiring and Training Report* (April 1990), 2.

White, Daniel R., *Trials & Tribulations—Appealing Legal Humor*. Highland Park, NJ: Catbird Press, 1989.

CONTRIBUTORS

Rebecca A. Albrecht is the Associate Presiding Judge of the Superior Court of Arizona in Maricopa County. She was appointed to the superior court bench in 1985. Judge Albrecht is the Past President of the Maricopa County Bar Association (MCBA), sits on the National Conference of Bar Presidents (NCBP) Executive Committee, and is a member of the ABA House of Delegates.

Sheila Anderson is a graduate of Duke University (A.B., 1984) and the Villanova University School of Law (J.D., 1989). She is currently an Assistant City Solicitor for the city of Pittsburgh. While in law school, Anderson served as a Summer Legal Intern for the Honorable William F. Hall, Jr., United States Magistrate, Eastern District of Pennsylvania, and later interned for the Honorable Vincent Cirillo, Superior Court of Pennsylvania. She has served as Judicial Law Clerk to the Honorable K. Streeter Lewis, Philadelphia Court of Common Pleas, and more recently, the Honorable James E. Rowley, President Judge, Superior Court of Pennsylvania.

Deborah L. Arron obtained her B.A. degree from the University of Washington in 1971, where she graduated magna cum laude. She graduated from UCLA Law School in 1975 and was a member of the *UCLA Law Review*. Arron practiced law for ten years in Seattle. In 1985, Arron closed her law practice to take a one-year sabbatical—from which she never returned! She now presents career-planning seminars to lawyers and law students nationwide.

Suzanne Baer is Assistant to the President of the Association of the Bar of the City of New York (ABCYN) for Minority Affairs. Prior to that she was the Senior Assistant Dean, Office of Career Services, at Hofstra University School of Law from 1990 to 1992, and the Director of Career Services at New York Law School from 1983 to 1990.

Donna M. Ballman is a solo practitioner in Coral Gables, Florida. Her practice includes commercial litigation, employment discrimination, and election law. Her book, *The Florida Election Law Handbook*, published by the American Political Institute, is in its second edition.

333

Lee Ann Bellon is the founder of Bellon & Associates in Atlanta, Georgia, and specializes in providing creative human-resource solutions to law firms and corporate legal departments.

Brion A. Bickerton is President of Bickerton & Gordon, Attorney and Executive Placement Consultants, in Boston. Bickerton & Gordon recruits lawyers for law firms and corporations, principally in the New England area. Bickerton was formerly a corporate and international attorney for the Boston law firm of Bingham, Dana & Gould and practiced in its London and Boston offices. He also clerked in the Massachusetts Federal District Court and was the Chief Law Clerk to the Justices of the Massachusetts Superior Court.

Kathleen Brady, Assistant Dean and Director of Fordham University School of Law's Career Planning Center, has been involved with career planning and placement for lawyers since 1986. She is an active member of the NALP and serves on three committees at the ABCNY: Recruitment of Lawyers, Lawyers in Transition, and Law Student Perspectives.

Gary A. D'Alessio, a lawyer and a Certified Professional Consultant, is the President and founder of Chicago Legal Search, Ltd., a firm specializing in legal search, placement, and consulting for law firms, corporations, and financial institutions primarily in the Chicago metropolitan area. He received his B.S.B.A. cum laude from Villanova University in 1976 and his J.D. from Tulane University Law School in 1980. He co-chaired the Careers Committee of the Young Lawyers Section of the Chicago Bar Association (CBA) for two years.

Mindy Friedler is a consultant in the Chicago office of Hildebrandt, Inc. Her areas of expertise include practice management, associate training and development, strategic planning, and quality management. She is a graduate of the New York University School of Law.

Randi G. Frisch is the founder and President of Legal Works, located in Los Angeles, California. She practiced law prior to becoming a legal recruiter. Frisch received her B.A. in History from the University of California, Los Angeles, in 1978. She received her J.D. in 1981 from Loyola Law School in Los Angeles.

Richards Gordon is a former banking and real estate partner with the Boston law firm of Wayne, Lazares & Chappell and a commercial loan officer with Bank of New England. He is a principal of Bickerton & Gordon, Attorney and Executive Placement Consultants, of Boston.

Laura J. Hagen received her B.A. in 1972 and her J.D. with honors in 1976 from the University of Texas at Austin. She also received an LL.M. from the Harvard Law School. Hagen is a principal in, and founder of, the Chicago office of Major, Wilson & Africa, a national legal search and consulting firm. Hagen is a member of the Board of Directors of the National Association of Legal Search Consultants (NALSC).

Gwen Baumann Harrell is Director of Career Services at Southern Methodist University (SMU) School of Law in Dallas, Texas. Harrell was previously employed as Associate General Counsel to Elcor Corporation in Dallas, and as Associate Counsel to Bayly, Martin & Fay International, Inc., in Fort Worth, a privately held group of insurance brokers. A 1984 graduate of the University of Florida College of Law, Harrell chaired the ABA-YLD Corporate Counsel Committee in 1992–1993.

Phyllis Hawkins is President of the Phoenix-based search firm of Phyllis Hawkins & Associates, Inc. The firm also maintains an office in the Detroit area. Hawkins received both her B.A. and M.A.Ed. from Arizona State University. A legal recruiter since 1984, she is a Vice-President and a Board Member of the NALSC.

Ronald L. Hirsch, author of the *State of the Legal Profession 1990* and *At the Breaking Point: The Emerging Crisis in the Quality of Lawyers' Health and Lives—Its Impact on Law Firms and Client Services*, served as the principal investigator for the National Survey of Career Satisfaction/Dissatisfaction conducted by the ABA-YLD in 1984 and 1990. Hirsch recently left his position as ABA-YLD Staff Director to form a consulting practice directed toward working with bar associations to improve the profession through the knowledge gained from survey research. He is a graduate of the University of Chicago Law School.

Irene Honey is the Director of Career Services and Alumni Relations for the University of Colorado School of Law. Her professional background includes several years of working in higher education as a career-development counselor and administrator. Prior to her position in Colorado, Honey worked at both private and public universities in Washington, D.C., New York, and New England. Her graduate degree is from Syracuse University and her undergraduate degree is from Georgetown University.

Mary Ann Hoopes is an honors graduate of Georgetown University Law Center in Washington, D.C., and Barat College in Lake Forest, Illinois. She currently serves as Deputy Legal Counsel for the Executive Office for U.S. Attorneys, U.S. Department of Justice.

Deborah Howard is the Director of Career Services at New York Law School. She received her B.A. from Harvard University in 1979 and her J.D. from Northeastern University School of Law in 1982.

Carol M. Kanarek is a partner in the New York City firm of Kanarek & Shaw, which provides placement, outplacement, and management consulting services to law firms. She served as Chairperson of the ABA-YLD Career Issues Committee from 1986–1988. During her tenure as Committee Chair, Kanarek edited the first edition of *Changing Jobs*.

Beth L. Kaufman is a partner in Schoeman, Marsh & Updike, New York, New York. Kaufman has been active in the ABCNY since 1978 and currently is Chair of its Committee on Law Student Perspectives.

Susan E. Kraybill trained and worked as a professional recruiter in New York City, first with Wells Legal Search, Inc., where she rose to become a department head, and later with Catalyst Legal Resources, Inc., for which she established and managed a branch office in Atlanta. Kraybill entered professional search after attending college in the Cleveland area and working for a major New York law firm in an administrative capacity.

David S. Machlowitz is Counsel for Siemens Corporation and serves as General Counsel to its Medical Division in Tselin, New Jersey. A 1977 graduate of Yale Law School, Machlowitz is a member of the Board of Directors of the New Jersey Chapter of the American Corporate Counsel Association (ACCA) and also has served as an officer and Director of the New York Chapter and Chair of its Environmental Law Committee.

Debra J. Madsen is the Assistant Dean of the University of Wyoming College of Law. She received her B.A. from the University of Texas and her J.D. from the University of Idaho. After graduating from the University of Idaho College of Law, she worked for Texas Instruments in Austin, Texas, specializing in computer law. She has been the Assistant Dean at the University of Wyoming since 1986.

Michael K. Magness is a partner in Magness & Wehmann Management Consultants, which provides consulting assistance and training programs to legal employers in the areas of lawyer recruitment, management, supervision, training, and professional development. Magness is active in the ABA and has held positions in the ABA-YLD and the Law Practice Management, General Practice, and Legal Education Sections.

Robert A. Major, Jr., received his B.A. in 1973 from Stanford University and his J.D. in 1976 from the University of Texas at Austin, where he served as an editor of the *Texas Law Review*. From 1976 to 1981, he was an associate with Wilmer, Cutler & Pickering in Washington, D.C. After a year as counsel to Saga Corporation in Menlo Park, California, he established Robert A. Major Jr. & Associates in 1982 as the predecessor firm to Major, Wilson & Africa.

Sandra G. Mannix, a Goucher College Phi Beta Kappa graduate, has been a Consultant with the attorney search firm of Cathy Abelson Legal Search since 1991. The Philadelphia firm specializes in the recruitment and placement of both associates and partners with firms, corporations, and financial institutions. She previously served as Vice-President of Student Affairs, Pennsylvania College of Podiatric Medicine, and Director of Admissions/Financial Aid, Villanova University School of Law.

Hillary J. Mantis is Associate Director of the Career Planning Center at Fordham University School of Law and a career counselor in private practice. Formerly, she was Associate Director of Career Counseling at New York Law School. She is a graduate of Brown University and Boston College Law School. Mantis is the Chairperson of the ABA-YLD Career Issues Committee for 1993–1994. In addition, she is Chair of the New York County Lawyer's Association (NYCLA) Committee on Lawyer Placement, Subcommittee Chair of the ABCNY Special Committee on Law Student Perspectives, and serves as the NALP's liaison to the ABA Section on Law Practice Management.

Margaret Kuroda Masunaga graduated from the University of California at Berkeley and received her J.D. at McGeorge School of Law, University of the Pacific, in Sacramento, California. She is currently the Deputy Corporation Counsel for the Kona Branch of the Office of the Corporation Counsel, County of Hawaii, in Kealakekua, Hawaii. She served as the District Representative for Hawaii and Alaska to the Executive Council of the ABA-YLD in 1992–1994.

Londell McMillan received his B.S. from Cornell University in 1987 and his J.D. from New York University in 1990. He is a lawyer with the law firm of Gold, Farrell & Marks in New York City.

Heidi L. McNeil is a partner with the Phoenix, Arizona, law firm of Snell & Wilmer, specializing in commercial and products liability litigation and Native American law. She received her B.A. from the University of Iowa in 1981 and her J.D. from the University of Iowa in 1985. McNeil served as Chairperson of the ABA-YLD Career Issues Committee in 1992–1993 and is serving as an ABA-YLD Director for the 1993–1994 bar year. She also has held various leadership positions in the Maricopa County Bar and State Bar of Arizona Associations.

Anthony Monahan, Editorial Director of Magazine Productions, Ltd., Seattle, is a former Staff Editor of *Barrister*, the magazine of the ABA-YLD. His chapter was adapted from his article, "Are You At Loose Ends?" which appeared in *Barrister*, Spring of 1991.

Gary A. Munneke is an Associate Professor of Law at Pace University School of Law in White Plains, New York, where he teaches courses in Law Practice Management, Torts, and Professional Responsibility. Prior to joining the Pace faculty in 1988, he served on the faculty of Widener University School of Law and the University of Texas School of Law. A 1973 graduate of the University of Texas School of Law, Munneke serves as Chair of the ABA's Law Practice Management Section Publishing Board.

Anne Neal began her legal career as a litigator with Semmes, Bowen & Semmes, a large firm in Baltimore. She enjoyed her limited trial experience, but tired quickly of the "paper." Neal went to Karen Williamson and Associates, the local search firm, to evaluate her options. Thereafter, the firm opened a Washington, D.C., office and became Williamson & Neal. Neal spends the majority of her time now in the Baltimore office.

Sandra O'Briant of O'Briant Legal Search has an M.A. in Education and was the Assistant Director of a tutorial program at Arizona State University prior to relocating to California and beginning work at an executive search firm in Beverly Hills. As a principal in her own firms since 1979, she has placed both partners and associates. She is on the Board of Directors for the NALSC.

Celia Paul is the Founder and Director of the career counseling firm, Celia Paul Associates. She received a master's degree from Columbia University in 1968 and serves on the faculty of New York University.

Joanna Piepgrass is an associate at the firm of Swift & Associates. She received her B.A. with honors (English) from Carleton College/University of Southern Maine and will be attending CUNY law school.

Maureen A. Provost has been working with lawyers in career transition since 1979 as a career planning professional in three law schools, in private practice, and as an associate development professional for a large New York firm. In March of 1992, Provost became Assistant Dean for Career Development at St. John's University School of Law. Provost has been active in the National Association for Law Placement (NALP) since 1980, serving as president of the organization during 1988–1989.

Kathy D. Pullins earned a B.A., magna cum laude, in English in 1985 and a J.D. in 1988 from Brigham Young University. She is a trained mediator in domestic relations and acts as an arbitrator for landlord/tenant disputes. In addition, she is an adjunct faculty member at Utah Valley Community College. Pullins served as Director of Career Services and Alumni Relations at Brigham Young University Law School from 1988 until she was named Assistant Dean in 1990.

Larry Richard is the president of Richard Consulting Group, Inc., a Philadelphia consulting firm focusing on communication, motivation, and human-resources issues in law firms. Dr. Richard earned his J.D. degree from the University of Pennsylvania Law School and his Ph.D. degree in psychology from Temple University. His doctoral research examined the relationship between personality differences (as measured by the Myers-Briggs Type Indicator) and job satisfaction among U.S. lawyers.

Carol Richardson is a principal in Omega Attorney Placement in Seattle, Washington. Founded in 1988, Omega Attorney Placement serves the Pacific Northwest and is a division of Organizational Architects, Inc., a human-resource development company established in 1980.

Jeanne Q. Svikhart has provided legal career counseling since 1968 when she became the Placement Director at George Washington University National Law Center. Prior to establishing White Svikhart & Associates, she was an administrator at Arent, Fox, Kintner, Plotkin & Kahn in Washington, D.C., for 13 years. Svikhart was one of the founding members of the NALP in 1971.

Catherine V. Swift is president of Swift & Associates, Legal Search Consultants, in Portland, Maine. She has more than 14 years of experience in law firm administration and recruitment. Prior to founding Swift & Associates in 1988, Swift served as Director of Legal Staff at Cadwalader, Wickersham & Taft in New York City; as Director of the recruitment program at Winthrop, Stimson, Putnam & Roberts in New York City; and as hiring consultant to several other law firms. Swift received her B.A. with honors (Sociology/Criminal Justice) from Boston University in 1978.

Lisa Tessler is the Director of Career Services and Chair of the Legal Studies Advisory Group at Bowdoin College. She formerly served as the Associate Director for Placement at New York University School of Law.

Jane Thieberger is the Assistant Dean for the Office of Career Counseling and Placement at the New York University School of Law, having joined the law school in 1975.

Pat Bowers Thomas is a partner in the Los Angeles firm of Beckwith Thomas & Fanning. Thomas specializes in lawyer search and placement for national and international law firms and corporations. She also provides consulting services (strategic planning, salary evaluation, market surveys, etc.) to this clientele.

Dr. Abbie W. Thorner is currently Assistant Dean for Career Services and Publications at Georgetown University Law Center. She has previously served as the law center's Director of Career Services, as the Recruitment Administrator at a large Washington, D.C., law firm, and as Director of Student Affairs and Placement for the University of Georgia School of Law. Dean Thorner is a Past President of the NALP, an organization for whom she served as Employer-Director, Northeast Regional Coordinator, Publications Committee Chair, and Conference Consultant. She also has represented that organization as a member of the NALP and the Association of American Law Schools (AALS) Joint Task Force on Recruitment Reform.

Marilyn Tucker, Director of the Office of Career Services, has been at Georgetown University Law Center for more than ten years. In addition to her activities at the Law Center, Tucker is active in the NALP and is a member of the Forum on Hiring for Prentice-Hall's *The Lawyer Hiring and Training Report*. She also was recently an At-Large Director of the AALS Section on Student Services.

Shelley L. Wallace is founder and president of The Wallace Law Registry, a nationwide legal placement agency that specializes in the temporary and permanent placement of lawyers and paralegals. Wallace graduated from Brown University, magna cum laude, and from Hofstra University School of Law with honors. Before founding The Wallace Law Registry in 1987, Wallace practiced commercial and appellate litigation with the New York City law firm of Gainsburg, Gottlieb, Levitan & Cole.

Ellen Wayne is the Director of Career Development and Placement at the New England School of Law in Boston, Massachusetts. She currently serves as Chair of the ABA General Practice Section Committee on Professional Competence and Liability. She is also a founding and active member of the AALS Section on Student Services.

Carolyn M. Wehmann is a partner in Magness & Wehmann Management Consultants. Her expertise is in cost-effective management of lawyer personnel, designing innovative solutions to management and recruitment problems, and conducting practical skills seminars for lawyers and administrators. Wehmann's professional activities include a role in the NALP, in which she has served as Recruitment Practices Committee Chair, Northeast Regional Coordinator, and a frequent conference speaker.

Christine White has been involved in legal career counseling since 1971 when she was Assistant Dean and Placement Director at Villanova University School of Law. Later, she was Executive Director at Steptoe & Johnson in Washington, D.C. Since 1984, she has provided outplacement counseling to 40 law firms and several companies in Washington, D.C. White has an M.A. in counseling from Cornell University. White was a founding member of the NALP in 1971.

James M. Wilson, Jr., graduated from Phillips Academy, Andover, Massachusetts, in 1968 and received his B.A. in 1972 and his J.D. in 1975 from the University of Texas, where he served as an editor of the *Texas Law Review*. From 1976 to 1979, he was an associate with Andrews & Kurth in Houston, after which he served as counsel to Summa Corporation in Las Vegas, Nevada, until 1981. From 1981 to 1984, he was Assistant General Counsel of Transco Energy Company in Houston, and from 1984 to September of 1986, he was Vice President and General Counsel of Cenergy Corporation in Dallas. In 1986, he joined Robert A. Major, Jr., and Martha Fay Africa in the founding of Major, Wilson & Africa, an international legal search firm.

Rita D. Zaslowsky is the Director of Placement at the University of Denver College of Law and is responsible for career-planning/job-hunting facilitation for an enrollment of more than 1,000 students. Prior to her present position, Zaslowsky was the Assistant Director of Human Resources for the largest law firm in the Rocky Mountain region. In addition, she was a partner in a consulting firm specializing in law firm management issues and lawyer recruitment. Zaslowsky has done graduate work in Industrial Relations at Loyola University of Chicago. Her undergraduate degree is from the University of Illinois, Champaign-Urbana.

Selected Books From...

THE SECTION OF LAW PRACTICE MANAGEMENT

Order Form

Qty	Title	LPM Price	Regular Price	Total
_____	ABA Guide to Int'l Business Negotiations (511-0331)	$ 74.95	$ 84.95	$_____
_____	ACCESS 1994 (511-0327)	29.95	34.95	$_____
_____	Breaking Traditions (511-0320)	64.95	74.95	$_____
_____	Changing Jobs, 2nd Ed. (511-0334)	49.95	59.95	$_____
_____	Flying Solo, 2nd Ed. (511-0328)	59.95	69.95	$_____
_____	How to Start & Build a Law Practice, 3rd Ed. (511-0293)	32.95	39.95	$_____
_____	Last Frontier (511-0314)	9.95	14.95	$_____
_____	Law Office Staff Manual (511-0307)	79.00	89.00	$_____
_____	Leveraging with Legal Assistants (511-0322)	59.95	69.95	$_____
_____	Making Partner (511-0303)	14.95	19.95	$_____
_____	Planning the Small Law Office Library (511-0325)	29.95	39.95	$_____
_____	Practical Systems (511-0296)	24.95	34.95	$_____
_____	Results-Oriented Financial Management (511-0319)	44.95	54.95	$_____
_____	A Short Course in Personal Computers (511-0302)	14.95	24.95	$_____
_____	Survival Skills for the Practicing Lawyer (511-0324)	39.95	49.95	$_____
_____	Through the Client's Eyes (511-0337)	69.95	79.95	$_____
_____	The Time Trap (511-0330)	14.95	14.95	$_____
_____	TQM in Action (511-0323)	59.95	69.95	$_____
_____	When a Professional Divorces (511-0326)	49.95	59.95	$_____
_____	Winning with Computers, Part 1 (511-0294)	89.95	99.95	$_____
_____	Winning with Computers, Part 2 (511-0315)	59.95	69.95	$_____
_____	Winning with Computers, Parts 1 & 2 (511-0316)	124.90	144.90	$_____
_____	Win-Win Billing Strategies (511-0304) 89.95	99.95	$_____	
_____	Women Rainmakers' 101+ Best Marketing Tips (511-0336)	14.95	19.95	$_____
_____	WordPerfect® in One Hour for Lawyers (511-0308)	9.95	14.95	$_____
_____	WordPerfect® Shortcuts for Lawyers (511-0329)	14.95	19.95	$_____
_____	Your New Lawyer, 2nd Ed. (511-0312) 74.95	84.95	$_____	

*HANDLING

$ 2.00-$9.99 .... $2.00
10.00-24.99 .... $3.95
25.00-49.99 .... $4.95
50.00 + ... $5.95

**TAX

DC residents add 5.75%
IL residents add 8.75%
MD residents add 5%

SUBTOTAL: $_____
*HANDLING: $_____
**TAX: $_____

TOTAL: $_____

PAYMENT

☐ Check enclosed (Payable to the ABA)   ☐ Bill Me

☐ Visa   ☐ MasterCard   Account Number:_____-_____-_____-_____

Exp. Date: _____ Signature _____

Name_____

Firm_____

Address_____

City_____State_____ZIP_____

Phone number_____

Mail to: ABA, Publication Orders, P.O. Box 10892, Chicago, IL 60610-0892

PHONE: (312) 988-5522
Or FAX: (312) 988-5568

BOOK

CUSTOMER COMMENT FORM

Title of Book:_____

We've tried to make this publication as useful, accurate, and readable as possible. Please take 5 minutes to tell us if we succeeded. Your comments and suggestions will help us improve our publications. Thank you!

1. How did you acquire this publication:

☐ by mail order   ☐ at a meeting/convention   ☐ as a gift

☐ by phone order   ☐ at a bookstore   ☐ don't know

☐ other: (describe)_____

Please rate this publication as follows:

	Excellent	Good	Fair	Poor	Not Applicable
Readability: Was the book easy to read and understand?	☐	☐	☐	☐	☐
Examples/Cases: Were they helpful, practical? Were there enough?	☐	☐	☐	☐	☐
Content: Did the book meet your expectations? Did it cover the subject adequately?	☐	☐	☐	☐	☐
Organization and clarity: Was the sequence of text logical? Was it easy to find what you wanted to know?	☐	☐	☐	☐	☐
Illustrations/forms/checklists: Were they clear and useful? Were there enough?	☐	☐	☐	☐	☐
Physical attractiveness: What did you think of the appearance of the publication (typesetting, printing, etc.)?	☐	☐	☐	☐	☐

Would you recommend this book to another attorney/administrator? ☐ Yes ☐ No

How could this publication be improved? What else would you like to see in it?

_____
_____
_____

Do you have other comments or suggestions?_____

_____
_____

Name_____

Firm/Company_____

Address_____

City/State/ZIP_____ Phone_____

Firm Size_____ Area of specialization_____

We appreciate your time and help.

Fold

NO POSTAGE
NECESSARY
IF MAILED
IN THE
UNITED STATES

BUSINESS REPLY MAIL
FIRST CLASS   PERMIT NO. 16471   CHICAGO, ILLINOIS

POSTAGE WILL BE PAID BY ADDRESSEE

AMERICAN BAR ASSOCIATION
PPM, 8TH FLOOR
750 N. LAKE SHORE DRIVE
CHICAGO, ILLINOIS 60611-9851

Fold